Catalogue Of The Library Of The American Philosophical Society: Held At Philadelphia For Promoting Useful Knowledge

American Philosophical Society. Library

CATALOGUE

OF THE

LIBRARY

OF THE

AMERICAN PHILOSOPHICAL SOCIETY,

HELD AT PHILADELPHIA

FOR

PROMOTING USEFUL KNOWLEDGE.

PUBLISHED BY ORDER OF THE SOCIETY.

PHILADELPHIA:
PRINTED BY JOSEPH R. A. SKERRETT.

1824.

LIST OF THE OFFICERS

OF THE

AMERICAN PHILOSOPHICAL SOCIETY,

FOR THE YEAR 1824.

President.

ROBERT PATTERSON.

Vice Presidents.

WILLIAM TILGHMAN,
PETER S. DUPONCEAU,
ZACCHEUS COLLINS.

Secretaries.

R. M. PATTERSON,
ROBERT WALSH, JUN.
GEORGE ORD,
WILLIAM H. KEATING.

Counsellors.

THOMAS JEFFERSON,
WILLIAM MACLURE,
NICHOLAS COLLIN,
WILLIAM MEREDITH,
NATHANIEL CHAPMAN,
ROBERT HARE,
WILLIAM HEMBEL, JUN.
CLEMENT C. BIDDLE,
HORACE BINNEY,
JOHN QUINCY ADAMS,
JOHN SERGEANT,
WILLIAM RAWLE.

Curators.

THOMAS SAY,
WILLIAM E. HORNER,
JAMES MEASE.

Treasurer.

JOHN VAUGHAN.

BOARD OF OFFICERS.

Chairman—PETER S. DUPONCEAU.
Secretary—R. M. PATTERSON.

Historical and Literary Committee.

Chairman—WILLIAM TILGHMAN.
Corresponding Secretary—PETER S. DUPONCEAU.
Recording Secretary—JOHN VAUGHAN.

Library Committee.

MATHEW CAREY,
ADAM SEYBERT,
PETER S. DUPONCEAU.

Librarian.

JOHN VAUGHAN.

CONDITIONS

OF THE

MAGELLANIC PREMIUM.

M. John Hyacinth De Magellan, of London, having sometime ago offered as a donation, to the American Philosophical Society held at Philadelphia for promoting useful knowledge, the sum of two hundred guineas, to be by them vested in a secure and permanent fund, to the end that the interest arising therefrom should be annually disposed of in premiums, to be adjudged by the society, to the author of the best discovery, or most useful invention, relating to navigation, astronomy, or natural philosophy, (mere natural history only excepted,) and the society having accepted of the above donation, hereby publish the conditions, prescribed by the donor, and agreed to by the society, upon which the said annual premiums will be awarded.

1. The candidate shall send his discovery, invention, or improvement, addressed to the President, or one of the Vice-Presidents of the society, free of postage or other charges; and shall distinguish his performance by some motto, device or other signature, at his pleasure. Together with his discovery, invention, or improvement, he shall also send a sealed letter, containing the same motto, device or signature, and subscribed with the real name, and place of residence of the author.

2. Persons of any nation, sect, or denomination whatever, shall be admitted as candidates for this premium.

3. No discovery, invention, or improvement shall be entitled to this premium, which hath been already published, or for which the author hath been publicly rewarded elsewhere.

4. The candidate shall communicate his discovery, invention, or improvement, either in the English, French, German, or Latin language.

5. All such communications shall be publicly read, or ex-

hibited to the society, at some stated meeting, not less than one month previous to the day of adjudication; and shall at all times be open to the inspection of such members as shall desire it. But no member shall carry home with him the communication, description, or model, except the officer to whom it shall be intrusted; nor shall such officer part with the same out of his custody, without a special order of the society for that purpose.

6. The society having previously referred the several communications, from candidates for the premium then depending, to the consideration of the twelve counsellors and other officers of the society, and having received their report thereon, shall, at one of their stated meetings in the month of December, annually, after the expiration of this current year, (of the time and place, together with the particular occasion of which meeting, due notice shall be previously given, by public advertisement,) proceed to the final adjudication of the said premium: and after due consideration had, a vote shall first be taken on this question, viz. Whether any of the communications then under inspection be worthy of the proposed premium? If this question be determined in the negative, the whole business shall be deferred till another year: but if in the affirmative, the society shall proceed to determine by ballot, given by the members at large, the discovery, invention, or improvement, most useful and worthy; and that discovery, invention, or improvement, which shall be found to have a majority of concurring votes in its favour shall be successful; and then, and not till then, the sealed letter accompanying the crowned performance shall be opened, and the name of the author announced as the person entitled to the said premium.

7. No member of the society who is a candidate for the premium then depending, or who hath not previously declared to the society, either by word or writing, that he has considered and weighed, according to the best of his judgment, the comparative merits of the several claims then under consideration, shall sit in judgment, or give his vote in awarding the said premium.

8. A full account of the crowned subject shall be published

by the society, as soon as may be after the adjudication, either in a separate publication, or in the next succeeding volume of their transactions, or in both.

9. The unsuccessful performances shall remain under consideration, and their authors be considered as candidates for the premium, for five years next succeeding the time of their presentment; except such performances as their authors may, in the mean time, think fit to withdraw. And the society shall, annually, publish an abstract of the titles, object or subject-matter of the communications so under consideration; such only excepted as the society shall think not worthy of public notice.

10. The letters containing the names of authors whose performances shall be rejected, or which shall be found unsuccessful after a trial of five years, shall be burnt before the society, without breaking the seals.

11. In case there should be a failure, in any year, of any communication worthy of the proposed premium, there will then be two premiums to be awarded in the next year. But no accumulation of premiums shall entitle an author to more than one premium, for any one discovery, invention or improvement.

12. The premium shall consist of an oval plate of solid standard gold, of the value of ten guineas; on one side thereof shall be neatly engraved a short Latin motto, suited to the occasion, together with the words——The premium of John Hyacinth de Magellan, of London, established in the year 1786. And on the other side of the plate shall be engraved these words. Awarded by the A. P. S.———for the discovery of——A. D.———

And the seal of the society shall be annexed to the medal, by a ribbon passing through a small hole at the lower edge thereof.

CONDITIONS

OF THE

SURPLUS

OR

EXTRA-MAGELLANIC PREMIUM.

Mr. De Magellan having fixed at ten guineas the sum to be annually disposed of as a premium according to the strict terms of the donation, and the Magellanic fund having been so managed as to produce an annual surplus, the society, with a view to promote as far as may be in their power, the liberal intentions of the doner, have determined that the said

SURPLUS-MAGELLANIC FUND

shall be employed, in the first instance, according to the strict conditions of the donation, if a sufficient number of deserving candidates shall have applied for the same; otherwise, that such surplus, or so much thereof as cannot be applied as above, be awarded by the society to the authors of useful inventions or improvements, on any subjects within the general view of the Magellanic donation, or to the authors of such communications as may lead to such inventions or improvements, and which communications may be deemed worthy of the premium. The premium to consist of a Gold Medal of the value of not less than twenty, nor more than forty-five dollars; or the same sum in money, at the option of the candidate, accompanied with a suitable diploma on parchment, with the seal of the society, and "may be awarded at such stated meeting of the society, as shall be agreed to at a previous stated meeting; due notice thereof being given to the members."

REGULATIONS

RESPECTING THE

SURPLUS-MAGELLANIC PREMIUM.

Every communication offered for the Magellanic premium, and which has not obtained it, shall be taken into consideration for the surplus premium.

All the rules and regulations established for the Magellanic premium, shall be conformed to with respect to the surplus premium, except wherein changed by the regulations; unless in some very special cases for the rewarding of some essentially useful discovery or improvement, two-thirds of the members of the society present at a meeting appointed for the awarding of the Surplus-Magellanic premium, shall by their votes taken by ballot or otherwise direct.

The Surplus-Magellanic premium shall not be exclusively applied to actual inventions or improvements, but may also extend to such valuable communications within the general view of the donation, as may lead to useful discoveries, inventions or improvements.

INTRODUCTION

TO THIS

CATALOGUE.

THE Committee who have been appointed, in conjunction with the Librarian, to prepare a Catalogue of the Library of this Society, have performed that duty with all the care and attention in their power. They have had two objects principally in view, the one that the members might be able to find the books that they should want with the greatest possible ease, the other that those students who may wish to avail themselves of our collection, might see at one glance all that we possess relating to the subjects of their particular researches.

To obtain this last end, particularly, the Committee have been obliged to introduce many divisions and subdivisions into this Catalogue. It may be thought by some that there are too many; but it must be observed, that this library is yet in its infancy, and that when it shall have increased, (as is expected,) to a large number of books and manuscripts, these subdivisions, with such alterations and amendments as the state of the library at the time shall require, will be found to be highly useful and convenient.

It was found impossible to adopt an uniform method throughout, and although it might appear like a novelty, the Committee thought it best to arrange the books under each division according to a method suited to the respective subjects. Thus the memoirs and transactions of learned societies, are classed in the order of the names of the places where those institutions are established, as London, Paris, Philadelphia, alphabetically. Biographical works follow each other in the same order, by the names of the distinguished men whose lives and actions have been thought worthy of being recorded. Historical documents, and books and pamphlets on local and occasional politics, are classed in the order of their dates, certain medical treatises in that of the diseases that they respectively treat of, and Philological works auxiliary to the study of different languages, in the order of those idioms, alphabetically arranged. When no particular arrangement was required, the order of the author's names was followed, anonymous works, when sufficiently numerous, being separately classed. At the end of the whole is a complete alphabetical list of the names of the authors whose works are contained in this Catalogue, with references to the pages where they are to be found.

The Committee acknowledge that they have not seen any catalogue of foreign or American libraries precisely so arranged; they have ventured on an experiment, not, however, without mature reflection, and with a strong hope that this method will be found useful in practice. Should it turn out otherwise, they flatter themselves that in a few years the number of the books of this library will have so encreased, as to require a new catalogue, in which the faults of the present one will be avoided.

One of the greatest advantages of the one now presented, is that it will be easy to know by its means what books we principally want in each department. It is hoped that the friends of science in these United States will contribute all in their power to supply the deficiencies; the more so as students have never been, and it is believed will never be, debarred the use of our books in aid of their scientific inquiries. It is hoped also by this means, to raise a *National Library*, for the promotion of the study of the different branches of human knowledge. Every friend to his country is interested in the success of this liberal undertaking.

MATHEW CAREY,
ADAM SEYBERT,
PETER S. DUPONCEAU, } *Committee.*
JOHN VAUGHAN, *Librarian.*

Philadelphia, March, 1824.

TABLE OF CONTENTS.

I. MEMOIRS AND TRANSACTIONS OF SCIENTIFIC AND LITERARY INSTITUTIONS.

II. ASTRONOMY.

III. MATHEMATICS.

IV. NATURAL PHILOSOPHY.

V. CHEMISTRY.

VI. NATURAL HISTORY.

VII. RURAL AND DOMESTIC ECONOMY.

VIII. MEDICINE AND SURGERY.

IX. RELIGION.

X. MORAL SCIENCES.

XI. JURISPRUDENCE.

XII. BIOGRAPHY.

XIII. HISTORY AND CHRONOLOGY.

XIV. HISTORICAL DOCUMENTS.

XV. POLITICAL ECONOMY AND STATISTICS.

XVI. LOCAL AND OCCASIONAL POLITICS,

XVII. COMMERCE AND MANUFACTURES.

XVIII. NAVIGATION.

XIX. MILITARY ART.

XX. GEOGRAPHY AND ETHNOGRAPHY.

XXI. PHILOLOGY.

XXII. ARCHÆOLOGY AND BIBLIOGRAPHY.

XXIII. LITERATURE AND FINE ARTS.

XXIV. MISCELLANEA.

XXV. SUPPLEMENT,

CATALOGUE, &c.

I. MEMOIRS AND TRANSACTIONS OF SCIENTIFIC AND LITERARY INSTITUTIONS.

1. Memoirs and Transactions. 2. Academical Discourses.

1. MEMOIRS AND TRANSACTIONS.

Albany. 530. Transactions of the Society for promoting Agriculture and useful Arts in the State of New York, 3 vol. 1801—1814.

531. Memoirs of the Board of Agriculture of the State of New York, 2 vol.—1821-3.

Batavia. 395. Transactions of the Batavian Literary Society of Arts and Sciences, vol. 8th, 1816.

Bath. 517. Transactions of the Bath and West of England Society, 14 vols.—1783 to 1814.

Belfast. 383. Q. Select papers of the Belfast Literary Society, 1st and 2d Fascicula. vol. 1. 1808.

Berlin. 326. Q. Nouveaux Mémoires de l'Académie Royale des Sciences & Belles Lettres, 17 vol. 1770—1775, 1786—1801.

327. Q. Abhandlungen der Königlichen Akademie der Wissenchafften in Berlin, 1812 to 1819, 4 vol.

239. Q. Monats-schrift der Akademie der Künste und mechan. Wissen. zu Berlin, 1788.

Berne. 1470. Der Schweitz. Gesellschaft Samml. von Landwirthschaftlichen Dingen, 4 vol. Zurich, 1760, 1. Abhandlungen der Œconomischen Gesell. zu Berne gesammelt, 17 vol. 1762—1773.

1471. Neue Sammlung Physisch-Œconomischer schriften, 3 vol. Berne and Zurich, 1779, 1782-5.

1472. Neueste Sammlung, &c. vol. 1, Berne, 1796.

1473. Mém. & Obs. recueillies par la Soc. Œcon. de Berne, 1762—5, 4 vol.

Bologna. 345. Q. Commentarii de Bononiensi Scient. & Art. Instituto atque Academiâ, 1757—1784, 4 vol.

Bologna. 279. *Q.* Memorie dell'Istituto Nazionale Italiano.
Classe di Fisica e Mat. vol. 1, 2, 1806—1810.
Classi di Mor. Pol. Litt. Belle arti, &c. Vol. 1. parts 1, 2, 1809—1813.

Boston. 366. *Q.* Transactions of the American Academy of Arts and Sciences, 1785—1821, 4 vol.

808, 9. Collections of the Massachusetts Historical Society, O. Series, 1 a 10, 1792 to 1809—N. Series, 1 a 10, 1814 to 1823.

620. Memoir of the Boston Atheneum, with the act of incorporation and organization of the institution. Boston, 1807.

549. Communications of the Mass. Medical Society, 1808—13, 2 vol.

256, 276. Communications made to the Massachusetts Society for promoting Agriculture. Boston, 1803—5.

Brussels. 338. *Q.* Nouv. Mém. de l'Acad. Roy. des Sci. & Belles Lett. tom. 1. 1820.

339. *Q.* Mém. sur les questions proposées par L'Acad. Roy. 1813—1816, & qui ont remporté le prix, 1817.

Calcutta. 367. *Q.* Asiatic Researches: or Transactions of the Society instituted in Bengal, for inquiring into the History and Antiquities, the Arts, Sciences and Literature of Asia, 14 vols. Calcutta, 1788—1822.

996. Same work reprinted. 6 vols. London, 1801.

Copenhagen. 298. *Q.* Det Kongelige Danske Videnskabers-Selskabs Skrivter, 1802—1810, 6 vols.

Q. Oversigt over det Kongel. Danske Vidensk. Selsk. Arbeid, &c. 1815—1821.

384. 14. *Q.* Analyse des Travaux de la Soc. Roy. Vétérinaire de Copenhague, 1815.

Dijon. 298 Mémoires de l'Académie de Dijon, 2 vol. 1769, 1774.

Dublin. 376. *Q.* Trans. of the Roy. Irish Acad. vols. 1. a 9, 1787—1803.

1316. Trans. of the Dublin Soc. 1799 a 1810, 8 vols.
Catalogue of Plants cultivated in their Botanical garden, by I. Underwood, 1804.

Edinburgh. 379. *Q.* Trans. of the Roy. Soc. of Edinb. vol. 1–9, 1788 a 1823, 9 vols.

378. *Q.* Trans. of the Soc. of Antiquaries of Scotland, vol. 1, 1792.

377. *Q.* MSS. Minutes of the Organization of the Ant. Soc. by Lord Buchan, and an account of its progress, by W. Smellie, 1782.

284. Laws of the Edinburgh Soc. for the investigation of Nat. Hist. Edinburgh, 1788.

Florence. 97. *F.* Saggi di naturali Esperienze fatte nell'Academia del Cimento, 1691.

Goettingen. 341. *Q.* Commentarii Soc. Reg. Sci. vol. 1 a 4, 1751—1754.

342. *Q.* Novi Commentarii, vol. 1 a 8, 1769—1777.

Q. Commentationes Soc. Reg. Sci. vol. 1 a 14, 1778—1799.

343. *Q.* Commentationes recentiores, vol. iii. iv. 1814, 1818.

Haarlem. 1474. Verhandelingen van de Hollandsche Maatschappy der Weetenschappen te Haarlem, 30 vol. 1754 a 1793.

1475. Natuurkundige Verhand. &c. te Haarlem, 1 vol. in 2 pts. 1799—1801. Amsterdam.

Werktuig en Wiskundige Verhand. &c. te Haarlem, 1802. Amsterdam.

Havana. 18. Mem. de la Real Soc. Economica, 4 vol. 1817—1820.

Leeds. 369. *Q.* Introd. Disc. to the Leeds' Philos. & Liter. Soc. By C. T. Thackrah, 1821.

Leipsic. 328. *Q.* Opuscula Omnia actis Eruditorum Lipsiensibus inserta, &c. vol. 1. 1682-1687—vol. 3, 1699-1708—vol. 4, 1701 1710. 2d vol. wanting. Venet. 1740—1743.

Lisbon. 160. *F.* Memorias da Academia Real das Sciencias de Lisboa, 2 vol. Lisboa, 1797, 1799.

438. *Q.* Mem. Economicas da Acad. &c. para adiantomento da Agric. das. Artes e da Industria em Portugal, 3 vols. 1791.

117. Mem. de Agricultura premiadas pela Acad. 1787—8, 2 vols.

453. *Q.* Breves Instrucções da Academia, para formar hum museo nacional, 1781.

439. *Q.* Memorias de Litteratura Portugueza, publicadas pela Real Acad. das Sciencias, 7 vol. Lisboa, 1792—1806.

London. 374. *Q.* Trans. Roy. Soc. Lond. vol. 5 a 30, 1670 to 1719—43 a 79, 1741—1789, and index to vols. 1 a 70, all bound in 63 vols. Wanting the four first volumes; also vols. 31 to 42, from 1720 to 1740; vol. 55 for 1765; vol. 65 for 1775; the second part of vol. 78 for 1788, and the subsequent volumes to 1800 inclusive, except vol. 79 for 1799, which is in this Library.

371. *Q.* Trans. Roy. Soc. London, 1801—1822, 22 vols.

373. *Q.* Abridg. of Trans. of Roy. Soc. to the end of 1700, by J. Lowthrop, 3 vols.—from 1700 to 1720, by H. Jones, 2 vols.—from 1720 to 1732, by J. Gray, 2 vols.—from 1732 to 1744, by J. Martyn, 2 vols.

372. *Q.* History of the Royal Society of London, by Thomas Birch, 4 vol. Lond. 1756—7.

490. Narrative of the dissensions and debates in the Royal Society. London, 1784.

124. *Q.* Memoirs of the Astronomical Society, vol. 1. 1822.

London. 241. Regulations of the Astronomical Society of London, established Feb. 8, 1820. London, 1820.

105. Q. Trans. of the Geological Society, first series, 1811 a 1821. 5 vol. 3 vol. plates—Second Series, vol. 1, 1822.

363. Q. Trans. Linnean Soc. 1791—1807, 8 vol.

169. Q. Trans. Horticultural Soc. 1792 a 1823, 5 vol.

217. Trans. of the Soc. of Arts, Manuf. and Comm. 1783 a 1822, (wanting 36, 1818,) 40 vols.

371½. Q. Charter and Bye-Laws of the Royal Institution of G. Britain, with list of proprietors, 1800.

1558. Journal of the Roy. Inst. vol. 1, 1802.

1559. Journal of the Sciences and the Arts, (R. I.) 1816—1823, 15 vols.

375. Q. Archæologia, or Miscellaneous tracts relating to antiquity, published by the Society of Antiquarians of London, 1779—1823, 20 vols.

423. Account of the Society for the improvement of Naval Architecture. London, 1792.

1640. Memoirs of the London Medical Society, instituted in the year 1773. vol. 3. Lond. 1792.

1664. Transactions of the Royal Humane Society, vol. 1. London.

Annual Reports made to the same, 4 vols. of pamphlets bound together. London, various dates.

263. Annual Reports of the Humane Society of London, 1801, 1803.

384. 15. Q. Account of the origin of the Board of Agriculture and its progress, by the President. London, 1796.

Madrid. 67. Q. Memorias de la Real Academia de la Historia, 1796—1805, 4 vols.

65. Q. Oraciones de la Real Acad. de la Historia, 1759—1783.

66. Q. Oraciones Funebres, &c. Estatutos de la R. A. Catalogo de los asociados, 1792—1803.

1496. Fastos de la R. Acad. de la Hist. 1739—1741, 3 vol.

1494. Coleccion de las Obras de Eloquencia y de poesia, premiadas por la Real Academia Española. Madrid, 1779.

Manchester. 515. Mem. of the Literary and Philosophical Society of Manchester, 1st ser. 1705—1802, 5 vols. in 7.

516. Same work, 2d ser. 1805—1813, 2 vols.

Milan. 335. Q. Atti della Società Patriotica di Milano, vol. 1. 1783.

Newhaven. 522. Mem. of the Connecticut Society of Arts and Sci. vol. 1, 1810—13.

239. Observations made by the Medical Society of Newhaven County. Newhaven, 1788.

N. York. 370. Q. Trans. of the Lit. and Phil. Society, vol. 1, 1815.

825. Collections of the New York Historical Society, 1809—1814, 2 vol.

N. York. 620. Charter and By-Laws of the American Academy of Arts, instituted Feb. 1802, with an account of the statues, busts, and paintings belonging to the Academy. New York, 1815

735. Charter, Constitution, and Bye-laws of the Lyceum of Natural History at New York, incorporated April 20, 1818. New York, 1823.

636. Observations on the establishment of the college of Physicians and Surgeons in the city of New York, by Dav. Hosack. New York, 1811.

636. Ordinances of the college of Physicians and Surgeons of the Western District of the State of New York, 1813.

636. Supplementary Charter of the College of Physicians, and Surgeons, with other ordinances relative to that institution. New York, 1811.

614. An Historical Sketch of the Origin, Progress, and Present State of the College of Physicians and Surgeons of the University of the State of New York. New York, 1813.

635. Address of the general Committee of the Board of Agriculture of the State of New York to the County Agricultural Societies. New York, 1820.

Paris. 354. Q. Mémoires de l'Académie Royale des Sciences, de 1666 a 1699, 11 vols. in 14. Paris, 1733.

354. Q. Histoire et Mémoires de l'Académie Royale des Sciences de 1699 a 1789—96 vols. & 9 vol. de Tables des matières. Paris, 1732—1793.

350. Q. Recueil des pièces qui ont remporté les prix de l'Académie (des Sciences.) 1720 a 1772, 9 vols.

351. Q. Machines & inventions approuvées par l'Académie, 1666 a 1774, 7 vols.

352. Q. Mémoires de Mathematiques et de Physique, présentés à l'Académie par divers savants & lus dans leurs assemblées, 1750—1786, 11 vols.

353½ Regiæ Scientiarum Academiæ Historia, autore J. B. Duhamel, 1697.

353. Q. Choix des Mem. de l'Acad. Roy. des Inscription & Belles Lettres de Paris, imprimés a Londres, 1777, 3 vol.

357. Q. Mém. de l'Institut National des Sciences & Arts de l'an 6 a l'an 12. 5 vol. de 3 parties.—Sc. Mor.& Pol.—Math. and Phys.—Litt. & Beaux-Arts, 15 vol. Rapports, 4 vol.

357. Q. Mém. de la Classe Math. & Phys. 1806 a 1815, 14 vols.

357. Q. Mém. de l'Acad. Roy. des Scien. de l'Institut de France, 1816—18, 3 vol.

357. Q. Mém. de l'Institut Royal de France, classe d'Hist. et de Litt. Anc. 1815—18, 4 vols.

358. Q. Mémoires présentés à l'Inst. des Sc. Belles Lett. & Arts par divers Savans 1806—11, 2 vols.

Paris. 359. *Q.* Mém. du Bureau de Consultation des Arts. vol. 1, 1793.

360. *Q.* Collec. Académiques ou Mem. Actes, &c. des plus célèbres Acad. & Sav. Partie Française, 1754 a 1774, 5 vols.

361. *Q.* Idem partie Etrangère, 1755 a 1774, 12 vols.

238. Raports des Commissaires de l'Académie des Sciences & de la Société de Médecine, sur le magnétisme animal. Paris, 1784.

395. *Q.* Recueil de pièces qui ont concouru pour les prix de l'Acad. Roy. de Chirurgie, vol. 1, 1753.

362. *Q.* Annales du Museum National, d'Hist. Nat. 1802—13, 20 vols.

263. *Q.* Mém. du Museum National d'Hist. Nat. 1815—22, 8 vols.

1062. Mém. &c. lus dans l'Acad. Celtique sur les antiquités Celtiques, Gauloises & Françaises, 1807—10, 5 vols.

1063. Mém. &c. lus dans la Soc. Roy. des Antiquaires de France, sur les Antiquités Nationales & Etrangeres, 1817—21, 3 vols.

322. Discours d'ouverture de la Soc. Asiatique, établie eu 1822. Par le Baron Silvestre de Sacy, President.

Mémoires lus à la Soc. Asiatique.

Sur l'origine du papier monnaye, par Jules Klaproth.

Sur l'identité des Ossètes & des Alains par le même.

304. Notice Historique des travaux de la Société Géographique, pendant l'an 1822, par Malte-Brun. Discours par le même.

324. Bulletin de la Societé de Géographie, No. 2.

Prix proposés par la Société Géographique en 1822.

1164. Mémoires du Musée de Paris. Paris, 1785.

394. *Q.* Histoire de la Société Royale de Médecine, années 1776—1781 & 1783, 5 vols.

303. Compte rendu à la Société d'Agric. du Départ. de la Seine d'une experience tentée et des succès obtenus contre la Morve et le Tarcin. Paris, 1811.

396. *Q.* Journal de l'Ecole Polytechnique, publié par le conseil d'instruction & administration de cet établissement, vol. 1, 2, 4, 7. Paris, an. 3—8.

397. *Q.* Bulletin des Sciences de la Société Philomatique de Paris, 1791—1804, 3 vol.

397½ *Q.* Nouveaux Bulletins de la même Société, vol. 1, 1807—1809.

Philadelphia. 364. *Q.* Trans. Amer. Philos. Soc. O. Ser. 1771—1809, 6 vols.

365. *Q.* Same, N. Ser. vol. 1, 1818.

Philadelphia. 879. Trans. of the Hist. and Litt. Committee of the Americ. Phil. Soc. 1819.

228. Journal of the Academy of Natural Sciences, 3 vols. 1817—1823. Philadelphia.

244. 354. Act of Incorporation and Laws of the Philad. Med. Soc. Philadelphia, 1793—1797.

879. 1672. Transact. of the College of Physicians of Philadelphia, vol. I. 1793.

1292. Trans. of the Philad. Agric. Soc. Philad. 1808—1818, 4 vol.

244. 263. Laws of the Philadelphia Society for promoting Agriculture. Philad. 1788, 1789.

696. Memorial of the Philadelphia Society for promoting Agriculture to the Legislature of Pennsylvania.

640. Charter, by-laws, and standing resolutions of the Pennsylvania Academy of the Fine Arts. Philadelphia, 1813.

Pisa. 330. *Q.* Historia Acad. Pisanæ auct. Fabronio, 1791—5, 3 vols.

329. *Q.* Observationes Siderum habitæ Pisis in Specula Academica a 1765 ad 1790, 3 vols.

Port-au-Prince. 381. Mémoires du Cercle des Philadelphes, vol. 1, 1788.

Prague. 303. *Q.* Abhandlungen der Boehmischen Gesellschaft der Wissenschaften, 1785.

Richmond. 635. Memoirs of the Society of Virginia for Promoting Agriculture. Richmond, 1818.

278. Mémoires, statuts & prospectus concernant l'Académie des Sciences établie à Richmond en Virginie. Présenté au Roi, par le Chevalier Quesnay de Beaurepaire. Paris, 1788.

Rotterdam. 384. 2. *Q.* Plan en Grondwetten van het Bat. Genoots. der Proefondervindelyke Wysbegeerte te Rotterdam. Rotterdam, 1788.

62. *Q.* Verhandelingen van het Bataafsch Genootschap der Proefondervindelyke Wysbegeerte te Rotterdam, 1774 a 1798, 12 delen, gebonden in 6.

Nieuwe Verhandelingen, &c. 1800—1812, 4 vols.

Stockholm. 340. *Q.* Mém. de l'Acad. Roy. des Sci. de Stockholm, 1740 a 1772, 29 vols. abrégés & traduits par Keralio. Paris, 1772.

377. Kongl. Vetenskaps Academiens nya Handlingar, 1780 a 1822, 43 vols.

378. Aors Berättelser om Vetenskapernas Framsteg, afgifne af Kongl. Vetenskaps-Academiens Embetsman, 2 vol. 1821—1822.

378½. Svenska Läkare-Sällskapets Handlingar, 5th vol. 1788.

380. Aors Berättelse om Svensk. Läk. Sällsk. Arbe-

ten, til 6 Oct. 1818, af Sekret. Chr. Carlander, 1818.

Stockholm. 379. Exposition des opérations faites en Lapponie pour la détermination d'un Arc du Méridien de 1801 a 1803, par Ofverbom, Svanberg, Holmquist & Palander, rédigée par J. Svanberg, 1805.

St. Petersburg. 271. Q. Commentarii Soc. Sci. Imp. Petropolitanæ, 1726 a 1746, 14 vols.

272. Q. Novi Commentarii, 1747 a 1769, 14 vol. in 15.

273. Q. Acta Acad. Sci. Imp. Petr. 1777 a 1782, 12 vols.

Nova Acta, 1783 a 1802, 15 vols.

274. Q. Mém. de l'Acad. Imp. des Sci. de St. Petersbourg, 1803 a 1818, 8 vols.

Turin. 331. Q. Miscell. Philos. Math. Soc. Privatæ Taurinensis, 1759 to 1773, 5 vols. (suspended until 1784.)

Mém. de l'acad. des Sciences de Turin, 1784—1800, 6 vols.

Mém. de l'Acad. Imp. des Sci. Litt. & Beaux-Arts, 1801—12, 5 vols.

Soi. Phys. & Mathém. 1801—12, 5 vols.

Mém. de l'Acad. Roy. des Sci. de Turin, 1813—21, 4 vols. [In all 25 vol.]

332. Q. Annales de l'observatoire de l'Acad. de Turin. Par Vassali Eandi, 1809—11.

Valencia. 27½. Q. Estatutos de la Soc. Economica de Amigos del Pays de Valencia, 1785.

Instituciones Economicas de la Sociedad, Primera Parte, 1777.

Extracto de las Actas, 1785—1791.

Junta Publica de la Real Sociedad de Valencia, 1799—1801, 12 vols. in 3.

Verona. 333. Q. Memorie di Matematica e Fisica della Soc. Italiana, 1782—4, 2 vol. in 3.

Upsal. 379½. Q. Nova Acta Regiæ Soc. Scient. Upsaliensis, vol. 7 and 8, 1815—21.

Worcester, (Mass.) 620. An account of the American Antiquarian Society, incorporated Oct. 24, 1812. Published by order of the Society. Boston, 1813.

878. Archæologia Americana. Transactions of the American Antiquarian Society, vol. 1. Worcester, 1820.

2. ACADEMICAL DISCOURSES.

620. *Beck, (Theod. R.)* An annual Oration delivered by appointment before the Society for the Promotion of Useful Arts, at the Capitol in the City of Albany, 3 Feb. 1813. Albany, 1813.

384, 5. Q. *Biddle, (Owen)* An Oration delivered 2d March, 1781, before the American Philosophical Society, on the rise, progress, and advantages of Learning and Science, and the means of rendering them more general. Philadelphia, 1781.

696. *Biddle (Nicholas)* An Address delivered before the Philadelphia Society for promoting Agriculture, 15th Jan. 1822. Philadelphia, 1822.

671. *Bond, (Thomas)* Anniversary Oration delivered May 21st before the American Philosophical Society, held in Philadelphia for the Promotion of Useful Knowledge for the year 1782. Philadelphia.

635. *Chaumont, (J. D. Le Ray de)* An Address delivered before the Agricultural Society of Jefferson County, (New York.) Dec. 29th, 1817. New York, 1817.

370. Q. *Clinton, (De Witt)* An Introductory Discourse delivered before the Literary and Philosophical Society of New York, 4th May, 1814. New York, 1815.

701. *Cutbush, (Edward)* An Address delivered before the Institute for the promotion of Arts and Sciences at Washington on the 11th Jan. 1817. Washington, 1817.

737. *Davie, (Wm. R.)* An Address delivered before the South Carolina Agricultural Society at their anniversary meeting held in Columbia on the 8th of December, 1818. Columbia, S. C. 1819.

237. *Du Ponceau, (Peter S.)* A Discourse on the early History of Pennsylvania, delivered before the American Philosophical Society, June 6th, 1821. Philadelphia, 1821.

701. *Holmes, (Abiel)* An Address delivered before the American Antiquarian Society in Boston at their second anniversary, October 24, 1814. Boston, 1814.

640. *Hopkinson, (Joseph)* Annual Discourse delivered before the Pennsylvania Academy of Fine Arts, 1810. Philadelphia, 1810.

730. *Hosack, (David)* An inaugural Address delivered before the New York Historical Society on the 9th of February, 1820. New York, 1820.

685. *Jarvis, (Samuel F.)* A Discourse on the religion of the Indian tribes of North America, delivered before the New York Historical Society, Dec. 29, 1819. New York, 1820.

620. *Jenks, (William)* An Address to the American Antiquarian Society, on their first anniversary, Oct. 23, 1813. Boston, 1813.

635. *Logan, (George)* An Address on the errors of husbandry in the United States, delivered before the Philadelphia

Society for promoting Agriculture, at their annual meeting, January 14, 1818. Philadelphia, 1818.

635. *Madison, (James)* An Address delivered before the Agricultural Society of Albemarle, (Virginia,) May 12, 1818. Richmond, 1818.

284-2 Q. *Matlack, (Timothy)* An Oration on Agriculture, delivered March 16th, 1780, before the American Philosophical Society. Philadelphia, 1780.

635. *Mease, (James)* An Address on the progress of Agriculture with hints for its improvements in the United States delivered before the Philadelphia Society for promoting Agriculture at their annual meeting, January 14th, 1817. Philadelphia, 1817.

635. ——— ——— Address on the subject of establishing a Pattern Farm in the vicinity of Philadelphia, delivered before the Philadelphia Society for promoting Agriculture. Philadelphia, 1811.

700. 730. *Morris, (Gouv.)* An inaugural Discourse, delivered before the New York Historical Society 4th September, 1816, the 206th anniversary of the discovery of New York. New York, 1816.

635. *Peters, (Richard)* A Discourse on agriculture, delivered before the Philadelphia Society for Promoting Agriculture, at their annual meeting the 9th of January, 1816. Philad. 1816.

736. ——— ——— Address delivered before the Philadelphia Society for Promoting Agriculture, at its annual meeting on the 23d of January, 1823. Philadelphia, 1823.

635. *Rawle, (William)* An Address delivered before the Philadelphia Society for Promoting Agriculture, Jan. 19, 1819. Philad. 1819.

384-9. Q. *Rittenhouse, (David)* An Oration delivered before the American Philosophical Society, Feb. 24, 1785, on the rise and progress of Astronomy. Philad. 1775.

696. *Rose, (Robert H.)* An Address delivered before the Agricultural Society of Susquehanna County, (Pennsylvania,) at its organization, Dec 6, 1820. Montrose, (Penn.) 1820.

384-10. Q. *Rush, (Benjamin)* An Oration delivered 27th Feb. 1786, before the American Philosophical Society on the influence of physical causes on the moral faculty. Philad. 1786.

537. ——— ——— A comparison between the diseases and remedies of the N. American Indians and those of the civilized nations.

620. *Schultz, (Benjamin)* An Oration delivered before the Mosheimian Society, July 23d, 1795. Philad. 1795.

384-5. *Smith, (Rev. Wm.)* An Oration delivered Jan. 22, 1773, before the American Philosophical Society, on the utility of learned societies. Philad. 1773.

635. *Tilghman, (William)* An Address delivered before the Philadelphia Society for Promoting Agriculture, Jan. 18, 1820. Philad. 1820.

384–16. Q. *Waterhouse, (B.)* Discourse on the principle of vitality, before the Humane Society. Boston, 1790.

730. *Wheaton, (Henry)* An anniversary Discourse delivered before the New York Historical Society, December 28, 1820. New York, 1821.

For Eulogiums and Funeral Orations delivered by order of, and before Scientific Societies, see Title BIOGRAPHY.

II. ASTRONOMY.

1. Theoretical Astronomy.
2. Practical Astronomy.
3. Astronomical Tables and Almanacs.

1. THEORETICAL ASTRONOMY.

458. *Alcmar, (Adr. Met.)* Primum mobile, Astronòmicè, Sciographicè, Geometricè, et Hydrographicè exsplicatum. Amsterdam, 1633.

304. *Anonymous.* The Anti-Newtonian; or a true system of the universe; with diagrams of explanation, proving the magnetic needle to have a centre meridian attraction between the poles of the world, &c. London, 1823.

139. Q. *Bailly.* Histoire de l'Astronomie ancienne. Paris, 1775.

140. Q. ——— Histoire de l'Astronomie moderne, 2 vol. Paris, 1779.

695. *Bennet, (S.)* A new explanation of the ebbing and flowing of the sea, upon the principles of gravitation. New York, 1816.

454. *B. V. L.* Versuch einer geschichtlichen Darstellung der Fortschritte der Sternkunde im verflossenen Decennio. Gotha, 1811.

469. *Carlini, (Francesco)* Esposizione d'un nuovo metodo di costruire le tavole astronomiche. Milano, 1810.

52. Q. *Cassini de Thury.* La Meridienne de l'observatoire de Paris, verifiée dans toute l'étendue du Royaume par des nouvelles observations. Paris, 1744.

453. *C. G. S.* Le Zodiaque expliqué, ou recherches sur l'origine & la signification des constellations de la sphère Grecque, traduit du Suédois. Paris, 1809.

158. Q. *Costard, (George)* History of Astronomy, with its application to geography, history and chronology. London, 1767.

470. *Delambre.* Abrégé d'astronomie, ou leçons élémentaires d'astronomie, théorique & pratique. Paris, 1813.

141. Q. ——— Histoire de l'Astronomie ancienne. Paris, 1817.

142. Q. ———Astronomie théorique et pratique, 3 vol. Paris, 1817.

474. *Dionis du Séjour*. Essai sur les phénomènes relatifs aux disparitions périodiques de l'anneau de Saturne. Paris, 1776.

472. *Ferguson.* Astronomy explained upon Newton's principles, with notes and supplementary chapters, by David Brewster, 2 vol. and a vol. of plates. Philad. 1817.

150. Q. *Gauss, (Carol. Fred.)* Theoria motus corporum coelestium in sectionibus conicis solem ambientium. Hamburgi, 1809.

440. *Gregory, (David)* The Elements of Physical and Geometrical Astronomy. Translated into English by M. Stone, 2 vols. London, 1726.

473. *Gummerie, (John)* Elementary Treatise of Astronomy. Philadelphia, 1822.

440. *Halley, (Dr.)* Synopsis of the astronomy of the Comets, (at the end of the 2d vol. of Gregory's Elements of Astronomy.) See *Gregory*. London, 1726.

137. Q. *La Place*. Exposition du Système du Monde. Paris, 1800.

138. Q. — —— Traité de Mécanique Céleste, 3 vol. Paris, 1800.

125. *Le Gendre*. Nouvelles méthodes pour la détermination des orbites des comètes. Paris, 1806.

83. F. *Maskelyne*. Astronomical observations made at the Royal Observatory at Greenwich, 2 vols. London, 1774, 1783.

437. *Maupertuis*. La figure de la terre, déterminée par les observations de M. de Maupertuis & autres savants, faites par ordre du Roi au Cercle Polaire. Paris, 1738.

439. Same work, translated into English. London, 1738.

237. *Minto, (Walter)* Researches into some parts of the Theory of the Planets. London, 1783

239, 247. *Oliver, (Andrew)* Essay on Comets. Salem, 1772.

136. Q. *Pingré*. Traité des Comètes, 2 vol.

384, 18. Q. *Stevens*. Mém. explicatif sur la sphère Caucasienne, & sur le Zodiaque. Paris, 1813.

292. *Woodward, (A. B.)* Considerations on the substance of the Sun. Washington, 1801.

493½. *Young, (Thomas)* Elementary Illustrations of the celestial mechanics of La Place. London, 1821.

2. PRACTICAL ASTRONOMY.

1401. *Anon*. Annuli Astronomici instrumenti, cum certissimi tum commodissimi usus, ex variis authoribus. Lutetiæ, 1557.

241. —— Method of finding a true meridian line useful in placing sun dials, &c. London, 1795.

384, 18. Q. *Arnold*. Instruction concerning Arnold's Chronometer or Time-keepers.

39. Q. *Bouguer*. Figure de la Terre, determinée par les observations de Messrs. Bouguer & de la Condamine. Paris, 1749.

241. *Brosius, (F. X.)* New method of finding the latitude by double altitudes of the sun. Cambridge, 1815.

384, 23. Q. *Caldas, (F. J. de)* Descripcion del observatorio Astronomico de Santafé de Bogotà, situado en el Jardin de la Real Expedicion Botanica. 1808.

47. Q. *Cassini de Thury.* Relation de deux voyages faits en Allemagne par ordre du Roi, par rapport à la figure de la Terre pour déterminer la grandeur des degrés de longitude & autres objets. Paris, 1763.

45. Q. *Cassini, Méchain, & Legendre.* Exposé des Opérations faites en France en 1787 pour la jonction des observatoires de Paris & de Greenwich. Paris, 1790.

Chappe d'Auteroche, see *Martin.*

41. Q. *Condamine, (la)* Mesure des trois prémiers degrés du Méridien dans l'Hémisphère austral. Paris, 1751.

384, 2. Q. *De Bruhl.* Three Registers of a Pocket Chronometer. London, 1784.

384, 23. Q. *De L'Isle.* Projet de la mesure de la Terre en Russie, lû dans l'assemblée de l'académie des Sciences de St. Petersbourg, le 21 Janvier 1737. St. Petersb. 1737.

384. Q. *Dollond, (Peter)* Some account of his discovery which led to the grand improvement of refracting telescopes. London, 1789.

468. *Dunn, (Samuel)* Introduction to Practical Astronomy. London, 1774.

292. *Ellicott, (A.)* Several methods by which meridional lines may be found. Philadelphia, 1796.

55. Q. *Gentil, (Le)* Voyage dans les mers de l'Inde à l'occasion du passage de Vénus sur le disque du soleil, Juin, 1761. 2 vol. Paris, 1779.

363. *Hoppe, (E.)* An Explanation of his improved Sextant. London, 1804.

436. *Jones, (William)* The description and use of the new Portable Orrery. London, 1794.

241. ——— ——— Methods of fixing a true meridian line useful in placing horizontal Sun-dials, setting Watches, &c. London, 1795.

384, 16. Q. *Lambert, (William)* Abstracts of Calculations to ascertain the Longitude of the Capitol. Washington, 1817.

619. ——— ——— Calculations for ascertaining the Latitude north of the Equator, and the Longitude west of Greenwich Observatory in England, of the Capitol at the City of Washington, in the U. States of America. Washington, 1805.

695. ——— ——— Message of the President of the U. States, transmitting a Report of William Lambert on the Longitude of the Capitol of the U. States, Jan. 9th, 1822. Washington, 1822.

384, 1. Q. *Le Roi.* Recherches sur les Longitudes depuis 1730. Paris, 1773.

237. *Ludlow, (Rev. Mr.)* The Theory of Hadley's *(Godfrey's)* Quadrant, and Directions for the use of it. London, 1771.

437. *Mackay, (Andrew)* Theory and Practice of the Longitude. London, 1793.

461. ——— ——— Theory and Practice of finding the Longitude, 2 vols. London, 1810.

235. Q. *Magellan, (L. F.)* Collection de différens traités sur des instrumens d'Astronomie, physique, &c. Londres, 1779.

384, 1. Q. ——— ——— Lettre sur une pendule de son invention.

42. Q. *Maire et Boscovisch.* Voyage astronomique & géographique dans l'état de l'église. Paris, 1770.

46. Q. *Martin, Chappe d'Auteroche, & Pingré.* Mémoire sur le passage de Vénus. Paris, 1767.

241. *Maskelyne.* Instruction relative to the ensuing transit of the planet Venus over the Sun's disk, on the 3d of June, 1769. London, 1768.

459. ——— Answer to a pamphlet of Thomas Mudge, jun. relating to certain time-keepers, and vindicating the conduct of the Astronomer Royal, &c. London, 1792.

384, 2. Q. ——— Concerning the Latitude and Longitude of the Royal Observatory at Greenwich. London, 1787.

488. *Maupertuis.* Degré du Méridien entre Paris & Amiens déterminé. Paris, 1740.

135. Q. *Mayer, (Christian)* Expositio de Transitu Veneris ante discum solis, 23 May, 1769. Petropoli.

156. Q. ——— ——— Methodus longitudinum promota. 1770.

384, 4. Q. ——— ——— Directio Meridiani Palatini. Heydelbergæ, 1774.

384, 4. Q. ——— ——— Observ. occultationis Saturni retrò lunam, 1775.

Pingré, see *Martin.*

384, 18. Q. *Rouy, (C. H.)* Mécanisme Uranographique Portatif. Milan, 1812.

45. Q. *Roy, (William)* An account of the mode proposed to be followed in the Trigonometrical operation for determining the relative situation of the Royal Observatories of Greenwich and Paris, with observations on the magnitude and figure of the earth. London, 1787

384, 19. Q. *Toennies, (F. G.)* Calculum differentiæ Longitudinum Geographicum, &c. Berolini, 1816.

239. *West, (Benj.)* Observ. of Venus upon the Sun. Providence, 1769.

---

3. ASTRONOMICAL TABLES AND ALMANACS.

324. Q. *Argoli* Ephemerides, 3 vol. Leyden, 1659.

1788. *Bode, (J. C.)* Astromisches Jahrbuch, 1795—1807, 1809—1817, 22 vol. Berlin.

1789. ——— ——— Sammlung astronomischer Abhandlungen, 3 vol. Berlin, 1793.

1790. ——— ——— Erläuterungen über die Einrichtung und den Gebrauch seiner astronomischen Jahrbücher. Berlin, 1811,

469. *Carlini, (Francesco)* Tavole della equazione del centro e riduzione all'Eclittica pei quattro novi pianeti. Milano, 1818.

134. Q. *De la Lande.* Ephémérides des mouvemens célestes 1775—1784. Paris, 1774.

539. Q. *Grew, (T.)* Tables of the Sun and Moon, fitted to the Meridian of Philadelphia, MS.

149. *Halley, (Edmund)* Astronomical Tables. London, 1752.

384, 2. Q. *Herschel.* Catalogue of one thousand new nebulæ and clusters of stars. London, 1786.

471. *Kunze, (John C.)* Table for calculating the great eclipse, 1806. New York.

160. Q. *Lindenau, (Bernhard de)* Tabulæ Martis novæ, correctæ ex Theoriâ Gravitatis. Eisenberg, 1811.

160½. Q. ——— ——— Tabulæ Veneris novæ, correctæ ex Theoriâ Gravitatis. Gothæ, 1810.

148. Q. *Mendoza Rios, (Joseph de)* A Complete Collection of Tables for Navigation and Nautical Astronomy. London, 1809.

1791. *Schumacher, (H. C.)* Distances of the Moon's centre from the four planets, Venus, Mars, Jupiter, and Saturn, for 1823 and 1824, 2 vol. Copenhagen, 1821.

153. Q. *Zach, (Franc. de)* Tabulæ motuum solis novæ et correctæ. Gothæ, 1792.

154. Q. ——— ——— Fixarum præcipuarum stellarum catalogus novus. Gothæ, 1790.

152. Q. ——— ——— Tabulæ speciales aberrationis et nutationis in ascensionem rectam et declinationem, 2 vol. 1800.

ANONYMOUS.

1793. The Nautical Almanac and Astronomical Ephemeris for the years 1774, 1798, 1802, 1804, 1805, and 1812, 6 vols. London.

1870. The Nautical Almanac for 1803, 1811—14, 5 vols. New Brunswick.

1871. The Nautical Almanac for 1814, (Blunt's Edition.) New York, 1813.

1787. Connaissance des Temps, 1735, 1766, 1774, 1776—1785, 1789, 1792, 1800, 1802—1805, 1807, 1810—1816, 1820—25, 41 vol. Paris.

1792. Almanaque Náutico y Efemérides Astronomicas para el Año de 1804. Madrid, 1802

456. Q. Ephem. Nauticas para o merid. de Lisboa, 1789 a 1798, 10 vols.

241. The names and situations of the Constellations, to which is added the names of the principal stars therein. Published by order of the board of longitude. London, 1816.

151. Q. Tables for correcting the apparent distance of the moon and a star from the effects of refraction and parallax. Cambridge, 1772.

III. MATHEMATICS.

1. Algebra and Arithmetic.
2. Geometry in general.
3. Infinitesimal Calculus.
4. Mathematical Tables.
5. Miscellaneous.

1. ALGEBRA AND ARITHMETIC.

202. Q. *Bezout.* Théorie générale des équations algébriques. Paris, 1719.

496½. *Euler.* Elémens d'Algèbre, traduits de l'Allemand par J. G. Garnier, 2 vol. Paris, 1807.

201. Q. *La Grange.* Traité de la résolution des équations numériques de tous les degrés. Paris, 1808.

125. Q. *Le Gendre.* Théorie des Nombres. Paris, 1808.

142. F. *Kersey, (John)* The Elements of that Mathematical Art commonly called Algebra. Expounded in four Books. London, 1673.

310. Q. *Kirkby, (John)* Arithmetical Institutions, containing a Complete System of Arithmetic, Natural, Logarithmical and Algebraical, in all their branches. London, 1735.

448. *Patterson, (Robert)* A Treatise of Practical Arithmetic, intended for the use of Schools. Pittsburg, 1818.

448½. *Value, (Victor)* Arithmetic, theoretical and practical, wherein the fundamental principles of the Science are explained in a perspicuous and familiar manner. Philadelphia, 1823.

1420. *Vinall, (John)* The Preceptor's Assistant, or Students Guide, being a Systematical Treatise of Arithmetic, both vulgar and decimal, calculated for the use of Schools, Counting-houses and private families. Boston, 1798.

117. Q. *Waring, (Edward)* Miscellanea Analytica de Æquationibus Algebraicis & curvarum proprietatibus. Cantab. 1762.

118. Q. ——— ——— Meditationes Analyticæ, Editio Secunda, cum additionibus. Cantab. 1785.

119. Q. ——— ——— Meditationes Algebraicæ, Edit. Tert. recensita and aucta. Cantab. 1782.

2. GEOMETRY IN GENERAL.

483. *Adams, (George)* Geometrical and Graphical Essays, with plates. London, 1797.

98. F. *Briggs, (Henry)* Trigonometria Britannica, seu de Doctrinâ Triangulorum, Libri Duo—Posterior ab Henrico Gillibrand, Astronom. Prof. in Colleg. Greshamensi apud Londin. Goudæ, 1633.

122. *Cabral, (Estevaõ)* Tratado de Agrimensura, lido na academia Real das Sciencias. Lisboa, 1795.

478. *Carnot, (L. N. M.)* De la corrélation des figures de Géometrie. Paris, 1801.

198. Q. *Cowley, (John Lodge)* An Illustration and Mensuration of Solid Geometry, revised, corrected, and augmented by William Jones. London, 1787.

503½ Q. *Garvies, (J. G.)* Elements de Geométrie analytique. Paris, 1808.

Gillibrand, see *Briggs*.

477. *Gregory, (David)* A Treatise of Practical Geometry. Edinburgh, 1766.

475. *Gummere, (John)* A Treatise on Surveying in theory and practice, to which is prefixed a perspicuous system of Plane Trigonometry. Philadelphia, 1814.

457. *Howard, (John A.)* A Treatise of Spherical Geometry. New Castle, (England,) 1798.

1400. *Keil, (John)* Elements of Trigonometry. Dublin, 1726.

435. *Larkin, (N. J.)* An Introduction to Solid Geometry and the study of Chrystallography. London, 1820.

503. *Legendre*. Elements de Géométrie. Paris, 1813.

476. *Playfair, (John)* Elements of Geometry. Boston, 1814.

106. Q. *Proclus*. His Philosophical and Mathematical Commentaries on the first book of Euclid's Elements, to which are added a history of the Restoration of Platonic Theology, by the latter Platonists, and a translation from the Greek of Proclus's Theological Elements, by J. Taylor, 2 vols. London, 1792.

116. Q. *Waring, (Edward)* Proprietates Algebraicarum Curvarum; primum editæ, anno 1762. Edit. sec. Lond. 1772.

484. *West, (John)* Elements of Conic Sections. New York, 1820.

---

3. INFINITESIMAL CALCULUS.

456. *Agnesi, (Mademoiselle)* Traités élémentaires du calcul differentiel & du calcul intégral, traduits de l'Italien; avec des additions. Paris, 1775.

128. Q. *Arbogast, (F. L. M.)* Du calcul des dérivations. Strasburg, 1800.

444. *Carnot, (L. N. M.)* Réflexions sur la Métaphysique du calcul infinitésimal. Paris, 1797.

498. Same work, 2d edit. Paris, 1813.

455. *Cousin*. Leçons de calcul différentiel & de calcul intégral, 2 vol. Paris, 1777.

127. Q. ——— Traité du calcul differentiel. Paris, 1796.

494. *Du Borguet, (J. B. E.)* Traités Elémentaires de calcul différentiel & de calcul intégral, indépendans de toutes notions de quantités infinitésimales & de toutes limites, 2 vol. Paris, 1810.

130. Q. *Euler*. Introduction à l'analyse infinitésimale, traduit

du latin avec des notes & des éclaircissemens, par J. B. Labey, 2 vol. Paris, 1796.

129. Q. *La Croix.* Traité du calcul différentiel, 3 vol. Paris, 1797.

200. Q. *La Grange.* Théorie des fonctions analytiques, contenant les principes du Calcul différentiel. Paris, an V.

493. —— —— Leçons sur le Calcul des fonctions. Paris, 1806.

126. Q. *Le Gendre.* Exercices du Calcul intégral, 3 vol. Paris, 1811.

384, 19. Q. *L'Hopital.* Analyse des infiniment petits. Paris, 1781.

237. *Ludlam, (Rev. Mr.)* Essay on ultimate Ratios, and on the power of the Wedge. Cambridge, 1770.

431. *Rowe, (John)* An Introduction to the doctrine of Fluxions. London, 1767.

118. *Stockler, (F. de Borja Garção)* Compendio da theorica dos limites, ou Introducção ao methodo das fluxões. Lisboa, 1794.

439. *Woodhouse, (Robert)* A Treatise on Isometrical problems and the Calculus of Variations. Cambridge, (England) 1810.

4. MATHEMATICAL TABLES.

241. *Anon.* An Essay on the origin and use of the Tables of Latitude and Departure. Dublin, 1770.

119. —— Taboas que contem os Logarithmos dos numeros naturaes, desde 1 atè 43200. Printed in 1804.

147. Q. *Burckhardt, (J. Ch.)* Table des Diviseurs pour tous les nombres de 1, 2, & 3 millions, ou plus exactement depuis 1 à 3,036,000, avec les nombres prémiers qui s'y trouvent. Paris, 1817.

485. *Callet, (Francis)* Tables of Logarithms, containing the logarithms of all numbers from 1 to 108,000, the logarithms, sines and tangents to every second, for the five first degrees, to every ten seconds, for all the degrees of a quadrant of the circle, and to every ten thousandth part, according to the new centesimal division. Also three new tables of logarithms to 20, 48, and 61, places of figures, and several other tables, useful in ascertaining the longitude at sea, &c. Translated from the French, by D. B. Warden. Paris, 1809.

486 *Hutton, (Charles)* Mathematical Tables, containing the common, hyperbolic, and logistic logarithms, and sines, tangents, secants, and versed sines, both natural and logarithmic. With several other tables. 4th edition. London, 1804.

455. Q. *Lambert, (J. H.)* Supplementa Tabularum logarithmicarum & trigonometricarum, cum versione introductionis Germanicæ in Latinum Sermonem. Curante Antonio Felkel. Olisipone, 1798.

462. *Mackay, (Andrew)* A collection of Mathematical Tables for the use of students. London, 1804.

288. *Oltmans, (J.)* Tables Hypsométriques portatives, servant aux calculs des hauteurs au moyen de la formule Barométrique de M. de la Place. Paris, 1811.

146. Q. *Taylor, (Michael)* Tables of Logarithms of all numbers from 1 to 101,000, and of the sines and tangents to every second of the quadrant. With a preface and precepts for the explanation and use of the same. By Nevil Maskelyne. London, 1792.

5. MISCELLANEOUS.

150½ F. *Anon.* Calculations, with the principles and data, on which they are instituted, relative to an act of parliament for raising a fund for the widows and children of the ministers of the church, &c. Published by order of the trustees. London, 1748.

449. *Archimedes.* Oeuvres d'Archimède, Traduites par Peyrard, 2 vol. Paris, 1808.

429. *Berard, (J. B.)* Mélanges Physico Mathématiques. Paris, 1801.

195. Q. *Bernouilli, (John)* Opera omnia, 4 vol. Lausannæ, 1742.

197. Q. ——— ——— Ars conjectandi. Basilæ, 1713.

505. *Delambre.* Rapport historique sur les progrès des sciences mathématiques depuis 1789. Paris, 1810.

133, Q. *De Moivre, (A.)* The doctrine of chances, or a method of calculating the probability of events in play. London, 1718.

384, 23. *Gerling, (C. L.)* Methodi projectionis orthographicæ ad calculos parallacticos facilitandos explicatio. Göttingæ, 1812.

109. Q. *Hutton, (Charles)* Philosophical and Mathematical Dictionary, 2 vols. London, 1815.

110. Q. ——— ——— Tracts Mathematical and Philosophical. London, 1786.

481. ——— ——— Tracts on Mathematical and Philosophical subjects, 3 vols. London, 1812.

593½. *La Place.* Essai Philosophique sur les probabilités. Paris, 1816.

504. *Lindenau, (Bernard De)* Tables Barométriques pour faciliter le calcul des nivellements, & des mesures des hauteurs par le Baromètre. Gotha, 1809.

500. *Mansfield, (J.)* Essays, mathematical and physical, containing new theories and illustrations on some important and difficult subjects. Newhaven, 1816.

384, 2. Q. *Maskelyne.* Account of an Instrument for measuring small angles. London, 1778.

495. *Milne, (Joshua)* A Treatise on the valuation of annuities, and assurances on lives and survivorships, 2 vols. London, 1815.

396. *Q.* *Polytechnic School of France.* Journal de l'Ecole Polytechnique vol. II. IV. VII. Paris, 1796—1808.

491. *Price, (Richard)* Observations on reversionary payments, or schemes for providing annuities for widows, &c. 2 vols. London, 1782.

384, 18. *Q.* *Rochon.* Recherches sur la mesure des Angles.

95. *F.* *Salisbury, (Thomas)* Mathematical Collections and Translations, from the original copies of Galileus and other famous modern authors. London, 1667.

121. *Q.* Scriptores Logarithmici. tomi. 3. London, 1791.

199. *Q.* *Simpson, (Thomas)* Opera quodam reliqua. Glasg. 1776.

446. ——— ——— Select Exercises for young proficients in the Mathematics. London, 1752.

50. *Q.* *Souciet, (E.)* Observations mathématiques, astronomiques, géographiques, chronologiques & physiques, tirées des anciens livres Chinois. Paris, 1729.

127. *Stockler, (J. B. Garção)* Ensaio historico sobre a origen e progressos das Mathematicas em Portugal. Pariz, 1819.

1602. *Sturmi, (Joh. Cristoph.)* Mathesis Enucleata. Nurembergæ, 1695.

501. *Webber, (Samuel)* Mathematics compiled from the best authors, and intended to be the text-book of the course of private lectures, in the university at Cambridge, 2 vols. Boston, 1801.

155. *Q.* *Williams, Mudge,* and *Darby's* account of the trigonometrical survey carried on in 1791, 1792, 1793, and 1794. London.

IV. NATURAL PHILOSOPHY.

1. General Treatises.
2. Electricity and Magnetism.
3. Meteorology and Pneumatics.
4. Optics.
5. Hydrostatics and Hydraulics.
6. Coins, Weights, and Measures.
7. Machines and Instruments.
8. Miscellaneous.

1. GENERAL TREATISES.

1122. *Adams, (George)* Lectures on Natural and Experimental Philosophy, 4 vols. and Atlas. London, 1799.

1738. *Brisson, (Mathurin Jaques)* Traité élémentaire ou principes de Physique, 3 vol. Paris, 1800.

1739. ——— ——— Elements ou principes Physico-Chymiques pour servir de suite aux principes de Physique. Paris, 1800.

216. *Q.* *Desaguliers, (T. T.)* Course of Experimental Philosophy, 2 vols. London, 1745.

1124. *Ewing, (John)* Natural and Experimental Philosophy. Philadelphia, 1809.

480. *Francœur, (L. B.)* Traité élémentaire de mécanique. Paris, 1804.

1126. *Haüy, (R. T.)* Traité élémentaire de Physique, 2 vol. Paris, 1806.

1125. —— —— Elementary Treatise on Natural Philosophy, 2 vols. London, 1807.

240. Q. *Jones, (William)* First Principles of Natural Philosophy. Oxford, 1762.

450. *Keill, (J.)* Introductio ad veram physicam, seu Lectiones Physicæ, habita in Academiâ Oxoniensi. Londini, 1799.

497½. *Monge, (Gasp.)* Traité élémentaire de Statique à l'usage des écoles de la Marine; 5e edition, revue par Hachette. Paris, 1810.

218. Q. *Muschenbroek. (P. Van)* Introductio ad philosophiam naturalem; 2 vol. Lugduni Batam. 1762.

157. Q. *Newton.* Philosophiæ naturalis principia mathematica. Londini, 1726.

1414. *Nollet, (l'Abbé)* Leçons de Physique expérimentale, 6 vol. Paris, 1775.

443. *Poisson, (S. D.)* Traité de Mécanique, 2 vol. Paris, 1811.

1515, 43. *Priestley, (Joseph)* Heads of Lectures on a Course of Experimental Philosophy. London, 1794.

396. Q. *Prony.* Leçons de Mécanique Analytique, données dans l'École Impériale Polytechnique. Paris, 1810.

—— Mécanique Philosophique, ou analyse raisonnée des diverses parties de la Science de l'équilibre & du mouvement, 7e & 8e Cahier. Paris, an 8.

382. Q. *Rutherforth, (T.)* System of Natural Philosophy, 2 vols. London, 1748.

---

2. ELECTRICITY AND MAGNETISM.

349. *Anon.* Remontrance des malades aux médecins de la faculté de Paris à cause de leur conduite à l'égard de Mesmer & le magnétisme animal. Amsterdam, 1785.

643. *Abbot, (Joel)* An essay on the central influence of magnetism. Philadelphia, 1814.

232. Q. *Æpini, (F. U. T.)* Tentamen theoriæ electricitatis & magnetismi. Petropoli.

107. Q. *Aldini, (Jean)* Essai théorétique & expérimental sur le Galvanisme. Paris, 1804.

96. F. *Beccaria, (Giambattista)* Lettere à G. B. Beccari, dell'-Elettricismo. Bologna, 1758.

384, 1. Q. —— —— Della Elettricità. Turin, 1775.

8. Q. —— —— Elettricismo artifiziale. Turin, 1772.

8. Q. —— —— De atmosphæra Electricâ. Turin, 1769.

8. Q. *Bertholon, (l'abbé)* Mem. sur le moyen de se preserver, de la foudre. Montpellier, 1777.

434. *Bond, (Henry)* Longitude found; a Treatise shewing an easy way to find the longitude by the use of the magnetic inclinatory needle, latitude being known. London, 1676.

1127. *Cavallo, (Siberdas)* Treatise on magnetism in theory and practice. London, 1795.

1128. ——— ——— Treatise on Electricity. London, 1782.

237. *Churchman, (John)* Explanation of the Magnetic Atlas. Philadelphia, 1790.

384, 8. Q. *Detienne.* Sur l'amélioration des mach. électr. 1775.

384, 8. Q. ——— Sur l'augmentation de la Force de l'électr. Paris, 1775.

384, 8. Q. ——— Sur les moyens de perfectionner les isolemens des machines électriques. Paris, 1779.

231½. Q. *Franklin.* Experiments and observations on electricity. London, 1774.

241. *Hare, (Robert)* An essay on the question whether there be two electrical fluids according to Du Faye, or one according to Franklin. Philadelphia.

695. ——— ——— Animadversions on Dr. Patterson's review of his Theory of Galvanism.

695. ——— ——— A memoir on some new modifications of Galvanic apparatus, with observations in support of his new theory of Galvanism.

643. ——— ——— A new Theory of Galvanism, supported by some experiments and observations, made by means of the Calorimotor. Philadelphia, 1819.

695. ——— ——— Strictures, in reply to remarks on the Calorimotor, published at different times in the American Medical Recorder. Philadelphia, 1820.

384, 8. Q. *Hartley, (D.)* Account of the Method of securing buildings and ships against fire. London, 1774.

1129½. *Haüy, (R. T.)* Expos. raisonnée de la théo. de l'Electricité & du Magnétisme. Paris, 1787.

251. *Henley, (William)* Romayne's letter to B. Franklin on atmospherical electricity and remarks communicated by W. Henley. London, 1772.

1130. *Humboldt.* Expériences sur le Galvanisme, & en général sur l'irritation des fibres musculaires & nerveuses. Paris, 1799.

384, 18. Q. *Humboldt* & *Biot.* Sur les variations du magnétisme terrestre à differentes latitudes. Paris, an 13.

384. Q. *Ingen-Housz, (Jean)* Lettre à Molitor, sur l'influence de l'Electricité sur les végétaux. 1788.

1129. *Jallabert.* Experiences sur l'Electricité. Geneve, 1748.

384, 8. Q. *Le Roy.* Exper. on Electricity. London, 1779.

233. Q. *Mahon, (Charles Viscount)* Principles of Electricity. London, 1779.

265. *Marat.* Recherches Physiques sur le feu. Paris, 1780.

1130½. *Meade, (William)* Outlines of the origin and progress of Galvanism. Dublin, 1805.

1635. *Mesmer.* Précis historique des faits relatifs au magnétisme animal. Londre, 1781.

237. *Nairne, (E.)* Directions for using the electrical machine. London, 1764.

1515, 6. *Priestley, (Joseph)* Introduction to the study of Electricity. London, 1773.

384, 3. Q. ——— ——— Account of a new electrom. London, 1773.

266. Q. ——— ——— History and present state of Electricity, 5 vols. London, 1775.

1160. *Rabiqueau, (Ch.)* Le spectacle du Feu élementaire ou cours d'électricité expérimentale. Paris, 1753.

384, 2. Q. *Stanhope, (Ch. Earl)* Remarks on Brydone's account of a remarkable thunder storm. London, 1787.

1131. *Sue, (P.)* Histoire du Galvanisme. Paris, 1802.

1101. *Walker, (Ralph)* Treatise on Magnetism, with a description of the meridional and azimuth compass. London, 1794.

322. Q. *Wavran, (C. L. B.)* Essai de Physique présenté au docteur Franklin, MS.

384, 8. Q. *Wilson, (Benjamin)* Experiments and observation on the nature and use of conductors. London, 1777

384, 8. Q. —— Mém. sur la forme des barres, ou conducteurs Métalliques. Paris, 1773.

---

3. METEOROLOGY AND PNEUMATICS.

1155. *Anon.* Meteorological Essays concerning the origin of springs, generation of rain, and production of wind. London, 1715.

1154. —— General chronological history of the air, weather, seasons, meteors, &c. for 250 years, 2 vols. 1749.

247. —— The Air Balloon, or a treatise on the Aerostatical globe invented by Montgolfier. London, 1787.

262. *Blanchard.* Journal of my forty-fifth ascension, being the first performed in America. January 9, 1793. Philadelphia, 1793.

78. Q. *Cavallo, (Tiberius)* Treatise on the nature and property of air. London, 1781.

1203. *Dalton, (John)* Meteorological observations and essays. London, 1793.

231. Q. *De la Luc, (J. I.)* Recherches sur les modifications de l'atmosphère. Geneve, 1772.

206. Q. *De Saussure.* Essais sur l'hygrométrie. Neuchâtel, 1783.

384, 4. Q. *Fontana, (Felice)* Ricerche Fisiche Sopra l'Aria Fissa. Firenze, 1775.

1162. *Forster, (Thomas)* Researches about atmospheric phenomena. London, 1815.

494. Q. *Jefferies.* Narrative of his aerian voyage with Blanchard. London, 1786.

1187. *Kirwan, (Richard)* Estimate of the temperature of different latitudes. London, 1787.

384, 4. Q. *Moscati, (P.)* Lettera al Sigr. de Saussure con la descrizione d'un Atmidometro, &c.

1157½ *Müller, (W. E.)* Ausserordenttiche Wärme und Kälte, in Sommern und Wintern seit 500 Jahren, nach Bremischen, Hamburgischen und Oldenburgischen Chroniken, und mehrerer anderweitigen Thermometer—Beobachtungen seit 100 Jahren; nebst einige Resultaten über ihre Perioden, und Einwirkung auf die Menschheit. Bremen, 1823.

384, 5. Q. *Pugh.* Observations sur la pesanteur de l'atmosphére. Rouen, an 8.

1156. *Van Swinden, (J. H.)* Observations sur le froid rigoureux de Janvier, 1776. Amsterdam, 1778.

1157. ——— ——— Dissertation sur la comparaison des thermomètres. Amst. 1778.

338. *Volta, (Alessandro)* Lettere sull'aria infiammabile nativa delle paludi. Milano, 1767.

4. OPTICS.

114. Q. *Adams, (George)* Essays on the Microscope. London, 1798.

115. Q. ——— ——— Essays on the Microscope, Plates belonging to.

355. Q. *De la Chambre.* Nouvelles observations & conjectures sur l'Iris. Paris, 1650.

1170. *Delaval, (Edward Hussey)* Enquiry into the cause of the permanent colours of opake bodies. Warrington, 1785.

384, 2. Q. *Dolland, (Peter)* Account of the discovery of refracting telescopes. London, 1789.

502. *Emerson, (W.)* Elements of Optics. London, 1768.

384, 4. Q. *Gruber.* Physicalische abhandlung über die Stralenbrechung, &c. Dresden, 1787.

384, 2. Q. *Herschel.* Investigation of the cause of that indistinctness of vision, which has been ascribed to the smallness of the optic pencil. London, 1786.

239. *Lincoln, (Charles)* Double Microscope described. London.

239. ——— ——— Directions to use solar apparatus. London.

239. ——— ——— Description of a Pocket Microscope. London.

384, 1. Q. *Jeaurat.* Mem. sur les Lunettes Displantidiennes. Paris, 1779.

384, 3. Q. *Maskelyne.* An attempt to explain a difficulty in the theory of vision. London, 1789.

288. *Opoix.* Examen de la théorie des couleurs, (rapport fait à l'académie des sciences.) Paris, 1810.

1515, 6. *Priestley, (Joseph)* Introduction to the theory and practice of perspective. London, 1780

Smith, (Robert) A Complete System of Optics. Cambridge, (Eng.) 1736.

5. HYDROSTATICS AND HYDRAULICS.

286. *Anon.* Notes sur le Bélier Hydraulique, extraites du Journal des mines, No. 63, vol. 13. Paris, 1806.

1599. —— Traité du mouvement des eaux. Paris, 1700.

112. Q. *Belidor.* Architecture Hydraulique, 4 vol. Paris, 1737.

196. Q. *Bernouilli, (Daniel)* Hydrodynamica, sive de viribus & motibus fluidorum commentarii. Argentor, 1738.

384. ii. Q. *Bralle.* Réponse à des mém. de Perrier sur la Machine de Marly. Paris, 1814.

1123. *Bremontier, (N. Th.)* Recherches sur le mouvement des Ondes. Paris, 1809.

384. ii. Q. *Brunet, (Ainé)* Mém. relatif au changement de la Machine de Marly. Paris, 1807.

1161. *Cotes, (Roger)* Hydrostatical and Pneumatical Lectures. London, 1775.

111. Q. *De Prony.* Nouvelle Architecture Hydraulique, 2 vol. Paris, 1790.

433. *Du Buat.* Principes d'Hydraulique, 2 vol. Paris, 1786.

111½ Q. *Fabre.* Essai sur la manière la plus avantageuse de construire les machines hydrauliques, & en particulier les moulins à bled. Paris, 1783.

707. *Merrick, (S. V.)* A description of the patent improved fire-engines, and other hydraulic machines invented by Jacob Perkins, and manufactured at Philadelphia.

286. *Montgolfier, (Joseph)* De l'utilité du Bélier Hydraulique. Paris, 1805.

384. ii. Q. *Perrier.* Mém. sur la Machine de Marly. Paris, 1807—1811.

217. Q. *Switzer, (Steph.)* Introduction to a general system of hydrostatics and hydraulics, 2 vols. in one. London, 1729.

384. ii. Q. *Sokolnicki, (General)* Descrip. d'une trombe Hydraulique pour le desséchement des Marais. Paris, 1811.

1169. *Zimmerman, (E. A. G.)* Traité de l'élasticité de l'eau & d'autres fluides. Amsterdam, 1780.

---

6. COINS, WEIGHTS AND MEASURES.

887. *Adams, (J. Q.)* Report to Congress on the subject of weights and measures. Washington, 1821.

85. Q. *Arbuthnot, (John)* Tables of ancient coins, weights and measures, explained and exemplified in several dissertations by John Arbuthnot, with an Appendix containing observations, by Benjamin Longwith. London, 1754.

241. *Aubry.* Le système des nouvelles mesures de la République Française mis à la portée de tout le monde. Paris, an 7.

238. *Bonne, (M.)* Principes sur les mesures en longueur & en capacité sur les poids & les monnoyes, dépendans du

mouvement des astres principaux & de la grandeur de la terre. Présenté à l'assemblé nationale. Paris, 1790.

357. Q. *Delambre.* Base du système métrique décimal, 1806—10, 3 vols.

241. *Carney, (Jean Alex.)* Mémoire sur les noms des poids & mesures. Montpellier, an. 2.

Congress of the United States. Report of a select committee on the subject of fixing a standard of weights and measures, read January 25, 1819.

538. *French Republic.* Instructions sur les mesures déduites de la grandeur de la terre, uniformes pour toute la République, & les calculs relatifs à leur division décimale. Par la commission temporaire des poids & mesures Républicaines; en exécution des Décrets de la Convention Nationale. Edition originale. Paris, an 2.

241. *Helvetic Government.* Schriften, Maasse und Gewichte betreffend der Helvetischen Regierung vorgelegt; Gedruckt auf Befehl des Vollziehungs. Rathes, 1801.

241, 608. *Jefferson, (Thomas)* Report of the Secretary of State on the subject of establishing an uniformity of weights, measures and coins in the United States. New York, 1790.

131. Q. *Lesparat.* Métrologie Constitutionelle & primitive, comparées entre elles & avec la métrologie d'ordonnances, 2 vol. Paris, 1801.

44. Q. *National Institute of France.* Discours prononcés à la barre des deux conseils du corps législatif au nom de l'Institut National des Sciences & des Arts, lors de la présentation des Etalons prototypes du mètre & du kilogramme, & du rapport sur le travail de la commission des poids & mesures. Imprimés par ordre des deux Conseils. Paris, an. 7.

241. *Senate of Pennsylvania.* Report on the subject of weights and measures, read in the Senate, March, 1, 1822. Mr. Raguet, Chairman.

379. *Svanberg, (J.)* Exposition des opérations faites en Lapponie pour la détermination d'un Arc du Méridien en 1801 a 1803, par Ofverbom, Svanberg, Holmquist & Palander, rédigée par J. Svanberg. 1805.

---

7. MACHINES AND INSTRUMENTS—STEAM ENGINE.

351. Q. *Academy of Sciences.* Machines approuvées par l'Académie Royale des Sciences, 7 vol. Paris, 1735.

205. Q. *Anon.* Projet d'une nouvelle méchanique. Paris, 1687.

330. —— An Address to the mining interest of Cornwall, on the subject of Boulton & Watt's and Hornblower's engines. Truro, 1792.

99. F. *Bion.* The construction and principal uses of mathematical

instruments. Translated from the French, by Edmund Stone. London, 1758.

143. Q. *Borguis, (T. A.)* Traité complet de Mécanique appliquée aux arts, 4 vol. Paris, 1818.

479. *Camus, (M.)* A treatise on the teeth of wheels, pinions, &c. for the various purposes of machinery. Translated from the French. London, 1806.

397. *Evans, (Oliver)* The abortion of the young Steam Engineers' guide, containing an investigation of the principles, construction, and power of the steam-engine, &c. and of five patented inventions. Philadelphia, 1805.

330. *Fitch, (J.)* The original steam-boat supported, or a reply to J. Rumsey's pamphlet, showing the true priority of J. Fitch, and the false datings, &c. of J. Rumsey. Philadelphia, 1788.

651. *Fulton, (Robert)* Report on the practicability of navigation with steam-boats on the southern waters of the United States. New York, 1813.

222. F. *Komarzewski, (M. de)* Mémoire sur un graphomètre souterrain. Paris, an xi.

237. *Ludlam*. Essay on ultimate ratios, and on the power of the wedge. Cambridge, 1770.

237. *Nicholson, (William)* Description of an instrument for measuring the gravity of bodies. Warrington, 1785.

384, 2. Q. *Magellan, (J. H. de)* Descrip. d'une nouvelle machine de Dynamique, inventée par Atwood. Londres, 1780.

339. *Masterman*. Description of Masterman's patent rotatory steam-engine. London, 1822.

464. *Mountaine, (William)* A description of the lines drawn on Gunter's scale, as improved by Mr. John Robertson, and executed by Messrs. Nairne and Blunt, with their use and application to navigation and astronomy. London, 1778.

302. *Pattu*. Description d'une vis d'Archimède à double effet destinée aux irrigations & aux épuisemens. Caen, 1815.

274. *Rumsey, (J.)* Short treatise on the application of steam. Philadelphia, 1788.

670. ——— ——— Plan wherein the power of steam is fully shown, by a new constructed machine for propelling boats or vessels, against the most rapid streams or rivers. 1788.

251 ——— ——— Plan of propelling boats by steam, and raising water to work grist mills. Berkley County, (Virginia,) 1788.

274. ——— ——— Explanations and annexed plates on improvements in the mechanics, viz. new constructed boiler, grist-mill, &c. Philadelphia, 1788.

——— ——— Explanation of a steam-engine, and the method of applying it to propel a boat. Philadelphia, 1788.

266. *Smeaton, (Q.)* Experimental Enquiry concerning the natural powers of wind and water to turn mills and other machines. London, 1794.

302. *Tarbé*. Rapport sur la vis d'Archimède à double effet. Caen, 1816.

384, 5. Q. *Tod, (A. J.)* Mémoire sur une machine à creuser & curer les canaux, inventée par les fréres Eckhardt.

330. *Wilson, (T.)* A comparative statement of the effects of Boulton & Watt's steam-engines with Newcommen's and Hornblower's. Truro, 1792.

8. MISCELLANEOUS.

344, i. Q. *Bacon*. Lord Verulam's Works, 5 vols. London, 1765.

108. Q. *Bertholet*. La Mécanique appliquée aux Arts, aux Manufactures, à l'Agriculture, & à la Guerre, 2 vol. Paris, 1782.

320. Q. *Boyle, (Robert)* His Works, 3 vols. London, 1738.

384, 14. Q. *Colden, (Cadwalader)* The principles of action in matter, the gravitation of bodies, and the motion of the planets. London, 1751.

254. *Elliott, (J.)* Philos. observ. on the senses of vision and hearing, with a treatise on harmonic sounds, and an essay on combustion and animal heats. London, 1780.

86. Q. *Feuillée, (Louis)* Journal des observations physiques, mathématiques, & botaniques, tom. 1. Paris, 1714.

906. *Franklin, (Benjamin)* His Works, 6 vols. Philadelphia, 1818.

——— ——— Political, miscellaneous, and philosophical pieces, with plates. London, 1779.

1606. *Hamilton, (Hugh)* Philosophical Essays. London, 1767.

1102. *Hooper, (W.)* Rational Recreations, in which the principles of numbers and natural philosophy are explained, 4 vols. London, 1794.

349. Q. *Humboldt, (Alex. de)* Nivellement barométrique fait dans les régions Equinoxiales du nouveau continent en 1799—1804. Paris, 1809.

243. *Gentzkenii, (Fred.)* Physica Hypothetica, pro demonstrandis rerum naturalium phenomenis. Kilonii, 1721.

1100. *Ingenhousz*. Nouvelles Expériences sur divers objets de physique, tom. 2. Paris, 1789.

1190. ——— Vermischte schriften physisch-medicinischen inhalts, 2 vol. Vienna, 1784.

1556. *Nicholson, (William)* Journal of Natural Philosophy, Chemistry, and the Arts, 32 vols. 1802—1812.

384. 19. Q. *Riccati*. Delle Corde ovvero Fibre elastiche; Schediasmi Fisico-Mathematici. Bologna, 1767.

671. *Rittenhouse, (David)* Philosophical papers by.— London, 1787.

491. Q. *Rozier*. Journal de Physique rédigé par—94 vol. Paris, 1773—1822.

432. *Stanat, (William)* Doctrine of projectiles. Dublin, 1733.

97. *F.* Saggi di naturali esperienze fatti nella academia del Cimento. Firenze, 1691.
551. *Silliman, (Benjamin)* American Journal of Science, 6 vols. New York, 1819—1823.
266. *Smeaton, (John)* New fundamental experiments upon the collision of bodies.
1560. *Thomson, (Thomas)* Annals of Philosophy, 16 vols. London, 1813—1820.
Same Work, (new series) 4 vols. London, 1822.
1562. *Tilloch, (Alexander)* Philosophical Magazine, 17 vols. London, 1798—1803.

ANONYMOUS WORKS.

382. Annales de Chimie & de Physique, 20 vol. Paris, 1816—1822.
1566. Edinburgh Philosophical Journal, Nos. 1 a 15. Edinburgh, 1819—1823.
334. *Q.* Raccolta d'opuscoli sulle Scienze e sulle Arti. Milan, 1779.
384. i. *Q.* Journal des inventions, découvertes, &c. dans les Sciences, &c. tome 2. Cahier 97. Paris, an. 3.
1408. Mathematical Magick, or the wonders that may be performed by mechanical geometry. London, 1648.

V. CHEMISTRY.

1. General Treatises.
2. Essays on particular subjects.
3. Miscellaneous.

1. GENERAL TREATISES.

1199½ *Accum, (Fred.)* System of Theoretical and Practical Chemistry, with an appendix containing a view of the late doctrines and discoveries in Chemistry, by Thomas Cooper, 2 vols. Philadelphia, 1814.
1184. *Anon.* A Brief outline of Modern Chemistry.
1632. —— Conversations on Chemistry. Philadelphia, 1806.
1633. The same, Second Edit. enlarged. Philadelphia, 1809.
1211. *Bache, (Franklin)* System of Chemistry for the use of Students in Medicine. Philadelphia, 1819.
1204. *Bertholet.* Essai de Statique Chimique, 2 vol. Paris, 1803.
209. *Q.* *Bœrhaave.* Elements of Chemistry, being his original Lectures. Translated from the Latin by Timothy Dallowe, London, 1735.

1739. *Brisson, (Mathurin-Jacques)* Elèments ou Principes Physico-Chimiques, destinés à servir de suite aux principes de Physique, à l'usage des Ecoles Centrales. Paris, 1800. See Title VI. NATURAL PHILOSOPHY, § 1. General Treatises.

1189. *Brownrigg, (William)* Art of making Common Salt. London, 1748.

1628. *Cutbush, (James)* Philosophy of Experimental Chemistry, 2 vol. Philadelphia, 1813.

1198. *Chaptal.* Elémens de Chymie, 3 vol. Paris, 1795.

1201. Same work, English Translation. Philadelphia, 1801.

1202. *Dalton, (John)* A new System of Chemical Philosophy. Manchester, 1808.

1186. *Davy, (Sir Humphrey)* Elements of Chemical Philosophy. Philadelphia, 1812.

1185. ——— ——— Lectures on Chemical Philosophy. Philadelphia, 1804.

1740. *Fourcroy.* Système des Connaissances Chimiques, 10 vol. Paris, 1800.

1480. *Foronda, (Valentin de)* Lecciones ligeras de Chimica. Madrid, 1791.

1200. *Gellert, (E. E.)* Metallurgic Chemistry. London, 1776.

1212. *Gorham, (John)* The Elements of Chemical Science, 2 vols. Boston, 1819.

1208. *Henry, (William)* The Elements of Experimental Chemistry. London, 1815.

1207. Same work; fourth American edition, with notes, by John Redman Coxe. Philadelphia, 1817.

1618. *Jacobs, (W. S.)* Student's Chemical pocket Companion. Philadelphia, 1802.

1177 *Lewis, (William)* A Course of practical Chemistry. London, 1746.

1176. *Parker, (Samuel)* A Chemical Catechism of the application of Chemistry to the arts, for the use of young people, artists, tradesmen, and the amusement of leisure hours. Philadelphia, 1807.

1209. ——— ——— Same work, with notes, illustrations, and experiments. London, 1819.

1630. ——— ——— Rudiments of Chemistry. London, 1822.

1629. *Parkinson, (James)* Chemical Pocket Book. Philadelphia, 1802.

1196. *Smith.* Institutes of Experimental Chemistry, 2 vols. London, 1759.

315. Q. *Stahl, (Geo. Ern.)* Fundamenta Chymiæ Dogmaticæ, rationabilis & experimentalis. Norimb. 1732.

1206. *Thenard, (L. J.)* Traité de Chimie Elémentaire, théorique & pratique. Paris, 1811.

1199. *Thomson, (Thomas)* A system of Chemistry, 4 vols. Philadelphia, 1818.

1627. ——— ——— Elements of Chemistry. Philad. 1810.

2. ESSAYS ON PARTICULAR SUBJECTS.

384, 23. Q. *Anon.* Reclamation sur l'article du rapport du jury concernant la fabrication de la soude. Paris.

736. *Abrams, (Isaac)* The powers of Chymistry in relation to things visible and invisible. Philadelphia, 1801.

301. *Addie, (John)* Hints respecting the construction and some uses to which bags capable of confining atmospheric air may be applied. Stockton, 1809.

Adet, see *Hassenfratz.*

384, 22. Q. *Bambrilla, (De)* Mém. sur la distillation du bois. 1811.

236. Q. *Bories.* Mémoire sur la manière de déterminer les titres ou degrés de spirituosité des eaux de vie & esprits de vin. Montpellier, 1774.

736. *Cooper, (Thomas)* Introductory lecture on Chemistry, delivered at the College of South Carolina in Columbia, January, 1820. Columbia, 1820.

1167. ——— ——— Philosophical Tracts.
1. Introductory Lecture. Carlisle, 1800.
2. Information concerning Gas-lights. Philadelphia, 1816.
3. Connexion between Chemistry and Medicine. Philadelphia, 1818.
4. Introductory Lecture on Chemistry. Philad. 1817.
5. Introductory Lecture on Chemistry. Columbia, 1820.

1178. *Cossigny, (T. F. C.)* Récherches physiques & chimiques sur la fabrication de la poudre à canon. Paris, 1807.

643. *Coxe, (John Redman)* Observations on combustion and acidification, with a new theory of those processes: founded on the conjunction of the Phlogistic and Antiphlogistic doctrines. Philadelphia, 1811.

350. *Curaudau, (F. R.)* Observations générales sur le gaz muriatique oxigéné. Paris, 1810.

1158. *Ellis, (Daniel)* Enquiry into the changes induced on atmospheric air by the germination of seeds, the vegetation of plants, and the respiration of animals. Edinburgh, 1807.

295. *Fontallard, (De)* Essai d'un art de fusion à l'aide du Feu ou air vital, traduit de l'allemand d'Ehrman, suivi des memoires de Lavoisier sur le même Sujet. Strasb. 1797.

1168. *Fulhame, (Mrs.)* Essays on Combustion. London, 1794.

1716. *Guyton Morveau.* Traité des moyens de desinfecter l'air & de prévenir la contagion. Paris, 1805.

384, 8. Q. *Hartley, (David)* Account of experiments made with the fire-plates. London, 1776.

254, 643. *Hare, (Robert)* Memoir on the supply and application of the blow pipe. Philadelphia, 1802.

695. ——— ——— Strictures on Clark's Blow-pipe. Philadelphia, 1820.

1188. *Hassenfratz & Adet.* Method of Chemical nomenclature proposed by Guyton de Morveau, Lavoisier, Bertholet, and Fourcroy—to which is added a new system of chemical characters adapted to the said nomenclature. Translated from the French, and the chemical names adapted to the genius of the English language, by James St. John. London, 1788.

317. Q. *Hausen, (Solomon)* Vollständiger Müntz-Meister und Müntz-Wardein. Frankf. am Mayn, 1765.

1163. *Hales, (Stephen)* Statical Essays, containing vegetable staticks, 2 vols. London, 1731.

1182. *Hall, (Harrison)* Hall's Distiller, adapted to the use of farmers. Philadelphia, 1813.

1194. *Huggins, (Bryan)* Experiments on acetous acid, fixable air, dense inflammable air, &c. &c. London, 1786.

1175. *Kirwan.* Essai sur le Phlogistique & sur la constitution des acides. Paris, 1788.

384. i. Q. *Ingenhousz.* Sur la constr. de l'Eudiomètre de Fontana.

Lavoisier, see *Fontallard.*

384, 17. Q. *Lettsom, (John Coakly)* Synop. of Chemical characters adapted to the new nomencl. by Hassenfratz and Adet. London, 1797.

1515, 45. *Maclean, (John)* Two lectures on combustion, containing an examination of Dr. Priestley's considerations on the doctrine of Phlogiston, and the decomposition of water. Philadelphia, 1797.

1212½ *Macneven, (William James)* Exposition of the Atomic Theory of Chymistry, and the doctrine of definite proportions. New York, 1819.

307. *Magellan, (J. H. de)* Description of a glass apparatus for making mineral waters, together with a description of some new Eudiometers, for ascertaining the wholesomeness of respirable air. London, 1777.

237. ——— ——— Same work. London, 1783.

265. *Marat.* Recherches Physiques sur le feu. Paris, 1780.

100. Q. *Marum, (M. Van)* Description de quelques appareils chimiques. Haarlem, 1798.

384, 13. Q. *Murray, (John)* Experiment on Muriatic Gas, &c. Edinburgh, 1818.

384, 5. Q. *Peacock, (James)* Account of a method of filtration by ascent. London, 1793.

384, 4. Q. *Peyla, (L.)* Maniera di fare le Candelette Fosforiche.

1515, 43. *Priestley, (Joseph)* Réflexions sur la doctrine du Phlogistique, par Adet. Philadelphie, 1797.

——7, 11. ——— ——— Experiments and observations on different kinds of air, 6 vols. London, 1776.

—— 43. ——— ——— Doctrine of Phlogiston. Northumberland, 1800, 1803.

—— 45. *Rupp, (Theop. L.)* Remarks on Dr. Priestley's experiments and observations, relating to the Analysis of atmospherical air, &c.

1195. *Scheele, (Charles William)* Chemical observations and experiments on air and fire. London, 1780.

260. *Smith, (James)* Manière de bonifier parfaitement les mauvaises eaux à bord des bâtimens. Suivie de considérations

chimiques sur le procédé épuratoire & quelques autres systêmes analogues, par Barry. Paris, an 9.

620. *Smith, (Thomas P.)* A sketch of the revolution in chemistry. Philadelphia, 1798.

1157. *Van Swinden, (J. H.)* Dissertation sur la comparaison des thermomètres. Amsterdam, 1778.

300. *Vauquelin.* Manuel de l'essayeur. Paris, 1812.

368. *Wedgwood, (Joseph)* Description and use of a thermometer for measuring the higher degrees of heat from a red heat, up to the strongest that vessels of clay can support. London, 1785.

3. MISCELLANEOUS.

376. Annales de Chymie, ou Recueil de Mémoires concernant la Chymie, & les arts qui en dépendent, 96 vol. Paris, 1790—1815.

382. Annales de Chymie & de Physique, 20 vol. Paris, 1816—1822.

1625. *Anon.* Chemische Versuche und Beobachtungen. *(No imprint or date.)*

1197. *Bergman, (Sir Torbern)* Physical and Chemical Essays, translated from the original Latin, with notes and illustrations, by Edmund Cullen. London, 1788.

1205. *Gay Lussac & Thenard.* Recherches Physico-Chimiques, 2 vol. Paris, 1811.

1191. *Lavoisier.* Opuscules physiques & chymiques. Paris, 1774.

208. Q. *Newman, (Caspar)* His Chemical Works abridged and methodized by William Lewis. London, 1759.

1626. *Scheele, (C. W.)* Mémoires de Chymie, 2 vol. Paris, 1785.

1210. *Ure, (Andrew)* A Dictionary of Chemistry on the basis of Mr. Nicholson, 1 Amer. Ed. with notes, by B. F. Bache. Philadelphia, 1819.

VI. NATURAL HISTORY.

1. In General.
2. Animal Kingdom.
3. Vegetable Kingdom.
4. Mineral Kingdom.

1. IN GENERAL.

1266. *Anderson, (James)* Recreations on Agriculture, Natural History, Arts, &c. 2 vols. London, 1799.

224. *Barton, (Benjamin S.)* Archæologia Americanæ telluris; Collectanea et Specimina, or Collections with Speci-

mens for a series of memoirs on certain extinct animals and vegetables of North America, Part I. Philadelphia, 1814.

262. *Beauvois, (Palissot de)* Catalogue raisonné du Muséum de C. W. Peale. (See *Peale*, p. 35.) Philadelphia.

1226. *Blumenbach.* Handbuch der Naturgeschichte. Goettingen, 1797.

365. ———— Beyträge sur Naturgeschichte. Goettingen, 1790.

365. ———— Von den Federbusch-Polypen in den Göttingschen Gewassern.

365. ———— Ueber die Liebe der Thiere.

1216. ———— Manuel d'Histoire naturelle, 2 vol. Metz, 1803.

385. *Q.* ———— Specimen Historiæ Naturalis, ex auctoribus classicis præsertim poetis illustratæ, eosque vicissim illustrantis. Goettingen, 1816.

247. *Q. Bonnet, (Charles)* Œuvres d'Histoire naturelle & de Philosophie—10 vol. Neuchatel, 1779.

1213. *Buffon.* Histoire naturelle générale & particulière, 127 vol. Paris, 1800.

223. *Q. Buffon & d'Aubenton.* Histoire naturelle, générale & parculière, avec la description du Cabinet du Roi, 5 vol. Paris, 1749—1778.

420. *Camper, (Pierre)* Œuvres de, qui ont pour objet l'histoire naturelle, la physiologie & l'anatomie comparée, 3 vol. Paris, 1803.

18. *F.* ——— ——— Planches pour les Œuvres de. Paris, 1803.

384, 22. *Q. Camper, (Adrien)* Mémoire sur quelques parties moins connues du Squelette des Sauriens fossiles de Maestricht. Paris, 1812.

289. ——— ——— Description du Musée de P. Camper. Amsterdam, 1811.

25. *F. Catesby, (Marc.)* Natural History of Carolina, 2 vols. London, 1771.

70. *F. Cavanilles, (Anto. Jos.)* Observaciones sobre la Historia Natural, &c. del Reyno de Valencia, 2 vol. Madrid, 1795.

77. *F. Chaisneau, (Charles)* Atlas d'Histoire naturelle. Paris, an 11.

164. *Q. Dillenius, (John Jac.)* General History of land and water, &c. mosses, and corals. London, 1768.

295. *Dolomieu.* Mémoire sur les Tremblemens de Terre de la Calabre en 1783. Rome, 1784.

1521. *Fabricius, (Jean Albert)* Théologie de l'eau. Paris, 1743.

1159. *Hales, (Stephen)* Considerations on the causes of earthquakes. London, 1750.

1239. *Hill, (John)* Essays on Natural History and Philosophy. London, 1752.

140. *F. Hooke, (R)* Micrographia, or some physiological description of minute bodies made by magnifying glasses. London, 1667.

229. *Humboldt, (Alex. de)* Essai géognostique sur le gisement des roches dans les deux Hémisphères. Paris, 1823.

309. *Kentish, (Richard)* An Essay on the method of studying Natural History. London, 1787.

365. *Kielmeyer, (Carl Fried.)* Ueber die verhältnisse der organischen kräfte, unter einander in der Reihe der verschiedenen organisationen, die geseze und folgen dieser verhältnisse. 1793.

1097. *Knight, (William)* Facts and observations towards forming a new theory of the earth. Edinburgh, 1819.

509½. *Lawrence, (Wm.)* Lectures on Physiology, Zoology, and the Natural History of Man. London, 1819.

288. *Leavenworth.* Essai sur l'influence de nos vents variables sur la température des saisons. Paris, 1807.

495. Q. *Leeuwenhoek, (Anthony)* Arcana Naturæ, 2 vol. Lugduni Batavorum, 1696.

384, 18. Q. *Lescallier.* Notes sur le climat de la Ligurie. 1808.

1274. *Lettsom, (John Coakley)* The Naturalists and Traveller's Companion. London, 1779.

276. *Luc, (J. A. de)* Abrégé de Principes & de faits concernants la Cosmologie & la Géologie. Brunswic, 1803.

1096. ——— ——— Lettres physiques & morales sur l'Histoire de la Terre & de l'Homme—5 vol. A la Haye, 1771.

241. Q. *Nemnich.* Natural Hist. Lexicon, 2 theil. Hamburg, 1795.

242. Q. ——— Polyglottes Lexicon der Naturgeschichte. Hamburg, 1798.

1134. *O'Gallagher, (Felix)* Investigation of the first principles of Nature, 2 vols. London, 1784.

244. *Peale, (C. W.)* Discourse Introductory to a course of Lectures on the Science of Nature. Philadelphia, 1800.

244. *Peale, (C. W.)* and *Beauvois.* A scientific and descriptive Catalogue of Peale's Museum. Philadelphia, 1796.

67. F. *Pisonis, (Gulielmi)* De Indiæ utriusque re naturali et medicâ. Amstelod. 1658.

66. F. *Plinii Secundi.* Historia Mundi Naturalis. Francofurti ad Moenum, 1582.

1455. ——— ——— Selecta quædam ex Plinii Secundi historiâ naturali. Warringtoniæ, 1776.

686. *Rafinesque, (C. S.)* Circular Address on Botany and Zoology, followed by the prospectus of two periodical works, Annals of Nature and Somiology of North America. Philadelphia, 1817.

686. ——— ——— Annals of Nature. First annual number for 1820.

323. Q. *Regii, (Hen.)* Philosophia Naturalis. Amstelod. 1654.

384, 12. Q. *Richard, (L. C.)* Examen Critique de quelques Mém. Anatomico-Physiologico-Botaniques. Paris.

104. *Romans, (Bernard)* Natural History of East and West Florida. New York, 1774.

215. Q. *Gravesande, (James William 'S)* Mathematical Elements of Natural Philosophy. Translated from Latin by J. T. Desaguliers, 2 vols. London, 1747.

1238. *Stillingfleet, (Benj.)* Miscellaneous Tracts relating to Natural History, Husbandry, and Physic. London, 1762.

1262. *Smellie, (William)* Philosophy of Natural History. Philadelphia, 1791.

1274. *Smith, (John Coakley)* Tracts relating to Natural History. London, 1798.

1224. *Soulavie, (Girard)* Histoire naturelle de la France Meridionale, 7 vol. Paris, 1780.

1192. *Spallanzani.* Opuscules de Physique, animale & végétale. Traduit de l'Italien & augmenté d'une Introduction sur les découvertes microscopiques dans les trois règnes, par Jean Senebier, 2 vol. Genèva, 1777.

171. Q. *Stackhouse, (John)* Nereis Britannica, continens species omnes fucorum in insulis Britannicis crescentium. Oxonii, 1816.

384, 4. Q. *Volta.* Observazioni di Storia Naturale sul viaggio da Fiorenzola à Velleja.

93. *Volney.* View of the soil and climate of the United States. Philadelphia, 1804.

447. *Whiston, (William)* Theory of the Earth. London, 1697.

856. *Williamson, (Hugh)* Observations on the Climate of different parts of America. New York, 1811.

ANONYMOUS WORKS.

640. Catalogue of the natural productions and curiosities which compose the collections of the Cabinet of Natural History in New York. New York, 1804.

1215. Essai sur l'Histoire Naturelle de St. Domingue. Paris, 1776.

583. Histoire Naturelle & Politique de la Pennsylvanie. Paris, 1768.

265. Mémoire instructif sur la manière de rassembler & préparer les diverses curiosités d'historie naturelle. Lyon, 1757.

215. Nouveau Dictionnaire d'Histoire Naturelle, appliquée aux arts, 36 vol. Paris, 1816—19.

1099. Nouveau systime du Monde, 3 vol. MS.

1243. Tabellen des ganzen Naturalien kabinets des Freyherrn von Hüpsch. Cöln, 1797.

---

2. ANIMAL KINGDOM.

65. F. *Anon.* Memoirs for a Natural History of Animals, translated from the French by Alexander Pitfield. London, 1688.

686. Report of a Committee of the Linnæan Society of New England, relative to a large marine animal supposed to be a serpent, seen near Cape Ann, Massachusetts, in August, 1817. Boston, 1817.

384, 20. Q. *Albers, (J. C.)* Beyträge zur Anatomie und Physiologie der Thiere. Bremen, 1802.

1265. *Anderson.* History of Quadrupeds. New York, 1804.

13. F. *Audibert, (J. B.)* Histoire naturelle des singes & des makis. Paris, 1812.

40½. F. *Audibert & Viellat.* Histoire naturelle des oiseaux dorés. Paris, 1802.

1264. *Azara, (Don Felix d')* Essais sur l'Histoire naturelle des quadrupèdes de la province de Paraguay, 2 vol. Paris, 1801.

224. *Barton, (Benj. S.)* Some account of the Syren Lacertina, and other species of the same genus of amphibious animals, in a letter to John Gottlieb Schneider. Philadelphia, 1808.

384, 17. Q. *Blumenbach.* Observations on some Egyptian mummies. 1794.

365, ——— Ueber die Liebe der Thiere. *(no imprint, no date.)*

385. Q. ——— Quatuor Decades collectionis suæ craniorum diversarum gentium illustrata. Gotting. 1790—1800.

1259. *Bowditch, (T. Edward)* Analysis of the natural classification of mammalia. Paris, 1821.

1258. ——— ——— An Introduction to the Ornithology of Cuvier, for the use of students and travellers. Paris, 1821.

384, 17. Q. *Brand, (Thomas)* Case of a boy who had been mistaken for a girl. London, 1787.

245. Q. *Brisson.* Le règne animal divisé en IX classes. Paris, 1756.

165. Q. *Brongniart, (Alexander) & Ans. Ga. Desmarets.* Histoire Naturelle des Crustacées Fossiles sous les rapports Zoologiques & Géologiques. Paris, 1822.

46. F. *Buffon.* Histoire Naturelle des Oiseaux, 5 vol. the three last consisting entirely of Plates. (Imprimerie Royale.) Paris, 1772.

289. *Camper, (A. G.)* Voorstel eener verbeterde classificatie in de reptilia, bekend onder den naam van Hagedissen en Slangen.

19. F. *Camper, (Pierre)* Description anatomique d'un Eléphant mâle. Paris, 1802.

1407. *Charas.* New Experiments on vipers. London, 1673.

1685. *Combe, (George)* Essays on Phrenology. Philada. 1822.

421. *Cuvier.* Tableau élémentaire de l'histoire naturelle des animaux. Paris, 1798.

222. Q. ——— Recherches sur les ossemens fossiles de quadrupèdes, 4 vol. Paris, 1812.

686. *Dandridge Peck, (William)* Natural History of the Slug-worm. Boston, 1799.

222½ Q. *Dalman, (Joh. Wilk.)* Analecta Entomologica, cum Tabulis IV. Æneis. Holmiæ, 1823.

375. *Desmarest, (A. G.)* Première Décade Ichthyologique, ou Description de dix espèces de poissons nouvelles, ou imparfaitement connues, habitant les côtes de l'Isle de Cuba. Paris, 1823.

1263. *Dodd, (James S.)* Essay towards a Natural History of the Herring. London, 1752.

403. *Easton, (James)* Human Longevity, recording the name, age, place of residence, and years of 1712 persons who attained a century and upwards, from A. D. 66 to 1799. Salisbury, 1799.

1260. *Fabricii, (Johan. Chris.)* Entomologia Systematica. Hasniæ, 1792.

242. *Fontana.* Ricerche Fisiche Sopra il veleno della vipera. Lucca, 1767.

338. ——— Ricerche Fisiche intorno alla salubrità dell'aria. Milano, 1775.

1162. *Forster, (Thomas)* Observations on the brumal retreat of the Swallow. London, 1813.

47. F. *Gariga, (Joseph)* Descripcion del esqueleto de un quadrupedo muy corpulento y raro. Madrid, 1796.

422. *Girard, (T.)* Anatomie des animaux domestiques, 2 vol. Paris, 1807.

249. Q. *Godart, (John)* Of Insects. York, 1682.

305. Q. *Gouan, (Antonio)* Historia Piscorum, Lat. & French. Strasburg, 1770.

1638. *Haller, (De)* Exposition des phénomènes relatifs à la génération. Paris, 1774.

253. Q. *Hermann.* Tabula Affinitatum animalium. Argentorati, 1783.

144½ Q. *Horsfield, (Thomas)* Zoological Researches in Java and the neighbouring islands, Nos. 1, 2, 3, 4, 5. London, 1821—1822.

384, 5. Q. *Hosack, (David)* Observations on Vision. London, 1794.

468. Q. *Hunter, (John)* Observations on certain parts of the animal Œconomy. London, 1786.

384, 3. Q. ——— ——— Anatom. Observ. on the Torpedo. London, 1774.

76. F. *Johnston.* Theatrum universale omnium animalium quadrupedum, 3 vol. Rothomagi, 1768.

384, 9. *Lacepède.* Disc. d'ouverture du cours de Zoologie de l'an IX.

1255. *Lamarck.* Histoire Naturelle des animaux sans Vertèbres, 6 vol. Paris, 1815.

289. *Latreille, (P. A.)* Histoire Naturelle des Salamandres de France. Paris, 1800.

289. *Le Gallois,* Rapport fait à la Société de médecine sur son mémoire, ayant pour titre: Recherches expérimentales sur le principe du mouvement & du sentiment, & sur son siège dans les mammifères & les reptiles. Paris, 1808.

1520. *Lesser, (M.)* Théologie des Insectes, traduit de l'Allemand avec des remarques par P. Lyonnet, 2 vol. Paris, 1745.

384, 22. Q. *Le Sueur, (Charles A.)* Notice de quelques Poissons découverts dans les lacs du Haut-Canada durant l'été de 1816.

Le Sueur, see *Péron.*

1256. *Linneus.* Institutions of Entomology, translated from the Latin, by Thomas Patterson Yeats. London, 1773.

243. Q. *Malpighi, (Marc.)* Dissertatio de Bombyce. Lond. 1669.

321. *Messheimer, (Fred. Val.)* A Catalogue of insects of Pennsylvania. Hanover, York County, 1806.

24½. F. *Merian.* Dissertation sur les Insectes de Surinam. La Haye, 1726.

15. F. *Monro, (Alexander)* The Structure and Physiology of Fishes explained and compared with those of man and other animals. Edinburgh, 1735.

1214. *Montfort, (Denis de)* Conchyliologie systèmatique, & classification des coquilles, 2 vol. Paris, 1808.

384, 14. Q. *Neergaard, (J. W.)* Commentatio Anat. Physiol. sistens an verum organorum digestioni inservientium Discrimen inter animalia Herbivora, Carnivora, & Omnivora reperiatur. Gottingæ, 1804.

244. Q. *Pallas.* Naturgeschichte merkwürdiger Thiere. Berlin, 1776.

386. Q. ——— Novæ species quadrupedum è glirium ordine. Fasciculus Primus. Erlangæ, 1778.

1241. *Paykull, (Gustavi)* Fauna Suecica, tom. I. Upsaliæ.

1246. ——— ——— Monographia Histeroidum. Upsaliæ, 1811.

254. *Peale, (Rembrandt)* Account of the Skeleton of the mammoth. London, 1802.

254. ——— ——— Hist. Disquisition on the Mammoth. London, 1803.

221. Q. *Pennant, (Thomas)* Arctic Zoology, 3 vols. Lond. 1792.

220. Q. ——— ——— History of Quadrupeds, 2 vols. London, 1793.

384, 22. Q. *Peron & Le Sueur.* Sur les Méduses du genre équorée.

384, 3. Q. *Pringle, (John)* Discourse on the torpedo. London, 1775.

161. Q. *Rusconi, (Mauro)* Descrizione anatomica degli organi della circolazione delle larve delle salamandre aquatiche. Pavia, 1817.

162. Q. ——— ——— Del proteo Anguino di Laurenti Monografia. Pavia, 1819.

1275. *Saint, Hilaire, (Geoffroy)* Philosophie Anatomique avec 116 figures. Paris, 1818.

686. *Say, (Thomas)* American Conchology. Philada. 1817.

235. ——— ——— Description of the land and fresh water shells of the United States. Philadelphia, 1819.

248. *Smith, (Samuel Stanhope)* Essay on the variety of the complexion and figure of the human species. Philadelphia, 1787.

527. Same work. New Brunswick, 1810.

255. Q. *Sœmmering.* Ueber den crocodilus priscus, oder ueber ein in Baiern versteint gefundenes schmalkieferiges krokodilus. *(No imprint, no date.)*

1637. *Spallanzani.* Expériences pour servir à l'histoire de la génération des animaux & des plantes. Genève, 1785.

302. *Spengler, (L.)* Extraits d'un mémoire sur les propriétés de l'Ivoire, traduit du Danois par Bruin-Neergaard. Paris, 1809.

1218. *Stewart, (L.)* Elements of the natural history of the animal kingdom, 2 vols. Edinburgh, 1817.

79. *F.* *Swammerdam.* Historia Insectorum. Leyd. 1737.

40. *F.* Same work in English. London, 1758.

74. *F.* *Topsell, (Edward)* History of four-footed beasts and serpents, from Gessner and other authors. London, 1658.

14. *F.* *Vieillot, (L. P.)* Histoire naturelle des oiseaux de l'Amérique Septentrionale, 2 vol. Paris, 1807.

384, 3. *Q.* *Walsh, (John)* Electric property of the torpedo. London, 1774.

72. *F.* *Willoughby.* The Ornithology of Francis Willoughby, translated into English with additions, by John Ray. London, 1778.

78. *F.* *Wilson, (Alex.)* American Ornithology, or the natural history of the birds of the United States, with plates, 9 vols. Philadelphia, 1808—1814.

1648. *Wintringham, (Clifton)* Enquiry on some parts of the animal structure. London, 1740.

246. *Q.* *Zimmermann, (E. A. G.)* Specimen Zoologiæ Geographicæ quadrupedum. Lugd. Batav. 1777.

---

3. VEGETABLE KINGDOM.

1242. *Acharius, (Erick)* Methodus quâ omnes detectos Lichenes redigere tentavit. Stockholm, 1803.

1240. *Agardh, (Carol. A.)* Synopsis Algarum Scandinaviæ. Lundæ, 1717.

1290. *Anderson, (James)* A Treatise on peat moss. Edinburgh, 1794.

1234. *Anon.* Genera et species plantarum vocabulis characteristicis definita. Marienwerder, 1781.

1231. —— Notions Elémentaires De Botanique. Dijon, 1781.

284. —— Observationes Botanicæ, genera and species filicum illustrantes.

224. *Barton, (Benj. S.)* Flora Virginica, sive plantarum, præcipuè indigenarum Virginiæ Historia inchoata, pars I. Philadelphia, 1812.

236. ———— ———— Elements of Botany, 2 vols. Philadelphia, 1812.

384, 12. *Q.* *Barton, (Wm. P. C.)* Floræ Philadelphicæ Prodromus. Philadelphia, 1815.

219. ———— ———— Compendium Floræ Philadelphicæ, 2 vols. Philadelphia, 1818.

686. ———— ———— Some accounts of a plant used in Lancaster

County, Pennsylvania, as a substitute for chocolate, and which appears to be the Holcus Bicolor of Willdenow's Species Plantarum; read to the Philadelphia Linnæan Society, October 17th, 1816, by Wm. P. C. Barton. Philadelphia, 1816.

1247. *Bergii, (Petri Jonæ)* Descriptiones Plantarum ex Capite Bonæ Spei. Stockholmiæ, 1767.

230. *Bigelow, (Jacob)* Florula Bostoniensis. Boston, 1814.

226. ——— ——— American Medical Botany, 6 vols. 1817.

1236. *Brisseau Mirbel, (C. F.)* Exposition de la théorie de l'organisation végétale. Paris, 1809.

1237 ——— ——— Traité d'Anatomie & de Phisiologie végétale, 2 vol. Paris, 1802.

1222. *Chomel, (P. J. B.)* Abrégé de l'histoire des plantes usuelles. Paris, 1782.

384, 22. Q. *Correa de Serra.* Note sur la valeur du Périsperme considéré comme caractère d'affinité des Plantes.

384, 12. Q. ——— ——— Vûës carpologiques, suite de ses observ.

284. *Cubières.* Mémoire sur l'érable à feuilles de Frêne ou Acer Negundo. Versailles, 1804.

284. ——— Mémoire sur le Genèvrier Rouge de Virginie. Versailles, 1805.

284. ——— Mémoire sur les Micocouliers ou Celtis de Linnée. Versailles, 1808.

452. Q. *Dalla Bella, (J. A.)* Mem. sobre a Cultura das Oliveiras. Coimbra, 1786.

De Candolle, See *Lamarck.*

1250. *Desfontaines.* Tableau de l'Ecole Botanique du Muséum d'Histoire Naturelle. Paris, 1804.

384, 3. Q. *Dicquemare.* Essay on Sea-Anemonies. London, 1774.

384, 12. Q *Dufour, (Leon)* Revision du Genre Opégraphe de la Flore Française. 1818.

362. Q. *Duhamel du Monceau.* La Physique des Arbres, 2 vol. Paris, 1758.

232. *Elliot, (Stephen)* Sketch of the Botany of South Carolina and Georgia, vol. 1. Charleston, 1821.

384, 2. Q. *Ellis, (John)* Hist. account of Coffee. London, 1774.

80. F. *Evelyn.* Sylva, or a Discourse on Forest Trees. London, 1806.

168. Q. Same work, 2 vols. York, 1812.

284. *Féburier.* Mémoire sur les Fausses-Teignes ou Gallerias de la Cire. Versailles, 1810.

284. ——— Observations sur la Végétation de la Tulipe. Versailles, 1809.

284. ——— Essay sur les Phénomènes de la Végétation. Versailles, 1812.

284. Q. *Forster, (John Rein. & George)* Characteres generum plantarum quas in itinere ad insulas Maris Australis collegerunt, descripserunt & delinearunt, annis 1772—1775. Londini, 1776.

170. Q. *Gærtner, (Joseph)* De fructibus & seminibus plantarum, 3 vol. and one of plates. Stutgardiæ, 1788.

686. *Green, (Jacob)* An Address on the Botany of the United States, delivered before the Society for the promotion of Useful Arts, on the 9th of February, 1814, with a Catalogue of plants indigenous to the state of New York. Albany, 1814.

121. *Grisley, (Gabriel)* Viridarium Lusitanicum, à D. Vandelli Linneanis nominibus illustratum; Jussu Academiæ in lucem editum. Olisipone, 1789.

1227. *Haworth, (A. H.)* Synopsis Plantarum succulentarum. Londini, 1812.

741. *Hosack, (David)* Catalogue of Plants contained in the Botanic Garden at Elgin in the vicinity of New York. New York, 1806.

686. ——— ——— Hortus Elginensis, or a Catalogue of Plants, indigenous and exotic, cultivated at the Elgin Botanic Garden in the vicinity of the city of New York. New York, 1811.

686. ——— ——— A statement of facts relative to the establishment and progress of the Elgin Botanic Garden, and the subsequent disposal of the same to the state of New York. New York, 1811.

685. *Humboldt, (Alex.)* Ideen zu einer Physiognomik der Gewächse. Tübingen, 1806.

1193. *Ingenhousz, (Jean)* Expériences sur les Vegetaux, 2 vol. Paris, 1787.

1225. *Jussieu, (Ant. Laur)* Genera Plantarum secundum ordines naturales disposita. Paris, 1789.

172. Q. *Kops, (Jan)* Flora Batava, afgebeeld door J. C. Sepp & Zoon, 4 vol. Amsterdam.

1220. *Lamarck & De Candolle.* Flore Française, ou descriptions succinctes de toutes les plantes qui croissent naturellement en France, 6 vol. Paris, 1815.

384, 17. Q. *Lescallier.* Descrip. Bot. du Chiranthodendron, arbre du Mexique. Paris, 1805.

384, 17. Q. *Lettsom, (John Coakley)* Natural History of the Tea-Tree. London, 1799.

24. F. *L'Héritier, (Carol. Ludov.)* Stirpes novæ illustratæ; Fasciculi 2 a 6. Paris, 1784.

1277. *Linné, (Caroli à)* Amœnitates Academicæ, 10 vol. Erlangæ, 1787.

1272. ——— ——— Species Plantarum, edit. quarta, curâ Willdenow, 5 vol. in 6. Berolini, 1797.

321. *Logan, (Jac.)* Experimenta meletemata de Plantarum generatione, Latin and English. London, 1747.
The author was Provincial Secretary of Pennsylvania, under William Penn.

252. Q. *Loureiro, (Joannis de)* Flora Cochinchinensis, 2 vol. in one. Ulyssipone, 1790.

671. *Marshall, (H.)* Arbustrum Americanum; the American Grove, or, an alphabetical catalogue of forest trees and

shrubs, natives of the American United States, arranged according to the Linnæan system. Philade. 1785.

225. *Michaux, (Fs. André)* Histoire des Arbres Forestiers de l'Amérique Septentrionale, 3 vol. with plates. Paris, 1810.

225½. ——— ——— North American Sylva; (being the above work in English, with additions) 7 vols. with plates. Paris, 1819—1820.

16. F. ——— ——— Histoire des Chênes de l'Amérique. Paris, 1801.

251. Q. ——— ——— Flora Boreali Americana, 2 vol. Paris, 1803.

92. ——— ——— Voyage à l'ouest des monts Alleghanys dans les Etats de l'Ohio, du Kentucky, & du Tennessee. Paris, 1804.

643. ——— ——— Rapport fait à la Société d'Agriculture sur ses voyages, par M. Correa de Serra & autres. Paris, 1809. Philadelphia, 1817.

26. F. *Miller, (J.)* Illustratio Systematis sexualis Linnæi, Latin and English. London, 1777.

1233. ——— ——— Botanicum Officinale. London, 1722.

222. *Muhlenberg, (Henry)* Catalogus Plantarum Americæ Septentrionalis. Lancaster, 1813.

223. ——— ——— Descriptio uberior Graminum et Plantarum Calamariarum Americæ Septentrionalis.

1249. *Murray.* A System of Vegetables, according to their classes, orders, genera and species. Litchfield, 1782.

167. F. *Nassy, (David)* Discours sur la question, si les recherches des Botanistes modernes, ont produit plus ou moins d'utilité pour le genre humain que celle des anciens. MS. 1794.

——— ——— Histoire de la découverte, & des vertus du Tikimma, plante de Surinam & de la Guiane, MS. 1794.

1273. *Necker, (Nat. Jos.)* Elementa Botanica, 4 vol. Neuwied, 1790.

218. *Nuttall, (Thomas)* Genera of North American Plants, 2 vols. Philadelphia, 1818.

384, 12. Q. *Palissot de Beauvois.* Notice sur une Nouv. Experience relative à l'écorce des Arbres. Paris, 1811.

384, 12. Q. ——— ——— Nouv. Observ. sur la fructification des Mousses & des Lycopodes. Paris, 1811.

1608. *Pechey, (John)* Complete Herbal. London, 1707.

1270. *Petersoon, (D. H.)* Synopsis Methodica Fungorum Gottingæ, 1801.

1526. *Petit Thouars, (Aubert du)* Essais sur l'organisation des plantes considérée comme résultat du Cours annuel de la végétation. Paris, 1806.

1278. *Pulteney, (Richard)* General View of the writings of Linnæus. London, 1781.

231. *Pursh, (Fred.)* Systematic arrangement and description of the plants of North America, 2 vols. London, 1814.

321. *Paykull, (Gust. de)* Monographia Stapylinorum Suecise. Upsaliæ, 1789.

384, 13. Q. *Raffeneau delile.* Disc. sur les effets d'un Poison de Java appellé Upas tienté, &c. Paris, 1809.

1219. *Relhan, (Richard)* Flora Cantabrigiensis. Cantabrigiæ, 1785.

321. *Rhode, (Mic.)* Monographiæ Cinchonæ generis tentamen. Gottingæ, 1804.

384, 12. Q. *Richard, (L. C.)* Analyse Botanique des Embryons Endorhizes ou Monocotyledons, & particulièrement des Graminées. Paris, 1811.

233. ——— ——— Botanical Dictionary, translated from the French, by Martyn, Smith, &c. Newhaven, 1817.

261. Q. *Rubio, (Simon de Roxas Clemente y)* Ensayo sobre las variedades de la vid commun que vegetan in Andalucia. Madrid, 1801.

264. *Ruiz, (Hipolito)* Quinologia o tratado del Arbol de la Quina o Cascarilla, con su descripcion y la de otras especies de Quinas nuevamente descubiertas en el Peru. Madrid, 1792.

264. ——— ——— Disertacion sobre el aspecto, cultivo, comercio y virtudes de la famosa planta del Peru nombrada Coca. Lima, 1794.

1235. ——— ——— *& J. Pavon,* Systema vegetabilium Floræ Peruvianæ & Chilensis. Madrid, 1798.

39. F. *Rumph, (G. E.)* Herbarium Amboinense, ed. John Burman, 6 vol. Latin and Dutch. Amsterd. 1750.

325. *Rush, (B.)* An Account of the Sugar Maple-tree of the United States, and of the method of obtaining sugar from it. Philadelphia, 1792.

1279. *Saint Hilaire, (Jan.)* Plantes de la France, 4 vol. Paris, 1808.

384, 4. Q. *San Martino, (Giamb. da)* Sopra la nebbia dei vegetabili. Vicenza, 1785.

1221. *Savi, (Gaetano)* Botanicon Etruscum sistens plantas in Etruria sponte crescentes. Pisis, 1808.

1232. *Scholler, (Fred. Ad.)* Flora Barbiensis. Lipsiæ, 1775.

384, 22. Q. *Schræder, (H. A.)* Commentatio de Halophytis Pallusi, respectu imprimis ad salsolam & suadam habito. Gottingæ, 1810.

384, 22. Q. ——— ——— Monographia generis verbasci. Gottingæ, 1813.

163. Q. *Schweinitz, (L. D. de)* Synopsis Fungorum Carolinæ Superioris.

686, 736. ——— ——— Specimen Floræ Americæ septentrionalis cryptogamicæ, or a Specimen of a systematic arrangement and description of the cryptogamous plants of North America. Raleigh, 1821.

250. Q. *Seguier, (J. F.)* Bibliotheca Botanica; accessit Bibl. Bot. Jos. Ant. Bumaldi, seu Ovidii Montalbani, curâ Gronovii. Lugd. Bat. 1760.

1228. *Smith, (Ever. Jac.)* Compendium Floræ Britannicæ. Londani, 1816.

1244. *Smith, (James Edward)* Introduction to Physiological and Systematical Botany. Philadelphia, 1814.

248. *Q. Smyth.* Botanologia Universalis Hibernica. Dublin.

224. *F.* ——— Icones plantarum Japonicorum, Nos. 1 & 5. Upsal, 1794—1805.

1257. *St. Pierre, (Bernardin de)* Botanical harmony delineated; or applications of some general laws of nature to plants. Translated by Henry Hunter. Worcester, (Mass.) 1797.

208. *Suter, (Johan Rud)* Flora Helvetica, 2 vols. Zurich, 1802.

1248. *Thunberg, (Carol. Petr.)* Flora Carpensis sistens plantas Promontorii Bonæ Spei. Upsaliæ, 1807.

1276. *Turpin, (J. F.)* Essai d'une iconographie élémentaire & philosophique des végétaux. Paris, 1820.

334, 22. *Q.* ——— ——— Mémoire sur l'inflorescence des graminées & des cypérées, comparée avec celle des autres végétaux sexifères, suivi de quelques observations sur les disques. Paris, 1819.

1316. *Underwood, (J.)* Catalogue of plants cultivated in the Botanical Garden of the Dublin Society. Dublin, 1804.

1223. *Ventenat, (E. P.)* Tableau du règne végétal selon la methode de Jussieu, 4 vol. Paris, 1800.

304. *Q. Viborg, (Eric)* Botanisk-œkonomisk afhandling om Byg-get. Kiobenhaven 1788.

384, 12. *Q. Wade, (Walter)* Observations on round-headed Buddlea, and sweet-scented holcus. Dublin, 1804.

1245. *Westring, (Joh. P.)* Svenska Lafvarnas Färghistoria. Första Bandet. Stockholm, 1805.

1229, 1230. *Weiss, (Frid. Gul.)* Plantæ cryptogamicæ Floræ Gottingensis. Gottingæ, 1770.

1271. *Willdenow, (Carl. Lud.)* Enumeratio plantarum Horti Regii Botanica Berolinensis, 2 vol. Berolini, 1809.
See above *Linné*, No. 1277, p. 42.

1203. *Wilkinson, (G.)* Experiments and observations on the Cortex Salicis Latifoliæ, or Broad-Leafed Willow Bark, with observations on the different species of Cinchona, &c. Newcastle, 1803.

CATALOGUES, &c. (Anonymous.)

1252. Catalogue of the plants in the Botanic Garden at Liverpool. Liverpool, 1808.

384, 23. *Q.* Synopsis plantarum Horti Botanici Musei Regii Florentini, 1801.

209. Synopsis of the genera of American plants. Georgetown, 1814.

284. Tableau de l'Ecole de Botanique du Jardin des Plantes de Paris. Paris, 1800.

---

4. MINERAL KINGDOM.

1116. *Anon.* Essai sur la théorie des volcans d'Auvergne. Clermont, 1802.

1098. *Anon.* Observations faites dans les Pyrénées, pour servir de suite à des observations sur les Alpes. Paris, 1789.

1631. *Accum, (Frederick)* Analysis of minerals. Philad. 1809.

1103. —— ——— Manual of analytical mineralogy, 2 vols. London.

82. F. *Agricola, (George)* De re metallicâ. Basileæ, 1657.

1109. *Aikin, (Arthur)* A Manuel of Mineralogy. Philadelphia, 1815.

103. Q. *Babington, (William)* New System of Mineralogy in the form of catalogue, after the manner of Baron Born's Systematical Catalogue of the fossils of Miss Honorée de Raab. London, 1799.

1117. *Bergman, (J.)* Manuel du Minéralogiste, ou Sciographie du règne mineral, traduit par Mongez. Paris, 1784.

686. *Bigelow, (Jacob)* Some account of the White Mountains of New Hampshire.

1454. *Boetius, (Anselmus)* Gemmarum et lapidum Historia, quam olim edidit Anselmus Boetius de Boot, cum Commentariis Adriani Toll. Lugd. Bat. 1636.

1113. *Born, (Baron Inigo)* Travels through the Bannat of Temeswar, Transylvania and Hungary, describing the mines and mountains of those countries, translated from the German. London, 1777.

104. Q. *Bournon.* Traité de Minéralogie, 3 vol. London, 1808
4 vol. Paris, 1818.

1105. *Breislak, (Scipion)* Voyages Physiques & Lithologiques dans la Campanie, traduits de l'Italien, par Pommereuil, 2 vol. Paris, 1801.

1142. ——— ——— Institutions Géologiques, traduites de l'Italien par J. L. Capmas, 3 vol. avec un vol. de cartes & planches. Milan, 1818.

1114. *Brisson, (Math. James)* Elements of Natural History and Chymical Analysis of mineral substances. London, 1800.

1146. *Brochant, (A. T. M.)* Traité élémentaire de Minéralogie suivant les principes du Prof. Werner, 2 vol. avec un de cartes & planches. Paris, 1808.

1140. *Brogniart, (Alexander)* Traité élémentaire de Minéralogie avec des applications aux Arts, 2 vol. Paris, 1807.

521. *Bruce, (Archibald)* The American Mineralogical Journal, vol 1. New York, 1814.

300. *Buch, (Leopold de)* Essai d'une description Minéralogique des environs de Landeck, traduit de l'Allemand. Paris, 1805.

384, 22. Q. *Camper, (Adrien)* Mém. sur quelques parties moins connues du squelette des sauriens Fossiles de Maestricht. Paris, 1812.

302. *Cavallo, (Tiberius)* Explanation and index of two mineralogical tables. London, 1786.

1148. *Cleaveland, (Parker,)* Elementary Treatise on Mineralogy and Geology. Boston, 1814.

1149. The same, second edition, 2 vols. Boston, 1822.

686. *Cooper, (Thomas)* Syllabus of Lectures on the elements of Geological Mineralogy. Columbia, 1821.

1121. *Cronstedt, (Axel. Fred.)* An Essay towards a system of mineralogy, 2 vols. London, 1788.

274 *Cullen, (C.)* Chemical Analysis of Wolfram, and examination of a new metal which enters into its composition by J. Joseph and F. de Luyart, translated from the Spanish. London, 1785.

1509. *Cuvier.* Essay on the Theory of the Earth, translated from the French, with mineralogical notes, by Jamieson, and observations on the geology of North America, and a description of the organic remains found in that part of the world, by S. L. Mitchell. New York, 1818.

227. *Dana, (J. & S. L.)* Outlines of the Mineralogy and Geology of Boston and its vicinity. Boston, 1818.

1110. *Daubuisson.* Account of the Basalts of Saxony, with an account of the origin of Basalts in general. Edinburgh, 1814.

384, 18. Q. *Desmarest, (A. G.)* Mém. sur deux genres de coquilles Fossiles cloisonnées & à siphon. Paris, 1817.

1217. *Dillwyn, (Lewis Weston)* A Descriptive Catalogue of recent shells, arranged according to the Linnæan method, with particular attention to the Synonymy, 2 vols. London, 1817

304. *D'Omelius d'Halloy.* Observations sur un essai de cartes Géologiques de la France, des Pays-Bas & des contrées voisines, avec une carte. Paris, 1823.

1120. *Edwards, (George)* Elements of Fossilogy, or an arrangement of fossils into classes, orders, genera, and species. London, 1796.

1104. *Engestrom, (Gustave d')* Guide du voyageur aux carrières & mines de Suède. Stockholm, 1796.

1115. *Faujas-St. Fond.* Essai de Géologie, ou mémoires pour servir à l'Histoire naturelle du Globe, 3 vol. Paris, 1803.

300. ——— ——— Histoire Naturelle des Roches de Trapps, considérée sous les rapports de la Géologie & de la minéralogie. Paris, 1813.

1113. *Ferber, (John James)* Mineralogical account of Bohemia. London, 1777.

318. *Fischer de Waldheim, (G.)* Essai sur la Pellegrina ou la perle incomparable des Frerès Zozima. Moscow, 1818.

318. Q. *Fischer, (Gotthelf)* Onomasticon du systême d'oryctognosie, servant de base à l'arrangement des minéraux du Muséum de l'Université Impériale de Moscow. (Russe & Français.) Moscow, 1811.

384, 22. Q. ——— ——— Notice des Fossiles du gouvernement de Moscow. Moscow, 1809.

300. ——— ——— Essai sur la Turquoise & sur la calaite. Moscow, 1816.

318. ——— ——— Same work. Moscow, 1818.

71. F. *Galitzin, (Le Prince Demetri de)* Recueil de noms par ordre alphabetique appropriés aux terres, pierres, &c. Brunswick, 1802.

319. Q. The same work. Brunswick, 1801.

384, 4. Q. *Gruber*, (*T.*) Versuche uber die ausdünstung des wassers im leeren Raume des Barometers und Abprellung auf erwärmten Flächen. Dresden, 1789.

384, 9. Q. *Hatschett*, (*Charles*) Anal. of a mineral substance from North America. London, 1802.

1112. *Haüy*. Essai d'une théorie sur la structure des crystaux. Paris, 1784.

1144. —— Traité de Minéralogie, 4 vol. avec un vol. de cartes & planches. Paris, 1801.

1145. —— Tableau comparatif des résultats de la Cristallographie & de l'analyse chimique relativement a la classification des minéraux. Paris, 1809.

1141. —— Traité des caractères physiques des pierres precieuses. Paris, 1817.

1143. —— Traité de Cristallographie, suivi d'une application des principes de cette science à la détermination des espèces minerales, 2 vol. avec un vol. de cartes & planches. Paris, 1822.

384, 22. Q. —— Sur des Cristaux de Pyroxène des environs de New York. Paris, 1812.

1651. *Herman*, (*Bened. Fr. John*) Naturgeschichte des Kupfers. St. Petersburg, 1790.

1139. *Holmes*, (*T. H. H.*) A Treatise on the Coal Mines of Durham and Northumberland. London, 1816.

102. Q. *Jameson*, (*Robert*) Mineralogy of the Scottish Isles, 2 vols. Edinburgh, 1800.

1137. —— —— System of Mineralogy, 3 vols. Edinburgh, 1804.

1152. —— —— Treatise on the external character of minerals. Edinburgh, 1805.

228. Q. *Jars*, (*G.*) Voyages Métallurgiques, ou observations sur les mines & forges de fer, &c. 3 vol. Paris, 1774.

686. *Keating*, (*W. H.*) Considerations on the art of mining. Philadelphia, 1821.

686. —— —— Account of the Jeffersonite, a new mineral discovered at the Franklin Iron Works, near Sparta, N. J. Philadelphia, 1822.

1136. *Kirwan*, (*Richard*) Elements of Mineralogy, 2 vols. London, 1794.

1135. —— —— Geological Essays. London, 1799.

1151. *Klaproth*, (*Martin Henry*) Analytical Essays towards promoting the chemical knowledge of mineral substances, 2 vols. London, 1801.

1412. *Köhler*, (*A. M.*) *and C. A. S. Hoffman*. Neues Bergmannisches Journal, 3 vols. Freyberg, 1795.

347½. Q. *Kursten*, (*L. G.*) Tablas mineralogicas dispuestas segun los descubrimientos mas recentes e ilustradas con notas. Traducidas al Castellano por D. Andres Manuel del Rio. Mexico. 1804.

384, 18. Q. *Lescallier*. Fragment sur la géologie de la Guadeloupe. an. 13.

75. F. *Lister*, (*Anth.*) Historia conchyliorum et tabularum anatomicarum. Oxonii. 1770.

1147. *Lucas, (T. A. H.)* Tableau méthodique des espèces minérales, 2 vol. Paris, 1806.

1138. *Martin, (William)* Outlines of an attempt to establish a knowledge of extraneous fossils on scientific principles. Macclesfield, 1809.

1150. *Mawe, (John)* Mineralogy of Derbyshire. London, 1802.

746. *Meade, (William)* A chemical analysis of the waters of New Lebanon, in the state of New York. Burlington, N. J. 1818.

553½. *Mease, (James)* A geological account of the United States, comprehending a short description of their animal, vegetable and mineral productions, antiquities and curiosities. Philadelphia, 1807.

101. Q. *Monnet.* Traité de l'exploitation des mines, traduit de l'Allemand. Paris, 1773.

384, 18. Q. *Monteiro.* Observations sur la composition & la structure du Pyroméride globaire. 1814.

1106. *Phillips, (William)* An elementary introduction to the knowledge of mineralogy. London, 1816.

300. *Pinkerton, (J.)* Esquisse d'une nouvelle classification de minéralogie, traduite de l'Anglais, par J. Janssen. Paris, 1803.

249. *Pini, (Ermenegildo)* Osservazioni mineralogiche su la miniera di Ferro di Rio ed altre parti dell' Isola d'Elba. Milano, 1777.

482. *Playfair, (John)* Illustrations of the Huttonian theory of the earth. Edinburgh, 1802.

302. *Rochon, (Alexis)* Mémoire sur le micromètre de cristal de roche pour la mesure des distances & des grandeurs. Paris, 1807.

1119. *Romé de l'Isle.* Cristallographie, ou description des formes propres à tous les corps du règne mineral, 4 vol. Paris, 1783.

846. *Schoolcraft, (H. B.)* A view of the Lead Mines of Missouri, including some observations on the mineralogy, geology, geography, antiquities, soil, climate, population, and productions of Missouri and Arkansas. New York, 1819.

321. *Schöpf, (John Dav.)* Beyträge zur mineralogischen Kenntniss des Œstlichen Theils von Nord Amerika und seine Gebürge. Erlangen, 1787.

229. Q. *Schultter, (Christophe André)* De la Fonte des Mines des fonderies, &c. traduit de l'Allemand & augmenté de plusieurs procédés & observations, par Hellot, 2 vol. Paris, 1750.

384, 4. Q. *Spallanzani.* Lettera al Marchese Lucchesini. Pavia, 1783.

1111. ——— Travels in the Two Sicilies, and some parts of the Apennines, 4 vols. London, 1798.

302. *Struve, (H.)* Méthode analytique des fossiles fondée sur leurs caractères extérieurs. Paris, 1798

300. *Tondi.* Tableau d'oréognosie ou Connaissance des Montagnes ou Roches. Paris, 1811.

230. Q. *Vauquelin.* Manuel de l'essayeur. Paris, 1800.

384, 4. Q. *Volta.* Saggio analitico sullo acque minerali di S. Colombano.

1118. *Walleri, (John Gottsch.)* Systema mineralogicum, quo corpora mineralia in classes, ordines, genera & species describuntur, 2 vol. Vindobonæ, 1778.

686. *Warne, (W.)* Natural and artificial mineral waters of Schooley's Mountains. New York, 1811.

368. *Watson, (White)* An explanation of a tablet representing the strata in Derbyshire. Sheffield, 1791.

1107. *Werner, (A. G.)* Nouvelle théorie de la formation des filons, traduite de l'Allemand, par J. F. Daubuisson. Paris, 1802.

1108. ——— ——— A treatise on the external characters of fossils. Translated from the German, by Thomas Weaver. Dublin, 1805.

203. Q. *Whitehurst, (John)* An inquiry into the original state and formation of the earth, deduced from facts and laws of nature, first edit. London, 1778.

203½. Q. ——— ——— His works, edited by C. Hutton. London, 1792.

1714. *Wild, (F. S.)* Essai sur la Montagne Salifère du gouvernement d'Aigle, situé dans le Canton de Berne. Genéve, 1788.

1133. *Williams, (John)* The Natural History of the Mineral Kingdom 2d ed. by J. Millar, 2 vols. Edinburgh, 1810.

643. *Woodhouse.* Reply to Seybert's Strictures on his Essay concerning the Perkiomen Zinc Mine. Philadelphia.

369. *Zollickoffer, (William)* A Treatise on the Prussiate of Iron. Frederick, Md. 1822.

PERIODICAL WORKS.

383. Journal des mines, publié par l'agence des mines du Gouvernment Français, 38 vol. Paris, 1795—1815.

384. Annales des mines ou recueil de mémoires sur l'exploitation des mines, redigée par le conseil général des mines. 7 vol. Paris, 1816—1822.

VII. RURAL AND DOMESTIC ECONOMY.

384, 3. Q. *Anderson, (J.)* General View of the Agriculture of Aberdeen. Edinburgh, 1794.

309. *Anderson, (James)* Letters to Sir Joseph Banks on the subject of Cochineal Insects, discovered at Madras. Madras, 1788.

309. ——— ——— Correspondence for introducing Cochineal Insects, &c. Madras, 1791.

309. ——— ——— Continuation of letters on the progress and establishment of the culture of silk on the coast of Coromandel. Madras, 1792.

384, 10. Q. ——— ——— Soins à observer pour la conservation des Insectes Cochenille, sur mer.

252. *Arthaud.* Dissert. sur le papier & Recherches sur les moyens de le conserver de la piqûre des insectes, faites par le cercle des Philadelphes au Cap François. Port-au-Prince, 1788.

624. *Boissier de Sauvages* and *Pullein.* Directions for the management of silk worms, extracted from their treatises. Philadelphia, 1770.

256. *Bucknall, (T. S. D.)* The Orchardist, or a system of close pruning and medication for establishing the science of orcharding. London, 1797.

696. *Beatson, (Alex.)* A New System of Cultivation without lime, or dung, or summer fallows. Philad. 1821.

384, 1. Q. *Belin de Villeneuve.* Mém. sur un nouvel équipage de Chaudières à Sucre. Paris.

262. *Binns, (J. A.)* Treatise on Practical Farming. Fredericktown, 1803.

256. *Bordley, (J. B.)* Sketches on Rotations of Crops. Philadelphia, 1792.

1287. ——— ——— Essays and Notes on Husbandry and Rural Affairs, 2d ed. Philadelphia, 1801.

384, 4. Q. *Bruni, (G.)* Diss. sulla Potatura de'Gelsi. Milan, 1784.

354. *Carver, (James)* A Treatise on the age of the horse. Philadelphia, 1818.

354. ——— ——— On the importance of the veterinary science. 1817.

354. ——— ——— Remarks and observations on the epidemic catarrh in horses which prevailed in this city during 1815–16, and now on the Lancaster line. Philadelphia.

286. *Chaptal, (J. A.)* Observations sur l'art de faire le vin. Paris, 1807.

254. *Clavering, (Robert)* Essay on the construction and building of Chimnies. London, 1793.

384, 1. Q. *Cointeraux.* L'Architecture Rurale, & la Ferme qui a remporté le prix en 1789. Paris.

384, 1. Q. ——— Chauffage économique & dissert. sur les Cheminées des Anciens. Paris, 1792.

1284. ——— Ecole d'Architecture Rurale, contenant divers traités sur l'utilité des bâtiments en pisé & la maniere des les construire. Paris, an 2.

286. ——— L'art de bâtir rendu familier. Paris, 1809.

249. *Commerel, (De)* Mém. & Instruc. sur la culture, &c. de la Betterave. Paris, 1798.

211. *Cointe, (J. Le)* La Cuisine de Santé, 3 vol. Paris, 1790.

364. 12. Q. *Cossigni.* Mém. sur les plantations de cannes à sucre dans le Midi de la France. Paris, 1808.

1268. *Coxe, (William)* On the Cultivation of Fruit Trees. Philadelphia, 1817.

544. Q. *Crescentiis, (Petri de)* Opus ruralium commodorum; German translation, printed in 1493. *Title page and a few of the first pages wanting.*

1283. *Culley, (George)* Observations on live stock. Dublin, 1789.

1322. *Davies, (David)* Case of the labourers in husbandry stated and considered. Dublin, 1796.

384, 13. Q. *De la Roche, (F. S.)* Expér. sur les effets qu'une forte chaleur produit dans l'économie rurale. Paris, 1806.

258. Q. *Deplanazu.* Œuvres d'agriculture & d'économie rurale. Paris, 1801.

384, 1. Q. *D'Etienne.* Mém. sur la découverte d'un ciment impénétrable à l'eau. Paris, 1782.

256. *Dettmar Basse.* De l'utilité & de la culture de l'Acacia Robinia. Paris, an 9.

384, 5. Q. *De Witt, (Benjamin)* A Memoir on the Onondaga salt-springs and salt manufactories in the state of New York. Albany, 1798.

1527. *Douette Richardot, (Nicolas)* De la pratique de l'agriculture. Paris, 1806.

318. *Doulcet, (A. J. B. L.)* Mémoire sur la destruction des forêts & les effets qui en résultent. Auxerre, 1821.

276. *Eddows, (R.)* Account of the wheat-moth or Virginia-fly. Philadelphia, 1805.

384, 2. Q. *Ellis, (John)* Observations on preserving seeds. London, 1773.

1529. *Feburier.* Traité sur les abeilles. Paris, 1810.

242. *Fontana, (Felice)* Osservazioni sopra la Ruggine del Grano. Lucca, 1767.

384, 1. Q. ——— ——— Saggio di osservazioni sopra il falso ergot e Tremella. Firenze, 1775.

1267. *Forsyth, (William)* A treatise on the culture and management of Fruit Trees, with an introd. and notes by W. Cobbett. Philadelphia, 1802.

384, 10. Q. *Grégoire.* Essai sur l'état de l'agric. en Europe, au 16me Siècle. Paris, an 12.

384, 15. Q. *Griggs.* General View of the Agriculture of the county of Essex. London, 1794.

384, 4. *Harasti, (P. Gaetano)* Descrizione d'un' Arnia, presentata alla Soc. patriot. di Milano. *(No date.)*

384, 21. Q. *Högermüller, (Von)* Wünsche und vorschläge zur errichtung eines Erziehungs-Instituts für Diensbothen. Wien, 1810.

1323. *Holt, (John)* General View of the Agriculture of the County of Lancaster. London, 1795.

1286. *Houghton, (John)* Husbandry and Trade improved, 4 vols. London, 1727.

260. Q. *James, (John)* Theory and Practice of Gardening. London, 1712.

367. *Isaac, (J.)* The General Apiarian, wherein is a method of obtaining the produce of bees. Exeter, 1799.

1293. *Johnson, (S. W.)* Rural Economy, containing a treatise on Pisé building. New Brunswick, 1806.

1288. *Kent, (Nathaniel)* Hints to gentlemen of landed property. London, 1775.

247. *Kirwan, (Richard)* Treatise on Manures. London, 1796.

256. ——— ——— Essay on Manures. Dublin, 1801.

1398. ——— ——— The Manures most advantageously applicable to the various sorts of soil. London, 1808.

318. *Lambry.* Exposé d'un moyen mis en pratique pour empécher la vigne de couler & hâter la maturité du raisin. Paris, 1818.

1531. *Lasteyrie.* Traité sur les bêtes-à-laine d'Espagne. Paris, 1799.

1530. ——— Du Pastel, de l'indigotier, &c. Paris, 1811.

1532. ——— Du Cotonnier & de sa culture. Paris, 1808.

384, 5. Q. *Le Bon, (Philippe)* Sur les thermolampes ou poëles qui chauffent & éclairent avec économie. Paris, 1802.

361. *Lemoine, (Léonor)* Cours de culture des arbres à fruit & de la vigne des jardins. Paris, 1801.

1289. *M'Mahon, (Bernard)* American gardener's calendar. Philadelphia, 1806.

166. Q. *M'William, (Robert)* Essay on the origin and operation of the Dry Rot. London, 1818.

696. *Mease, (James)* Address on the subject of establishing a pattern farm, in the vicinity of Philadelphia. Philadelphia, 1818.

1254. *Menonville, (Thierry de)* Traité de la culture du nopal & de l'éducation de la cochenille, 2 vol. Paris, 1787.

1528. *Mitterpacher, (Ludovico)* Elementi di agricultura, 2 vol. Milano, 1784.

256. *Moore, (Thomas)* The great error of American agriculture exposed, and hints for improvement suggested. Baltimore, 1801.

256. ——— ——— Essay on the most eligible construction of ice-houses. Baltimore, 1803.

252. *Moreau de Saint Mery.* Essai sur la manière d'améliorer l'éducation des chevaux en Amérique. Philade. 1795.

384, 15. Q. *Naismyth, (John)* Observations on the different breeds of sheep, and the state of sheep farming in the southern districts of Scotland. Edinburgh, 1795.

696. *Parkes, (Samuel)* A letter to the farmers and graziers of Great Britain to explain the advantages of using salt in the various branches of agriculture, and in feeding all kind of farmer's stock, 1st ed. London, 1819.

1285. ——— ——— The same. Philadelphia, 1819.

——— ——— On the use of sugar for fattening cattle. London, 1808.

——— ——— On the laws relative to salt in Great Britain. London, 1817.

1172. *Parmentier, (A. A.)* Aperçu des resultats obtenus de la fabrication des syrops & des conserves de raisins, dans le cours des années 1810 & 1811. Paris, 1812.

624. *Peters, (Richard)* Agricultural inquiries on Plaster of Paris. Philadelphia, 1797.

1724. *Philadelphes, (Cercle des)* Recherches sur les maladies épizootiques de Saint Domingue. Cap François, 1788.

384, 4. Q. *Ponti, (P. F.)* Descr. d'una machina per isgombrare il terreno da' sassi. Milan.

1173. *Roard, (J. L.)* Traité sur la culture de la vigne. Paris, 1806.

384, 15. Q. *Robertson, (Thomas)* Outline of the General Report upon the size of farms, and upon the persons who cultivate farms. Edinburgh, 1796.

1328. *Robertson, (George)* General View of the Agriculture of Mid-Lothian. Edinburgh, 1795.

384, 18. Q. *Rochon, (A.)* Mém. sur l'emploi des gazes métalliques, pour rendre les édifices incombustibles. Paris, 1812.

1174. *Rozier.* Mémoire sur la manière de faire les vins de Provence. Lausanne, 1771.

259. Q. —— Dictionnaire d'agriculture & d'économie rurale, 2 vol. Nismes, 1804.

384, 6. Q. —— Descr. du Moulin Hollandais pour extraire l'huile des graines.

1294. —— Traité sur la meilleure manière de cultiver la navette & le Colsat. Paris, 1774.

1499. *Schmalz, (Fried.)* Erfahrungen im Gebiete der Landwirthschaft. Vierter Band. Leipz. 1820.

256. Q. *Scriptores* rei rusticæ veteres Latini, 2 vol. Leipz. 1773.

384, 15. Q. *Sinclair, (John)* A general view of the agriculture of the northern counties and Islands of Scotland. London, 1795.

384, 15. Q. *Somerville, (Robert)* Outlines of the fifteenth chapter of the proposed General Report from the Board of Agriculture on the subject of Manures. London, 1795.

384, 18. Q. *Thouin, (A.)* Essai sur l'économ. rurale. Paris, 1805.

318. —— —— Instruction sur l'établissement des pépinières. Paris, 1821.

1280. *Tuke, (John)* General view of the agriculture of the North Riding of Yorkshire. London, 1800.

1533. *Tupputi, (Dominique)* Réflexions succinctes sur l'état de l'agriculture. Paris, 1807.

635. *Washington, (George)* Letters to Art. Young and John Sinclair, containing an account of his husbandry. Alexandria, 1803.

513. *Willich, (A. F. M.)* Domestic Encyclopedia, edited by Dr. Mease, 5 vols. Philadelphia, 1803.

514. —— —— Same work, edited by Thomas Cooper, 3 vols. 1821.

276. *Young, (Arthur,)* Rural Economy, or essays on the practical parts of husbandry, also rural Socrates. Lond. 1776.

387. —— —— Annals of Agriculture, 3 vols. London, 1784.

ANONYMOUS WORKS.

Agriculture. 696. Address to the Citizens of Pennsylvania on the importance of a more liberal encouragement of Agriculture. Philadelphia, 1818.

256. Communications made to the Board of Agriculture in Great Britain on the culture of potatoes. Published by order of the Massachusetts Society for Promoting Agriculture. Boston, 1798.

635. Examination into the expediency of establishing a Board of Agriculture in the state of New York. New York, 1819.

696. Queries to Agriculturists to acquire local and statistical information.

Economical Society of Philad. 636, 708. Report of the Committee on Domestic Economy, to the Pennsylvania Society for the promotion of Public Economy, on a new method of sweeping chimnies, read on November 10, 1817. Philadelphia, 1817.

Fishery. 1411. L'art de la Pêche à la ligne. Paris, 1816.

Food for Cattle. 316. Facts and experiments on the use of sugar in feeding cattle, with hints for the cultivation of waste lands. London, 1809.

Foot-plough. 248. A letter on the construction and use of the improved Foot-plough, by an Essex Farmer. London, 1784.

Hemp. 316. Istruzione per la cultivazione e preparazione della Canapa nella Lombardia. Milano, 1790.

Horses. 240. Essay on improving the breed of horses in America. Philadelphia, 1795.

Horticulture. 384, 17. *Q.* Grove-Hill, a rural and horticultural sketch. London, 1804.

257. *Q.* Le parfait Jardinier.

Husbandry 81. *F.* The Complete Farmer, or a Dictionary of Husbandry, by a Society of Gentlemen. London, *no date.*

1291. Gleanings from the most celebrated books on husbandry, gardening, and rural affairs. Philadelphia, 1803.

276. Notes on Farming, ascribed to Charles Thomson. New York, 1787.

1282. The rural Socrates; an account of Kliyogg, a philosophical Farmer. Hallowell, (Maine,) 1800.

Live-Stock. 316. Remarks on Live-Stock and relative subjects. Edinburgh, 1806.

Reaping. 384, 4. *Q.* Della Falce da Mietere il Grano.

Sheep. 696. The Constitution of the Merino Society of the Middle States of North America; premiums proposed for 1812 and 13, &c. Philad. 1811.

Wine & Brandy. 1183. De la Fermentation des vins & de la meilleure manière de faire de l'eau-de-vie. Lyon, 1770.

VIII. MEDICINE AND SURGERY.

1. Medicine in general.
2. Anatomy and Physiology.
3. Theory and Practice of Physic in general.
4. Treatises and Essays on particular Diseases.
5. Surgery and Obstetrics.
6. Materia Medica and Therapeutics.
7. Miscellaneous.

1. MEDICINE IN GENERAL.

356. *Bouté, (S. G. G.)* Essai sur l'histoire & les avantages des institutions cliniques. Paris, 1803.

412. *Cabanis.* Du degré de certitude dans la médecine. Paris, 1803.

1668. ——— Same work, translated from the French, by R. La Roche. Philadelphia, 1823.

413. ——— Coup d'œil sur les révolutions & sur la réforme de la médecine. Paris, 1804.

238. *Coste.* De antiquâ medico-philosophiâ orbi novo adaptandâ. Lugd. Bat. 1783.

1619. *D'Iharcé.* Erreurs populaires sur la médecine. Paris, 1783.

1721. *Lettsom, (J. C.)* Hints designed to promote beneficence, temperance, and medical science, 3 vols. London, 1801.

354. *Ramsay, (David)* A review of the improvements, progress, and state of medicine in the 18th century. Charleston.

537. *Rush, (Benjamin)* Observations on the duties of a physician, and the methods of improving medicine. Philadelphia, 1789.

2. ANATOMY AND PHYSIOLOGY.

356. *Anon.* Garçon & fille hermaphrodites vûs & dessinés d'après nature. Paris, 1773.

22. F. *Albini, (B. G.)* Explicatio tabularum anatomicarum. Leidæ Batavorum, 1744.

1647. *Alpinus, (Prosper)* De præsagiendâ vitâ & morte ægrotorum libri vii. cum præfatione, H. Boerhaave. Lugd. Bat. 1710.

1717. *Bell, (Charles)* Engravings of the Arteries, illustrating the second vol. of the Anatomy of the Human Body, and serving as an introduction to the surgery of the arteries. First American Edition. Philadelphia, 1812.

1660. *Bichat, (Xavier)* Physiological Researches upon life and death, translated from the French. Philadelphia, 1809.

526. *Blumenbach, (J. F.)* A short System of Comparative Anatomy, translated from the German by W. Lawrence, with an Introduction and Notes, by the translator. London, 1807.

1652. ——— —— Geschichte und Beschreibung der Knochen des menschlichen Körpers. Göttingen, 1786.

418. ——— —— Elements of Physiology, 2 vols. in 1. Philadelphia, 1795.

414. *Cabanis.* Rapports du physique & du moral de l'homme, 2 vol. Paris, 1805.

420. *Camper, (Pierre)* Œuvres de—qui ont pour objet l'Anatomie comparée, la Physiologie, &c. 3 vol. Paris, 1803.

Coates, see *Lawrence*.

1685. *Combe, (George)* Essays on Phrenology. Philad. 1822.

1595. *Condie, (David T.)* Course of examinations in Anatomy, Physiology, &c. Philadelphia, 1818.

415. *Crawford, (A.)* Experiments and Observations on Animal Heat, and the Inflammation of combustible bodies. London, 1788.

470. Q. *Cruikshank, (William)* The Anatomy of the absorbing vessels in the Human body. London, 1786.

419. *Cuvier.* Leçons d'anatomie comparée, 2 vol. Paris, 1800.

384, 13. Q. *De la Roche.* Mém. sur l'influence que la température de l'air exerce dans les phénomènes chimiques de la respiration. 1812.

384, 18. Q. *Dufour, (Leon)* Recher. Anatom. sur les Scolies. Paris, 1818.

356. *Flourens.* Analyse de la Philosophie Anatomique. Paris, 1819.

353. *Forster, (Guliel.)* Dissertatio de Aëre Marino ejusque in Corpus humanum efficaciâ. Halæ, 1787.

1655. *Gavard, (Hyacinthe)* Traité de Splanchnologie, suivant la méthode de Desault. Paris, 1801.

303. *Gentilini di Cefalonia.* Lettera sull'uso primario della Tuba Eustachiana. Pavia, 1808.

1639. *Graaf, (R. de)* De virorum organis generationi inservientibus. Lugd. Bat. 1668.

353. *Hendy, (James)* An Essay on glandular secretion, containing an experimental enquiry into the formation of the pus. London, 1775.

1723. *Hewson, (William)* Experimental inquiries on the lymphatic system, &c. London, 1774.

525½. *Horner, (W. E.)* Lessons in Practical Anatomy. Philadelphia, 1823.

736. *Lawrence, (J. O'B.)* and *B. H. Coates.* An account of some further experiments to determine the absorbing power of the veins and lymphatics.

1661. *Lawrence, (William)* Introduction to comparative anatomy and physiology. London, 1816.

509½. ——— ——— Lectures on Physiology, Zoology, and the Natural History of Man. London, 1819.

27. F. *Mascagni, (P.)* Vasorum lymphaticorum corporis humani historia & ichnographia. Senis, 1787.

1694. *Morgan, (Johannis)* Πύοποιησις, Seu Tentamen Medicum de puris confectione. Edinburgi, 1763.

1687. *Pole, (Thomas)* Anatomical Instructor. London, 1790.

1693. *Roebuck, (Jarvis)* Experiments on the Bile. Philadelphia, 1801.

1696. *Smith, (Hugh)* Essays physiological and practical on the nature and circulation of blood, and the effects and uses of blood-letting. London, 1761.

1622. *Spallanzani.* Expériences sur la digestion, traduites en François & précédées de considérations sur la méthode de l'auteur par Jean Sénebier. Genève, 1784.

545. Q. *Tarin.* Dictionnaire Anatomique. Paris, 1753.

249. *Trent, (Joseph)* Inquiry into the effects of light in respiration. Philadelphia, 1800.

1686. *Warren, (John C.)* A comparative view of the Sensorial and Nervous System. Boston, 1822.

1614. *Winslow.* Exposition anatomique de la structure du corps humain, 4 vol. Paris, 1766.

525. *Wistar, (Caspar)* A System of Anatomy, 2 vols. Philadelphia, 1811.

1616. *Wright, (Thomas)* The Human Muscles. Dublin, 1791.

3. THEORY AND PRACTICE OF PHYSIC IN GENERAL.

359. *Alexander, (William)* Experimental Essays on the external application of antiseptics, on the doses and effects of medicines, and on diuretics and sudorifics. London, 1768.

1646. *Allen, (John)* Practice of Physic, 2 vols. London, 1740.

1735. *Barnwell, (William)* Physical investigations and deductions, relative to the nature and remedies of diseases proceeding from a vitiated atmosphere. Philadelphia, 1802.

303. *Bigeon, (L. F.)* Observations qui prouvent que l'abus des remèdes surtout de la saignée & des évacuans du canal alimentaire est la cause la plus puissante de notre destruction prématurée, des maux & des infirmités qui la précèdent. Dinan, 1812.

548. Q. *Boerhaave.* MS. Lectures taken under the dictation of, 3 vols.

384, 1. Q. *Carminati, (Bassiano)* Ricerche sulla Natura & sugli usi del Succo Gastrico in Med. ed in Chirurg. Milano, 1785.

1663. *Colombier, (M.)* Code de Médecine Militaire pour le service de terre, 4 vol. Paris, 1772.

551. Q. *Drelincourt, (Carol)* Opuscula Medica. Hagæ Comitum, 1727.

384, 20. Q. *Fomento, (F. M.)* De Publicâ Valetudine tuendâ. Taurini, 1793.

1665. *Fothergill, (A.)* On the preservation of the lives of the inhabitants of Great Britain. London, 1783.

469. Q. *Fothergill, (John)* His Works, with some account of his life by Dr. Lettsom. London, 1784.

1295. *Gregory.* Dissertation on the influence of a change of climate in curing diseases. Translated from the Latin, by W. P. C. Barton. Philadelphia, 1815.

1657. *Hartmann, (J. J.)* Tydelig underrættelse om de mæst gångbara Sjukdomar, &c. Abo, 1765.

1615. *Hippocratis* Aphorismi, ad mentem ipsius artis usum & mechanismi rationem expositi, 2 vol. Paris, 1724.

532. *Hosack, (David)* A system of Practical Nosology. New York, 1818.

471. Q. ——— ——— Observations on the laws governing the communication of contagious diseases. New York, 1815.

1153. *Huxham.* Observations on the air and epidemic diseases, from 1728 to 1748, 2 vols. London, 1759.

1650. *Kämpf, (Johannes)* Von einer neuer methode die hart nackigsten Krankheiten zu heilen. Leipzig, 1786.

1610. *Lobstein, (J. F. Daniel)* General guide for practising physicians. Philadelphia, 1823.

1180. *Macbride, (David)* Experimental essays on medical and philosophical subjects. London, 1767.

1179. *Mayow, (Joh.)* Tractatus quinque medico-physici. Oxonii, 1674.

930. *Miller, (Edward)* The medical works of—collected and accompanied with a biographical sketch of the author. New York, 1814.

1726. *Moseley, (Benjamin)* Medical Tracts—on Sugar—the Cow Pox—the Yaws—the Plague and Yellow Fever—Hospitals—Prisons—Bronchocele, &c. London, 1800.

550. Q. *Neuter, (G. P.)* Fundamenta Medicinæ Theoretico-Practicæ. Argentorati, 1718.

1701. *Peale, (Charles W.)* Epistle to a friend on the means of preserving health. Philadelphia, 1803.

1641. *Percival, (Thomas)* Medical, philosophical and experimental Essays. Warrington, 1789.

1645. *Quincy, (John)* See *Sanctorius.*

539. *Rush, (Benjamin)* Six Introductory Lectures to Courses of Lectures upon the Institutes and Practice of Medicine. Philadelphia, 1801.

537. ——— ——— Medical Enquiries, 4 vols. Philadelphia, 1805.

1645. *Sanctorius.* Medicina Statica, being the aphorisms of Sanctorius, translated into English with large explanations; to which is added Dr. Keil's Medicina Statica Britannica, with remarks and explanations, and also Medico-Physical Essays, by John Quincy, M. D. 2d edit. London, 1720.

384, 21. Q. *Sinclair.* Code of Health and Longevity.

362. *Townshend, (Joseph)* The Physicians Vade Mecum, being a compendium of Nosology and Therapeutics. London, 1794.

355. *Waterhouse, (B.)* Cautions to young persons concerning health. Cambridge, (Mass.) 1805.

546. Q. *Willis, (Thomas)* Opera Medica et Physica. Lugd. 1676.

---

4. TREATISES AND ESSAYS ON PARTICULAR DISEASES.

Angina Suffocativa. 352. An Enquiry into the nature, cause and cure of the Angina Suffocativa, by S. Bard. N. York, 1771.

Armies, (Diseases of.) 1339. The Diseases incident to Armies, with the method of cure, by Baron Van Swieten, to which are added, the nature and treatment of gunshot wounds, by W. Ranby, and directions to sea-surgeons in engagements, and preventatives of the scurvy at sea, by W. Northcote. Philadelphia, 1776.

123. Compilaçaõ de reflexões de Sanches, Pringle, Monro, Van Swieten e outros acerca das doenças dos exercitos, por A. A. das Neves. Lisb. 1797.

Asphyxia. 246. Preservative Plan, or hints for the preservation of persons exposed to those accidents which suddenly suspend or extinguish vital action, by A. Fothergill. London, 1798.

384, 13. Q. Essay Physiologique sur la cause de l'Asphyxie par submersion, par M. Berger. Paris, 1805.

246. Methode de traiter tous les hommes décédés, afin de rappeller à la vie ceux qui ne sont morts qu'en apparence, par M. de Hüpsch. Cologne, 1789.

124. Avisos interesantes sobre as mortes apparentes. Lisboa, 1790.

Bile, (Diseases of the.) 353. An essay on the disease of the bile, by William White. London, 1777.

Catarrh. 303. Memoire sur les fluxions de Poitrine, par Louis Valentin. Nancy, 1815.

Children, (Diseases of.) 1676. A treatise on the diseases of children, with directions for the management of infants from the birth, by Michael Underwood, with notes by a physician of Philadelphia. Philade. 1818.

384, 20. Q. Abhandlungen uber die Coxalgie, oder das sogenannte Freywillige Hinken der kinder, von J. C. Albers. Wien, 1807.

Croup. 384, 20. Q. Commentatio de tracheitide infantum, vulgò *Croup* vocatâ, autore J. A. Albers. Lips. 1816.

365. Ueber eine die Schnellste hülfe erfordernde art von Husten, und von beschwerden, beym athmen oder über den Croup, von J. A. Albers. Bremen, 1804.

365. Abhandlung über den Kropff, so wie es sich in verschiedenen theilen von Nord Amerika häufig findet, von Benjamin S. Barton, übersetzt von Wilhelm Liebsch. Göttingen, 1802.

Cutaneous Diseases. 1644. A treatise of diseases incident to the skin, by Daniel Turner. London, 1726.

Diabetes. 262. Case of Diabetes, with an historical sketch of that disease, by Thomas Girdlestone. Yarmouth, 1799.

Diarrhœa. 384, 13. Q. Dissertation sur une espèce particulière de diarrhée, par M. Dalmas. Paris, 1808.

Dysentery. 352. An essay on dysentery, by ——Ball. N. York, 1796.

Elephantiasis. 357. Rapport des commissaires de la Societé Royale de Medecine sur le mal rouge de Cayenne ou eléphantiasis. Paris, 1785.

349. Verhandeling over de melaatsheid. Uit het Latyn vertaald, door G. W. Schelling. Utrecht, 1771.

Endemic Diseases. 349. *Anon.* Observations sur les maladies des nègres. *(No imprint, no date,)*

359. *Baker (George)* Essay concerning the cause of the endemial colic in Devonshire. London, 1767.

861. *Chalmers.* Account of the weather and diseases of South Carolina, 2 vols. London, 1776.

1732. *Clark, (Thomas)* On the nature and cure of the fevers and diseases of the East Indies and of America. Edinburgh, 1801.

1037. *Cleghorn.* On the epidemical diseases of Minorca. London, 1779.

1634. Same work. Philadelphia, 1809.

417. *Currie, (William)* Historical account of the climates and diseases of the United States. Philadelphia, 1792.

1734. ——— ——— View of the diseases most prevalent in the United States. Philadelphia, 1811.

1705. *Ewell, (James)* Planter's and mariner's medical companion. Philadelphia, 1807.

384, 9. Q. *Girdlestone, (Tho.)* Diss. de Hepatite Indiæ Orientalis. Lug. Bat. 1787.

216. *Hilary, (William)* On the diseases of the West India Islands. London, 1766.

368. Q. *Hunter, (George)* Essay on the diseases incident to Indian seamen or Lascars on long voyages. Calcutta, 1804.

402. *Johnson, (James)* On the influence of tropical climates on European constitutions, 2 vols. Philadelphia, 1821.

416. *Lind, (James)* Essay on the diseases incidental to Europeans in hot climates. London, 1777.

1702. *Mann, (James)* Medical Sketches on the campaigns of 1812, 1813, 1814, with a dissertation on dysentery, and observations on the winter epidemic denominated *Peripneumonia Notha*, as it appeared at Sharon and Rochester in the state of Massachusetts. Dedham, (Mass.) 1816.

1727, 1728. *Mosely, (Benjamin)* A treatise on tropical diseases, and on military operations, and on the climate of the West Indies, London, 1792, 4th ed. London, 1803.

350. *Tennent, (John)* Physical Enquiries, discovering the mode of translation in the constitutions of northern inhabitants on going to, and for some time after arriving in, southern climates. London, 1742.

26, 291. *Unanue, (Hipolito)* Observaciones Sobre el clima de Lima, y Sus influencias en los Seres organizados, en especial el hombre. Lima, 1806, 1815.

Fevers. 1643. A Discourse concerning fevers, by Daniel Turner. London, 1739.

618. An Essay on Fevers, more particularly those of the Common-continued and Inflammatory sorts, by Lionel Chalmers. Charleston, 1767.

351. A Dissertation on simple Fever, or on fever consisting of one paroxysm only, by George Fordyce. London, 1794.

1733. Observations on the Causes and Cures of Bilious Fevers, by William Currie. Philadelphia, 1799.

352. Reflections on the inflammatory character of Fevers, by Lyman Spalding. New York, 1817.

369. A Treatise upon the Typhus Fever, by George Buchanan. Baltimore, 1789.

1680. Practical illustrations on Typhus Fever, of the common continued fever, and of inflammatory diseases, &c. By John Armstrong, with notes, by Nathan Potter. Philadelphia, 1821.

1658. Essai sur la fièvre miliaire, par M. Gastellier. Paris, 1773.

351. An account of the Scarlet Fever and Sore throat: or Scarlatina Anginosa, by W. Withering. Birmingham, 1793.

See *Yellow Fever.*

Gout. 1617. An Enquiry into the nature, causes and cure of the Gout, and of some of the diseases with which it is connected, by John Gardiner. Philadelphia, 1793.

358. Reflections and observations on the Gout, by James Jay. London, 1772.

Hemoptysis. 355. Medical Dissertations on Hemoptysis, or the spitting of blood, and on suppuration, by John Ware. Boston, 1820.

Hydrocephalus. 351. Letters concerning the internal Dropsy of the Brain, by William Patterson. Dublin, 1794.

Hydrophobia. 239, 1692. A dissertation on the bite of a mad dog, by James Mease. Philadelphia, 1792.

384, 5. Q. On curing the bite of a mad dog, by De Mederer. *(No imprint, no date.)*

1692. Observations on the arguments of Professor Rush in favour of the inflammatory nature of the disease produced by the bite of a mad dog, by James Mease. Philadelphia, 1801.

1656. R. Hamilton's Bemerkungen über die mittel wider den Biss toller Hunde, und anderer wütenden thiere, nebst widerlegung des Irrthums vom Wurmnehmen, aus dem Englischen übersezt und mit einigen Anmerkungen begleitet von Dr. C. F. Michaelis. Leipz. 1787.

369. A case of hydrophobia successfully treated, by John Shoolbred, with an appendix containing two cases, treated by F. Tymen. Cupar, (Scotland) 1813.

Pleurisy. 369. An Essay on the Pleurisy, by John Tennent. Williamsburg, 1740.

Plague. 384, 21. *Q.* Observ. on the increase and decrease of different diseases, and particularly of the plague, by William Heberden, jun. London, 1801.

130. Observations sur la maladie appellée peste, par Assalini. Paris, 1801.

384, 13. *Q.* De la manière dont la peste se communique aux animaux & à l'homme, par M. Bonnissant. Paris, 1812.

125. Peste de Lisboa, em 1569. Lisboa, 1801.

125. Advertencias dos meios que os particulares podem usar para preservar-se da peste, conforme à o que tem ensinado a experiencia. Publicadas por ordem da Academia das Sciencias. 2 Edição, à que se ajunta o opusculo de Thomaz Alvarez e Garcia de Salzado sobre a peste de Lisboa em 1569. Lisboa, 1801.

212. *Q.* Act of the British parliament and order in council respecting quarantine. 1805.

384, 10. *Q.* Collezione di Notificazioni, e ordini per la deputazione di Sanità in Livorno. 1804.

Poisons. 534. A General System of Toxicology, translated from the French of Orfila, by Joseph G. Nancrede. Philadelphia, 1817.

1620. A Treatise on the adulterations of food and culinary poisons, by Frederick Accum. Philadelphia, 1820.

1696. Observations and Experiments on the poison of lead, by Thomas Percival. London, 1774.

351. Cautions concerning the poison from using lead and copper vessels, &c and the method of detecting them, by A. Fothergill. Bath, 1790.

1624. Ueber die Bleyglasur unserer töpferwaare, von G. A. Ebell. Hanover, 1794.

Scurvy. 1649. An Enquiry into the source from whence the symptoms of the Scurvy and of putrid fevers arise, by Francis Milman. London, 1782.

1339. Preservatives of the Scurvy at sea, by William Northcote. Philadelphia, 1776.

Small Pox. 1731. An Enquiry how to prevent the Small Pox, by John Haygarth. Bath, (Eng.) 1801.

354. Account of an Epidemic Small Pox which occurred in Cupar in Fife in 1817, by H. Dewar. Cupar, 1817.

384, 5. *Q.* Diss. med. de opt. meth. Variolas inoculandi à Lud. Valentin. Nanceii, 1786.

207. *Q.* Memoires pour servir à l'histoire de l'inoculation de la petite vérole, par la Condamine. Paris, 1768.

384, 20. *Q.* Analyse & Tableaux de l'influence de la petite vérole sur la mortalité, par M. Duvillard. Paris, 1806.

1730. Medical Transactions, containing tracts chiefly relating to the small pox and other contagious diseases, by John Haygarth, 4 vol. Bath, (England,) 1801.

Syphilis. 1679. A Treatise on the Venereal Disease, by John Hunter; with an Introduction and Commentary, by Joseph Adams. First American edition. Philadelphia, 1818.

467. *Q.* Same work. London, 1786.

1678. Practical Observations on Venereal Complaints, by F. Swediaur. Edinburgh, 1788.

359. Same work. New York.

1683. A practical dissertation on the Venereal Disease, by Daniel Turner. London, 1727.

1668. Historical and critical observations on Syphilis, by A. J. L. Jourdan, translated from the French, by R. La Roche. Philadelphia, 1823.

Tetanos. 252. Dissertation & observations sur le Tétanos, publiés par le Cercle des Philadelphes au Cap-François. 1786.

Vaccine. 384, 9. *Q.* On the origin of the Vaccine Inoculation, by Edward Jenner. London, 1801.

301, 354. A letter to Wm. Dillwyn on the effects of Vaccination in preserving from the small-pox, by Edward Jenner. Philadelphia, 1818.

1612. Jennerian Discovery, or a concise view of all the most important facts which have hitherto appeared concerning the Vaccine or Cow-pock, by C. R. Aikin. London, 1801.

1611. A popular view of Vaccine Inoculation, with the practical mode of conducting it, by Joseph Adams. London, 1807.

384, 5. *Q.* Lettsom's observations on the Cow-pock. London, 1801.

1613. A practical treatise on Vaccine or Cow-pock, by Samuel Scofield. New York, 1810.

Practical observations on Vaccination, by John Redman Coxe. Philadelphia, 1802.

Vaccine. 354. Report to the Royal Jennerian Society. London, 1804.

274. Rapport de la Commission instituée à Milan, pour faire des observations & expériences sur la Vaccine. Traduit de l'Italien par N. Heurteloup. Paris, 1802.

850. Bericht einer von der Classe der Physischen und Mathematischen Wissenchaften niedergestzten Commission zur untersuchung der methode, durch die Kuhpocken für die wirklichen Pocken zu schützen.

274. An historical account of the Vaccine Inoculation, written originally in English, and translated into Chinese by Sir George Staunton, published in the said language under the name of Gnewqua, the responsible editor. Canton.

1718. Publications on the Vaccine, containing inter alia: Rappórt sur la Vaccine, par A. Aubert—Waterhouse's history of the Kine-pox—Woodville's and Dunning's observations, and Currie's letters on the same—Resultats de l'inoculation de la Vaccine, par Valentin—Woodville's report of a series of cases of Vaccine inoculation—Rapports sur les Vaccinations pratiquées en France en 1806 & 1807, 2 vol.

Worms. 1642. A Natural and Medicinal History of Worms bred in the bodies of men and other animals, done from the Latin of D. Le Clerc. London, 1721.

Yellow Fever. 274. Facts and observations relative on the nature and origin of the Pestilential Fever which prevailed in this city in 1793, 1797, and 1798, by the College of Physicians of Philadelphia. Philadelphia, 1798—1806.

537. Observations upon the origin of the malignant bilious or yellow fever in Philadelphia, by Benjamin Rush. Philadelphia, 1799.

330. An impartial review of that part of Dr. Rush's publication, entitled, "An account of the bilious remitting yellow fever, as it appeared in Philadelphia in 1793, by William Currie. Philadelphia, 1794.

1711. Collection of publications on the yellow fever—Containing inter alia—Account of the fever at Philadelphia in 1793, by M. Carey—Description of the same, by William Currie—History of the yellow fever at New York in 1795, by Alexander Hosack, jr.—Analysis of the Black vomit by Isaac Cathrall, 2 vols. Philadelphia.

1712. Traité de la Fièvre Jaune, par Jean Devèze. Paris, 1820.

252. Recherches & observ. sur les causes & les effets de la maladie épidémique qui a regné à Philadelphie en 1793, par le même.

246. Same work in English. Philadelphia, 1794.
1714. Traité de la fièvre jaune d'Amérique, par Louis Valentin. Paris, 1803.
216. Observations on the changes of the air, and the yellow fever, by Dr. Hillary. London, 1766.
1708. A Memoir on Contagion, more especially as it respects the yellow fever, by Nathaniel Potter. Balti, 1818.
1710. A Treatise on the plague and yellow fever, by James Tytler. Salem, 1799.
646. A Treatise on Malignant Fevers, with an attempt to prove its non-contagious nature, by Stubbins Firth. Philadelphia, 1804.
339. Observations on the Yellow Fever, by Anthony Plantou. Philadelphia, 1822.
352. Observations on Febrile contagion, and on the means of improving the medical police of the city of New York, by David Hosack. New York, 1820.
1709. Letters and documents respecting the Yellow Fever. Baltimore, 1820.
274. Report on the Malignant Disease which prevailed in the city of New York in the autumn of 1805, by E. Miller. New York, 1806.
355. A concise History of the autumnal Fever which prevailed at Wilmington in 1802, by John Vaughan. Wilmington, (Del.) 1803.
384, 20. *Q.* Constantii Didier Commentatio Medica de Febre Flavâ Americanâ. Gottingæ, 1800.
1713. Breve descripcion de la Fiebre Amarilla padecida en Cadiz, en 1800—1804, por J. M. de Arejula. Madrid, 1806.
274. Osservazioni Mediche sulla malattia febrile dominante in Livorno, da Gaetano Palloni. Livorno, 1804.

OMITTED ABOVE.

Goitre. 224. Memoir concerning the disease of the goitre, as it prevails in different parts of North America, by Benjamin S. Barton. Philadelphia, 1800.

5. SURGERY AND OBSTETRICS.

459. *Anon.* Recueil des pièces qui ont concouru pour le prix de l'Académie Royale de Chirurgie. Paris, 1753.
353. *Adams, (W.)* Official papers relating to operations performed at Greenwich on several of the pensioners for ascertaining the efficacy of the new modes of treatment practised by W. Adams for the cure of cataract. Published by order of the directors.
350. *Baudeloque, aîné.* Recherches & réflexions sur l'opération Césarienne. Paris, an 7.
1670. *Burns, (John)* The Principles of Midwifery, including the

diseases of women and children, 3d American Edition, with notes by Thomas C. James, 2 vols. Philada, 1813.

549. Q. *Cooke, (James)* Mellificium Chirurgiæ, or the Marrow of Chirurgy. London, 1685.

1681. *Cooper, (Astley)* and *Travers, (Benjamin)* Surgical Essays, Parts I. and II. First American Edition. Philadelphia, 1821.

355. *Dewees, (William P.)* An essay on the means of lessening pain in cases of difficult parturition. Philada. 1819.

524. *Dorsey, (John)* Elements of Surgery, 2 vols. Philadelphia, 1813.

1674. *Hamilton, (Alexander)* Outlines of the Theory and Practice of Midwifery. Edinburgh, 1784.

362. *Herholdt, (Joh. Dan.)* Commentatio de vitâ, imprimis foetus humani ejusque morte sub partu. Hauniæ, 1802.

68. F. *Hernandez, (Fran.)* Rerum medicarum novæ Hispaniæ Thesaurus. Romæ, 1651.

1677. *Hunter, (John A.)* Treatise on the blood, inflammation, and gunshot wounds. Philadelphia, 1817.

466. Q. ——— ——— Natural History of the human teeth. London, 1778.

1671. *James, (Thomas C.)* A Synopsis of the various kinds of difficult parturition. Philadelphia, 1816.

1725. *Lafargue.* L'Art du Dentiste. Paris, 1802.

1659. *Larrey, (D. J.)* Mémoires de chirurgie militaire & de campagne, 3 vol. Paris, 1812.

384, 20. Q. *Loder, (J. C.)* Oratio inauguralis novi Theatri Anatomici Moscuæ; Latin and Russian, with an engraved plan. Moscow, 1819.

350. *Pelletan, (Ph. J.)* Observations sur un osteo-sarcôme de l'humerus simulant un aneurisme. Paris, 1815.

1339. *Ranby, (John)* The nature and treatment of gunshot wounds. Philadelphia, 1776.

303. *Richerand, (Le Chevalier)* Account of resection of the ribs and Pleura. Translated by T. Wilson. Philada. 1818.

262. *Saucerotte.* De la conservation des Enfans pendant la grossesse. Paris, an 4.

1673. *Smellie, (W.)* A Treatise on the Theory and Practice of Midwifery, 3 vols. London, 1762.

30. F. *Sœmmering, (Sam. Tho.)* Icones embryonum humanorum. Francofurti ad Moenum, 1799.

359. *Thomassin.* Sur l'extraction des corps étrangers des playes. Strasb. 1788

384, 17. Q. *Turnbull, (William)* A case of extra uterine gestation of the ventral kind. London, 1791. Philadelphia, 1819.

1634. *Wilson, (J.)* Pharmacopœia Chirurgica, or a manual of Chirurgical Pharmacy. Philadelphia, 1818.

---

6. MATERIA MEDICA AND THERAPEUTICS.

244. *Anon.* Account of the Philadelphia Dispensary, April 12, 1786. Philadelphia, 1802.

359. *Alexander, (William)* Experimental essays on the following subjects.
I. On the external application of antiseptics in putrid diseases.
II. On the doses and effects of medicines.
III. On diuretics and sudorifics. London, 1768.

224. *Barton, (Benjamin S.)* Collections for an essay on the Materia Medica of the United States. Philadelphia, 1801.

264, 5. Q. *Barton, (W. P. C.)* Vegetable Materia Medica, with plates, 2 vols. Philadelphia, 1817—1823.

283. *Beddoes, (Thomas)* On factitious airs as medicinal, addressed to J. Watt. Clefton, 1795.

283. ——— ——— Description of a Pneumatic apparatus.

301. ——— ——— and *James Watt.* Considerations on the medical use, and on the production of factitious airs. Bristol, 1795.

246. *Berkeley, (Robert)* An Inquiry into the modus operandi of that class of medicines called sedatives. Philadelphia, 1800.

350. *Björnlund, (B.)* Materia Medica Selecta. Aboæ, 1797.

330. *Brande, (Aug. Evr.)* Experiments and observations on the Angostura bark. London, 1793.

362. *Chamberlaine, (William)* A Practical Treatise on the efficacy and safety of Stizolobium or Cowhage. (The dolichos pruriens of Linnæus,) internally administered in diseases occasioned by worms. London, 1804.

512½. *Chapman, (Nath.)* The Elements of Therapeutics and Materia Medica, 3d ed. revised and much improved 2 vols. Philadelphia, 1823.

1653. *Chrestien, (A. J.)* De la méthode iatroliptique, ou observations pratiques sur l'administration des remèdes à l'extérieur dans les maladies internes. Montpellier, an 12.

357. *Cosnier, Malvet, &c.* Rapport sur les avantages reconnus de la nouvelle méthode d'administrer l'électricité dans les maladies nerveuses. Paris, 1783.

1707. *Coxe, (John R.)* The American Dispensatory. Philadelphia, 1806.

1703. *Crawford, (Alexander)* An experimental enquiry into the effects of tonics and other medical substances, on the cohesion of the animal fibre. London, 1816.

1729. *Currie, (James)* Medical Reports on the effects of water, cold and warm, as a remedy in fever and other diseases. Philadelphia, 1808.

361. *Currie, (William)* Abridgment of his work on the use of water in diseases of the human frame, and on fever, opium, &c. Augusta, (Maine.)

384, 10. Q. *Decandolle.* Essai sur les propriétés médicales des plantes. Paris, 1804.

523. *Eberle, (John)* A Treatise of the Materia Medica and Therapeutics, 2 vols. Philadelphia, 1822.

384, 13. Q. *Faculté de Médecine de Paris.* Bulletin sur l'emploi du zinc. 1813.

384, 12. *Q. Fleming*. Catalogue of Indian medicinal plants with their names in the Hindostan and Sanscrit languages.

358. *Fowler, (Thomas)* Medical Reports of the effects of tobacco principally to its diuretic quality in the cure of Dropsies and Dysuries. London, 1785.

1609. *Graves, (Robert)* Pocket Conspectus of the London and Edinburgh Pharmacopœias. Philadelphia, 1803.

303. *Gondret, (L. Fr.)* Considerations sur l'emploi du feu en Médecine. Paris, 1818.

1675. *Hamilton, (James)* Observations on the utility and administration of purgative medicines in several diseases. Philadelphia, 1818.

1667. *Hawes, (James)* An account of Dr. Goldsmith's illness, so far as relates to the exhibition of James's powders. London, 1780.

1695, 9. *Horsfield, (Thomas)* An Experimental dissertation on the Rhus Varnix, Rhus Radicans, and Rhus glabrum. Philadelphia, 1798.

1736. *Laffecteur*. Sur les effets du rob anti-syphilitique. Paris, 1810.

357. *Mayault*. Réflexions sur quelques préparations chymiques appliquées à l'usage de la médecine. Paris, 1779.

1181. *Meade, (William)* An experimental enquiry into the chemical properties and medicinal qualities of the principal mineral waters of Ballston and Saratoga. Philadelphia, 1817.

1704. *Pharmacopœia* of the Massachusetts Medical Society. Boston, 1808.

741. ———— Simpliciorum & efficaciorum in usum Nosocomii militaris, ad exercitum foederatarum Americæ civitatum pertinentis. Philadelphia, 1778.

350. ———— Suecica. Holmiæ, 1790.

533. ———— of the United States of America. Boston, 1820.

350. *Robiquet*. Analyse de la Réglisse. Paris, 1809.

355. *Rouelle, (John)* A complete treatise on the Mineral Water of Virginia. Philadelphia, 1792.

537. *Rush, (Benjamin)* Experiments and observations on the Mineral Waters of Philadelphia, Abington, and Bristol. Philadelphia, 1773.

537. ———— A comparison between the diseases and remedies of the North American Indians and those of civilized nations.

239. *Ruspini, (Barth.)* Account of his Balsamic Styptic. London, 1791.

1621. *Russel, (Richard)* A Dissertation on the use of Sea Water in the diseases of the glands, translated from the Latin by Andrew Leuthold. London, 1760.

409. *Salazar, (Don Thomas de)* Tratado del Uso de la Quina. Madrid, 1791.

1623. *Sans, (l'Abbe)* Guérison de la paralysie par l'électricité. Paris, 1778.

259. *Shoepf, (J. D.)* Materia Medica Americana, potissimum Regni vegetabilis. Erlangæ, 1787.

1715. *Smyth, (James Carmichael)* The effect of nitrous vapour in preventing and destroying contagion—with an Introduction respecting the nature of the contagion which gives rise to the Hospital Fever. Philadelphia, 1799.

357. Q. *Tavares, (F.)* Advert. sobre os abusos das Agoas Mineraes das Caldas da Rainha, 1791. See *Withering.*

350. *Valli.* Lettre à Astier, sur la découverte de la vertu antifermentescible de l'oxide rouge de mercure. Paris.

1722. *Withering, (William)* An account of the Fox Glove, and some of its medical uses. Birmingham, 1785.

458. Q. ——— ——— Analyse Chimica da Agoa das Caldas da Rainha, Em Portugues e Ingles. 1795. See *Tavares.*

1607. *Zollickoffer, (William)* A Materia Medica of the United States. Baltimore, 1819.

---

7. MISCELLANEOUS.

550. The American Medical and Philosophical Register, 4 vols. New York, 1811—1814.

536. The Philadelphia Medical and Physical Journal, edited by B. S. Barton, vols. 2 and 3. Philadelphia, 1805.

311. The American Medical Recorder, edited by John Eberle, 5 vols. Philadelphia, 1818—1822.

704. Amerikanische Annalen der Arzneykunde, Naturgeschichte, Chemie und Physik, von Dr. J. A. Albers—incomplete. Bremen, 1803.

1662. Bibliothek for Læger, 2 Hafter. Kiöbenhavn, 1821.

363. The Charleston Medical Register for 1802, by David Ramsay. Charleston, 1803.

509. The Eclectic Repertory and Analytical Review, Medical and Philosophical, by a Society of Physicians, 10 vols. Philadelphia, 1811—1820.

507. The Edinburgh Medical and Physical Commentaries, 10 vols. Edinburgh, 1774—1785.

507½. Same work, decade II. vol. 7. 1793.

636. The New England Journal of Medicine and Surgery, April, 1816, vol. 5, No. 2, containing some account of Harvard University, in Cambridge, Massachusetts.

529. The New York Medical Repository, edited by Samuel L. Mitchill and Edward Miller, 15 vols. New York, 1804—1812.

508. The Philadelphia Medical Museum, edited by John Redman Coxe, 7 vols. Philadelphia, 1805—1811.

1706. The Philadelphia Medical Dictionary, by John Redman Coxe. Philadelphia, 1808.

512. The Philadelphia Journal of the Medical and Physical Sciences, edited by Nathaniel Chapman, 6 vols. Philadelphia, 1820—1822.

1190. Vermischte Schriften physisch-medicinischen Inhalts, von Johann Ingenhousz; Uebersetzt, und herausgegeben von N. C. Molitor, 2 vols. Wien, 1784.

552½. The Western Quarterly Reporter of Medical, Surgical, and Natural Science, edited by John D. Godman, No. 1—6. Cincinnati, 1822.

243. Inaugural Theses and Dissertations on various Medical and other subjects, from 1664 to the end of the 17th century.

547. Q. Dissertationes Inaugurales Medicæ ad Academiam. Lugduni Batavorum, 1725—1732.

1699. Thesaurus Medicus, sive Dissertationum in Acad. Edin. ad rem medicam pertinent. delectus à Gulielm. Smellie, 3 vol. Edinburgh, 1778.

1695. Inaugural Theses, Essays, and Dissertations by Graduates in Medicine in the University of Pennsylvania, 16 vols. Philadelphia, 1761—1820.

1697. Inaugural Dissertations by Graduates in Medicine in the College of New York. New York, 1797—1813.

1700. Inaugural Dissertations by Graduates in Medicine in the University of Pennsylvania and other medical schools in the United States, selected and published by Charles Caldwell, M. D. 2 vols. Philadelphia, 1805.

465. Mémoire sur les Hôpitaux de Paris. Paris, 1788.

636. Medical Police of the City of Boston. Boston, 1808.

353. Reports of deaths in the City and County of New York for 1818. New York, 1819.

IX. RELIGION.

1. Sacred Writings.
2. Liturgies, Catechisms, Confessions of Faith, &c.
3. Ecclesiastical History, and documents thereto belonging.
4. American Churches.
5. Theological and Religious Writings.
6. Controversial Writings.
7. Bible and Missionary Societies.

1. SACRED WRITINGS.

1346. Biblia Sacra, Hebraicè, cum punctis. Amstelod. 1732.

478. Q. Biblia Sacra, tam veteris quam novi Testamenti, cum apocryphis; adjectæ sunt Lectiones variæ selectæ, Hebraicè & Græcè. Curâ C. B. Michaelis. Zullichav. 1741.

472. Q. The Holy Bible, containing the Old and New Testament, in the Arabic language. Newcastle-upon-Tyne, 1811.

473. Q. Same in Syriac, printed for the B. & F. Bible Society. London, 1816.

471½. Q. The Holy Bible, containing the Old and New Testament, translated out of the original tongues, and with the former translations diligently compared and revised, with marginal notes and references. Philadelphia, 1803.

1352. The Holy Bible. Printed for the British and Foreign Bible Society. London, 1804.

1370. The same. Duodecimo. London, 1804.

1344. The same. Octavo. London, 1815.

1350. The same. Duodecimo. London, 1815.

42. *F.* La Sainte Bible, qui contient le Vieux & le Nouveau Testament avec les notes de la Bible Flamande de Diodati & autres. Publiée par Desmarets, père & fils. Amsterdam, Elzevir, 1669.

1354. *Q.* La Sainte Bible, imprimée sur l'édition de Paris de l'année 1805. Ed. Stéréot. aux frais de la Société Biblique Angl. & Etrangère. Londres, 1814.

1353. La Sainte Bible, Traduction de Sacy. Imprimée aux frais de la Société Biblique Russe. St. Petersb. 1817.

479. *Q.* Biblia Española, por Cassiodoro Reyna. This translation is generally known by the name of the *Bible of the Bear*, because the figure of a bear is printed on the frontispiece, which has made bibliographers suppose that it was printed at Berne. But it seems now admitted that it was published at Basil in 1569. *(Title page wanting.)*

1348. Die Bibel, oder die ganze Heilige Schrift des alten und neuen Testaments, nach Luthers Uebersetzung, auf Kosten der Britt. und Ausländ. Bibel Gesellsch. London, 1813.

1358. The same. London, 1814.

481. *Q.* Biblia, thet ær all then Heliga Skrift, på Svensko, medh Summarier, Concordantier, &c. Stockholm, 1706, 1715.

474. *Q.* The Bible and New Testament in the Armenian language, printed for the Russian Bible Society. St. Petersb.

1347. Same in Illyrian. Printed as above. St. Petersb. 1819.

1355. Same in Slavonic. Printed as above. St. Petersb.

1356. Same in the Finnish language. Printed as above. St. Petersb. 1817.

1346. Same in the Welch language. Printed for the British and Foreign Bible Society. London, 1814.

1359. Same in the same language. Caer grawnt, 1813.

537. *Q.* Mamusse Wunnetupanatamwe, &c. The Bible and New Testament, translated into the Massachusetts Indian language, by John Eliot. With an Indian grammar prefixed. Cambridge, (Mass.) 1666.

538. The same, second edition. Cambridge, (Mass.) 1680.

190. *F.* Daniel, Secundùm Edit. LXX. Interpretum, ex Tetraplis desumptam. Ex Codice Syro-Estranghelo Biblioth. Ambrosianæ Syriacè edidit, Latinè vertit, præfatione notisque illustravit Caietanus Bugatus. Mediol. 1788.

301. *Q.* Codex Syriaco Hexaplaris Ambrosiano Mediolanensis, editus & Latinè versus à Matth. Norberg. Lond. Goth. 1787.

1351. Psalterium Davidis, Æthiopicè. Impensis Sodalitii ob Biblias in Mag. Brit. atq. alibi evulgandas instituti. London, 1815.

1345½. Η ΚΑΙΝΗ ΔΙΑΘΗΚΗ. Novum fœdus, cum versione latinâ, Secundum curam J. Leusdenii et Griesbachii editum ab H. A. Aitton. Lugd. Bat. et Amstelod. 1809.

1349. The New Testament of our Lord and Saviour Jesus Christ. Translated from the original Greek, appointed to be read in churches. Stereotype edition. Printed for the B. & F. Bible Society. Cambridge.

1345. The New Testament in an improved version upon the basis of Abp. Newcome's new translation. London, 1808.

1690½. The New Testament and the Psalms, written in short hand, MS.

1367. Le Nouveau Testament de N. S. Jesus Christ. Ed. Stereot. Publié par la Soc. Bibl. Angl. & Etrang. Londres, 1807.

1368. El Nuevo Testamento de N. S. Jesu Christo. Bermondsey, (Inglaterra) 1813.

1365. O Novo Testamento, isto he, O Novo Concerto de Nosso fiel Senhor e redemptor Jesu Christo. Traduzido na lingoa Portugueza. Chelsea, (Inglaterra) 1817.

1364. Il nuovo Testamento del nostro Signore Gesù Cristo, ediz. stereot. Shacklewell, (Inghilterra) 1816.

1376. Das Neue Testament unsers H. und H. Jesu Christi. Verdeutscht von Dr. Martin Luther. Auf kosten der Russichen Bibel-gesselchaft. St. Petersb. 1819.

1372. Nowy Testament pana Naszego Jesuza Christusa, *(Polish.)* From the vulgate by Jacob Wuyka, of the Society of Jesus. Published by the Russian Bible Society. Moscow, 1809.

1373. The same, published as above. St. Petersb. 1819.

1360. Det nye Testamente, oversat fra grundsproget; Udgivet efter den Danske Bibel oversættelses fiortende Udgave. Trykt paa des Brit. og Udent. Bibel-Sælskabs Bekostnung. London, 1814.

1374. Η' καινὴ διαθήκη τȣ κυρίȣ καὶ σωτῆρος Ἰησȣ Χριςȣ̃. Μεταφρασθεῖσα εἰς κοινὴν διάλεκτον, *(Romaic.)* Published by the Russian Bible Society. St. Petersburgh, 1817.

1375. The same, published by the B. & F. Bible Society. London, 1814.

477. Q. Novum Testamentum Domini et Salvatoris nostri Jesu Christi è græcâ in Persicam linguam, à V. R. Henrico Martyn translatum in Urbe Schiraz—Sumptibus Soc. Bibl. Ruthenicæ typis datum. Petrop. 1815.

475. Q. The New Testament in the Armenian language. Published by the Russian Bible Society. St. Petersburgh.

476. Q. The same in the Grusinian, *(Georgian)* language. Published as above. St. Petersburgh.

1361. The same in the Tartar language. Published as above. Astrachan, 1818.

480. Q. The same in the Samogitian language. Published as above. Wilna, 1816.

1357. The same in the Esthonian language. Published as above. St. Petersburgh, 1815.

1366. The same in the Manks language. Published by the B. & F. Bible Society. London, 1815.

1369. The same in the Gaelic or Erse language. Published as above. Edinburgh, 1813.

1362. The same in the Irish language. Published as above. Shacklewell, 1815.

482. *Q.* The Gospels of St. Matthew and St. John, in the Mongul language. Published by the Russian Bible Society. St. Petersburgh.

483. *Q.* The Gospel of St. John, in the Calmuck language. Published as above. St. Petersburgh.

1363. The Gospels of St. Matthew, St. Luke, and St. John, translated into the language of the Esquimaux Indians of the Coast of Labrador, by the Missionaries of the *Unitas Fratrum.* Published by the B. &. F. Bible Society. London, 1813.

1378. The three Epistles of the Apostle John, translated into Delaware Indian, (with the text opposite,) by C. F. Dencke. Published by the American Bible Society. New York, 1818.

ETHNICK RELIGIONS.

1438. The Alcoran of Mahomet, translated out of Arabique into French by Du Ryer, and newly Englished. London, 1649.

1436½. L'Ezour-Vedam, ou Anciens Commentaires du Vedam. Traduits du Sanscretan par un Brame, 2 vol. Yverdun, 1778.

---

2. LITURGIES, CATECHISMS, CONFESSIONS OF FAITH, &C.

Bible Christian Church. 1585½. The offices of the Bible Christian Church. Manchester, (Eng.) 1817.

Church of England. 1572. The Book of Common Prayer and Administration of the Sacraments, &c. according to the use of the Church of England, with occasional prayers and sentences of scripture. Formerly collected and translated into the Mohawk language, under the direction of the Society for the propagation of the Gospel in foreign parts. A new edition. To which is added, The Gospel according to St. Matthew, translated into the Mohawk language, by Capt. Joseph Brandt, an Indian of the Mohawk nation. (The English text opposite.) London, 1787.

1583. The order of the morning and evening prayer, and administration of the sacraments, and some other offices of the church. With a collection of prayers and some sentences of Holy Scripture. Collected and translated into the Mohawk language under the direction of the late Rev.

W. Andrews, H. Barclay, and J. Ogleby, formerly missionaries from the Society for propagating the gospel in foreign parts to the Mohawk Indians. New York, 1769.

1574. The morning and evening prayer, litany, church catechism, family prayers, and several chapters of the Old and New Testament, translated into the *Mahaque* Indian language. By Lawrence Claesse, interpreter to William Andrews, missionary to the Indians, from the Society for the propagation of the gospel in foreign parts. New York, 1715.

1574½. Same work, with MS. translations and notes in English and German by the Rev. Chr. Pyrlæus.

1573. *Leabhar*, &c. The Liturgy of the Church of England, with David's Psalter in the Irish language. London, *(no date.)*

Greek Church. 276. Q. Liturgy of the Greek church in the Armenian language.

135. The Russian Catechism, composed and published by order of the Czar, to which is annexed, a short account of the church government and ceremonies of the Muscovites. Second edition. London, 1725.

297. Q. The rites and ceremonies of the Greek Church in Russia, by John Glen King, D. D. London, 1772.

Lutheran Church. 1594. Kirchen Ordnung der Augspurgischen confession zugethanen gemeinde in St. Mary's, Savoy. London, 1743.

Presbyterian Church. 1437. Constitution of the Presbyterian Church in the United States. Philadelphia, 1821.

Quakers. 520. Q. The Book of Discipline of the Society of Friends in Pennsylvania and New Jersey, as revised and established in 1719. MS. from an ancient copy in the possession of T. Matlack, Esq. Philadelphia, 1820.

R. Catholic Church. 1439. MS. Breviary, on parchment, illuminated capitals. *(No title page, no date.)*

1544. Officia B. Virginis & SS. Martyrum—MS. on parchment, with elegant illuminated pictures. *(No title page, no date.)*

533. Q. Catecismo Brazilico da Doctrina Christãa, com o ceremonial dos sacramentos, &c. Composto (em lengoa Brazilica,) por Padres doutos da Companhia de Jesus. Emendado pelo P. Bartholomeo Deleam. Lisboa, 1686, MS. copy.

Unitas fratrum. 1585. A Collection of Hymns, for the use of the Christian Indians of the Missions of the United Brethren in North America. (In the Delaware language.) By the Rev. David Zeisberger. Philadelphia, 1803.

1567½. E Hime neoia te Parau Haamaitai, e te arue i te Atua, (Hymns in the Otaheitian language.) Tahiti, printed at the Windward Missionary press, 1822.

---

3. ECCLESIASTICAL HISTORY AND DOCUMENTS THERETO BELONGING.

272. *Anon.* Index Librorum ad celebranda Sacra Sæcularia Reformationis Ecclesiasticæ Tertia. Berolini, 1821.

1445. —— Taxæ Cancellariæ Apostolicæ. Sylvæ-Ducis, 1526.

315. *Ashworth, (John)* An account of the rise and progress of the Unitarian Doctrine, in several places. Rochdale, 1817.

118. F. *Bedæ, (Venerabilis)* Historia Ecclesiastica gentis Anglorum. Cantab. 1643.

1433. *Buchanan, (Charles Christian)* Researches in Asia, with notices on the translation of the Scriptures into the Oriental languages. New York, 1812.

271. *Cloyne, (Bishop of)* Present state of the church of Ireland. Dublin, 1787.

Felix, (Minucius) see *Tertullian.*

685. *Holmes, (Abr.)* An Historical Sketch of the English translations of the Bible. 1815.

1577. *Lieberkuhn, (Sam.)* The History of our Lord and Saviour Jesus Christ, comprehending all that the four Evangelists have recorded concerning him. Translated into the Delaware Indian, by the Rev. David Zeisberger, Missionary of the United Brethren. New York, 1821.

1435. *Miller, (Robert)* History of the propagation of the gospel and the overthrow of paganism, 2 vols. London, 1731.

136. *Plato,* (Metropolitan of Moscow) The present state of the Greek church in Russia, or a summary of Christian divinity. Translated from the Sclavonian, with a preliminary memoir and an appendix, by Robert Pinkerton. New York, 1815.

272. *Rimius, (H.)* A candid narrative of the rise and progress of the Hernnhutters, commonly called Moravians. London, 1753.

1371. *Royaumont.* L'Histoire du Vieux & du Nouveau Testament, par le Sieur de Royaumont, Prieur de Sombreval. St. Brieuc, 1802.

1377. Testamen çaharreco eta Berrico Historioa, (being the above work translated into the Basque language.) 2 vols. Bayonne, 1775.

115. F. *Sewel, (William)* The History of the rise, increase, and progress of the Christian people called Quakers. London, 1725.

1448. *Tertulliani* Apologeticus & ad Scapulam liber. Accessit M. Minucii Felicis Octavius. Cantab. 1686.

670. *Weygard, (J. A.)* The whole system of the XXVIII articles of the Evangelical unvaried confession presented

at Augsburgh, to the emperor Charles V. by the Protestant princes and states, translated by J. A. Weygard. New York, 1755.

Zeisberger, see *Lieberkuhn*.

---

4. AMERICAN CHURCHES, (IN ORDER OF DATES.)

1620—1698.

124. *F.* Magnalia Christi Americana, or the Ecclesiastical History of New England, from 1620 to 1698, by the Rev. Cotten Mather. London, 1702.

1763.

679. Verses on Dr. Mayhew's book of observations on the charter and conduct of the society for the propagation of the gospel. Providence, (New England) 1763.

This and many of the following pamphlets relate to the controversy respecting an American episcopacy.

1764.

679. An answer to Dr. Mayhew's observations on the charter and conduct of the society for the propagation of the gospel, by Dr. Secker, Archbishop of Canterbury. London, 1764.

676. A Review of Dr. Mayhew's Remarks. *(No title page, probably printed at Boston.)*

689. The charter of the United Episcopal churches in Philadelphia, granted June 14, 1765, and also bye-laws and resolutions of the vestry of the said churches. Philadelphia, 1813.

1765.

676. A Defence of the Episcopal Government. *(No title page, probably printed at Boston.)*

1767.

676. An appeal to the public in behalf of the Church of England in America, by Thomas Bradbury Chandler, D. D. New York, 1767.

679. Remarks on certain passages in the bishop of Landaff's society sermon, by Charles Chauncey. Boston, 1767.

1768.

676. A Letter concerning an American bishop, &c. to Dr. Bradbury Chandler, in answer to the appendix of his appeal to the public, &c. 1768.

678. Dr. Chauncey's answer to Dr. Chandler's appeal to the public. Boston, 1768.

676. A Letter concerning an American bishop, &c. to Dr. Bradbury Chandler, in answer to the appendix of his appeal to the public, &c. Printed A. D. 1778.

1771.

679. An address from the clergy of New York and New Jersey to the episcopalians in Virginia, occasioned by some late transactions in that colony, relative to an American episcopate. New York, 1771.

678. The Appeal further defended in answer to the further misrepresentations of Dr. Chauncey, by Thomas Chandler. New York, 1771.

669. A Critical Commentary on Archbishop Secker's letter to H. Walpole, concerning bishops in America. Philadelphia, 1771.

1773.

649. An Appeal to the public for religious liberty, against the oppressions of the present day, by James Backus. Boston, 1773.

1777.

676. An Appeal in behalf of the Church of England in America, by the Rev. Thomas Bradbury Chandler. New York, 1777.

1778.

649. Government and Liberty described, and Ecclesiastical Tyranny exposed, by James Backus. Boston, 1778.

1780.

630. Observations sur l'origine, les principes & l'établissement en Amérique de la Société connue sous la dénomination de Quakers ou Trembleurs, par Ant. Benezet. Philadelphia, 1780.

1785.

675, 724. Journal of a Convention of the Protestant Episcopal Church of several states, held at Philadelphia in September and October, 1785. Philadelphia, 1785.

1786.

689. A Sermon delivered in Philadelphia on the 21st of June, 1786, at the opening of the convention of the Protestant Episcopal Churches in several states by William White. Philadelphia, 1786.

1787.

675. A Sermon delivered in Philadelphia, the 28th of May, 1787, at the first ordination held by the bishop of the Protestant Episcopal Church there, by Samuel Magaw. Philadelphia, 1787.

1797.

698. Constitution and rules to be observed and kept by the Friendly Society of St. Thomas's African Church of Philadelphia. Philadelphia, 1797.

1799.

267. Journal of the Convention of the Protestant Episcopal church. Philadelphia, 1799.

600. Journal of the Proceedings of the bishops, clergy and laity of the Protestant Episcopal Church in the United States of America, in a convention held at Philadelphia in June, 1799. Philadelphia, 1799.

1804.

261. Minutes of the General Assembly of the Presbyterian Church in the United States. Philadelphia, 1804.

1805.

817. An Account of the several Religious Societies in Portsmouth, New Hampshire, from their first establishment,

and of the ministers of each to the 1st of January, 1805, by Timothy Alden, jun. Boston, 1808.

1806.

649. A View of the Ecclesiastical Proceedings in the county of Windham, Connecticut, by J. Sherman. Utica, 1806.

1807.

689. A Charge to the clergy of the Protestant Episcopal Church in Pennsylvania, delivered in Philadelphia, May 27, 1807, by William White. Philadelphia, 1807.

1813.

689. Reports of the Board of Trustees of the Society for the advancement of Christianity in Pennsylvania, made January 6th, 1813. Philadelphia, 1813.

1817.

634. Extracts from the minutes of the proceedings of the fourteenth General Synod of the associate reformed church in North America, held at Philadelphia, 21st May, 1817. Philadelphia, 1817.

730. The Blessed Reformation; a Sermon preached in New York on the 31st of October, 1817, by the Rev. F. C. Schaeffer, on occasion of the celebration of the third centurial jubilee of the reformation commenced by Dr. Martin Luther. New York, 1817.

272. Der 31ste October 1817. Zum feyerlichen andenken an den 31sten October, 1517, mit Rührung begangen in der St. Michaelis und Zions gemeinde in Philadelphia, mit einer kurzen Anzeigen von Dr. Luthers frühern lebensjahren, und die Artikeln der Augsburgischen Confession. Philadelphia, 1817.

1818.

137. Journal of the Proceedings of the Protestant Episcopal Church in the State of South Carolina, held in Charleston, February, 1818. Charleston, 1818.

1819.

689. The Constitution of the Society of the Episcopal Church for the advancement of Christianity in Pennsylvania. Philadelphia, 1819.

634. Extracts from the minutes of the General Assembly of the Presbyterian Church in the United States, 1819. Philadelphia, 1819.

1820.

272. Grundverfassfung der Evangelisch Lutherische General Synode in den vereinigten Staaten von Nord America, nebst dem protocol der versammlung die sie entworfen. Baltimore.

687. Memoirs of the Protestant Episcopal Church in the United States of America, containing,

I. A Narrative of the organization, and of the early measures of the church.

II. Additional statements and remarks.

III. An appendix of original papers by William White. Philadelphia, 1820.

1822.

714. Extracts from the Minutes of the Proceedings of the nineteenth General Synod of the associate Reformed Church in North America, held at Philadelphia, May, 1822. Philadelphia, 1822.

688. Proceedings and Journals of the General Convention of the Protestant Episcopal Church in the United States of America. 1784—1822.

---

5. THEOLOGICAL AND RELIGIOUS WRITINGS.

944. *Abercrombie, (James)* Lectures on the Catechism and Liturgy of the Protestant Episcopal Church, and Sermons on various subjects. Philadelphia, 1798—1812.

310. *Barbauld, (Anna Lætitia)* Remarks on G. Wakefield's enquiry into the expediency and propriety of public and social worship. London, 1792.

1439½. *Baronius, (R.)* Philosophia Theologiæ ancillaris; hoc est pia & sobria explicatio quæstionum philosophicarum in disputationibus theologicis subindè occurrentium. London, 1658.

336. *Beattie, (James)* An Essay on the nature and immutability of truth, in opposition to sophistry and scepticism. London, 1773.

488. Q. *Bertaudus Petragoricus, (Joh.)* De cognatione S. Joannis Baptistæ cum filiabus & nepotibus beatissimæ Annæ, libri tres. Imprimebat Jodocus Badius Ascensius. Anno 1529.

490. Q. *Boehm, (Martin)* Kirchen Calender, in 13 Predigten verfasset. Wittenberg, 1671.

484. Q. *Bynaeus, (A.)* De Natali Jesu Christi. Amstelaedami, 1689.

1534. *Dupont de Nemours.* Sur les institutions religieuses dans l'intérieur des familles. Paris.

572. *Kersey, (Jesse)* On the fundamental doctrines of the Christian Religion. Philadelphia, 1815.

487. Q. *Limborch, (Phil.)* De Veritate Religionis Christianæ. Goudæ, 1687.

676. *Llandaff,* (Bishop of) A Sermon preached before the Society for the propagation of the Gospel, &c. Feb. 20, 1767. London, 1767.

267. *Magaw, (S.)* Sermon preached at the first ordination by the bishop of the Protestant Episcopal Church. Philadelphia, 1782.

745. *More, (Hannah)* Considerations on the Speech of M. Dupont in the National Convention of France, together with an address to the ladies, &c. of Great Britain and Ireland. Boston, 1794.

1590. *Paley, (William)* Natural Theology, or evidences of the existence and attributes of the Deity, collected from the appearances of nature. New York, 1820.

1515, 45. *Priestley, (Joseph)* Outline of the evidences of revealed religion. Philadelphia, 1797.

—— 44. —— —— Originality and superior excellence of the Mosaic Institutions. Northumberland, 1803.

—— 30. —— —— A serious Address to Masters and Families.

—— " —— —— Prayers for families, and forms of prayers for particular occasions.

—— " —— —— A Free Address to Protestant Dissenters as such, by a Dissenter. London, 1771.

—— " —— —— An Appeal to the professors of Christianity. London, 1775.

—— " —— —— Familiar Illustrations of certain passages of Scripture. London, 1772.

—— 34. —— —— Comparison of the Institutions of Moses, with those of the Hindoos, &c. Northumberland, 1799.

—— 35–38. —— —— History of early opinions concerning Jesus Christ, 4 vols. Birmingham, 1786.

—— 39. —— —— Discourses on various subjects. Birmingham, 1787.

—— 46. —— —— Doctrines of Heathen Philosophy compared with those of revelation. Northumberland, 1804.

—— 48. —— —— General History of the Christian church, 6 vols. Northumberland, 1803.

—— 49. —— —— Notes on all the books of Scripture, 4 vols. Northumberland, 1803.

—— 41. —— —— Familiar Letters to the Inhabitants of Birmingham. 1790.

—— 40. —— —— Forms of Prayers, &c. for the use of Unitarian Societies. Birmingham, 1783.

—— 44. —— —— Discourse on the evidence of the resurrection of Jesus. Birmingham, 1791.

—— 20, 21. —— —— Institutes of Natural and Revealed Religion, 2 vol. London, 1782.

—— 22, 23. —— —— Corruptions of Christianity, 2 vols. Birmingham, 1782.

—— 25–27. —— —— Theological Repository, 3 vols. London, 1771.

—— 29. —— —— Two Letters to Doctor Newcome on the duration of our Saviour's ministry. Birmingham, 1780.

—— " —— —— A Third Letter to the same. Birmingham, 1781.

—— " —— —— Doctrine of Divine Influence on the Human Mind. Bath, 1779.

—— " —— —— Sermon preached at Birmingham. 1781.

—— " —— —— Two Discourses on habitual devotion, and on the duty of not living to ourselves. Birmingham, 1782.

—— " —— —— Sermon preached at the New-Meeting at Birmingham. 1782.

—— 30. —— —— Catechism for children and young persons. London, 1781.

745. *Rochester, (Bishop of)* Critical disquisitions on the

Eighteenth Chapter of Isaiah in a letter to Edward King. Philadelphia, 1800.

573. *Say, (Thomas)* His life and writings. Philadelphia, 1796.

389. Q. *Simsonii.* Hieroglyphica Animalium quæ in Scripturis Sacris inveniuntur. Edinburgi, 1622.

937. *Smith, (Rev. W.)* His works, 2 vols. Philadelphia, 1803.

938. ——— ——— His discourses on various occasions in America. London, 1762.

630. *Tennent, (Gilbert)* His Sermons. Philadelphia, 1747—1752.

485. Q. *Til, (J. Van)* Malachias Illustratus. Lugduni Batavorum, 1701.

1413. *Volpilière, (de la)* Discours de la louange & de la gloire, où on prouve qu'elles appartiennent à Dieu & non aux hommes. Conformément au sujet proposé par l'Académie Françoise. Paris, 1672.

105. F. *Wilson, Baywell, & Simson.* A complete Christian Dictionary, wherein all the words mentioned in the Holy Scriptures are fully opened, expressed, and explained. London, 1678.

ANONYMOUS.

1747. The Christian's Magazine, vols. 1, 5, 6, 7. New York, 1806—1810.

272. Essay on the constitution of the Apostolic churches, considered in application to the churches of Christ in every age. New York, 1811.

342. A Key to the three first chapters of Genesis, opening to the most common understanding the production of the world, the creation, formation and fall of man, and the origin of evil. London, 1784.

1582. *Ehelittonhenk li Amemensak.* Sermons to children. Translated into the Delaware language, by David Zeisberger. Philadelphia, 1803.

1378. *Llyfr y Resolusion,* &c. The Book of Resolution, which teaches us all to do our best, and bestow all our attention and mind to be true Christians, &c. *(Welch.)* Llundain, 1684.

133. *Pisaniou Skiatomou,* &c. Instructions for the true knowledge of the Passion and Death of our Saviour. *(Ancient Russian.)* *No imprint or date.*

6. CONTROVERSIAL WRITINGS.

Arminians. 1512. Views of the controversy between the Calvinists and Arminians by the Rev. W. White, 2 vols. Philadelphia, 1817.

Buchanites. 342. Eight letters between the people called Buchanites, and a teacher near Edinburgh. Edinburgh, 1785.

Calvinists. 945. A careful and strict enquiry into the modern and prevailing notions of freedom of will, &c. by the Rev. Jonathan Edwards, 4th ed. Wilmington, (Del.) 1790.

621. The peculiar doctrines of the Gospel explained and defended, by Noah Webster. Newhaven, 1809.

Church Discipline. 1515, 28. View of the principles and conduct of the Protestant Dissenters, by Joseph Priestley. Lond.

—— " Address to Protestant Dissenters on the Lord's Supper, by the same. London, 1773.

—— " Address to Protestant Dissenters on the Church Discipline, by the same. London, 1770.

—— " Remarks on several publications relative to the Dissenters, in a letter to Dr Priestley, by a Dissenter. London, 1770.

—— " Letters to the author of the above remarks, by Joseph Priestley. London, 1770.

—— 29. Letter to a layman on the subject of Lindsey's proposal for a Reformed Church, by the same. London, 1774.

Church Ministry. 1601. De gradibus ministrorum evangelii liber, à Theo. Bezâ. 1592.

691. Letters addressed to the Rev. S. Miller, concerning the constitution and order of the Christian Ministry, by Thomas Y. How. Utica, 1808.

Congregationalists. 621. An inquiry into the right to change the ecclesiastical constitution of the Congregational churches of Massachusetts. Boston, 1816.

Divine Worship. 689. Thoughts on the singing of Psalms and Anthems in churches, by W. White. Philadelphia, 1808.

Divorce. 1442. Tractatio de repudiis & divortiis, à Theod. Bezâ. Genevæ, 1591.

Free-will. 1515, 19. Controversy with J. Palmer concerning the doctrine of necessity, by Joseph Priestley. London, 1779.

Infidelity. ——, 44. Observations on the increase of infidelity, by the same. Philadelphia, 1797.

——, 24. Letters to a philosophical unbeliever, by the same. London, 1780.

——, 42. Letters to Mr. Volney on his work, entitled Ruins, by the same, with Volney's answer. Philadelphia, 1797.

—— " Letters to the philosophers and politicians of France on Religion, by the same. Lond. 1793.

—— " Observations on the increase of Infidelity, by the same. Northumberland Town, 1795.

—— " Answer to Paine's Age of Reason, by the same. London, 1795.

Jesuits. 1446. Secret instructions of the Jesuits. London, 1723.

Jews. 681. A Looking Glass for the Jews, by George Fox, in the year of our Lord 1674. London, 1784

1741. Lettre politico-theologico-morale sur les Juifs, par D. Nassy. (French and Low Dutch.) Paramaribo, 1798.

Methodists. 1434. Portraiture of Methodism, by Jonathan Crowther. New York, 1813.

740. Three Letters to the Rev. Mr. Whitefield. Philadelphia, 1739.

Monastic Vows. 483½. *Q.* De votis monasticis, by Martin Luther. Wittemberg, 1521.

Presbyterians. 486. *Q.* Dangerous positions, &c. published and practised within this island, by S. Bancroft. London, 1640.

Prophecies. 1515, 44. Sermon on the present state of Europe, compared with ancient prophecies, by Joseph Priestley. London, 1794.

342. The Key of Prophecy, being the opening of the seals of the revealed will of God, by Robert Atkinson. London, 1782.

Prot. Epis. Church. 486½. *Q.* The unreasonableness of separation from the Church of England, by Stillingfleet. London, 1681.

631. A Friendly expostulation with all persons concerned in publishing a pamphlet, entitled, The Real Advantages which ministers and people may enjoy, especially in the colonies, by conforming to the Church of England, by J. Beach. New York, 1763.

645. An Address to the Ministers and Congregations of the Presbyterian and Independent persuasions in the United States of America, by a member of the Episcopal Church. 1790.

675, 724. The Case of the Episcopal Churches in the United States considered, by Dr. White. Philadelphia, 1782.

342. Letters containing an Apology for the Episcopal Church of Scotland, by George Gleig. Edinburgh, 1787.

690. Collection of pamphlets concerning a certain dispute which arose in the Protestant Episcopal Church at New York, between the Right Rev. Bishop Hobart and the Rev. John Cave Jones. 1811.

Quakers. 630. The Doctrine of Christianity as held by the people called Quakers indicated, in answer to Gilbert Tennent's sermon on the lawfulness of war. Philadelphia, 1748.

630. An Apology for the religious society called Free Quakers in the City of Philadelphia, showing that all churches who excommunicate, act inconsistently with the gospel of Jesus, by Samuel Wetherill. Philadelphia.

663. Narrative and appeal from certain proceedings against him of the Society of the People called Quakers, alleging a breach of discipline, &c. by John Evans. Philadelphia, 1811.

634. A Solemn Review of the custom of war. Philadelphia, 1815.

Reformation. 1689. Bellarminus enervatus, à Gulielm. Amesio. Amstelodami, 1628.

Roman Catholics. 1444. Assertion of the Seven Sacraments against Martin Luther, by Henry the Eighth. London, 1688.

621. Sundry documents submitted to the consideration of the Pewholders of St. Mary's Church, by the Trustees of that Church. Philadelphia, 1812.

709, 710. Various pamphlets concerning the differences between the Roman Catholics worshipping at St. Mary's Church in Philadelphia, occasioned by the suspension and excommunication of their pastor the Rev W. Hogan, in which various points of the discipline of the Roman Catholic Church are discussed. Philadelphia, 1821—1822.

951. Catholic Layman, being publications on the subject of a controversy between the Roman Catholic Bishop of Philadelphia and the Congregation of St. Mary's Church, respecting the right of patronage, the mode of inflicting Ecclesiastical censures, &c. by Mathew Carey. Philadelphia, 1822.

Scots Covenanters. 1598. Sermons on renewing and subscribing the National Covenant of Scotland. Glasgow, 1741.

Unitarians. 110. Letters to Dr. Priestley, occasioned by his late controversial writings, by M. Madan. London, 1787.

1515, 44. Unitarianism explained and defended, by J. Priestley. Philadelphia, 1796.

——, 50. Tracts in controversy with Bishop Horsley, by the same. London, 1815.

1510. Boston Unitarian controversy, by Samuel Worcester and W. E. Channing. Boston, 1815.

649. A statement of reasons for not believing the doctrines of Trinitarians respecting the nature of God, and the person of Christ, occasioned by Stuart's Letters to Channing. Boston, 1819.

713. Various pamphlets and discourses on the Unitarian and Trinitarian controversy. Philadelphia, &c. 1818—1822.

732. Answer to Dr. Wood's Reply in a second series of Letters addressed to Trinitarians and Calvinists, by Henry Ware. Cambridge, 1822.

310½. The Unitarian Christian's Apology for seceding from the communion and worship of Trinitarian Churches, by S. C. Fripp. Bristol, 1822.

Unitas Fratrum. 272. The plain case of the Representatives of the people known by the name of Unitas Fratrum. London, 1754.

---

7. MISSIONARY AND BIBLE SOCIETIES.

Great Britain. 81. Missionalia, or a collection of missionary pieces relating to the conversion of the heathen. London, 1727.

670. Charter for the Society for the propagation of the gospel. 1701.

676. An abstract of the Charter and proceedings of the Society for the propagation of the gospel, in London, from the 21st of February, 1766, to the 20th day of February, 1767. London.

670. Instructions from the society for the propagation of the gospel in foreign parts, to their missionaries in North America. London, 1756.

A Collection of papers printed by order of the Society for the propagation of the gospel in foreign parts. London, 1741.

1379. Reports of the British and Foreign Bible Society, 17 vols. 1805—1822.

364. Substance of the report delivered by the Directors of the Sierra Leone Company to the proprietors, 1794. Philadelphia, 1795.

Massachusetts. 695. Report of the executive committee of the Bible Society of Massachusetts, prepared for the Anniversary of the Society, June 2, 1814. Boston, 1814.

685. Report of the Committee of the Society for propagating the gospel among the Indians, read and accepted 7th November, 1816.

634. Report of the select Committee of the Society for propagating the Gospel among the Indians and others in North America, read November 4, 1819. Cambridge, 1819.

261. Discourse before the Society for propagating the Gospel among the Indians, &c. with a History of the said Society, by John Lathrop. Boston, 1804.

N. Hampshire. 693. Second report of the New Hampshire Bible Society, communicated to the Society at their annual meeting at Plymouth, September 22, 1813. Concord, 1813.

Pennsylvania. 634. Charter and By-laws of the Philadelphia Missionary Society, incorporated April 18th, 1814. Philadelphia.

693. Constitution, By-laws, and Annual Report of the auxiliary African Bible Society of the city of Philadelphia. Philadelphia, 1817

693. Constitution and Reports of the Female Bible Society of Philadelphia.
Philadelphia, 1814—1820.

692. Reports of the Bible Society established at Philadelphia, May 1, 1809.
Philadelphia, 1809—1822.

685. A Brief Account of the proceedings of the committee appointed in 1795, by the Yearly Meeting of Friends of Pennsylvania, New Jersey, &c. for promoting the improvement and gradual civilization of the Indian Natives.
Philadelphia, 1805.

634. Circular of the Standing Committee of Missions of the Presbyterian church. Philadelphia, 1804.

680. A Discourse concerning the conversion of the Heathen Americans, by William Smith.
Philadelphia, 1760.

Russia. 276. Q. Fourth Anniversary Report of the Russian Bible Society.

Unitas Fratrum. 852. History of the Missions of the United Brethren among the Indians of North America, by George Henry Loskiel. Translated from the German by C. J. Latrobe. London, 1794.

851. A Narrative of the Missions of the United Brethren among the Delaware and Mohegan Indians, by John Heckewelder. Philadelphia, 1821.

United States. 693. Constitution, Proceedings, and Reports of the American Bible Society, together with their address to the people of the United States.
New York, 1816—1821.

Communications relative to the progress of Bible Societies in the United States.
Philadelphia, 1813.

738. A report of the American Board of Commissioners for foreign missions, at the third annual meeting held at Hartford, September 16, 1812, with annual reports of the same.
Boston, 1812.

693. Report of the American Board of Commissioners for foreign missions. Boston, 1816.

X. MORAL SCIENCES.

1. Logic, Metaphysics and Ethics. 2. Education.

1. LOGIC, METAPHYSICS AND ETHICS.

169. *Anon.* Ἀποπέιρα ἀναλύσεως τοῦ νοουμένου ἑτεροίας παρὰ τὰς νῦν, &c. *(Romaic.)* Leipsick, 1817.

430. —— Principes Mathématiques de la loi naturelle. La Haye, 1779.

1410. *Bacon.* Essays or counsels civil and moral. London, 1639.

1450. *Baldesanus.* Stimuli virtutum adolescentiæ Christianæ dicati.

1511. *Beasley, (Fred.)* A search of truth, in the science of the human mind. Philadelphia, 1822.

242. *Boerhaave, (Herman)* Disputatio philos. de distinctione mentis à corpore, pro gradu doctoratûs habita. Lugd. Bat. 1690.

130. F. *Burton, (Robert)* The anatomy of melancholy, philosophically, medicinally, and historically opened and cut up, by Democritus, jun.
(Title page wanting, supplied in MS. but no date.)

370. *Condillac.* La logique, ou les prémiers développements de l'art de penser. Paris, 1796.
Same work in English, translated by Joseph Neef. Philadelphia, 1809.

1483. La misma Obra, traduzida al Castellano, por Don Valentin de Foronda. Madrid, 1800.

132. Q. *Condorcet.* Essai sur l'application de l'analyse à la probabilité des décisions. Paris, 1785.

1050½. ——— Outlines of an historical view of the progress of the human mind. Baltimore, 1802.

1513. *Cooper, (Thomas)* Tracts, ethical, theological, and political, vol. 1. Warrington, (England) 1789.

1251. *Delamétherie.* De la perfectabilité & de la dégénérescence des êtres organisés Paris, 1806.

1553. *Destutt de Tracy, (A. L. C.)* Elémens d'Idéologie, 4 vol. Paris, 1804.

1596. ΕΠΙΚΤΗΤΟΥ ΕΓΧΕΙΡΙΔΙΟΝ. Epicteti Enchiridion, Latinis versibus adumbratum, per Edwardum Ivie. Oxon. 1723.

1483. *Foronda, (Valentin de)* See *Condillac.*

1877. *Gros, (John Daniel)* Natural principles of rectitude for the conduct of man, in all states and situations in life. New York, 1795.

Ivie, see *Epictetus.*

1432. *Lavater, (J. C.)* Secret journal of a self observer, 2 vols. in one. London, 1770.

1525. *Maximus of Tyre.* Dissertations de Maxime de Tyr, Philosophe Platonicien, traduites sur le texte Grec, avec des notes critiques, &c. par J. J. Combes-Dounous, 2 vol. Paris, 1802.

224. F. *Montaigne, (Michel)* Essais de. Paris, 1652.

1541. *Neufchateau, (François de)* Conseils d'un père à son fils, imité des vers que Muret a écrits en Latin, pour l'usage de son neveu. Parme (Bodoni) 1801.
This is a poetical translation of Muret's work, to which is prefixed the original text, and an Italian and German translation in verse, are added.

1341. *Owen, (Robert)* New View of Society, or Essays on the formation of the human character. London, 1813.

1515, 14. *Priestley, (Joseph)* Hartley's Theory of the Mind, with Essays. London, 1775.

——, 15. —— —— Examination of Reid's Enquiry into the Mind, Beattie's Essay on Truth, and Oswald's Appeal in behalf of Religion. London, 1775.

——, 16. —— —— Disquisitions relating to Matter and Spirit. London, 1782.

——, 17. —— —— Doctrine of Philosophical Necessity. London, 1782.

——, 18. —— —— Discussion of the Doctrine of Materialism with Dr. Price. London, 1778.

538. *Rush, (Benjamin)* Essays, Literary, Moral, and Philosophical. Philadelphia, 1798.

552. Q. *Salesberiensis, (Johannes)* Policraticus, sive de nugis curialium & vestigiis Philosophorum. Paris, 1513.

158. F. *Salzedo, (Pedro Gonzales de)* Examen Veritatis. Bruxelles, 1673.

1440. *Scaliger, (J. C.)* De Subtilitate. Francof. 1582.

1507. *Tela, (Joseph)* The Philosophical Library, being a collection of ancient and modern MSS. and printed works, metaphysical, theological, historical and philosophical, containing the Lives and Morals of Confucius, Epicurus and others, 3 vols. London, 1818.

728. *Volney.* Catechism of Nature, translated from the French.

2. EDUCATION.

262. *Anon.* Essay on the means of improving public education, adapted to the United States. Frederick-Town, 1803.

636. —— Précis sur les Instituts d'Education de Mr. de Fellenberg, établis a Hofwyl, auprès de Berne (extrait du Journal d'Education.) Paris, 1817.

651. *Barlow, (Joel)* Prospectus of a National Institution to be established in the United States. Washington, 1806.

1534. *Dupont de Nemours.* Sur l'Education Nationale dans les Etats Unis d'Amérique. Paris, 1812.

1383. *Grivel.* Théorie de l'Education, 3 vol. Paris, 1775.

404. *Hamel, (Joseph)* Der gegenzeitige Unterricht Geschichte. Paris, 1818.

225 Q. *Hauy.* Essai sur l'éducation des aveugles. Paris, 1786.

684 *Hobson, (J.)* Prospectus of a plan of Instruction for the young of both sexes. Philadelphia, 1799.

400. *Knox, (Samuel)* Essay on the best system of liberal education. Baltimore, 1799.

1300. *Lancaster, (Joseph)* Improvements in education, as it respects the industrious classes of the community. London, 1805.

262. Same work, American edition. New York, 1804.

708. ——— ——— Letters on National subjects auxiliary to universal education and scientific knowledge. Washington, 1820.

1534. *Lasteyrie, (Charles de)* Nouveau système d'Education pour les Ecoles primaires adopté dans les 4 parties du monde. Paris, 1815.

1304. *Locke* on Education. Translated into Russian. Moscow, 1760.

454. Q. *Mello Franco, (Francisco de)* Tratado de Educaçaõ Fysica dos meninos. 1790.

324. *Pictet, (C.)* Lettre au général Vial sur les établissemens de Hofwyl. Laney, 1808.

1515, 43. *Priestley, (Joseph)* Discussion on Education, delivered to the supporters of the new college at Hackney. London, 1791.

——, 12. ——— ——— Miscellaneous observations relating to education, and the conduct of the mind. London, 1778.

324. *Rengger, (A.)* Rapport sur l'institut d'éducation des pauvres à Hofwyl. Paris, 1815.

724. *Rush, (Benjamin)* Thoughts upon female education. Philadelphia, 1787.

304 *Shaw, (Benjamin)* Brief exposition of the principles and details of the Lancasterian system of education.

615. *Smith, (Samuel)* Remarks on Education. Philadelphia, 1798.

724. *Swanwick, (John)* Thoughts on education. Philadelphia, 1787.

718. *Torres de Navarra, (Joseph Gonzalez)* Rasgo de ideas para instituir un seminario general de Educacion practica en la corte de España. Philadelphia, 1810.

324. *Villevieille, (Louis de)* The establishment of E. de Fellenberg at Hofwyl, considered with reference to their claim upon the attention of men in public stations, translated from the French. London, 1820.

615. *Wardlaw, (Ralph)* An essay on J. Lancaster's improvements in Education. Glasgow, 1810.

366. *Winchester, (Elhanan)* A plain political Catechism, intended for the use of schools in the United States of America. Philadelphia, 1796.

XI. JURISPRUDENCE.

1. Law of Nature and Nations.
2. Municipal Codes and Laws, and Commentaries thereon.
3. Criminal and State Trials.
4. Miscellaneous.

1. LAW OF NATURE AND NATIONS.

1065. *Azuni, (D. A.)* Droit Maritime de l'Europe, 2 vol. Paris, 1805.

1015. *Barton, (William)* A dissertation on the freedom of navigation and maritime commerce. Philadelphia, 1802.

1313. *Burlamaqui, (J. J.)* The principles of natural law, translated by Nugent. London, 1780.

1307. *Bynkershoek, (Cornelius Van)* A Treatise on the law of war, being the first book of his Quæstiones Juris Publici. Translated from the Latin original, with notes, by Peter S. Du Ponceau. Philadelphia, 1810.

638. *Dumoulin, (J. T.)* An essay on naturalization and allegiance. Washington, 1815.

631½. *Duane, (W. J.)* The Laws of Nations, investigated in a popular manner, addressed to the Farmers of the United States. Philadelphia, 1809.

——— see *Schlegel.*

Du Ponceau, see *Bynkershoek.*

638. *Hay, (George)* A Treatise on Emigration. Washington, 1814.

— Review of the above, ascribed to J. Lowell. Boston, 1814.

1310. *Jacobsen, (Frederick J.)* Laws of the Sea, with reference to maritime commerce during peace and war. Translated from the German, by William Frick. Baltimore, 1818.

Lowell, see *Hay.*

282. *Madison, (James)* Examination of the British doctrine which subjects to capture a neutral trade not open in time of peace.

628. *Pinckney, (Charles)* Three Letters published under the signature of a South Carolina Planter, containing
I. The case of Jonathan Robbins.
II. On the recent captures of American vessels by British Cruisers.
III. On the right of expatriation. Philadelphia, 1799.

638. *Plowden, (F.)* A Disquisition concerning the law of Alienage and Naturalization. Paris, 1818.

642. *Rush, (Richard)* American Jurisprudence, written and published at Washington, being a few reflexions suggested on reading "Wheaton on Captures." Washington, 1815.

255, 632. *Schlegel, (J. F. W.)* Neutral Rights, or an impartial examination of the right of search of neutral vessels under convoy, translated from the French by W. Duane. Philadelphia, 1801.

625. *Tilghman, (William)* The case of Alien Enemies considered and decided upon a writ of habeas corpus allowed on the petition of C. Lockington, an alien enemy, by Wm. Tilghman, Chief Justice of the Supreme Court of Pennsylvania. Philadelphia, 1813.

1315. *Vattel, (M. de)* The Law of Nations, or principles of the law of nature applied to the conduct and affairs of Sovereigns. Northampton, (Mass.) 1820.

1012. *Warden, (D. B.)* On the origin, nature, progress, and influence of consular establishments. Paris, 1813.

ORDINANCES AND DECREES.

384, 7. *Q.* Déclaration du Roi de France concernant la course sur les ennemis de l'Etat. Paris, 1778.

384, 7. *Q.* Réglement concernant la Navig. des Bâtimens Neutres. Paris, 1778.

384, 7. *Q.* Réglement concernant les Prises. Paris, 1778.

384, 7. *Q.* Réglement pour l'établis. du Conseil des Prises. Paris, 1778.

281. Decree of the Judge of the High Court of Admiralty of Great Britain in the Case of Fox and others, libelled for having violated the Orders in Council respecting neutral trade. 1811.

For further public acts respecting the law of nations, see the Laws of the United States, Collection of State Papers, and the title HISTORICAL DOCUMENTS, *passim.*

---

2. MUNICIPAL CODES AND LAWS, AND COMMENTARIES THEREON.

America and Europe. 90. Review of the Constitutions of the principal states of Europe and the United States of America, by M. de la Croix, 2 vols. London, 1792.

Austria. 311. The Emperor's (Joseph II.) new Code of Criminal laws, published at Vienna, 15th Jan. 1787, translated from the French. Dublin, 1787.

Barbadoes. 155. *F.* The Laws of Barbadoes. London, 1699.

China. 1549. Les loix fondamentales du Code pénal de la Chine, 2 vol. Paris, 1812.

Colombia. 718. Constitucion de la Republica de Colombia, impresa en la Villa del Rosario de Cúcuta en Agosto de 1821 y reimpresa en Filadelfia, en 1822.

31. *Q.* Cuerpo de Leyes de la Republica de Colombia, tomo I. (comprende la constitucion y leyes hasta el 14 de Octobre de 1821.) Bogotà, 1822.

Cundinamarca. 291. Constitucion de Cundinamarca, su Capital Santa Fé de Bogotà. 1811.

Denmark. 1453. Kong Christian V. Danske Lov. Kiöbenh. 1753.

England. 112½. *F.* Leges Anglo-Saxonicæ, Ecclesiasticæ et Civiles; accedunt leges Edwardi Latinæ, Gulielmi Conquestoris Gallo-Normannicæ, et Henrici I. Latinæ. Subjungitur H. Spelmanni Codex legum veterum ab ingressu Gulielmi I. usque ad annum IX. Henricii III. quas cum Codd. MSS. contulit, Notas, Versionem et Glossarium adjecit David Wilkins. London, 1721.

1384. The Constitution of England, or an account of the English government, by J. L. De Lolme. New York, 1792.

293. *Q.* Commentaries on the Laws of England, by William Blackstone, 4 vols. Oxford, 1766.

492. *Q.* Lectures on the Constitution and Laws of England, by Francis Stoughton Sullivan, 2d edit. with the additions of Gilbert Stewart. London, 1776.

France. 317. Constitution de la République Française proposée au peuple Français par la Convention Nationale. Paris, an. 3.

319. The French Constitution of 1793, with notes and remarks by Maria Aletta Hulshoff. New York, 1817.

1691. Les cinq Codes de l'Empire François. Amsterdam.

128. Codes de l'Empire François. Paris, 1811.

1010½. Commercial Code of France, translated into English, with notes, and the text opposite, by John Rodman. New York, 1814.

1417. Ordonnances de Louis XIV. de 1669 & 1673, avec commentaires par M. Jousse, Conseiller au Présidial d'Orléans. Paris, 1761.

384, 7. *Q.* Déclaration du Roi de France concernant l'abolition du Droit d'Aubaine. 1778.

384, 23. *Q.* Arrêt du Conseil d'Etat du Roi, concernant le Commerce étranger dans les Isles Françaises de l'Amerique. 1784.

Germany. 1312. Corpus Juris publici S. R. Imperii, 3 vol. Leipzick, 1794.

393. *Q.* Tractatus de Regimine Seculari Ecclesiastico; auctore Theod. Reinkingk. Francof. ad Mœn. 1659.

Hayti. 268. Constitution of Hayti. Aux Cayes, 1805.

Louisiana. 731. Report made to the general assembly on the plan of a penal code, by Edward Livingston. New Orleans, 1822.

731. Report to the Legislature on the revision of the penal code, by Edward Livingston, Moreau, Lislet and Derbigny. New Orleans, 1823.

Maryland 212. *F.* The Charter of Maryland, together with the proceedings in the two houses of assembly in 1722, 1723 and 1724, relating to the government and judicature of that province. Philadelphia, Bradford, 1725.

151. *F.* Laws of Maryland at large, by Thomas Bacon. Annapolis, 1765.

N. Hampshire. 799. Laws of the State of New Hampshire. Exeter, 1815.

N. Jersey. 135. *F.* Acts of the General Assembly of the State of New Jersey. Philadelphia, 1752.

N. York. 629. Laws of the Legislature of the State of New York, in force against the loyalists, &c. London, 1786.

Pennsylvania. *The Great Law*, enacted by the General Assembly of Pennsylvania, on the 10th of December, 1682, in LXIX. chapters. Extracted from the Archives of the State, by Redmond Conyngham, Esq. MS. *(Not numbered.)*

613. The Constitution of the Commonwealth of Pennsylvania. 1776.

748. The Constitution of the Commonwealth of Pennsylvania, as established by the general convention held at Philadelphia, 1776, to which is prefixed the Confederation of the United States of America. Philadelphia, 1781.

674. The Constitution of the Commonwealth of Pennsylvania, as established by the general convention. Philadelphia, 1784.

275. Constitution of the Commonwealth of Pennsylvania, as altered and amended, and proposed for consideration by the convention. Philadelphia, 1790.

1784. An abridgment of the Laws of Pennsylvania, by Collinson Read, 2 vols. Philadelphia, 1801—1804.

1783. Laws of the Commonwealth of Pennsylvania, republished by authority of the Legislature, with notes and references, by Charles Smith and Joseph Reed, Esqrs. 6 vols. Philadelphia, 1820—1822.

1785. A Digest of the Laws of Pennsylvania, with references to judicial decisions, by John Purdon. Philadelphia, 1818.

246. Collection of the penal laws of the Commonwealth of Pennsylvania. Philadelphia, 1801.

642. Report of the Committee of the Senate, appointed on the Judiciary system, in the year 1816.

275. Compilation of the poor laws of the State of Pennsylvania. Philadelphia, 1788.

Act for the consolidation and amendment of the poor laws, as far as they respect the poor of the city of Philadelphia. Philadelphia, 1806.

656. Experience the test of Governments; in eighteen essays, to aid the investigation of principles and operation of the Constitution and Laws of Pennsylvania, by Isaac Weaver, (a member of the Senate of Pennsylvania.) Philadelphia, 1807.

Portugal. 440. Q. Hist. Juris Civilis Lusitani. Liber singularis, Paschalis Jos. Mellii Freirii. Ulyssip. 1788.

441. Q. Institutionum Juris Criminalis Lusitani—Liber singul. Ejusd. Ulyssip, 1794.

442. Q. Institutionum Juris Civilis Lusitani—1 a 4, 1789—1793. Ejusd. 4 vols. Ulyssip. *(no date.)*

446. Q. Fontes Proximas da Compilaçaõ Filippina do se derivou o Codigo Filippino. Por J. J. Fereira Gordo. Ulyssip. 1792.

445. Q. Indice Chronol. remissivo da Legislaçaõ Portug. posterior a publicaçaõ do Codigo Filippino atè 1804. Por J. P. Ribeiro, 1805, 2 vol.

Rome. 1593. Justiniani Institutionum Libri IV. Amstel. 1669.

1297. Institutes of Justinian, translated from the Latin, with notes, by Thomas Cooper. Philadelphia, 1812.

Russia. 275. Code of Russian Laws, enacted in 1017. (In Russian.) Moscow, 1799.

134. Instructions données par Catherine II. à la Commission pour travailler à la rédaction d'un nouveau code de lois. Lausanne, 1769.

276. Q. Same work in English. London, 1768.

276. Q. Mémoire présenté par le Ministère de la Justice relativement à l'organisation de la Commission des lois, suivi d'un extrait des rapports présentés à S. M. J. sur les travaux de cette Commission. Prémière partie. St. Petersburgh, 1804.

Spain. 370. Constitucion Politica de la Monarquia Española promulgada en Cadiz 19 de Marzo de 1812. Cadix.

285. Constitution of the Spanish Monarchy, promulgated at Cadiz on the 19th of March, 1812. Philadelphia, 1814.

59 Q. Codigo de las Costumbres maritimas de Barcelona, vulgarmente llamado *Libro del Consulado*, traducido al Castellano por D. Antonio de Capmany y Monpalau, con su apendice conteniendo una coleccion de leyes y Estatutos Maritimos, 2 vol. Madrid, 1791.

Sweden. 306. Q. Codex Juris Vestrogothici ex vetusto Bibl. Reg.

Holmiens. MS. transscriptus, quem latinè vertit notisq. illustravit Ebbe Samuel Bring. Lundæ, 1818.

1452. Sveriges Rikes Lag; Gillad och antagen på Riksdagen, Aor 1734. Stockholm, 1766.

361. Forme du Gouvernement de Suède ratifiée par le Roi & les états du Royaume le 21 Avril 1772, avec les discours prononcés à la Diéte, à l'occasion de sa Clôture. Copenhague, 1775.

1058. Anmärkningar til Sveriges Rikes Siæ Lag; a Commentary on the Sea-Laws of Sweden, by Jacob Albrecht Flintberg. Stockholm, 1794.

Switzerland. 26. *Q.* Cours ou explication du Coustumier du pays de Vaud, par Gabriel Olivier. Lausanne, 1808.

United States. 612. Observations on the Articles of Confederation. of the Thirteen United States of America. New York.

556. Constitutions of the United States of America. Philadelphia, 1791.

12. *Q.* The same arranged and epitomized by W. D. Robinson. *(Published at Philadelphia in* 1820.

894. A defence of the Constitutions of the Government of the United States, by John Adams, 3 vols. London, 1787.

797. Laws of the United States, published by authority, 5 vols. Philadelphia, 1815.
Continuation of the same in 7 pamphlets to 1821.

800. A Digest of the Laws of the United States from 1789 to 1820, by Edward Ingersoll. Philadelphia, 1821.

11. *Q.* The same, arranged and epitomized, by W. L. Smith. Philadelphia, 1796.

12. *Q.* The same arranged and epitomized by W. D. Robinson. *(Published at Philadelphia in* 1820.*)*
For a more modern arrangement of the same subject, see M. Carey's atlas of the United States, Title GEOGRAPHY and ETHNOGRAPHY, §. MAPS and CHARTS.

Vermont. 798. Laws of the State of Vermont, by Tolman, 3 vols. Randolph, 1808.

Virginia. 223. *F.* The Acts of the General Assembly of Virginia, from 1660 to 1768. *(Title page wanting.)*

1343. Laws of Virginia of a public and permanent nature, 2 vols. Richmond, 1814.

S. CRIMINAL AND STATE TRIALS.

American.

212. *F.* John Peter Zenger, New York. *(Libel.)* 1735.

833. Pennsylvania State Trials, by William Hogan. Philadelphia, 1794.

697. Report of the Committee of the House of Representatives on the same. 1797.
601. William Blount, Senator. *(Impeachment.)* 1799.
911. John Fries. *(High Treason.)* 1800.
631½. Alexander Addison, Judge, Pennsylvania. *(Impeachment.)* 1803.
697. Samuel Chase, Judge of the Supreme Court of the United States, *(Impeachment)* his answer and pleas. 1805.
936. Shippen, Yeates, and Smith, Judges, Pennsylvania. *(Impeachment.)* 1805.
625. O. Selfridge, Massachusetts. *(Murder.)* 1806.
822. Smith and Ogden, New York. *(Aiding in Miranda's expedition.)* 1806.
934. Aaron Burr, *(High Treason,)* 2 vol. Philadelphia, 1808.
625. Lynn, Meigs, and others, Maine. *(Murder.)* 1810.
625. M'Clean and Graham, Pennsylvania, *(Conspiracy to extort money.)* 1812.
663. John H. Jones. *(Piracy.)* 1813.
663. William Butler. *(Piracy.)* 1813.
873. John Hodges. *(High Treason.)* 1815.
633. Case of Mr. Workman, New Orleans. *(Contempt of Court.)* Philadelphia, 1816.

Foreign.

244. Galileo, Rome. *(Heresy.)* 1633.
See also the same in *Coloniæ Anglicanæ illustratæ*, 384—10. *Q.* No. 14, p. 65.
1515, 30. Elwall, England, *(Heresy and Blasphemy.)* 1726.
311. John Wilkes, England. *(Libel.)* 1763.
221. *F.* John Horne, England. *(Libel.)* 1777.
327, 721. Thomas Paine, England. *(Libel.)* 1792.
311. P. W. Duffin and Thomas Lloyd, England, *(Libel.)* 1793.
311. Thomas Muir, Scotland. *(Sedition)* 1793.
663. J. B. Lacombe, Bordeaux, France. *(Exaction, prevarication, ultra-revolutionary conduct.)* An 2.
293. Charge delivered by C. J. Eyre, on the trials for *High Treason*, in Middlesex in 1794, with strictures on the same, answer, replies, &c. London, 1794.
293. Thomas Hardy, England, *(High Treason.)* 1794.
293. Hamilton Rowan, Ireland. *(Libel.)* 1794.
293. Maurice Margarot, Scotland. *(Sedition.)* 1794.
311. Thomas Walker and others, England. *(Conspiracy to overturn government.)* 1794.
331. R. Watt and R. Downie, Scotland. *(High Treason.)* 1794.
293. Speeches of T. Erskine on the trial of T. Williams for publishing the Age of Reason by T. Paine. Philadelphia, 1797.
347. William Orr, Ireland. *(Treason.)* 1798.
293. A. Hodge, Tortola. *(Murder.)* 1811.
311. Bellingham, England. *(Murder.)* 1812.

4. MISCELLANEOUS SUBJECTS.

Alluvious. 73, 873. Juridical and Polemical writings, by Thomas Jefferson, Edward Livingston, Peter S. Duponceau, and others, on the subject of the controversy respecting the tract of alluvion land at New Orleans, called the *Batture*. New Orleans and Philad. 1808, 1809, 1814.

Civil Law. 1306. Joh. Gottl. Heineccii Recitationes in elementa juris civilis. Vratislaviæ, 1765.

Colonial Legislation. 725. The examination of Mr. Maseres, late Attorney-General of Quebec, and now Baron of the Exchequer, and of Mr. Hey, the present Chief Justice of Quebec, at the Bar of Parliament, on the 3d of June, 1774.

Commercial and Maritime Law. 1340. Lex Mercatoria, by Wyndham Beawes. Dublin, 1794.

804. Reports of Decisions in the Court of Admiralty of Pennsylvania, by R. Peters, jr. 2 vols. Philadelphia, 1807.

1337. Judgments in the Admiralty Court of Pennsylvania, in four suits for maritime hypothecations. Philadelphia, 1789.

1742. Advice concerning bills of exchange, by John Marius. Philadelphia, 1790.

1311. The law of bills of exchange and promissory notes, by T. Cunningham. London, 1778.

290. Notice de la traduction du consulat de la mer de Boucher, par Lanjuinais. Paris, 1808.

Connecticut Claims. 273, 603. Charge of Judge Paterson to the Jury in the case of Van Horne's Lessee against Dorrance, tried at the Circuit Court for the United States, Philadelphia, 1795. Philad. 1796—1801.

273, 623. Report of the case of the Commonwealth vs. T. Coxe, on a motion for a Mandamus in the Supreme Court of Pennsylvania. Philadelphia, 1803.

273. Opinion of the Supreme Court of the United States in the case of the Lessee of H. J. Huidekoper vs. J. Douglas. Philadelphia, 1805.

Contested Elections. 721. Proceedings in the House of Representatives of the United States of America, respecting the contested election for the Eastern District of the state of Georgia. Philadelphia, 1792.

Escheats. 684. A Collection of the several Acts of Assembly relating to the Literary Fund, and to the appointment and duties of Escheators. Richmond, 1816.

Essays and occasional writings. 716. Letter to Dr. Blackstone; to which is prefixed Dr. Blackstone's Letter to Sir William Meredith. London, 1770.

384, 21. Q. Sketch of American Law, written for the American edition of the Edinburgh Encyclopedia, by Peter S. Duponceau.

642, 736. Reflections upon the Administration of Justice in Pennsylvania, by a Citizen, *(Richard Rush.)* Philadelphia, 1809.

323. Samson against the Philistines, or the Reformation of Lawsuits.

642. Considerations on the Abolition of the Common Law in the United States. Philadelphia, 1809.

Evidence. 298. The Catholic Question in America, whether a Roman Catholic clergyman be in any case compellable to disclose the secrets of auricular confession, decided at the Court of General Sessions in New York. New York, 1813.

664. Instructions of A. J. Dallas, Secretary of the Treasury, for levying the Direct Tax on land, furniture, &c. 1815.

1285. Thoughts on the Laws relative to Salt, by Samuel Parkes. London, 1817.

Interest on Money. 1517. Vindication of the Laws, limiting the rate of interest on loans, by Gilmer. Richmond, 1820.

Jurisdiction. 611. Case decided in the Supreme Court of the United States in February, 1793, on the question, "whether a state be liable to be sued by a private citizen of another state." Philadelphia, 1793.

602. Report of the case of the Commonwealth of Pennsylvania versus J. Smith, Marshal of the United States for the District of Pennsylvania. Philadelphia, 1809.

602. The whole proceedings in the case of Olmsted and others versus Rittenhouse's executrices, by Richard Peters, jun. Esq. Philadelphia, 1809.

873. Report of the case of Hunter v. Martin in the Virginia Court of Appeals on the question whether the Supreme Court of the United States can in certain cases reverse the decisions of the State Courts.

642. An argument before the Chancellor of Maryland in July, 1816, on the extent of the Chancellor's power, by H. M. Brackenridge. Baltimore, 1817.

Liberty of the Press. 364. Remarks on Zenger's Trial, taken out of the Barbadoes Gazette, for the benefit of the students of law and others in North America. Philadelphia, Keimer, 1737.

681. The same, first and second pages wanting.

628. An Essay on the Liberty of the Press, by Hortensius. Philadelphia, 1799.

294. Considerations sur la Liberté de la Presse, par J. P. Bertin. Paris, 1814.

244. Aristides on the liberty of the press, with the sen-

tence and recantation of Galileo. Extracted from Prynnes rights, &c. of English freemen, and Andrew Fletcher on Militia, published by the Constitutional Society, London, 1786, being part of vol. 2d.

Medical Jurisprudence. 1261. Leçons faisant partie du cours de Médecine légale par Orfila. Paris, 1821.

528. Tracts on Medical Jurisprudence, by divers English writers, edited by T. Cooper. Philadelphia, 1819.

Mines and Miners. 314. Q. Bruks—Idkares Städers och Borgerskaps Oemse Förmoner och Skyldigheter, i Stöd af författningar, af Jacob Albrecht Flintberg. Stockholm, 1788.

Miscellaneous Works. 939. The Works of the Hon. James Wilson, 3 vols. Philadelphia, 1804.

Parliamentary Practice. 584. A Manual of Parliamentary Practice for the use of the Senate of the United States, by Thomas Jefferson, 1st ed. Washington, 1801—2d ed. Lancaster, (Penn.) 1813.

Patent Rights. 1314. Essay on the law of patents, by Thomas Green Fessenden. Boston, 1822.

254. Treatise on the justice, policy, and utility of establishing an effectual system for assuring property in the works of genius, by Joseph Barnes. Philadelphia, 1792.

701. Exposition of part of the patent law, by a native born citizen of the United States, to which is added, reflections on the patent law. 1816.

701. Mode of taking out patents in the United States, by William Thornton. Washington, 1811.

Penal Laws. 246. An enquiry how far the punishment of death is necessary in Pennsylvania, with notes and illustrations by William Bradford. Philadelphia, 1793.

246. An account of the alteration and present state of the penal law of Pennsylvania, by Caleb Lownes. Philadelphia, 1792.

841. Cases in the general court of Virginia, respecting the penal laws. Philadelphia, 1815.

662. Report of the committee of the Society for the improvement of Prison Discipline and for the reformation of juvenile offenders. London, 1818.

642. The penitentiary plan, compared with the system of transportation to New South Wales, addressed to the English judges, by Jeremy Bentham. London, 1802.

Poor Laws. 1309. History of the poor, and their rights, duties, and laws respecting them, by Thomas Ruggles. London, 1793.

736. A Manual for the guardians of the poor of the city of Philadelphia and suburbs. Philadelphia, 1817.

Reports. 602. Reports of Cases adjudged in the Circuit Court of the United States for the third circuit, by John B. Wallace. Philadelphia, 1801.

606. Cases decided in the District and Circuit Court of the United States for the Pennsylvania district, and also a case decided in the District Court of Massachusetts, relative to the employment of British licences on board of the vessels of the United States. Philadelphia, 1813.

1296. Reports of Cases argued and determined in the Court of Chancery of the state of South Carolina, from the Revolution to December, 1813, inclusive, by Henry William De Saussure, 3 vols. Columbia, (S. C.) 1817

327. Proceedings in an action for debt, between C. J. Fox and J. Horne Tooke. London, 1792.

State rights. 651. History of the Steam-boat case discussed before the Legislature of New Jersey. Trenton, 1815.

" The rights of a State to grant exclusive privileges in Roads, Bridges, Canals, &c. vindicated. New York, 1811.

" Examination of the Chancellor's opinion in the case of Robert R. Livingston and Robert Fulton vs. James Van Ingen, Lansing, and others. Albany, 1812.

Study of the Law. 336. A Key to the Law, or an introduction to Legal Knowledge, by R. Hemsworth. London, 1765. *(An attempt to reduce the Common law into Aphorisms.)*

336. Reflections on the natural and acquired endowments requisite for the study of law, by Joseph Simpson. London, 1764.

721. An introductory lecture to a course of law lectures, by James Wilson. Philadelphia, 1791.

642. Extract from a letter to a student at law, recommending a course of studies, by Thomas Cooper. Carlisle, 1815.

1299. The study and practice of the law considered in their various relations to society. Portland, 1806.

Trial by Jury. 407. Observations on the Trial by Jury, by an American. *(William Barton.)* Strasburg, (Penn.) 1803.

339. Mémoire qui a remporté le prix l'an 10, sur cette question proposée par l'institut National "Quels sont les moyens de perfectionner en France l'institution du Jury," par M. Bourguignon. Paris, an 10.

XII. BIOGRAPHY.

1. General. 2. Particular.

1. GENERAL.

953. *Allen, (William)* An American Biographical, and Historical Dictionary. Cambridge, 1809.

1877. *Anon.* Nouveau Dictionaire Historique, ou Histoire abrégée de tous les Hommes qui se sont fait un nom par des talents, des vertus, des forfaits, des erreurs, &c. Avec des Tables Chronologiques pour réduire en Corps d'Histoire les Articles repandus dans ce Dictionaire. Par une Société de gens de Lettres, 8 vol. Caen, 1786.

109. F. *Bayle.* See title XIII. History and Chronology.

818. *Belknap, (Jeremy)* American Biography, 2 vols. Boston, 1794.

481. Q. *Beza, (Theodorus)* Icones, id est veræ imagines virorum Illustrium. Geneva, 1580.

288. Q. *Delaplaine.* Repository of the lives and portraits of distinguished Americans, 3 vols.

294. *Hormayr, (Joseph, Freiherr Von)* Biographische Züge ans den Leben Deutscher Männer vol. 1. Leipzig, 1815.

989. *Lempriere, (J.)* Universal Biography, 2 vols. New York, 1810.

542. Q. *Lozano, (Pedro)* Diccionario Historico Indico, por el P. Pedro Lozano, de la Comp. de Jesus, MS. This appears to be only part of a larger work, compiled on the plan of Moreri's Dictionary, and in a great measure biographical. It begins with letter G. and ends with letter L. It contains 408 pp.

Moreri, See title XIII. History and Chronology.

1447. *Pauli Jovii* Illustrium Virorum Vitæ. Basiliæ, 1559.

1515, 31. *Priestley, (Joseph)* Description of a Chart of Biography. London, 1778.

1515, 32. ——— ——— A description of a System of Biography. Philadelphia, 1803.

R. 1. ——— ——— A Chart of Biography in one sheet, 2 copies. *(No date.)*

946. *Sanderson, (John)* Biography of the Signers to the Declaration of Independence, 3 vols. *(To be continued.)* Philadelphia, 1820–3.

133. F. *Sedenius, (Juan)* Alphabeta de Varones illustres. Medina del Campo, 1551.

2. PARTICULAR.

[*In order of Subjects.*]

261. *Adams, (Samuel)* Funeral Discourse on his death, by Thomas Thatcher. Dedham, (Mass.) 1804.

658. *Barton, (Benjamin S.)* A Biographical sketch of his life, by W. P. C. Barton, M. D. read before the Philadelphia Medical Society. Philadelphia, 1816.

658. A Review of the same, and abstract in German, by J. A. Albers, M. D. 1817.

928. *Benezet, (Anthony)* His Life, by Roberts Vaux. Philadelphia, 1817.

34. Q. *Bodoni, (Giambattista)* Vita del Cavaliere. Parma, 1816.

384, 2. Q. *Bowdoin, (James)* Eulogy on, by John Lowell. Boston, 1791.

559. *Brainerd, (David)* His Life, by J. Styles. Boston, 1812.

283. *Brissot, (J. P. de Warville)* His Life, written by himself. Translated from the French. London, 1794.

920. *Brown, (Charles Brockden)* His Life, by Wm. Dunlap, 2 vols. Philadelphia, 1815.

1548½. *Camoens, (Luis de)* Memoires of his Life and Writings, by John Adamson, 2 vols. London, 1820.

1491. *Castro, (Dom Joaõ de)* Vida de, por Jacinto Freyre de Andrada, Nova Ediçaõ, acrescentada da vida do Autor. Paris, 1769.

1428. *Cervantes, (Miguel)* Su Vida, por Don Juan Antonio Pellicer. Madrid, 1800.

1497. *Charles VI. (Emperor of Germany)* Vida del Emperador Carlos VI. *(Anon.)* Madrid, 1742.

117, 2. F. *Columbus, (Christopher)* His Life, and the History of his Discovery of the West Indies, by his son, D. Ferd. Columbus, translated from the Italian. London, 1704.

643. ——— ——— Sermon funebre en Elogio del Señor Christobal Colon, por el Dr. J. A. Caballero. Philadelphia, 1803.

——— ——— Notice par M. Lanjuinais d'un ouvrage intitulé : Dissertazioni Epistolari bibliografiche sopra Cristoforo Colombo, da Francesco Cancellieri. Paris, 1811.

658. *Dallas, (Alexander James)* The Life of. Philad, 1817.

923½. *Decatur, (Stephen)* The Life of, by S. Putnam Waldo. Middletown, (Conn.) 1822.

447. Q. *Duarte, (Don, Infante de Portugal)* Vida de, por A. D. Rezende. 1789.

923. *Eaton, (General William)* The Life of. Brookfield (Mass.) 1813.

953½. *Eliot, (John)* A Biographical Dictionary, containing a brief account of the first settlers and other ancient characters of New England. Salem, 1809.

496. *Euler.* Lobrede auf, in der Versammlung der Kayserl. Akad. der Wissensch. zu St. Petersburg vorgelisen, von Nicolaus Fuss. Basil, 1786.

297. *Fayette, (la)* Statement of his own conduct and principles, from the French. London, 1793.

1396. *Ferdinand the Catholic*, (King of Spain) La politique de Don Ferdinaud le Catholique, traduit de l'Espagnol de Balthazar Gracien, avec des notes. Rotterd. 1732.

906. FRANKLIN, (BENJAMIN) Memoirs of the Life and Writings of, written by himself, and continued to the time of his death, by his grandson, William Temple Franklin, together with the whole of his political, philosophical, and miscellaneous works, 6 vols. Philadelphia. 1818.

248. ——— ——— Eulogium on, by the Rev. Dr. William Smith. Philadelphia, 1792.

275. ——— ——— Eloge civique de, prononcé an nom de la commune de Paris, par M. l'Abbé Fauchet. Paris, 1790.

922. *Fulton, (Robert)* Life of, by Cadwalader Colden. New York, 1817.

633. *Gerrald, (Joseph)* Biographical Anecdotes of. London, 1795.

282. Q' *Green, (Nathan)* Sketches of the life and correspondence of, by William Johnson, 2 vols. Charleston, 1822.

912. ——— ——— Memoirs of, by Charles Caldwell. Philadelphia, 1819.

658. *Hamilton, (Alexander)* A sketch of the character of, by Fisher Ames. Boston, 1804.

915. ——— ——— Collection of facts and documents, relative to the death of, by ——— Coleman. New York, 1804.

924. *Heath*, (Major General) Memoirs of his life, written by himself. Boston, 1798.

913. *Henry, (Patrick)* Sketches of the life of. by William Wirt. Philadelphia, 1817.

1007. *Herberstein, (Siegmund Freyherr von)* Mit besonder Rücksicht auf seine Reisen in Russland geschildert, von Friedrich Adelung. St. Petersb. 1818.

384, 10. Q. *Hobbes.* Vita Hobbesii. Lond. 1679.

1392. *Howard, (John)* Philanthropic labours of, by John Aikin. Philadelphia, 1794.

579. *Jackson*, (*General Andrew)* Memoirs of, by S. Putnam Waldo. Hartford, (Conn.) 1818.

962. *James I.* (King of Great Britain) Account of the life and writings of, after the manner of M. Bayle, by William Harris. London, 1753.

270. *Jefferson, (Thomas)* Address to the people of the United States, with an epitome and vindication of the public life and character of. Philadelphia, 1800.

274. *Jenner, (Doctor)* Notice biographique sur le Docteur Jenner, par Louis Valentin. Montpellier, 1805.

1744. *Johnson, (Samuel*, President of King's College, New York,) Life of, by Thomas Bradbury Chandler. New York, 1805.

994. *Jones, (Sir William)* Memoirs of the life, writings, and correspondence of, by lord Teignmouth. Philad. 1805.

1002. *Kouli Khan, (Thamas)* History of Nadir Shaw, formerly called Thamas Kouli Khan, by James Fraser. London, 1742.

658. *Kuhn, (Adam*, of Philadelphia, M. D.) Notice of, by one of his pupils. Philadelphia, 1818.

384, 9. Q. *Las Casas, (Barthol. de)* Apologie de, par M. Grégoire. Paris, an 8.

618. *Law, (Jonathan*, Governor of Connecticut,) Funeral Oration on, by Ezra Stiles. 1750.

384, 13. Q. *La Grange*. Précis Historique sur, par Virey. Paris, 1813.

308. *Laud, (Archbishop)* Some remarkable passages relating to, particularly of his affection for the church of Rome. London, 1812.

927. *Lay, (Benjamin*, and *Ralph Sandiford)* Lives of, by Roberts Vaux. Philadelphia, 1815.

574. *Lee, (General Charles)* Memoirs of. New York, 1792.

919. Same work. Dublin, 1792.

987. *Leo X*. The Life of, by William Roscoe, 4 vols. Philadelphia, 1805.

988. *Medici, (Lorenzo de')* The Life of, by William Roscoe, 3 vols. Philadelphia, 1803.

497. *Monge, (Gaspard)* Essai Historique sur les services & les travaux scientifiques de. Paris, 1819.

384, 21. Q. *Morris, (Robert*, first Minister of Finance of the United States,) The Life of, by James Mease. Philadelphia, 1821.

294. *Napoleon*. Oraison funèbre sur la tombe de, prononcé à Ste. Helène le 9 Mai, 1821, par le Maréchal Bertrand.

975. *Orrery, (Roger Boyle, Lord)* Memoirs of his life, at the beginning of the first vol. of the collection of his state-letters, by Thomas Morrice. London, 1743.

347. *Paine, (Thomas)* Life of, by Francis Oldys. Boston, 1796.

983. ——— ——— Life of, by James Cheetham. New York, 1809.

705. *Parsons, (Theophilus*, Chief Justice of Massachusetts,) A Sketch of the character of, by Isaac Parker. Boston, 1813.

926. Penn, (William) Life of, by Clarkson, 2 vols. Philadelphia, 1814.

925. ——— ——— Vie de, par Marsillac, 2 vol. Paris, 1791.

384, 23. Q. ——— ——— A Letter to, with his answer, in which he refutes the charge of his being a papist. London, 1688.

697. *Perry, (Commodore Oliver H.)* Documents in relation to the differences which subsisted between him and Capt. J. D. Elliot. Washington, 1821.

705. *Pinckney, (William)* A Sermon on his death, by Jared Sparks. Baltimore, 1822.

248. *Price, (Dr. Richard)* Discourse on the occasion of his death, by Joseph Priestley. London, 1791.

248. ——— ——— Address on his interment, April 26, 1791, by A. Kippis. London, 1791.

1515, 45. *Priestley, (Joseph)* The Life of, by John Corry. Birmingham, (England) 1804.

1515, 45. *Priestley, (Joseph)* Sermons on his death, at Northumberland, (Penn.) 1804, by W. Christie—at London, 1808, by Thomas Lindley—at Leeds, (Eng.) 1804, by W. Wood —at Hackney, (Eng.) 1804, by Thomas Belsham.

1515, 44. ——— ——— Letters to the inhabitants of Northumberland. Philadelphia, 1801.

—— " 722. ——— ——— Observations on his emigration to America. Philadelphia, 1814.

659. ——— ——— Remarks on the above. New York, 1795.

1515, 46. ——— ——— Letters in answer to his letters to the inhabitants of Northumberland. Newhaven, (Conn.) 1800.

1515, 51. ——— ——— His memoirs to the year 1795, with a continuation to the time of his decease, by his son J. Priestley; with observations on his writings by Thomas Cooper and W. Christie, 2 vols. Northumberland, (Penn.) 1806.

1514. ——— ——— Vindiciæ Priestléianæ, by Theophilus Lindsey. London, 1788.

1503. *Purgstall, (Grafen von)* Denkmal auf das Grab der beyden letzten Grafen von Purgstall, Gesetzt von ihrem freunde, Joseph von Hammer. Wien, 1821.

907. *Rittenhouse, (David)* Memoirs of, by William Barton. Philadelphia, 1813.

284. ——— ——— Eulogium on, by Dr. Benjamin Rush. Philadelphia, 1796.

307. *Rousseau, (Jean Jacques)* Relation des derniers jours de, & circonstances de sa mort, par le Bégue de Presle. London, 1778.

537. *Rush, (Dr. Benjamin)* An Eulogium in memory of, by W. Staughton. Philadelphia, 1813.

—— ——— ——— An Eulogium upon, by David Ramsay. Philadelphia, 1813.

—— ——— ——— Recollections of, by Dr. Lettsom. London, 1814.

512, 658. *Shippen, (Dr. William)* Eulogium on, by Dr. Caspar Wistar. Philadelphia, 1818.

921. *Stiles, (Rev. Ezra)* Life of, by Abiel Holmes, Boston, 1798.

666. *Toussaint Louverture,* (General in Chief of St. Domingo,) The life of, translated from the French, by Herbemont. Charleston, 1802.

1550, 1. *Turgot.* Mémoires de. Paris, 1810.

18. *Valli, (Eusebio)* Elogio del Dr. Eusebio Valli, leido en Junta de la Soc. Econ. de la Habana, el 22 de Nov. 1816, por el Dr. D. Tomas Romay. Habana, 1816.

254. Q. *Viretus.* Commentarium inservitururm Historiæ Pisani Vireti Bolandici Academici, Auctore Joh. Calvio. Pisis, 1787.

658. *Warren, (General John)* An Eulogy on the character of, by James Jackson. Boston, 1815.

908. WASHINGTON, (GEORGE) Life of, by John Marshall, 5 vols. And atlas. Philadelphia, 1804.

909. WASHINGTON, (GEORGE) Life of, by David Ramsay. New York, 1807.

908½. ——— ——— Life of, by Aaron Bancroft. Worcester, (Mass.) 1807.

245. ——— ——— Character of, by Charles Caldwell. Philadelphia, 1801.

741. ——— ——— The Will of, to which is annexed a schedule of his property directed to be sold. Alexandria, 1800.

910. ——— ——— His monuments of patriotism, containing a variety of official documents respecting him. *(No imprint, no date.)*

624. ——— ——— Fac simile of his handwriting, and sketches of his private character, by Richard Peters. *(No imprint, no date.)*

658. ——— ——— Funeral Oration on, delivered at New York, Feb. 20, 1800, by John M. Mason. New York, 1800.

" ——— ——— Oration on the sublime virtues of, delivered before the legislature of Massachusetts, Feb. 8, 1800, by Fisher Ames. New York, 1800.

705. ——— ——— Oration on the death of, delivered at Charleston, Jan. 15, 1800, by David Ramsay. Charleston, 1800.

" ——— ——— Eulogy on the death of, delivered at Newburyport, Jan. 2, 1800, by Thomas Paine. Newburyport, (Mass.) 1800.

715. ——— ——— Oration on the resignation of, including a short view of his life, character, and conduct, delivered in London, on the 29th of Nov. 1796, by John Gale Jones. London.

245. ——— ——— Oraison funèbre du frère George Washington, prononcée le 1er Janv. 1800, dans la loge Française l'Aménité, par Simon Chaudron. Philadelphia, 1801

966. *Watson, (R. Bishop of Llandaff)* Anecdotes of the Life of. Philadelphia, 1818.

569. *Whalley, Goffe, and Dixwell,* (Judges of King Charles I. of England) History of, by the Rev. Ezra Stiles. Hartford, (Conn.) 1794.

658, 705. *Williamson, (Hugh)* Biographical memoirs of, by David Hosack. New York, 1820—1821.

365. Q. *Wistar, (Dr. Caspar)* Eulogium in Commemoration of, delivered before the American Philosophical Society, 11th March, 1818, by William Tilghman. Philadelphia, 1818.

930½. ——— ——— Note nécrologique sur le Dr. Wistar, de Philadelphie, par M. Correa de Serra, MS. 1818.

930½. ——— ——— A tribute to the memory of the late Caspar Wistar, by his friend David Hosack. New York, 1818.

930½. ——— ——— An Eulogium on Caspar Wistar, delivered

before the members of the Philadelphia Medical Society, by Charles Caldwell. Philadelphia, 1818.

400. Q. *Yu, (the Great, Emperor of China)* Yu le Grand et Confucius, Histoire Chinoise, par M. Clerc. Soissons, 1769.

XIII. HISTORY AND CHRONOLOGY.

1. General. 2. Local and particular.

1. GENERAL.

109. F. *Bayle, (Pierre)* Dictionnaire Historique, seconde edition, 3 vol. Amsterd. 1702.

——— ——— Dictionnaire Historique, avec la vie de l'auteur, par Des Maizeaux, 4 vol. 5e Ed. La Haye, 1740.

——— ——— Supplément au même, par Chauffepié, 4 vol. Amsterd. La Haye, & Leyde, 1750—1756.

——— ——— Œuvres diverses, 4 vol. seconde edition. La Haye, 1727—1731.

425. Q. *Bergeron, (Pierre)* Abrégé de l'Histoire des Sarasins & Mahométans. Leide, 1729.

Chauffepié see *Bayle.*

43. F. *Blair, (John)* Chronology and History of the World. London, 1788.

1505. *Bucholarus, (Abraham)* Index Chronologicus, à mundo condito, usque ad annum nati Christi MDLXXX. Francof. 1612.

1534. *Du Pont de Nemours.* Mémoire soumis à la 3e Classe de l'Institut sur plusieurs Ouvrages Historiques & particulierèment sur celui de M. de Rulhière, intitulé "L'Anarchie de Pologne." Paris, 1810.

Franklin, see above, page 28, title NATURAL PHILOSOPHY, § 8. Miscellaneous.

1034. *Herodotus.* Translated from the Greek by Wm. Beloe, 4 vols. Philadelphia, 1814.

669. *Holwell, (J. Z.)* Interesting Historical Events relative to the provinces of Bengal, and the empire of Hindostan, part 2. London, 1767.

149. F. *Isaacson, (Henry)* Chronological series of the Four Monarchies. London, 1633.

344. *Miller, (Samuel)* A Retrospect of the 18th Century, 2 vols. New York, 1803.

91, 92, 93. *F. Moreri.* Le grand Dictionaire Historique, 10 vol. dont 4 de Suppléments. Paris, 1732—1749.

204. *Q. Newton, (Isaac)* The Chronology of the Ancient Kingdoms amended. London, 1728.

384, 17. *Q. Potocki, (Le Comte Jean)* Principes de Chronologie, pour les temps antérieurs aux Olympiades. St. Petersburgh, 1810.

1515, 33. *Priestley, (Joseph)* Description of a New Chart of History. London, 1781.

1515, 47. ——— ——— Lectures on History and General Policy, 2 vols. Philadelphia, 1803.

R. 2. ——— ——— A Chart of History, in one sheet, 2 copies. *(No date.)*

120. *F. Ralegh, (Walter)* History of the World. London, 1677.

121. *F. Ross, (Alex.)* History of the World, being a continuation of Raleigh's History. London, 1652.

1415. *Shallus, (Francis)* Chronological Tables for every day in the year; compiled from the most authentic documents, 2 vols. Philadelphia, 1817.

1550, 2. *Turgot.* Sur l'Histoire Universelle & les progrès de l'esprit humain. Paris, 1808.

131. *Volney, (C. F.)* Lectures on History, translated from the French. Philadelphia, 1801.

1515, 15. *Watts.* Historical Catechisms, with alterations, originally edited by Joseph Priestley. London, 1801.

ANONYMOUS WORKS.

1390. Histoire des prémiers âges du monde. Paris, 1778.

84. *F.* L'art de vérifier les dates des faits historiques, &c. par un Religieux Benédictin de la Congrégation de St. Maur, vol. 1. Paris, 1783.

112. Mnemonika, or Chronological Tablets, exhibiting in a methodical manner the most remarkable occurrences from the creation of the world to the present period. Baltimore, 1812.

2. LOCAL AND PARTICULAR HISTORY.

Africa. 347. *Anon.* A short Account of Algiers and its several wars against Spain, France, &c. with a concise view of the origin of the rupture between Algiers and the United States, &c. Philad. 1794.

1387. *Benezet, (Anthony)* Some Historical account of Guinea. Philadelphia, 1771.

America. 1. *Bartollozzi, (Francesco)* Ricerche istorico-critiche circa alle scoperte d'Amerigo Vespucci. Tirenze, 1789.

886. *Holmes, (Abiel)* American Annals, 2 vols. Cambridge, (Mass.) 1805.

68. Q. *Muñoz, (Juan)* Historia del Nuevo Mundo. tomo I. Madrid, 1793.

2. *Robertson, (William)* History of America, 4 vols. London, 1803.

3. ——— ——— Same work, Books IX. and X. Philadelphia, 1799.

553. *Snowden, (Richard)* History of North and South America. Philadelphia, 1809.

854. *Trumbull, (Henry)* History of the Discovery of America, of the landing of our forefathers at Plymouth, and of their remarkable engagements with the Indians in New England. Norwich, (Conn.) 1812.

Asia. 27. Q. *Hottinger, (J. H.)* Historia Orientalis, ex variis orientalium monumentis collecta. Zurich, 1651.

(This book contains an account of the rise and progress of Mahometism and other religions of the East.)

Barbadoes. 139. F. *Ligon, (Richard)* History of the Island of Barbadoes. London, 1673.

British Colonies. 889. *Anon.* The contest in America between Great Britain and France, by an impartial hand. London, 1757.

82. *Anon.* British Empire in America, containing the history of the discovery, settlement, progress, and state of the British Colonies in North America, 2 vols. London, 1741.

52. —— Memoirs relating to the history of the Islands of Cape Breton and St. Johns. London, 1760.

83. *Douglass, (William)* Summary, historical and political, of the British settlements in North America, 2 vols. Boston, 1749.

11. *Edwards, (Bryan)* History of the British Colonies in the West Indies, 4 vols. with an Atlas. Philadelphia, 1806.

61. *Rogers, (Major)* Journal during the war of 1756. London, 1765.

900. *Sanford (Ezekiel)* History of the United States before the Revolution, with some Account of the Aborigines. Philadelphia, 1819.

88. *Stokes, (Anthony)* View of the Constitutions of the British Colonies in North America and the West Indies. London, 1783.

811. *Whipple, (Joseph)* History of Acadie, Penobscott Bay and River, with a Geographical and Statistical view of the District of Maine. Bangor, 1816.

85. *Wynne.* General History of the British Empire in America, 2 vols. London, 1770.

Byzantine History. 52. *F. Leo Diaconus.* Leonis Diaconi historia scriptoresque alii ad res Byzantinas pertinentes. Paris, 1819.

Caribbee Islands. 57. *F. Davies, (John)* The History of the Caribbee Islands, with a Caribbean vocabulary. London, 1666.

Europe. 1394. *Anon.* Histoire politique du siècle, depuis la paix de Westphalie jusqu' à celle d'Aix-la-Chapelle, inclusivement, par de B. M. 2 vol. London, 1754.

1022. *Arnould.* Système maritime & politique des Européens pendant le 18e siècle. Paris, 1797.

341. *Belsham, (Wm.)* Two historical dissertations on the Silesian war, concluded by the treaty of Breslaw in 1742. London, 1800.

1089. *Russell, (William)* History of Ancient Europe, 2 vols. Philadelphia, 1801.

1090. ——— ——— History of Modern Europe, with a continuation to 1802, 6 vols. Philadelphia, 1800—1811.

105. *Malo de Lugue, (Eduardo)* Historia politica de los establecimientos ultramarinos de la Naciones Europeas, tomos I. y IV. *(Desunt* tom. II. and III. Madrid, 1784.

France. 320. *Cobbin, (J.)* Statements of the persecution of the Protestants in the South of France, since the restoration of the Bourbon Family. London, 1815.

1026½. *Gourgaud, (General)* The campaign of 1815, in France and Belgium, translated from the French. London, 1818.

To which is added, Observations sur la relation de la campagne de 1815, publiée par le Général Gourgaud, par le Maréchal de Grouchy. Philadelphie, 1818.

317. *Grouchy, (le Maréchal de)* Observations sur la relation de la campagne de 1815, publiée par le General Gourgaud. Philadelphie, 1818.

317. ——— ——— Doutes sur l'authenticité des mémoires historiques attribués à Napoléon. Philadelphie, 1820.

1025. *Hue, (François)* Dernières années du règne & de la Vie de Louis XVI. Paris, 1814.

1060. *La Baume, (Eugène)* Relation circonstanciée de la campagne de Russie. Paris, 1814.

1040. *Laskay, (J. C.)* Description of the medals struck by order of Bonaparte, commemorating the principal events of his reign. London, 1818.

1381. ***Mezeray.*** Histoire de France avant Clovis. Amsterdam, 1692.

1026. ***Napoleon.*** Mémoires Historiques de Napoléon, Livre IX. Philadelphie, 1820.

341. ***Petit,*** *(Joseph)* Marengo, or the campaign of Italy, by the army of reserve under command of the Chief Consul, Bonaparte. To which is added, a biographical notice of Gen. Desaix, by C. Foudras, both translated from the French. Philadelphia, 1801.

1027. ***Sainneville,*** *(Charrier)* Compte rendu des Evénements qui se sont passés a Lyon en 1816–17. Paris, 1818.

1024. ***Soulavie,*** *(Jean Louis)* Mémoires Historiques & Politiques du Règne de Louis XVI. 6 vols. Paris, 1801.

1021. ***Stephens,*** *(Alexander)* Wars of the French Revolution, 2 vols. Philadelphia, 1804.

1380. ***Velly, Villaret,*** and ***Garnier.*** Histoire de France, 30 vols. Paris, 1775.

Germany. 1053. ***Anon.*** Neue Chronik von Hamburg bis zum Jahre 1819. Hamburg, 1820.

320. —— A Particular Account of the transactions which took place in the City of Hamburg, during the first six months of 1813. Philadelphia, 1814.

1504. ***Frederick II.*** (King of Prussia.) Oeuvres Posthumes de Frederic II. 15 vols. Berlin, 1789.

1441. ***Gunther.*** Guntheri Poetæ Ligurini, de rebus gestis Imp. Cæs. Frederici primi, P. P. Aug. Cognomento Œnobarbi, sive Barbarossæ, Libri X. Tubingæ, 1508.

G. Britain. 89½. ***Andrews,*** *(John)* History of the War with America, France, Spain, and Holland, commencing in 1775, and ending in 1783, 4 vols. London, 1785.

280. Q. ***Aikin,*** *(John)* History of Manchester. London, 1795.

964. ***Anon.*** Relations and Observations, Historical and Political, upon the Long Parliament of England and the history and proceedings of the Independent party. London, 1648.

964. —— Anarchia Anglicana, or the History of Independency, (being a continuation of the above work, and bound with it.) London, 1649.

1388. —— Wars of England, Ireland, and Scotland, during the Reign of Charles I. London, 1706.

277. —— Sketch of the reign of George III. from 1780 to the close of the year 1790. London, 1791.

961. —— History of the English Sedition Acts. London, 1791.

G. Britain. 118, 1592. *F. Bedæ, (Venerabilis)* Historia gentis Anglorum. Lovæni, 1566.

1379½. *Evans, (Theophilus) Drych y prif Oesoedd yn Ddwy Ran.* The mirror of the first ages, in two parts; the first treats of the genealogy, and history, and manners of the Welch, before their conversion to Christianity; the second contains the history of the introduction of the gospel into Britain. Mwythig, 1716.

464. *Q. Gaitland, (Michael)* History of the Lives and reigns of the kings of Scotland. Dublin, 1722.

976. *Higgons, (Bevill)* Short View of English history. London, 1748.

6. *Q. Incerti Auctoris.* Emmæ, Anglorum Reginæ, Richardi I. ducis Normannorum filiæ, encomium, incerto Auctore, sed coætaneo. Item Gesta Gulielmi II. Ducis Normannorum, Regis Anglorum I. à Gulielmo Pictavensi contemporaneo scripta. London, 1783.

971. *Plowden, (Francis)* Historical Review of the state of Ireland, 5 vols. Philadelphia, 1805.

971½. ——— ——— The History of Ireland from its union with Great Britain in Jan. 1801, to Oct. 1810, 3 vols. Dublin, 1811.

339. *Vincent, (William)* Narrative of the late riots and disturbances in the cities of London and Westminster. London, 1780.

1605. *Virgilii, (Polydori)* Historiæ Anglicæ libri XXVI. Lugd. Bat. 1651.

William of Poictiers, see *Incerti Auctoris.*

Japan. 1386. *Charlevoix.* Histoire du Japon, 6 vol. Paris, 1754.

India. 341. *Hossein Khan, (Seid Gholam)* Extracts from a History of India, by Seid Gholam Hossein Khan. Translated from the original Persian. Calcutta, 1789.

Italy. 183. *Muratori.* Annali d'Italia dal principio dell'Era Volgare fino all'anno 1750, 20 vol. Roma, 1752.

94. *F. Vertot.* History of the knights of St. John of Jerusalem. *(Title page wanting.)*

Mexico. 91. *Q. Castillo, (Bernal Diaz del)* History of the Conquest of Mexico, translated from the Spanish, by Maurice Keating. London, 1800.

90. *Q. Clavigero.* History of Mexico, translated by C. Cullen, 2 vols. London, 1787.

19. *Robinson, (W. D)* Memoirs of the Mexican Revolution. Philadelphia, 1820.

58. *Q. Solis, (Antonio de)* Historia de la conquista de Mexico, 2 vol. Madrid, 1783.

Netherlands. 1052. *De Witt, (John)* The true interest and political maxims of the republic of Holland and West Friesland. London, 1702.

Paraguay. 163. *Anon.* Memoria Historica, politica y economica de esta provincia de Misiones e Yndios Guaranis, MS.

21. *Charlevoix.* History of Paraguay, 2 vols. London, 1769.

22. *Funes, (Gregorio)* Ensayo de la Historia civil del Paraguay, Buenos Ayres y Tucuman. Buenos Ayres, 1816.

Peru. 731. *Anon.* Peruvian Pamphlet, being an exposition of the administrative labours of the Peruvian government, from the time of its formation till the 15th of July, 1822. Translated from the Spanish. London, 1823.

98. *Garcilaso de la Vega.* Histoire des Incas du Perou, Traduite de l'Esp. 2 vol. Amsterd. 1715.

Philippine Islands. 63. *F. Murillo, (Pedro Velar de)* Historia de la provincia de Philipinas, segunda parte. Manilla, 1749.

62. *F. Salazar, (Vincinte de)* Historia de la provincia de el Santisimo Rosario de Philipinas. Manilla, 1742.

Poland. 981. *Komarzewski, (M. de)* Coup d'œil rapide sur les causes réelles de la décadence de la Pologne. Paris, 1807.

Portugal. 115. *Amaral, (Antonio Caetano de)* Observações sobre as principaes causas da decadencia dos Portuguezas na Asia. Lisboa, 1790.

1395. *Anonymous.* Historia de Portugal, 3 vol. Lisboa, 1788.

116. ——— Collecção dos principaes auctores da Historia Portugueza, com notas, 4 vol. Lisboa, 1806.

99. *Castañeda, (Herman Lopes de)* Historia del descubrimiento y conquista de la India por los Portugueses, traducida al Castellano. Amberes, 1554.

161. *F. Correa da Serra, (Joze)* Collecção de livros ineditos de Historia Portugueza, 3 vol. Lisboa, 1790.

115. *Conto, (D. de)* Obs. sobre as causas da decadencia dos Portuguezes en Asia. 1790.

448. *Q. Madre de Deos, (Fr. Gaspar da)* Mem. para a Historia da Capitania de St. Vincente, hoje S. Paulo. Brazil, 1797.

Rome. 1879. *Livii, (Titi)* Qui extant Historiarum Libri, 2 vol. Cantab. 1679.

Russia. 380. *Q. Le Clerc.* Histoire physique, morale, civile, & politique de la Russie ancienne, 3 vol. Paris, 1783–4.

381 *Q.* ——— Histoire physique, morale, civile, & politique de la Russie moderne, 3 vol. Paris, 1783—1793.

193. *Q. Manstein, (General)* Memoirs of Russia, historical, political, and military. London, 1770.

Russia. 23. Q. *Potocki, (Jean Comte de)* Histoire ancienne des gouvernements de Cherson & Podolie. St. Petersburgh, 1804.

132. *Voltaire.* History of the Russian Empire under Peter the Great, English translation, 2 vols. Berwick.

South America. 117, 4. F. *Techo, (Nic. del)* The history of the provinces of Paraguay, Tucuman, Rio-de-la-Plata, Parana, Guaira, and Chili, translated from the Latin. London, 1704.

Spain. 123. F. *Beawes, (Wyndham)* Civil, political, and commercial history of Spain and Portugal. London, 1793.

1382. *Estrada, (Famiano)* Segunda Decada de las guerras de Flandes, desde el principio del Govierno de Alexandro Farnese, Duque de Parma, traducida del Latin, por Melchior de Novar. Amberes, 1701.

348. Q. *Mariana.* Historia general de España, 9 vol. Valencia, 1783.

1488. *Moncada, (Juan de)* Expedicion de los Catalanes y Aragoneses contra Turcos y Griegos. Madrid, 1777.

980. *Power, (George)* History of the empire of the Musselmans in Spain and Portugal. London, 1815.

979. *Rocca, (De)* Memoirs of the war of the French in Spain, translated from the French. Philadelphia, 1820.

157. F. *Salazar de Mendoza.* Origen de las Dignidades Seglares de Castilla y Leon. Madrid, 1657.

Strada, see *Estrada.*

Sweden. 1402. *Blix, (Magnus)* Sweriges Statshwälfningar och hushållsanstalter, ifrån 1720 til 7921. Stockholm, 1795.

1545. *Hemsö, (Jacopo Gråberg di)* Saggio Istorico su gli Scaldi. Pisa, 1811.

Switzerland. 271. *Anon.* Authentic History of the origin and progress of the Revolution in Geneva. Philadelphia, 1794.

191. Q. *Planta, (J.)* History of the Helvetic Confederacy, 2 vols. London, 1800.

992. *Watteville, (A. L. de)* Histoire de la Confédération Helvétique. Yverdun, 1768.

UNITED STATES IN GENERAL.

United States. 793. *Allen, (Paul)* History of the American Revolution, 2 vols. Baltimore, 1819.

89½. *Andrews, (John)* History of the War with America, France, and Holland, commencing in 1775 and ending in 1783. London, 1785.

United States.

703. *Anon.* Accounts of the actions between the British and American vessels of war in 1812 and 1813.

918. —— Narrative of Gen. St. Clair's Campaign against the Indians in 1791. Philadelphia, 1812.

P. 1. Sketch of the Action on the heighths of Charlestown, 17th June, 1775, between his majesty's troops under Major General Howe and a large body of American Rebels, MS. drawing.

932. *Barbé-Marbois, (Marquis de)* Complot d'Arnold & de Sir Henry Clinton. Paris, 1816.

250. *Belknap, (Jerem.)* Letter to Dr. Kippis, contradicting his assertion that Congress had given orders to capture Captain Cooke, if he should be found at sea. Boston, 1795.

37. *Bonnet, (J. E.)* Etats Unis de l'Amérique à la fin du XVIII. siècle. Paris, *(no date.)*

44. *Botta, (Carlo)* Storia della Guerra dell' Independenza degli Stati Uniti d'America, 4 vol. Milano, 1819.

45. —— —— Histoire de la Guerre de l'Indépendance des Etats Unis d'Amérique, traduit de l'Italien, par L. de Sévelinges, 4 vol. Paris, 1812–3.

46. —— —— History of the War of the Independence of the United States, translated from the Italian by A. Otis, 3 vols. Philadelphia, 1820.

890½. *Clark, (Thomas)* Natural History of the United States, from the commencement of the revolutionary war to the present time, 2 vols. Philadelphia, 1814.

96. *Ebeling, (C. D.)* Erdbeschreibung und Geschichte von Amerika, 7 vol. Hamburg, 1793—1816.

89. *Gordon, (William)* History of the rise, progress, and establishment of the Independence of the United States, 2d Ed. 3 vols. New York, 1794

563. *Henry, (John Joseph)* History of the Campaign in Canada in 1775. Lancaster, 1812.

888. *Hubly, (Bernard)* History of the American Revolution, vol. 1. Northumberland, 1805.

78. *La Tour, (A. Lacarriere)* Historical Memoir of the war in West Florida and Louisiana, translated from the French, by H. P. Nugent, with an Atlas. Philadelphia, 1816.

864. *Lee, (Henry)* Memoirs of the war in the southern department of the United States, 2 vols. Philadelphia, 1812.

908. *Marshal, (John)* The Life of Gen. Washington, with an Atlas, 6 vols. Philadelphia, 1804.

124. *F. Mather, (Cotton)* Magnalia Christi Americana. London, 1702.

United States.

892. *Palmer, (T. H.)* The Historical Register of the United States, 1812—1814, 4 vols. Philadelphia, 1814—1816.

897. *Ramsay, (David)* History of the American Revolution, 2 vols. Philadelphia, 1779.

896. ——— ——— History of the United States from the first settlement to the year 1808, continued to the treaty of Ghent, by S. S. Smith, L. L. D. and other literary gentlemen, 3 vols. Philadelphia, 1818.

734. ——— ——— A Chronological Table of the principal events which have taken place in the English colonies now United States from 1601 till 1810. Charleston, 1811.

802. *Sullivan, (Thomas)* Journal of the operations of the American army, 1775 to 1778, MS.

561. *Thomson, (John Lewis)* Historical sketches of the late war. Philadelphia, 1816.

885. *Trumbull, (Benjamin)* A General History of the United States of America from the discovery in 1492 to 1792. Boston, 1810.

903. *Warren, (Mercy)* History of the rise, progress, and termination of the American Revolution, 3 vols. Boston, 1805.

929. *Wilkinson, (General James)* Memoirs of his own times, 3 vols. and Atlas. Philadelphia, 1816.

SEPARATE STATES.

Carolinas and Georgia.

1566. *Anon.* The History of the dividing line between Virginia and North Carolina, run in the year of our Lord, 1728. Ascribed to Dr. William Byrd, of Westover, one of the Commissioners on the part of Virginia, MS.

1567. The Secret History of the line, (ascribed to the same,) MS.

669. Account of the late intended insurrection among the blacks of the city of Charleston, published by authorization of the corporation of that city. Charleston, 1822.

857. *Anon.* Historical account of the rise and progress of the colonies of South Carolina and Georgia, 2 vols. London, 1779.

13. Q. *Lawson, (John)* The History of Carolina. London, 1714.

865. *M'Call, (Hugh)* History of Georgia, 2 vols. Savannah, 1811.

860. *Moultrie, (William)* History of the American Revolution so far as regards North and South Carolina and Georgia, 2 vols. New York, 1802.

858. *Ramsay, (David)* History of South Carolina, 2 vols. Charleston, 1809.

859. *Ramsay, (David)* History of the Revolution of South Carolina, 2 vols. Trenton, 1785.

855. *Williamson, (Hugh)* History of North Carolina, 2 vols. Philadelphia, 1812.

Connecticut. 820. *Trumbull, (Benjamin)* History of Connecticut, 2 vols. Newhaven, 1819.

Louisiana. 172. *F. Bernard de la Harpe.* Journal Historique concernant l'établissement des Français à la Louisiane, tiré des Mémoires de Mrs. d'Iberville & de Bienville, Commandans pour le Roi audit pays, & sur les découvertes & recherches de Mr. Bernard de la Harpe, nommé au commandement de la Baye St. Bernard, par Mr. Bernard de la Harpe, MS.

76. *Du Pratz, (Le Page)* History of Louisiana, or the western parts of Virginia and Carolina. Translated from the French. London, 1774.

74. *Vergennes, (le Comte de)* Mémoire historique & politique sur la Louisiane. Paris, 1802.

Maine. 801. *Sullivan, (James)* History of the province of Maine. Boston, 1795.

Maryland. 835. *Anon.* Papers respecting the Baltimore riots in 1812. Philadelphia, 1812.

834. *Bozman, (John Leeds)* Sketch of the History of Maryland. Baltimore, 1811.

Massachusetts. 595. *Anon.* A short narrative of the horrid massacre in Boston, perpetrated the 5th of March, 1770, with observations, &c. Boston, 1770.

812. *Hutchinson, (Thomas)* History of Massachusetts, 2 vols. Boston, 1795.

598. *Mauduit, (Israel)* A short view of the History of the Colony of Massachusetts Bay. London, 1774.

814. *Minot, (George Richards)* History of the Insurrections in Massachusetts. Boston, 1810.

813. ——— ——— Continuation of Hutchinson's History of Massachusetts Bay, 2 vols. in one. Boston, 1798.

New England. 557. *Hubbard, (William)* A Narrative of the Indian Wars in New England, from 1607 to 1667. Brattleborough, 1814.

124. *F. Mather, (Cotton)* Antiquities of the New-English History. London, 1702.

566. *Morse, (Jedidiah) and Parish, (Elijah)* History of New England. Newburyport, 1809.

806. *Neal, (Daniel)* History of New England to the year 1702, 2 vols. London, 1720.

565. *Prince, (Thomas)* A Chronological History of New England, in the form of annals, from the discovery by captain Gosnold in 1602 to the arrival of governor Belcher, in 1730. Boston, 1736.

567. *Robbins, (Thomas)* View of the first planters of New England. Hartford, 1815.

803. *Winthrop, (John)* Journal of transactions and occurrences in New England from 1630 to 1644. Hartford, 1790.

N. Hampshire. 816. *Belknap, (Jeremy)* History of New Hampshire, 3 vols. Boston, 1791

N. Jersey. 821. *Smith, (Samuel)* History of New-Jersey. Burlington, 1765.

N. York. 824. *Smith, (William)* History of the province of New York. Philadelphia, 1792.

Pennsylvania. 497½. *Q. Acrelius. Beskrifning om de Swenska forsamlingars,* &c. Description of the present and former state of the Swedish congregations in Pennsylvania, in the Swedish language. Stockholm, 1759.

832. *Anon.* Historical Review of the Constitution and Government of Pennsylvania, ascribed to B. Franklin. London, 1759.

269. —— Narrative of the murder of the Indians in Lancaster and Lancaster county. 1763.

645, 682. —— A Narrative of the late massacres in Lancaster county of a number of Indians, friends of this province, by persons unknown. Philadelphia, 1764.

347. —— Affecting History of the dreadful distresses of several persons, and an account of the destruction of the settlements at Wyoming. Philadelphia, 1794.

638. —— A report of the extraordinary transactions which took place at Philadelphia in February 1799, in consequence of a memorial from certain natives of Ireland to Congress, praying a repeal of the Alien Bill, by William Duane. Philadelphia, 1799.

741. —— A brief sketch of the origin and present state of the city of Philadelphia. Philadelphia, 1804.

829. *Brackenridge, (Hugh H.)* Incidents of the insurrection in the western parts of Pennsylvania. Philadelphia, 1795.

926. *Clarkson, (Thomas)* Memoirs of the private and public life of William Penn, 2 vols. Philadelphia, 1814.

For other works concerning William Penn, see title XII. Biography, *under his name, and see below, title* XIV. Historical Documents, § 1, Collections.

830. *Findley, (William)* History of the Western Insurrection. Philadelphia, 1796.

571. *Graydon, (Alexander)* Memoirs of a life chiefly

passed in Pennsylvania, within the last 60 years. Harrisburg, 1811.

831. *Proud, (Robert)* History of Pennsylvania, 2 vols. Philadelphia, 1797.

384, 16. Q. *Reed, (John)* Explanation of the Map (made by order of W. Penn) of the city and Liberties of Philadelphia. 1776.

1580. *Watson, (John)* Narrative of the Indian Walk, being a purchase of lands made of the Indians in Pennsylvania in 1756, MS.

Virginia. 840. *Burke, (John)* History of Virginia, with Jones's and Girardin's continuation, 4 vols. Petersburg, 1804.

575. *Campbell, (J. W.)* History of Virginia. Philadelphia, 1813.

Girardin, see *Burke*.
Jones, see *Burke*.

17. Q. *Keith, (William)* The History of the British Plantations in America, with a Chronological account of the most remarkable things which happened to the first adventurers in their several discoveries in that New World, Part I. containing the History of Virginia. London, 1738.

638. *Smith, (John)* The generall Historie of Virginia, New England, and the Summer Iles, from 1584 to 1626. Reprinted from the London Edition of 1629, 2 vols. Richmond, (Virginia) 1819.

837. *Stith, (William)* History of Virginia. Williamsburg, 1747.

Vermont. 819. *Williams, (Samuel)* History of Vermont, 2 vols. Burlington, 1809.

XIV. HISTORICAL DOCUMENTS.

1. Collections.
2. Separate Documents.
3. Historical Registers and Newspapers.

1. COLLECTIONS.

FOREIGN.

France. 1748. Procès verbaux de l'Assemblée Nationale, 49 vol. Paris, 1789—1791.

1023. Pieces imprimées d'après le décret de la Convention Nationale, du 5 Dec. 1792, 3 vol. Paris, 1793.

1009. Procès verbaux des Séances de la Chambre des Députés des Départements—Session de 1822, (Juin, Juillet & Août.) Paris, 1822.

Great Britain. 119. *F.* Rushworth's Historical Collections from 1628 to 1640, vols. 1 & 2. London, 1680.

1691½. *Reliquiæ Sacræ Carolinæ*, or the works of king Charles I. collected together and digested in order according to their several subjects. Hague, 1657.

975. A collection of the State Letters of the Right Honourable Roger Boyle, first Earl of Orrery, Lord President of Munster, in Ireland, from the Restoration to 1668, together with some other letters and papers of a different kind, particularly the life of the Earl of Orrery, by Thomas Morrice, 2 vols. Dublin, 1743.

590. Almon's Remembrancer, an impartial repository of public events from 1775 to 1784, 17 vols. London.

588. —— Prior Documents, a collection of authentic papers relative to the dispute between Great Britain and America, from 1764 to 1775. London, 1777.

Hayti. 667. Haytian Papers. A collection of the very interesting proclamations and the official documents, together with some account of the rise, progress, and present state of the kingdom of Hayti, by Prince Sanders. Boston, 1818.

Peru. 164. *F.* MS. Collection of Documents concerning the rebellion in Peru under the Indian Chief Tupac Amaro, in 1780, collected by J. R. Poinsett.

Spain. 1482. Diario de las Discusiones y actas de las Cortes de España, vol. 2. Cadiz, 1811.

410. Discusion del proyecto de decreto sobre el Tribunal de la Inquisicion. Cadiz, 1813.

DOMESTIC.

173. *F.* Copies of Records concerning the early settlements on Delaware river. 1. English records, from 1614 to 1682. 2. Dutch records, from 1630 to 1656. Extracted from the archives of the State of Pennsylvania, by Redmond Conyngham, Esq. MSS.

173½. *F.* Copies of Swedish Records, concerning the Colony of New Sweden, (now Pennsylvania and Delaware,) obtained from the archives of the Swedish government at Stockholm, by Jonathan Russell, Esq. (Swedish and French,) MSS.

194. *Q.* Historical Collections of State Papers, by Ebenezer Hazard, 2 vols. Philadelphia, 1792.

This collection contains Documents relative to the early History of the British Colonies, now United States.

1749. Journals of Congress from September 5, 1774, to October

21, 1788. First and original edition, 13 vols. incomplete; Vols. 3, 5, 6, 10, 11, wanting.

Same work, 2d edition, complete in 13 vols. Philadelphia, Folwell, 1800, 1801.

909½. Official Letters of G. Washington to Congress, vol. 1. New York, 1796.

610. Correspondence of the late President Adams in a series of letters. Boston, 1809.

1750. State Papers and public Documents from 2d of December, 1793, to the 2d of April, 1808, 16 vols.

177. *F.* Public Accounts of the United States, 1781—1784.

180. *F.* Collection of Bills before Congress, 1807—1808.

F. Financial Documents, 1798—1802.

F. Miscellaneous Documents, 1802—1809.

181. *F.* Presidents' Messages, Reports, and other miscellaneous State papers, 1807, 1814, 11 vols.

182. *F.* ——— 1813—1817, 10 vols.

183. *F.* Census of the United States, 1810 and 1820, 2 vols.

600, 632. Same, for 1790 and 1800.

891. A Collection of State papers and public documents of the United States, from the accession of George Washington to the presidency to the present time, published by Wait and Sons, 1st ed. 8 vols. Boston, 1815—1817.

176. *F.* Communications of the Executive of the United States, 1789—1792, 2 vols.

1751. The same, 1809 to 1810, 4 vols.

1752. ——— 1810 to 1811, 2 vols.

1753. ——— 1811 to 1812, 2 vols.

1754. ——— 1812 to 1813, 4 vols. (1st vol. wanting.)

1755. ——— 1813 to 1814, 7 vols.

1756. ——— 1814 to 1815, 5 vols.

1757. ——— 1815 to 1816, 5 vols.

1758. ——— 1816 to 1817, 5 vols.

1759. ——— 1817 to 1818, 10 vols.

1760. ——— 1818 to 1819, 12 vols.

1761. ——— 1819 to 1820, 16 vols.

1762. ——— 1820 to 1821, 17 vols.

179. *F.* Journals of the Senate of the United States, 1789—1792, 6 vols.

178. *F.* ——— of the House of Representatives, same period, 6 vols.

1755½. Collection of speeches delivered in Congress from 1794 to 1814.

162. *F.* A Collection of original letters from eminent characters during the revolutionary war, collected by the late Charles Pettit, deputy commissary general of the continental army, 12 vols. MS.

F. The Correspondence of the Hon. James Logan, with William Penn and others, with notes, by Deborah Logan, MS. *(Not numbered.)*

193. *F.* The Charter of the province of Pennsylvania and city of Philadelphia. Philadelphia, B. Franklin, 1742.

194. *F.* Votes and Proceedings of the House of Representatives of

the province of Pennsylvania, beginning the 4th of December, 1682, to September, 1776, 6 vol. Philadelphia, by B. Franklin, and H. Muller, 1752—1776.

225. *F.* A collection of Treaties between the Government of Pennsylvania and the Indian Nations, from 1721 to 1762, to which are prefixed: 1. The Royal Charter to W. Penn. 2. The frame of government, 1612. 3. The laws agreed upon in England. 4. Certain conditions or concessions. 5. The act of settlement, 1682. 6. The second frame of government, 1683. 7. The charter of the city of Philadelphia, 1701. 8. The new charter of privileges to the province, 1701. Philadelphia.

226. *F.* Another collection from 1742 to 1758.

195. *F.* Journal of the House of Representatives of the commonwealth of Pennsylvania, beginning the 28th of November, 1776, and ending the 20th of October, 1781. Philadelphia, 1782.

197. *F.* Journal of the Senate of the Commonwealth of Pennsylvania, commencing the 6th of December, 1791, to April 6, 1802, 12 vols. Philadelphia, 1802.

1780. Same from 1802 to 1822-3, 21 vols.

198. *F.* Journal of the House of Representatives of the commonwealth of Pennsylvania, from the 7th of December, 1790, to March 17, 1800, 10 vols. Philadelphia.

1781. Same, from 1802 to 1822-3, 21 vols.

1782. Official statements of the finances of Pennsylvania, from 1777 to 1822, 10 vols.

245. Correspondence of Thomas Jefferson, Secretary of State, with M. Hammond, Minister Plenipotentiary from Great Britain to the U. States of America, from 1791 to 1793.

665. Correspondence of J. R. Poinsett with the Secretary of State, on the affairs of South America. 1818.

255. Official Documents relative to transactions of the United States with the Barbary powers. Washington, 1802.

189. *Q.* A collection of Army Registers, Regulations, General Orders, &c. partly printed and partly original MSS. from 1801 to 1815.

1036. Collection of Public Documents and Essays on Subjects of Finance, but particularly of Banks, 3 vols. Philadelphia, Washington, and elsewhere, 1786—1822.

---

2. SEPARATE DOCUMENTS.

(In order of dates.)

1300.

8. *Q.* Liber Quotidianus Contrarotulationis Garderobiæ, anno regni regis Edwardi Primi vicesimo octavo, A. D. 1299 and 1300. Londini, 1787.

1478.

384, 17. *Q.* Lettre inédite de la Seigneurie de Florence au Pape Sixte IV. 21 Juillet. 1478.

1692.

672. The Charter granted by King William and Queen Mary,

to the inhabitants of Massachusetts-Bay, in New England, 7th Oct. 1692. Printed 1775.

1696.

243. Ausführliche Vorstellung was das Hoch-fürstl. hauss Würtemberg hat unbillig gelitten von der Cron Frankreich à tempore dess gebrochnen Still-stands bis hiehero. Stuttgart, 1696.

1703.

175. *F.* The original Cash Book of William Penn, containing the entries of his expenses from 1699 to 1703, MS.

1716.

174. *F.* The original rough minutes of the Executive Council of Pennsylvania from 1700 to 1716, both inclusive, from the papers of the family of James Logan, Secretary of the said Council, MS.

1724.

144. *F.* Ancient copy of the Charter granted by Sir William Keith to the town of Newcastle, Delaware, erecting it into a city, 28th of May, 1724, MS.

1755.

15. *Q.* The memorials of the English and French Commissaries concerning the limits of Nova Scotia or Acadia, with a Map. London, 1755.

1757.

65. A Memorial, containing a summary view of facts, with their authorities, in answer to the observations sent by the English Ministry to the Courts of Europe, translated from the French. Philadelphia, 1757.

626. Same work. New York, 1757.

1758.

166. *F.* Extracts from the original minutes of the Executive Council of Pennsylvania from 1748 to 1758, extracted by Thomas Sergeant, Esq. Secretary of State.

1764.

613, 682. A speech delivered in the House of Assembly of the province of Pennsylvania, May 24th, 1764, by J. Dickinson, on occasion of a petition, praying his majesty for a change in the government of this province. Philadelphia, 1764.

682. The same speech in the German language. Philad. 1764.

613. The Speech of Joseph Galloway, Esq. in answer to the speech of John Dickinson, Esq. delivered in the House of Assembly of Pennsylvania, May 24th, 1764, with J. Dickinson's reply. Philadelphia, 1764.

1765.

592, 630. Authentic account of the proceedings of the Congress held at New York, 1765, on the subject of the Stamp Act.

1766.

645. Examination of Doctor B. Franklin, before an august Assembly, relating the repeal of the Stamp Act, &c.

593. A list of the minority in the House of Commons, who voted against the bill to repeal the American Stamp Act. Paris, 1766.

593. Correct copies of the two protests, (11th of March and 17th of March, 1766,) against the bill to repeal the American Stamp Act of last session, with a list of speakers and votes. Paris, 1766.

660. Second protest, with a list of the votes against the bill to repeal the American Stamp Act of last session. Paris, (London) 1766.

1768.

617. Governor Bernard's intercepted letters, from 1763 to 1768.

1769.

595. A letter to the Earl of Hillsborough from Governor Bernard, General Gage, and his Majesty's Council for the Province of Massachusetts-Bay, with an Appendix. Boston, 1769.

1773.

716. The votes and proceedings of the Freeholders and other inhabitants of the town of Boston, in Town-meeting assembled 1772. Boston, 1773.

725. The Speeches of Governor Hutchinson to the General Assembly of the Massachusetts-Bay, at a session begun and held on the 6th of January, 1773. With the answers of his majesty's council and the Houses of Representatives, respectively. Boston, 1773.

1774.

599. Journal of the Proceedings of the Congress, held at Philadelphia, September 5, 1774. Philadelphia, 1774.

661, 673. Extracts from the votes and proceedings of the American Continental Congress held at Philadelphia, September 5, 1774. Philadelphia, 1774.

612, 673. Letter of the Congress of the United Colonies to the inhabitants of the Province of Quebec. Philad. 1774.

260. Proceedings of the first Provincial Convention of Pennsylvania, with instructions to their representatives in Assembly, prepared chiefly by John Dickinson.

596. The Bishop of St. Asaph's speech on the bill, for altering the charter of the Colony of Massachusetts-Bay. London, 1774.

727. The Petition and Memorial of the Assembly of Jamaica, to the king of Great Britain, (voted in Assembly on the 28th of December, 1774.) Philadelphia, 1775.

51. Proceedings of the British and other Protestant inhabitants of the province of Quebec, in order to obtain a House of Assembly in that province. London, 1774.

1775.

629. A Declaration by the Representatives of the United Colonies of North America now met in General Congress at Philadelphia, setting forth the causes and necessity of their taking up arms. Philadelphia, 1775.

673. An Address of the twelve United Colonies of North America to the people of Ireland. Philadelphia, 1775.

661. Debates in the English Parliament relative to American affairs.

616. Speeches in the last session of the present parliament, de-

livered by several of the principal advocates in the House of Commons in favour of the rights of America. New York, 1775.

616, 384, 16. Speech of the Earl of Chatham in the House of Lords, January 20, 1775, on a motion for an address to his majesty to give immediate orders for removing his troops from Boston. Philadelphia, 1775.

616. The Speech of E. Burke on moving his resolutions for conciliation with the Colonies, March 22d, 1775. New York, 1775.

616. Speech of E. Burke on American taxation, April 19, 1774. London, 1775.

616. Speech and motion made in the House of Commons on the 27th of March, 1775, together with a draught of a letter of requisition to the colonies, by D. Hartley.

644. Rules for establishing rank or precedence amongst the Pennsylvania Associators, military regulations for same recommended by Congress. 1775.

1776.

556. Declaration of American Independence, 4th of July, 1776.

270. Proceedings of the provincial conference of committees of the province of Pennsylvania, held at the Carpenters' Hall at Philadelphia, June 18 and 25, 1776. Philadelphia.

612. Charge on the rise of the American Empire, delivered to the Grand Jury for the district of Charlestown, by William H. Drayton. Charlestown, 1776.

670. Form of Prayer ordered by the British government to be used in all churches on the 13th of December, 1776, appointed as a day of fasting and prayer in consequence of the American *Rebellion*. London, 1776.

1777.

613, 630. An address to the inhabitants of Pennsylvania, by those freemen of the city of Philadelphia who are now confined in the Mason's Lodge, by virtue of a general warrant signed in council by the vice-president of the council of Pennsylvania. Philadelphia, 1777.

1778.

384, 7. *Q.* Traité d'Amitié & de Commerce entre la France & les Etats Unis d'Amérique. Paris, 1778.

616. Speeches of Governor Johnstone, Mr. Cruger, Captain Luttrell, Colonel Acland, H. T. Luttrell, and the Marquis of Granby, in favour of the rights of America.

645. A list of the general and staff officers, and of the officers in the regiments serving in North America under the command of William Howe. Philadelphia, 1778.

212. *F.* Proceedings of a general Court Martial held at White Plains in the State of New York, by order of H. E. Gen. Washington, for the trial of Major General St. Clair, August 25, 1778. Philadelphia, 1778.

1779.

661. Observations on the American Revolution, published by order of Congress. Philadelphia, 1779.

612. Report of commissioners for settling a cartel for the exchange of prisoners. Philadelphia, 1779.

645. A view of the evidence relative to the conduct of the American war under Wm. Howe, Viscount Howe, and General Burgoyne, as given before the House of Commons, to which is added, a collection of pieces, that have given rise to that important enquiry. London, 1779.

644. A vindication of the opposition of Verment to the Government of New York, and of their right to form into an independent state, by Ethan Allen. 1779.

740. Address of the Council of Pennsylvania, Joseph Reed, President, to the citizens, on the subject of the taking of all Salt in the hands of the Council. 1779.

384, 7. Q. Exposé des motifs de la conduite du Roi de France relat. a l'Angleterre. Paris, 1779.

1780.

645. Proceedings of the Board of General Officers held by order of General G. Washington, respecting Major André, Sept. 29, 1780.

670. Observations on certain commercial transactions in France, laid before Congress by Arthur Lee. Philadelphia, 1780.

384, 7. Q. Observations sur le mémoire Justificatif, de la Cour de Londres. Paris, 1780.

619, 670. Same work, translated from the French by Peter S. Du Ponceau. Philadelphia, 1781.

1781.

384, 9. Q. Compte rendu au Roi, par M. Necker. Paris, 1781.

1782.

669. A complete and accurate account of the very important debate in the House of Commons on July 9, 1782, in which the cause of Mr. Fox's resignation, and the great question of American Independence came under consideration. London, 1782.

616. Speech of Charles J. Fox on American Independence, spoken in the House of Commons on July 2, 1782. London.

1783.

660. Address and recommendations to the States by the United States in Congress assembled. Philadelphia, 1783.

669. The definitive treaty between Great Britain and the United States of America, signed at Paris the 3d day of September, 1783.

1784.

711. Questions sur lesquelles on souhaite de sçavoir les réponses de Monsieur Adhémar, de Monsieur de Lisle, & d'autres habitants de la province de Québec. London, 1784.

384, 9. Q. First and third Reports of a Committee of the House of Commons of Great Britain, appointed to enquire into the frauds on the revenue. London, 1784.

1785.

271. Proceedings in and out of Parliament on propositions re-

gulating the trade between Great Britain and Ireland, and Mr. Fox's speech in the House of Commons, May, 1785. London, 1785.

275. State of the accounts of the treasury of Pennsylvania, from the 1st Oct. 1702, to the 1st of Jan. 1785. Philad. 1785.

1786.

384, 3. Q. View of the debts and expenses of Pennsylvania, by John Nicholson, Comptroller General. 1786.

1787.

805. Journal, acts and proceedings of the Convention which formed the Constitution of the United States. Boston, 1819.

278. Speech of H. Flood in the House of Commons of Great Britain, Feb. 15, 1787, on the Commercial Treaty with France. Dublin, 1787.

384, 21. Q. An act imposing duties on goods and merchandise, imported in the State of New York, passed 11th of April, 1787.

1788.

815. Debates in the Massachusetts Convention on the Federal Constitution. Boston, 1808.

294. Tagebuch der Convention der Republik Pennsylvania. Philadelphia, 1788.

842. Debates and other proceedings of the Convention of Virginia for deliberating on the Federal Constitution. Richmond, 1805.

1789.

196. F. Minutes of the Convention of the Commonwealth of Pennsylvania, commenced the 24th of November, 1789, for the purpose of reviewing, altering and amending the Constitution of the State. Philadelphia, 1789.

721. Speech of William Pinckney in the House of Delegates of Maryland, in November, 1789, on a bill relative to the manumission of slaves. Philadelphia, 1790.

1790.

384, 11. Q. Mémoire du Peuple au Peuple, au rapport de huit des Comm. de l'Ass. Nat. par M. de Brie Serrant. Paris, 1790.

450. Q. Docum. Arabicos para a Hist Portug. dos copiados originaes da Torre do Tombo. Por J. de Sousa, 1790.

608. Report of the Secretary of the Treasury, made on the 13th of December, 1790, on the means of establishing public credit.

384, 10. Q. Etat des finances de St. Domingue depuis le 10 Nov. 1785, jusqu' au dernier Décembre, 1788, par M. Barbé de Marbois. Paris, 1790.

1791.

278. Debates on February 29, in the House of Commons of Great Britain on the cession of Oczakow by the Turks to Russia, and on an armament of Great Britain against Russia.

348. Report of the Secretary of the Treasury of the United States on the subject of manufactures, December 5, 1791. Dublin, 1792.

348. Report of the Secretary of the Treasury of the United States, (A. Hamilton,) on Manufactures, December 5, 1791. (Reprinted,) Dublin, 1792.

1792.

304. An inquiry into the causes of the insurrection of the Negroes in the island of St. Domingo, to which is added, observations of Garran Coulon on the same subject, translated from the French. London, 1792.

600. Report of the Secretary of State on the Cod and Whale Fishery, made to Congress, February 1, 1791. Philadelphia, 1792.

608. Report of the Secretary of the Treasury, respecting the Act imposing a duty on Spirits, &c. March 6, 1792.

1793.

384, 9. *Q.* First, second, and third reports from the Committee of the East India Company, relative to the export trade from Great Britain to the East Indies. 1793.

384, 16. *Q.* Correspondence relative to the renewal of treaties between the United States and France, and the supposed insults offered to the French flag. Philadelphia, 1793.

829. Correspondence between Thomas Jefferson and Mr. Hammond in 1791. Washington, 1793.

603. Report of the Secretary of State on the privileges and restrictions on the commerce of the United States in foreign countries. Philadelphia, 1793.

296. J. P. Brissot's report of the Committee of General Defence on the dispositions of the British government towards France, and on the measures to be taken, January 12, 1793. Translated from the French. London, 1793.

343. The trial of Louis XVI. late king of France, to which is subjoined a copy of his majesty's will, translated from the French. London.

1794.

319. Le Livre Rouge, or Red Book, being a list of private pensions paid from the public treasury of France, translated from the French. New York, 1794.

722, 603. The proceedings of the Executive of the United States respecting the insurgents in Pennsylvania, 1794. Philadelphia, 1794, 1795.

603, 641. The Speeches of Mr. Smith of South Carolina, delivered in the House of Representatives of the United States in January, 1794, on the subject of certain commercial regulations, proposed by Mr. Madison. Philadelphia, 1794.

259. The first report of the Committee of Secrecy of the House of Commons relative to the London Corresponding Society for constitutional information, May, 1794. London, 1794.

259. Idem, the first and second report of the Committee, &c. of the House of Lords, May, 1794. London, 1794.

269, 329. Vindication of Mr. Randolph's resignation. Philadelphia, 1794.

334. Rapport fait au nom du Comité de salut public par M. Robespierre sur les rapports des idées religeuses & morales aves les principes républicains & sur les fêtes nationales, 18 floréal an 2. Brest, 1794.

1795.

255, 603. Report of the Secretary of the Treasury on the 19th of January, 1795, containing a plan for the further support of public credit. 1795.

722. The Speech of Albert Gallatin in the H. of Representatives of the General Assembly of Pennsylvania on the important question touching the validity of the elections held in the four western counties of the State, on the 14th of October, 1794, with notes and an appendix, containing sundry Documents relative to the western insurrection. Philadelphia, 1795.

370. Proceedings of the Society of United Irishmen at Dublin. Philadelphia, 1795.

628. Speech of Thomas Paine, delivered in the French Convention, July 7, 1795.

299. ——— Boissy d'Anglas in the sitting of the 6th Fructidor, on the political situation of Europe, translated from the French. London, 1795.

251. Contract made by Anderson and Hobby with the legislature of Georgia, for the purchase of the western territory of that State. Augusta, 1799.

1796.

245. Washington's Address to the People of the United States, announcing his intention of retiring from public life. Philadelphia, 1796.

665. A Sketch of the Finances of the United States, by Albert Gallatin. New York, 1796.

744. Treaty of Amity, Commerce, and Navigation, between the United States and Great Britain, concluded at London, November 19, 1794, proclaimed at Philadelphia, on the 29th of February, 1796, with the President's proclamation. Philadelphia, 1796.

887½. Proceedings of the House of Representatives of the United States, respecting the Treaty Powers. Philadelphia, 1796.

255. Report of the Attorney General of the United States relative to the South Western Territory of the United States, charters, treaties, &c. Philadelphia, 1796.

657. Official and private correspondence of Major-General J. S. Eustace during the late war. Paris, 1796.

275. Report of a Committee of the Select Council of Philadelphia, Nov. 10th, 1796, on the present state of the finances of the city. Philadelphia, 1796.

1797.

905. Message from the President of the United States to Congress relative to the French Republic, 19th Jan. 1797. Philadelphia.

255. Documents relative to General Pinckney's reception in

France, &c. furnished by the President of the U. States. Philadelphia, 1797.

916. View of the conduct of the Executive of the United States, by James Monroe. Philadelphia, 1797.

648. A letter to Timothy Pickering, Secretary of State, from the Chevalier de Yrujo, Minister Plenipotentiary of his Catholic Majesty, dated July 11, 1797.

744. Papers relative to the late negociation at Lisle, laid before both houses of Parliament, by his Majesty's command. 1797.

1798.

715. President's Message, containing the instructions to, and despatches from the American Envoys to France. Philadelphia, 1798.

703, 719. The speech of Albert Gallatin, delivered in the House of Representatives of the United States, on the 1st of March, 1798, upon the foreign intercourse bill.

637. A short account of the principal proceedings of Congress in the late session, and a sketch of the state of affairs between the United States and France in July, 1798, in a letter from Robert Goodloe Harper, of South Carolina, to one of his constituents. Philadelphia, 1798.

637. Observations on the dispute between the United States and France, addressed by Robert G. Harper, of South Carolina, to his constituents in May, 1797. Philadelphia, 1798.

1799.

715. President's Message, including the Report of the Secretary of State on the transactions with France.

608. ——— ——— accompanying sundry papers relative to the affairs of the United States with the French Republic.

251. Proceedings of the commissioners for carrying into effect the sixth article of the treaty between His Britannic Majesty and the United States of America. Philadelphia, 1799.

1800.

384, 16. *Q*. Convention made on the 30th Sept. 1800, between the government of the United States and the French Republic. Washington, 1801.

611, 702. Proceedings of the Virginia Assembly on the answers of sundry states to their resolutions passed in December, 1798. Philadelphia, 1800.

744. Speech of John Marshall in the House of Representatives of the United States on the resolutions of Edward Livingston, relative to Thomas Nash, alias Jonathan Robbins. Philadelphia, 1800.

1801.

600. Accounts of the Treasurer of the United States from the 1st of Oct. 1800, to the 30th of June, 1801, inclusive. Washington, 1801.

601, 728. Views of the public debt, receipts, and expenditures of the United States, by Albert Gallatin. Philadelphia, 1801.

257. Proceedings of the General Society of Cincinnati, formation, laws, &c. Philadelphia, 1801.

1802.

600. Communication from the Secretary of the Treasury to the chairman of the committee appointed to investigate the state of the treasury. Washington, 1802.

703. The Speeches of Messrs. Giles and Bayard in the House of Representatives of the United States, February, 1802, on the bill received from the Senate, entitled, An act to repeal certain acts respecting the organization of the Courts of the United States. Boston, 1802.

367. Speech of M. Portalis in the French legislature on the subject of the Concordat. New York, 1802.

1803.

648. Report of a debate in the Senate of the United States, Feb. 1803, on certain resolutions concerning the violation of the right of deposit in the island of New Orleans, by Wm. Duane. Philadelphia, 1803.

657. Papers in relation to the official conduct of Winthrop Sargeant, Gov. of the Mississippi Territory. Boston, 1801.

1804.

631½. Report of a debate in the Senate of the United States on a resolution for an amendment in the Constitution relative to the mode of electing a President and Vice-President of the said States, by Wm. Duane. Philadelphia, 1804.

1805.

75. Q. Rapport de M. Gaudin, Ministre des Finances de France, sur l'administration des finances de l'empire Français pendant l'an 12. Paris, 1805.

269. Proceedings of the Pennsylvania Society of the Cincinnati, May, 1784. Philadelphia, 1785.

269. Proceedings of the same. 1805.

1806.

75. Q. Rapport de M. Gaudin, Ministre des Finances de France, sur l'administration des finances de l'empire Français, pendant l'an 13. Paris, 1806.

600. Report of the Committee of Ways and Means of the Corporation of Philadelphia, for the year 1806.

703. Mr. Madison's motion for commercial restrictions, January 3, 1794. Washington, 1806.

1807.

73, 1. Q. Comptes généraux du trésor public pour l'année 1807. Paris, 1808.

1808.

73, 1. Q. Administration des finances de l'Empire Français pour l'année 1808. Paris, *(no date.)*

743. Amendments of the Constitution of the United States, submitted for consideration by Mr. Hillhouse, April 12th, 1808.

281. Memorials of sundry merchants relative to the infringement of our neutral trade, and the resolutions of the Senate grounded thereon. Published by order of the Senate. Washington, 1808.

1809.

73, 1. Q. Comptes du trésor de l'Empire pour l'année 1809, présenté à S. M. l'Empereur & Roi par son Ministre du Trésor. Paris, 1811.

703. Documents relative to the Correspondence between the British Minister, Jackson, and the Secretary of State, Robert Smith, communicated by the President of the United States to Congress, November 29, 1809.

703. Message of Governor Snyder to the Legislature of Pennsylvania, December 7, 1809.

664, 743. Speech of Josiah Quincy, on the joint resolution approving of the conduct of the Executive of the United States in relation to the refusal to receive any further communication from the British Minister, 28th December, 1809.

384, 14. Q. Traité de paix entre les Rois de Danemark & de Suède, conclu à Jönköping, le 10 Décembre, 1809, Copenhague.

1810.

73, 2. Q. Comptes du Trésor de l'Empire pour l'année, 1810, présentés à S. M. l'Empereur & Roi par son Ministre du Trésor. Paris, 1812.

608. Report of the Secretary of the Treasury on American manufactures, 17th April, 1810. Brooklyn, (Long Island) *no date.*

608. Report of the Secretary of the Treasury on the subject of a National Bank. Washington, 1810.

931. Report of the Committee appointed to enquire into the conduct of General James Wilkinson, dated May 1, 1810. Washington, 1810.

712. Speech of Mr. Porter on internal improvements, delivered in the House of Representatives on the 8th February, 1810.

1811.

609. Address of Robert Smith, (late Secretary of State,) to the people of the United States. Baltimore, 1811.

697. Proceedings of a Court of Inquiry, held at the request of Commodore Rodgers in August, 1811, concerning the affair of the Little Belt.

602. Debate in the House of Representatives of Pennsylvania, on Mr. Holgate's resolutions relative to the Bank of the United States, January, 1811. Reported by W. Hamilton.

667. Relation des glorieux événemens qui ont porté leurs Majestés Royales sur le Trône d'Hayti, suivie de l'Histoire du Couronnement & du Sacre du Roi Henri I. & de la Reine, par le Comte de Limonade, au Cap-Henri, 1811.

1812.

281. Abstract of evidence before the House of Commons, against the orders in council, with the facts proved relative to the Commerce and Manufactures of the country. London, 1812.

654. A selection of Laws, &c. passed at the first session of the

12th Congress of the United States of America, illustrative of the present relative position of the United States and Great Britain. Philadelphia, 1812.

703. Speech of Josiah Quincy in the House of Representatives of the United States, January 25th, 1812, in relation to Marine protection. Alexandria, 1812.

606, 654. An Address of several members of the House of Representatives of the Congress of the United States, to their constituents on the subject of the war with Great Britain. Alexandria, 1812—Philadelphia, 1812.

654. Message of the Governor Griswold to the Legislature of Connecticut on the 25th of August, 1812. Newhaven, 1812.

654. Proceedings and Address of the Convention of Delegates to the people of New Jersey, July, 1812. Trenton.

1813.

73, 2. Q. Budget de l'exercice de 1813. Paris, *(no imprint, no date.)*

606. Speeches of Josiah Quincy and James Emott in the House of Representatives of the United States on the 5th of January, 1813, on the bill in addition to the act entitled "An act to raise an additional military force." Alexandria.

1814.

665. Message from the President of the United States of 31st January, 1814, transmitting a letter from the Secretary of War, accompanied with sundry documents, tending to explain the causes of the failure of the arms of the United States on the Northern frontier. Baltimore, 1814.

654. Report of the Committee appointed to inquire into the causes and particulars of the invasion of the city of Washington by the British forces in August, 1814, November, 1814. Washington, 1814.

654. Speech of Mr. Pickering in the House of Representatives of the United States on the 26th and 28th of February, 1814, on the bill to authorize a loan of twenty-five millions of dollars. Georgetown, 1814.

703. Speech of Artemas Ward, delivered in the House of Representatives of the United States, 5th of March, 1814, on a bill for the support of the military establishment of the United States for 1814. Washington, 1814.

657. Report of the Trial of Brigadier General William Hull, commanding the Northwestern army of the United States, by a Court Martial held at Albany, January, 1814. New York, 1814.

667. Manifeste du Roi Christophe d'Hayti, Septembre, 1814.

667. Notes à M. le Baron de Malouet en refutation du 4e volume de son ouvrage intitulé: Collection de Mémoires sur les colonies & particulièrement sur St. Domingue, par le Baron Vastey, Secrétaire du Roi Henry I. Cap-Henry, 1814.

667. Première Lettre du Baron de Dupuy Secrétaire du Roi Henri I. à H. Henry, auteur du pamphlet intitulé: Considéra-

tions offertes aux habitants d'Hayti, sur leur situation actuelle & sur le sort présumé qui les attend. Cap-Henry, Decembre, 1814.

667. 2de Lettre du même au même, du 20 Décembre, 1814.

1815.

75. *Q.* Proposition de la loi de finances pour l'année 1816. Discours du Ministre des Finances à la Chambre des Députés, & Rapport au Roi sur le projet de cette loi & sur la situation générale des finances. Paris, 1815.

652. Report on Banks, presented to the Legislature of the State of Virginia, on the 5th January, 1815.

654. An exposition of the causes and character of the war with Great Britain. *(Semi-official.)* Washington, 1815.

657, 917. Official correspondence with the Department of War, relative to the military operations of the American army under the command of Major General Izard, in 1814, and 1815. Philadelphia, 1816.

653. Governor Snyder's Message to the Legislature of Pennsylvania. 1815.

667. L'Olivier de la paix; Lettre du Comte de Limonade, Secrétaire d'Etat d'Haity au Géneral Petion, 1815.

1817.

654. Letter from the acting Secretary of War, transmitting information relative to the claims of the State of Massachusetts for paying off the expenses of the militia, February, 20, 1817. Washington, 1817.

183½. *F.* Accounts of the Receipts and expenditures of the United States, for the years 1797, 9—1800, 2, 5, 1807 to 1817.

1818.

665. Message from the President of the United States, transmitting the correspondence between the Department of State, and the Spanish Minister residing here, March 14, 1818. Washington, 1818.

665. Message from the President of the United States, transmitting copies of documents referred to in his communication in relation to the Seminole war, December 3, 1818. Washington, 1818.

1820.

699. Speeches of Mr. Sergeant, Mr. Taylor, and Mr. Tallmadge, in the House of Representatives of the United States on the Missouri question. 1820.

707. Speech of Mr. M'Lane in Congress, 26th April, 1820, on the proposed Tariff.

697. The parole and documents delivered before a Committee of the House of Representatives, appointed to inquire into the conduct of the Governor of Pennsylvania, 1820.

707. Report of the Committee of Merchants and others of Boston, on the Tariff. Boston, 1820.

707. The Memorial of a Convention of Delegates representing the Merchants and others interested in Commerce, assembled in Philadelphia, to the Congress of the United States, on the subject of duties and imposts. Philadelphia, 1820.

1821.

707. Report of the Committee on Manufactures of the Congress, on the various memorials praying for, and remonstrating against, an increase of the duties on imports, January 15, 1821.

733. Description of some of the medals struck in relation to important events in North America, before and since the Declaration of Independence by the United States, by James Mease. New York, 1821.

1822.

712. Views of the President of the United States on the subject of Internal Improvements, transmitted May 4, 1822. Washington, 1822.

735. Governor's Message delivered in the Legislature of Pennsylvania, read December 5th, 1822.

703. Report relative to executive patronage, read in the Senate of Pennsylvania, March 25, 1822.

737. Official report of the trials of sundry negroes charged with an attempt to raise an insurrection in the state of South Carolina. Charleston, 1822.

703. Anno Tertio Georgii IV. Regis, Chap. XLIV. An act to regulate the trade between His Majesty's possessions in America and the West Indies, and other places in America and the West Indies, (24th June, 1822.)

---

3. HISTORICAL REGISTERS AND NEWSPAPERS.

999. Asiatic Annual Register, 1806, 1809, 2 vols. London, 1809—11.

1564. Annuaire historique, politique & littéraire, par C. Lesur, années 1818, 1819. Paris.

883. The American Register, or general repository of history, politics, and science, (edited by Charles Brockden Brown,) 7 vols. Philadelphia, 1807—1811.

959. The American Weekly Messenger, 2 vols. Philadelphia, 1813—1815.

1746. The Examiner, containing political essays on the most important events of the times, public laws and official documents, Barent Gardenier, Editor, 4 vols. New York, 1813—1815.

958. Niles's Weekly Register, 23 vols. Baltimore, 1811—1823.

220. *F.* The Massachusetts Spy, or the Worcester Gazette, from October 30, 1788, to Dec. 31, 1817, 14 vols.

199. *F.* The Pennsylvania Chronicle and Universal Advertiser, from January 26, 1767, to January 25, 1768, by Goddard.

558. *Q.* The same, continued from Jan. 25, 1768 to Jan. 22, 1770, 2 vols.

200. *F.* The Pennsylvania Gazette, from January 14, 1768, to Feb. 1783, by Hall and Sellers, 2 vols.

201. *F.* The Pennsylvania Mercury and Universal Advertiser, from March 4, 1785, to December 31, 1785, by Eleazer Oswald.

202. *F.* The Independent Gazetteer, or the Chronicle of Freedom, from June 29, 1782, to November 1, by E. Oswald and D. Humphreys.

203. *F.* The Pennsylvania Evening Herald and the American Monitor, from Jan. 4, 1786, to Dec. 6, 1786, by E. Oswald.

204. *F.* Collections of Philadelphia Newspapers, 1777, 8, 9—1803, -6, 5 vols.

205. *F.* Gazette of the United States, from April 15, 1789, to April 10, 1790, by John Fenno. New York.

206. *F.* The Freemans' Journal, or the North American Intelligencer, from April 25, 1781, to July 13, 1785, by Francis Bailey, 2 vols. Philadelphia.

207. *F.* The Pennsylvania Journal and Weekly Advertiser, from January 7, 1768, to December 29, 1769, by William and Thomas Bradford.

From January 3, 1781, to December 26, by T. Bradford, and P. Hall.

From January 1, 1783, to December 31, 1783, by Thomas Bradford, 3 vols. Philadelphia.

208. *F.* The Pennsylvania Packet, or the General Advertiser, from Januury 19, 1779, to December 30, 1779, by J. Dunlap.

209. *F.* The same, from Feb. 18, 1782, to Dec. 31, 1790, 10 vols.
1782-3, by D. C. Claypole.
1784, by J. Dunlap.
1785-6—1788-90, by Dunlap and Claypole.

210. *F.* Dunlap's Daily Advertiser, from January 1, 1791, to December 31, 1791, 2 vols.

211. *F.* Relf's Philadelphia Gazette and Daily Advertiser, from January 1, 1812, to December 31, 1812.

557. *Q.* The Pennsylvania Gazette, from January 13, 1742-3, to February 11, 1745-6, by B. Franklin. Philadelphia.

559. *Q.* The American Weekly Mercury, from March 6, 1732-3, to February 19, 1733-4, by Andrew Bradford. Philadelphia.

561. *Q.* The Pennsylvania Evening Post, from January 1775, to December 31, 1776, 2 vols. by Benjamin Towne. Philadelphia.

560. *Q.* The Quebec Mercury, from January 1, 1814, to November 29, 1814, by Thomas Carey. Quebec.

24. Gazeta de Guatemala, from 1797 to 1802, 6 vols. Guatemala.

32. *Q.* Semanario del nuevo Reyno de Granada, des de el 8 de Enero hasta el 31 de Diciembre de 1809. Santafé de Bogotà.

893. The American Register, or a summary review of history, politics and literature, by Robert Walsh, jr. 2 vols. Philadelphia, 1817.

XV. POLITICAL ECONOMY AND STATISTICS.

1. Theory of Government.
2. Penal Laws.
3. Internal Improvements.
4. Domestic Manufactures.
5. Public Schools.
6. Relief of the Poor.
7. Slavery and the Slave Trade.
8. Statistics.

1. THEORY OF GOVERNMENT.

914. *Ames, (Fisher)* His Works. Boston, 1809.

1018 *Arnould.* De la Balance du Commerce. Paris, 1791.

318. *Bail.* Des Juifs au dix neuviéme Siecle ou considerations sur leur état Civil & Politique en Europe. Paris, 1816.

673. *Barton, (William)* Observations on the nature and use of paper credit. Philadelphia, 1781.

312. *Bentham, (Jeremy)* Observations on the restrictive and prohibitory Commercial system. London, 1821.

264. *Bielfeld, (Baron de)* Instituciones politicas; obra en que se trata de los Reynos de Portugal y España. Traducidas al Castellano por Don Valentin de Foronda. Burdeos, 1781.

606. *Bolman, (Erick)* Paragraphs on Banks. Philadelphia, 1810.

294, 707. *Chaptal, (le Comte)* Essay on Import duties and prohibitions. Translated from the French. Philadelphia, 1821.

279. *Clarkson.* Essai sur les désavantages politiques de la Traite des Negres, traduit de l'Anglais. Paris, 1814.

1301. *Colquhoun, (P.)* A Treatise on Indigence, a general view of the natural resources for productive labour. London, 1806.

515, 642. *Cooper, (Thomas)* Political Arithmetic, and propositions respecting the foundation of Civil Government. 1787.

1551. *Destutt de Tracy.* Commentaire sur l'Esprit des Loix de Montesquieu. Paris, 1819.

1298. ——— ——— Some work, translated into English. Philadelphia, 1811.

935. *Dickinson, (John)* His Political Writings, 2 vols. Wilmington, (Del.) 1801.

656. *Duane, (William)* Politics for American Farmers, being a series of tracts exhibiting the blessings of Free Government. Washington, 1807.

328. *Eden, (William)* Letters to the Earl of Carlisle, on Population, Revenue Laws, and Public Economy. London, 1779—1780.

1449. *Erasmus, (Desid.)* Principis Christiani Institutio. Lug. Bat. 1641.

547½. *Everett, (Alex. H.)* New ideas on population, with remarks on the theories of Malthus and Godwin. Boston, 1823.

1017. *Ferrier, (F. L. A.)* Du Gouvernement considéré dans ses rapports avec le Commerce. Paris, 1805.

401. *Filangieri.* La Scienza della legislazione, tom. I. e II. Napoli, 1781.

1481. *Foronda, (Valentin de)* Memorias sobre la edificacion de Hospitales. Madrid, 1793.

1484. ——— ——— Cartas sobre la Economica Politica, 2 vol. Madrid, 1789.

1493. ——— ——— Cartas sobre la Policia. Madrid, 1801.

906. *Franklin, (Benjamin)* His Works, 6 vols. Philadelphia, 1818.

807. ——— ——— Political, Miscellaneous, and Philosophical pieces, with plates. London, 1779.

543. *Ganilh, (Charles)* Enquiries on Political Economy, translated from the French, by D. Boileau. New York, 1812.

548. *Grellier, (J. J.)* History of the English National Debt from 1688 to 1800. London, 1810.

941. *Hamilton, (Alexander)* His Works, 3 vols. New York, 1810.

406. *Herrenschwand.* De l'économie, moderne. Paris, an 3.

327. *Hertzberg, (Baron de)* Two Discourses delivered at public meetings of the Royal Academy of Sciences and Belles Lettres at Berlin, in 1785 and 1786.

I. On the Population of States in general, and that of the Prussian dominions in particular.

II. On the true riches of States and Nations, the balance of Commerce, and that of Power. Translated from the French. London, 1786.

1502. *Jakob, (L. H. Von)* Die Staats Finanz Wissenchaft, Erster Band. Halle, 1821.

369. *Law, (John)* Money and trade considered, first published at Edinburgh, 1705. Glasgow, 1790.

544. *Malthus, (J. R.)* Principles of Political Economy. Boston, 1821.

546. ——— ——— On the Principle of Population, 2 vols. Washington, 1809.

547. Additions to the above. London, 1817.

259. *Mascall, (E. J.)* Tables of Duties, &c. under the act for the consolidation of the customs and other duties. London, 1787.

733. *Melish, (John)* Views on Political Economy from the description of the United States. 1822.

326. *Milton, (John)* A treatise of civil power in ecclesiastical causes. London, 1790.

345. *Mirabeau, (le Comte de)* Essai sur le despotisme.

642. *O'Cane, (Fr.)* The government and laws of every country are the effect, not the cause of the condition of the people. Charleston, 1819.

7. *Page, (P. F.)* Traité d'Economie politique & de commerce des colonies, 2 vol. Paris, 1802.

633. *Paine, (Thomas)* The Rights of Man; for the use and benefit of all mankind. London, 1795.

340, 633. ——— ——— Dissertation on first principles of government. London, 1795.

1330. *Pasley, (C. W.)* Essay on the military policy and institutions of the British empire. London, 1810.

543. Q. *Perez, (Antonio)* El Conocimiento de las Naciones. MS. Written in prison, 1599.

The author gives advice to Philip II. concerning the government of the different parts of the Spanish monarchy.

1745. *Petty, (William)* Political Arithmetic. London, 1699.

408. ——— ——— Essays on Political Arithmetic. London, 1699.

1515, 13. *Priestley, (Joseph)* Essay on the first principles of government. London, 1771.

541. *Ricardo, (David)* Principles of political economy and taxation. Georgetown, 1819.

542. *Raymond, (Daniel)* Thoughts on political economy. Baltimore, 1820.

519. *Rumford, (Benjamin, Count of)* Essays political, economical, and philosophical, 4 vols. Boston, 1798.

411. *Say, (Jean Baptiste)* Traité d'économie politique, 2 vol. Paris, 1819.

545. The same work, translated by Prinsep, with a translation of the Introduction and additional notes, by Clement C. Biddle. Boston, 1821.

392. ——— ——— Catéchisme d'Œconomie Politique, 2d ed. Paris, 1821.

411½. *Smith, (Adam)* An inquiry into the nature and causes of the wealth of nations, with notes and a supplement, by W. Playfair, and the life of the author, by Dugald Stewart, 2 vols. Hartford, (Con.) 1818.

335. *Towers, (Joseph)* A vindication of the political principles of Locke, in answer to the objections of Dr. Tucker. London, 1782.

1550. *Turgot, (Œuvres de)* 9 vol. Paris, 1810.

1036. *Various Authors.* Collection of essays and other publications concerning banks and banking, 3 vols. 1810—1821.

555. *Washington, (George)* His legacies, or collection of his most approved writings. Trenton, 1820.

942. *Webster, (Petatiah)* Political Essays on the nature and operation of money, public finances and other subjects. Philadelphia, 1791.

388. *Young, (Arthur)* Essays on the Spirit of Legislation which gained the premiums offered by the Economical Society of Berne, translated from the French. London, 1772.

390. ——— ——— Political Arithmetic. London, 1774.

ANONYMOUS.

5. Le triomphe du nouveau monde; Réponses Académiques, formant un nouveau système de confédération fondé sur

les besoins actuels des nations Chrétiennes commerçantes, 2 vol. Paris, 1785.

656. Considerations on the choice of public rulers, on the extent of their powers, and on the best means of securing the advantages and reforming the abuses of popular elections. New York, 1805.

1423. Conversations on Political Economy. Philadelphia, 1817.

1456½. Refutation of the principles of Machiavel.

270. An Essay on Credit, in which the doctrine of banks is considered. Philadelphia, 1786.

665. A view of the public debt on the 1st of January, 1790, and 1796, respectively.

---

2. PENAL LAWS.

384, 23. Q. *Barbé Marbois, (the Marquis de)* Continuation de la visite des Prisons du Département de la Seine-Inférieure, par un Membre de la Societé pour l'amélioration des Prisons, en Septembre, 1822. Paris, 1822.

1303. *Beccaria.* On crimes and punishments, translated from the Italian. London, 1785.

602. *Bradford, (William)* An enquiry how far the punishment of death is necessary in Pennsylvania, by William Bradford. To which is added, An account of the jail and penitentiary house of Philadelphia, by Caleb Lownes. Philadelphia, 1793.

266, 700. *Eddy, (George)* A view of the New York State Prison, in the city of New York. New York, 1801—1815.

252. *Liancourt, (La Rochefoucault)* Sur les Prisons de Philadelphie. 1796.

240. Same work, English translation. Philadelphia, 1796.

Lownes, see *Bradford.*

671. *Rush, (Benjamin)* An enquiry into the effects of public punishment upon criminals and upon society. Philadelphia, 1787.

325. ——— ——— On the punishment of murder by death. Philadelphia, 1793.

ANONYMOUS.

662. Description and historical sketch of the Massachusetts State Prison. Charlestown, 1816.

662, 700. A statistical view of the operation of the penal code of Pennsylvania; to which is added, a view of the present state of the Penitentiary and Prison of the city of Philadelphia. Philadelphia, 1817.

262, 662. Extracts and remarks on the subject of punishment and reformation of criminals, published by order of the Society established in Philadelphia for alleviating the miseries of public prisons. Philadelphia, 1790.

662. Report to the legislature of Massachusetts on Prisons, &c. 1817.

694. **Essays on Capital Punishments—various Reports on State Prisons and Penitentiary Systems—Treatises and Essays on prisons, vice, immorality, pauperism, and the means for preventing the same.** Philadelphia, Charleston, &c. 1810—1821.

662. The third report of the Society for the diffusion of knowledge respecting the punishment of death, and the improvement of prison discipline. London, 1816.

---

3. INTERNAL IMPROVEMENTS.

IN GENERAL.

184. Q. *Fulton, (R.)* Treatise on the improvement of canal navigation. London, 1796.

445. *Leach, (Edmund)* A treatise of universal inland navigation. London, 1791.

1538. *M'Adam, (Loudon)* Remarks on the present system of road-making. Baltimore, 1821.

240. *Peale, (C. W.)* Essay on wooden bridges. Philadelphia, 1797.

183. Q. *Phillips, (T.)* General history of inland navigation. London, 1792.

460. *Pope, (Thomas)* A treatise on bridge architecture. New York, 1811.

651. *Stevens, (John)* Documents tending to prove the superior advantages of rail-ways and steam-carriages over canal navigation. New York, 1812.

LOCAL IMPROVEMENTS.

FOREIGN.

France. 467. Histoire du Canal de Languedoc. Paris, 1805.

384, 11. Q. Mémoire & discussion sur les moyens de rendre le Doubs navigable, pour opérer la jonction du Rhône au Rhin, ou Système de Navigation fluviale, par P. Bertrand. Paris, 1804.

384, 11. Q. Plan d'une Navigation, pour communiquer par une route assez droite, de Paris, à Chartres, Vendôme, Angers, Nantes, &c. par une Societé d'Actionnaires, & Projet d'un Canal de Navigation interieure entre le Port de Brest & la Loire à Nantes, par Alexis Rochon. Paris, an 13.

Poland. 384, 14. Q. Notice Historique sur un Canal de dessèchement, executé en Pologne, par Michel Sokolnicki. 1780.

DOMESTIC.

Delaware. 263. Laws of the Legislatures of Maryland, Delaware, and Pennsylvania, respecting the Chesapeake and Delaware Canal. Philadelphia, 1803.

Delaware. 827. First general report of the President of the Chesapeake and Delaware Canal Company, June 4, 1804.
2d Report, June 3, 1805.
3d Report, June 2, 1806.

273, 734. Facts and observations respecting the Chesapeake and Delaware Canal. Philadelphia, 1805.

827. The memorial and petition of the President and Directors of the Chesapeake and Delaware Canal Company, to the House of Representatives of the United States, drawn up by Joshua Gilpin. 1805.

827. The Memorial and Petition of the President and Directors of the Chesapeake and Delaware Canal Company, to the House of Representatives of the Commonwealth of Pennsylvania, drawn up by Joshua Gilpin. 1805.

652. Letters to A. Gallatin, Secretary of the Treasury of the United States, and other papers relative to the Chesapeake and Delaware Canal, by J. Gilpin and H. Latrobe, with Mr. Gallatin's report respecting the same. Philadelphia, 1808.

828. A Memoir on the Rise, Progress, and Present State of the Chesapeake and Delaware Canal, accompanied with original Documents and Maps, by Joshua Gilpin. Wilmington, (D.) 1821.

734. Communication from the Chesapeake and Delaware Canal Company, and a report and estimate of William Strickland to the President and Directors. Philadelphia, 1823.

Maryland. 340. Acts passed at the General Assembly of Maryland concerning the navigation of the river Susquehanna. Baltimore, 1797.

653. Remarks on the intercourse of Baltimore with the Western country. Baltimore, 1818.

653. Executive communication to the Legislature of Maryland, 1818, on the subject of Turnpike roads. Annapolis, 1819.

N. York. 366. Report of the Directors of the Western Inland Lock-Navigation Company to the Legislature. Albany, 1798.

273. Observations on the proposed State Road, from Hudson's River to Lake Erie. New York, 1800.

652. Report of the Commissioners of the Legislature of the State of New York, to explore the route of an Inland Navigation, from Hudson's River, to Lake Ontario and Lake Erie. New York, 1811.

652. Remarks on the importance of the contemplated Grand Canal between Lake Erie and the Hudson River, by Atticus. New York, 1812.

652. Report of the Commissioners of the Legislature of the State of New York, on the subject of improving the Internal Navigation of that State. New York, 1812.

N. York. 652. Reports of the Commissioners of the Legislature of the State of New York on the 8th of March, 1814, on the subject of Roads and Canals. *(No imprint, no date.)*

729. The advantages of the proposed Canal from Lake Erie to Hudson's River, fully illustrated in a correspondence between Gouverneur Morris and R. Fulton. New York, 1814.

652. Memorial of the Citizens of New York in favour of a Canal Navigation between the great Western Lakes and the tide-waters of the Hudson. New York, 1816.

" Remarks on the proposed Canal from Lake Erie to the Hudson River, by Atticus. New York, 1816.

" A Serious Appeal to the Legislature of the State of New York on the subject of Canal Navigation. New York, 1816.

653. The Official Reports of the Canal Commissioners of the State of New York, and the Acts of the Legislature respecting Navigable Communications between the great Western and Northern Lakes, with a Map. New York, 1817.

" Considerations on the great Western Canal, with a view of its expense, advantages, and progress, by C. G. Haines. New York, 1818.

729. Annual Report of the Canal Commissioners of the State of New York, presented to the Legislature, 12th of March, 1821. Albany, 1821.

" A Letter to Brockholst Livingston, on the Lake Canal Policy of the State of New York, by Robert Troup. Albany, 1822.

Pennsylvania. 251. Historical Account of the Canal Navigation in Pennsylvania. Philadelphia, 1795.

250, 340. A Description of the River Susquehanna, with observations on the present state of its trade and navigation, and their practicable and probable improvement, ascribed to J. Adlum. Philadelphia, 1796.

650. Account of the Conewago Canal on the river Susquehanna, to which is prefixed the act for incorporating the Company. Philadelphia, 1798.

" Address of the Committee of the Delaware and Schuylkill Canal Company, to the Committees of the Senate and House of Representatives on the Memorial of said Company. Philadelphia, 1799.

273. Facts and Arguments respecting the great utility of Inland Navigation in America, by Turner Camac. Philadelphia, 1805.

650. An Address to the Citizens of Philadelphia, on the great advantages which arise from the trade of

the western country to the State of Pennsylvania and the City of Philadelphia, by Tarascon, jun. and James Berthoud. Philadelphia, 1806.

650. Letters addressed to the people of Pennsylvania, respecting the Internal Improvement of the Commonwealth, by means of Roads and Canals, by W. J. Duane. Philadelphia, 1811.

712. Addresses of the President and Managers of the Schuylkill Navigation, to the Stockholders and to the public in general, May 29, 1817. Philadelphia, 1818—1821.

653. Sketch of the Internal Improvements already made by Pennsylvania, illustrated by a Map, by Samuel Breck. Philadelphia, 1818.

" 712. Observations on the importance of improving the Navigation of the River Schuylkill for the purpose of connecting it with the Susquehanna, &c. and the Genessee Lakes and the Ohio, by Samuel Mifflin. 1818.

734. Reports of the Watering Committee, read in Select Council, November the 12th, 1818. Philadelphia, 1822, 1823.

695. Report of a Survey of a section of the River Delaware, from one mile below Chester to Richmond above Philadelphia, by David M'Clure. Philadelphia, 1820.

S. Carolina. 712. Plans and Progress of Internal Improvement in South Carolina, with observations on the advantages resulting therefrom to the Agricultural and Commercial interests of the State, reported by the Board of Works. Columbia, 1820.

737. Inland Navigation, plan for a great Canal between Charleston and Columbia, and for connecting our waters with those of the western country, by Robert Mills. Columbia, S. C. 1821.

United States. 652. Facts and Arguments respecting the great utility of an extensive plan of Land Navigation in America, by Turner Camac. Philadelphia, 1805.

" Report of the Secretary of the Treasury on the subject of public Roads and Canals, March 2, 1807. Washington, 1808.

608. Same work, 2d ed. Philadelphia, 1808.

712. Result of the Survey of the main Post Road from Robbinstown in Maine to St. Mary's in Georgia, made between June, 1812, and January, 1813.

" Report of the Committee on Roads and Inland Navigation, read in the House of Representatives of Pennsylvania, January 30, 1821.

" 734. Report on Roads, Bridges, and Canals, read in the Senate of Pennsylvania, March 23, 1822.

Vermont. 652. Copies of Letters to the Governor and Address to the Legislature of Vermont, respecting a Ship Canal from Lake Champlain to the River St. Lawrence, to which is added the case of the Ship and Cargo of the Olive Branch, by Ira Allen. Philadelphia, 1809.

Virginia. 712. A Comparative View of the four projected coastwise Canals, which are supposed by some to be in competition for the trade between Norfolk and North Carolina, by William Tatham. Norfolk, 1808.

652. Report on Internal Improvement, by the Committee of Roads and Internal Navigation of the State of Virginia, on the 28th of December, 1815.

653. Annual Report of the President and Directors of the Board of Public Works to the General Assembly of Virginia. Richmond, 1818.

712. Report of Thomas Moore to the Virginia Board of Public Works. Richmond, 1818.

" Annual and Supplementary Report of the President and Directors of the Board of Public Works, to the General Assembly of Virginia. Richmond, 1818, 1819.

737. Reports of the Civil and Military Engineer of the State of South Carolina, for the years 1818 and 1819.

---

4. DOMESTIC MANUFACTURES.

947. *Carey, (Mathew)* Addresses of the Philadelphia Society for the Promotion of National Industry. Philadelphia, 1819.

949. ——— ——— Same work, new Series, new edition. Philadelphia, 1822.

" ——— ——— An Appeal to Common Sense and Common Reason, intended to prove the injustice and impolicy of the existing Tariff. Philadelphia, 1822.

" ——— ——— The Letters of Hamilton, or an Address to the Citizens of the United States, on the tendency of our system of intercourse with foreign nations. Philadelphia, 1822.

951. ——— ——— The New Olive Branch, showing the identity of interest between Agriculture, Manufactures, and Commerce. Philadelphia, 1821.

665. *Coxe, (Tench)* A Memoir on the subject of the Cotton Wool cultivation, the Cotton Trade, and the Cotton Manufactures of the United States, with an addition thereto. Philadelphia, 1807.

671. ——— ——— An Address to the Assembly of the friends of American Manufactures. Philadelphia, 1787.

290. Q. *Coxe, (Tench)* A Statement of the Arts and Manufactures of the United States for the year 1810, digested and prepared from the official returns, by order of Government. Philadelphia, 1814.

244. *Logan, (George)* Letter to the Citizens of Pennsylvania, on the necessity of promoting Agriculture, Manufactures, and the Useful Arts. Philadelphia, 1800.

622. *Seybert, (Adam)* An Oration delivered on the 19th of May, 1809, at the Meeting of the Manufacturers and Mechanics of the City of Philadelphia. Philadelphia, 1809.

332. *Wansey, (Henry)* Wool encouraged without exportation, or Practical Observations on Wool and the Woollen Manufacture. London, 1791.

ANONYMOUS.

671. The plan of the Pennsylvania Society for the encouragement of Manufactures and the Useful Arts. Philadelphia, 1787.

650. An Address to the Assembly of the friends of American Manufactures. Philadelphia, 1787.

270. Observations on the Agriculture, Manufactures, and Commerce of the United States. New York, 1789.

651. Thoughts on the increasing wealth and National economy of the United States of America. Washington, 1801.

263, 646. A Communication from the Pennsylvania Society for the encouragement of Manufactures and the Useful Arts. Philadelphia, 1804.

651. An Essay on the Manufacturing interest of the United States. Philadelphia, 1804.

665. Constitution of the Philadelphia Society for the Promotion of American Manufactures. 1817.

707. Address of the American Society for the encouragement of Domestic Manufactures to the people of the United States. New York, 1817.

---

5. PUBLIC SCHOOLS.

FOREIGN.

1669. The History of the University of Edinburgh, from 1580 to 1646, by Thomas Craufurd. Edinburgh, 1808.

384, 23. Q. Joanneum, 2 ter, 7 ter, und 8 ter Jahrsbericht. Wien, 1818.

314. Observations on Brougham's bill, "for better providing the means of education for his majesty's subjects." London, 1821.

304. Compte de l'examen public du Lycée National de Haiti, rendu par Colombel. Port-au-Prince, 1820.

DOMESTIC.

Connecticut. 615. The Laws of Yale College in Newhaven in Connecticut. Newhaven, 1808.

684. Catalogus Senatus Academici in Collegio Yalensi, Novi-portus, in Republica Connecticutensi. Novi-portus, 1820.

Kentucky. " Theses Universitatis Transylvaniensis, 1822. Lexington, 1822.

" A Catalogue of the Officers and Students of the Transylvania University, Lexington, Kentucky, January, 1822.

" Catalogus Senatûs Academici, in Universitate Transylvaniensi. Lexingtoniæ, 1822.

735. Catalogue of the Officers and Students of Transylvania University, Lexington, Kentucky, January, 1823.

Maryland. 260, 615. Account of Washington College in the State of Maryland. Philadelphia, 1784.

684. Review of the Maryland report on the appropriation of public lands for schools. Baltimore, 1821.

Massachusetts. 636. The statutes of the University in Cambridge relating to the degree of doctor in medicine. Boston, 1811.

" Laws of Harvard College for the use of the students. Cambridge, 1816.

" Catalogus Universitatis Harvardianæ, 1818. Cantabrigiæ, 1818.

684. Catalogus Senatûs Academici in Universitate Harvardianâ Cantabrigiæ in Republicâ Massachusettensi. Cantabrigiæ, 1821.

N. Hampshire. 636. Statutes of Dartmouth University relating to medical graduation, passed August 25, 1812.

684. Address of Three Trustees of Dartmouth College to the Legislature of New Hampshire, 1816.

N. Jersey. 254, 600. Laws of the College of New Jersey. Philadelphia, 1802.

N. York. 615. Statutes of Columbia College as adopted by the Board of Trustees, June 13, 1811. New York, 1811.

636. An act to incorporate the members of the New York Institution for the instruction of the Deaf and Dumb, passed April 15, 1819; to which is added the By-laws. New York, 1819.

691. Documents respecting the Protestant Episcopal Theological Education Society in the state of New York. New York, 1820.

Pennsylvania. 615. Proposals relating to the education of youth in Pennsylvania. Philadelphia, 1749.

618. A brief history of the charitable scheme for instruct-

ing poor Germans in Pennsylvania, printed by B. Franklin. Philadelphia, 1755.

Pennsylvania. 723. A charge delivered May 17, 1757, at the first anniversary commencement in the College and Academy of Philadelphia, by W. Smith. Philadelphia, 1757.

631. Candid remarks on Dr. Witherspoon's address to the inhabitants of Jamaica and the other West India Islands. Philadelphia 1772.
(This work relates to the history of the College and Academy, now University of Pennsylvania.)

681. An address to the General Assembly of Pennsylvania in the case of the violated charter of the College, Academy, and Charitable School of Philadelphia, &c. Philadelphia, 1788.

615. Report of the Committee for the arrangement of the Schools in the University of Pennsylvania. Philadelphia, 1795.

" Rules and statutes of the University of Pennsylvania, 1811, 1820.

741. Constitution of the Society for the institution and support of Sunday Schools of the city of Philadelphia and the districts of Southwark and the Northern Liberties. Philadelphia, 1810.

708. Sketch of the origin and progress of the Adelphi School, established in the Northern Liberties of the city of Philadelphia, under the direction of the Philadelphia Association of Friends, for the instruction of poor children. Philadelphia, 1810.

636, 708. Report of the Committee on Public Schools to the Pennsylvania Society for the promotion of Public Economy, read at its meeting on November 10, 1817. Philadelphia, 1817.

708. A sketch of the origin and present state of the Philadelphia Society for the establishment of Charity Schools. *(No date, supposed about* 1820.*)*

" Annual Reports of the Board of Managers of the Philadelphia Society for the establishment and support of Charity Schools, with the annual report of the treasurer. Philadelphia, 1817—1820, 1823.

636. Act of the Legislature of Pennsylvania to provide for the education of children, at public expense, within the city and county of Philadelphia, March 6, 1818.

" 708. Annual Reports of the Controllers of the Public Schools of Philadelphia, 1819—1822.

708. Annual Reports of the Philadelphia Sunday and Adult School Union. Philadelphia, 1819—1822.

Pennsylvania. 700. The Constitution and By-laws of the Pennsylvania Institution for the Deaf and Dumb. Philadelphia, 1820.

" An account of the origin and progress of the Pennsylvania Institution for the Deaf and Dumb. Philadelphia, 1821.

684. Report on the subject of education, read in the Senate of Pennsylvania, March 1, 1822.

" Address delivered at the organization of the Faculty at Dickinson College, Jan. 15, 1822, by J. M. Mason. Carlisle, 1822.

736. Minutes of the Course of Chemical Instructions in the Medical Department of the University of Pennsylvania, first, second, and third part, by Robert Hare. Philadelphia, 1822—1823.

S. Carolina. 684. Address to the Graduates of the South Carolina College, 3d December, 1821, by Thomas Cooper. Columbia, 1821.

Virginia. 636. Sundry documents on the subject of a system of public education for the state of Virginia. Richmond, 1817.

" Proceedings and report of the Commissioners for the University of Virginia, presented December 8, 1818. Richmond, 1818.

684. Report of the President and Directors of Literary Fund to the General Assembly, December 19, 1818. Richmond, 1818.

" Proceedings and report of the Commissioners for the University of Virginia, presented December 8, 1818. Richmond, 1818.

---

6. RELIEF OF THE POOR.

702. *Adams, (John Q.)* An address to the members of the Massachusetts Charitable Fire Society, at their annual meeting, May, 28, 1802. Boston, 1802.

1682. *Barton, (W. P. C.)* A treatise containing a plan for the internal organization and government of Marine Hospitals in the United States. Two copies. Philadelphia, 1817.

314. *Brougham, (Henry)* A letter to Sir Samuel Romilly, upon the abuse of charities, with an appendix containing the minutes of evidence taken before the Education Committee. London, 1818.

1534. *Du Pont de Nemours.* Idées sur les secours à donner aux pauvres malades dans une grand ville. Philadelphie, (Paris) 1786.

——— Rapport sur les travaux de la Société Philanthropique. Paris, 1810.

Ruggles, see page 100.

1689. *Trimmer, (Mrs.)* The Œconomy of Charity. London, 1787.

643. *Valentin, (Louis)* Notice sur les établissemens de charité & de bienfaisance & sur l'hospitalité dans les Etats Unis de l'Amerique, lue dans l'académie de Marseille, 28 Août. 1808.

" ——— ——— Seconde & troisième notices sur les progrès des Sciences Physiques & Naturelles & sur les établissemens de bienfaisance dans les Etats Unis de l'Amérique. Marseille, 1809.

ANONYMOUS.

336. Observations on the number and misery of the poor, and on the general causes of poverty. London, 1765.

618. An account of the charitable corporation lately erected in Philadelphia, for the relief of the widows and orphans of clergymen of the Episcopal Church. Philadelphia, 1769.

680. Some account of the charitable corporation erected for the relief of the widows and children of clergymen in America. Philadelphia, 1770.

680. Rules and constitutions of the Society of the Sons of St. George. Philadelphia, 1772.

680. An abstract of the proceedings of the corporation for the relief of the widows and children of clergymen. Philadelphia, 1773.

344. An account of the benevolent institution for delivering poor married women, established Nov. 1779. London, 1783.

344. An account of the institution and proceedings of the guardians of the asylum at Lambeth, (England.) 1782.

344. Plan of the Surry Dispensary for administering advice and medicine to the poor. London, 1784.

344. The first report of the Philanthropic Society, instituted in London, 1788, for reforming the morals of the poor.

708. Plan for a school on an establishment similar to that of Ackworth, Yorkshire, Great Britain, within the limits of the (Friends') Yearly Meeting for Pennsylvania and New Jersey. Philadelphia, 1790.

325. A concise description of the Royal Hospital for Seamen at Greenwich. 1791.

1688. Description of the institution near York, (England,) for insane persons of the Society of Friends. Philadelphia, 1813.

700. Constitutions and By-laws of the Orphan Society of Philadelphia, instituted December 20, 1814; and annual reports of the same. Philadelphia, 1815.

662. Rules and regulations for the internal government of the Alms-house and House of Employment at Philadelphia, published, May, 1816. Philadelphia, 1816.

700. Constitution of the Widow's and Single Women's Society

of Philadelphia, instituted the 9th of January, 1817, and annual reports of the same. Philadelphia, 1817—1822.

700. Articles of the Saving Fund Society. Philadelphia, 1817.

" Observations on the utility and management of Saving Banks. Manchester, 1817.

" The Constitution, Plan, and By-laws of the Provident Institution for Savings in the town of Boston. Boston, 1818.

730. The first annual report of the Managers of the Society for the prevention of Pauperism in the City of New York, October 26, 1818. New York, 1818.

662. Report of a Committee to the New York Society for the prevention of Pauperism. New York, 1818.

314. Annals of Banks for Savings, containing an account of their rise and progress, reports and essays on their national importance, &c. together with more than sixty reports from more than sixty institutions in Great Britain and Ireland. London, 1818.

700. An act incorporating the Philadelphia Saving Fund Society. 1819.

" Fourth Report of the Directors of the American Asylum at Hartford, for the education and instruction of the Deaf and Dumb, May, 13, 1820. Hartford, 1820.

314. Report of the Committee of the House of Commons on the poor laws, (made 1819.) London, 1821.

---

7. SLAVERY AND THE SLAVE TRADE.

706. *Bacon, (E.)* Abstract of a Journal of E. Bacon, assistant agent of the United States to Africa, with an appendix &c. the whole showing the successful exertions of the British and American governments in repressing the Slave Trade. Philadelphia, 1821.

747. *Benezet, (Anthony)* A Caution and Warning to Great Britain and her colonies, in a short representation of the calamitous state of enslaved negroes in the British dominions. Philadelphia, 1766.

" —— —— A Mite cast in the Treasury, or observations on Slave-keeping. Philadelphia, 1772.

699. —— —— An affectionate address to the inhabitants of the British colonies in America. 1776.

280. *Clarkson, (Thomas)* An Essay on the impolicy of the African Slave Trade. Philadelphia, 1788.

706. *Coker, (Daniel)* Journal of Daniel Coker, a descendant of Africa, from the time of leaving New York on a voyage to Sherbro, in Africa, in company with three agents and about ninety persons of colour, with an appendix. Baltimore, 1820.

304. *Giudicelly, (l'Abbé)* Observations sur la traite des Noirs en

réponse au rapport de Courvoisier sur la pétition de J. Morenas. Paris, 1820.

645. *Glover, (———)* The evidence delivered on the petition presented by the West India planters and merchants to the House of Commons. London, 1775.

279. *Gregoire.* De la Domesticité, chez les peuples anciens & modernes. Paris, 1814.

" ——— De la Traite & de l'Esclavage des Noirs & des Blancs. Paris, 1815.

304. *Morenas, (J.)* Seconde Petition présentée aux deux chambres de France, contre la Traite des Nègres. Paris, 1821.

698. *Saunders, (Prince)* A Memoir presented December 11th, 1818, to the American Convention for promoting the abolition of Slavery. Philadelphia, 1818.

343, 699. *Webster, (Noah)* Effects of Slavery on morals and industry. Hartford, (Conn.) 1793.

725. *Wesley, (John)* Thoughts upon Slavery. London, 1774.

279. *Wilberforce, (W.)* Lettre à Talleyrand-Perigord au sujet de la traite des Nègres, traduite de l'Anglais. Londres, 1814.

698. *Winchester, (Elhanan)* The Reigning Abominations, especially the Slave Trade, considered in a discourse delivered in Fairfax County, Virginia, the 30th of December, 1774. London, 1788.

ANONYMOUS.

364. An Epistle of the Yearly Meeting of the Society of Friends, cautioning and advising against the buying and keeping of Slaves. Philadelphia, 1754.

699. A Serious Address to the Rulers of America, on the inconsistency of their conduct respecting Slavery, forming a contrast between the encroachments of England on American liberty. Trenton, 1783.

698. Rules for the regulation of the Society for the relief of free Negroes, and others, unlawfully held in bondage, instituted in Philadelphia, in the year 1784. Philadelphia, 1784.

239, 680. The Constitution of the Pennsylvania Society for promoting the abolition of Slavery. Philadelphia, 1788.

747. A short sketch of the evidence for the abolition of the slave trade, delivered before a committee of the House of Commons. Philadelphia, (Reprinted) 1792.

" The debate on a motion for the abolition of the slave trade in the House of Commons, 2d April, 1792. London, 1792.

280. Memorial presented to the Congress of the United States by the Societies for the Abolition of Slavery, &c. Philadelphia, 1792.

747. A serious expostulation with the members of the House of Representatives of the U. States (on the slave trade.) Philadelphia, 1793.

257. Constitution, &c. of the Society for the Abolition of Slavery. Act of incorporation, laws of United States and of Pennsylvania respecting the same, Philadelphia, 1800.—Minutes of Delegates, from 1795 to 1803.

698. Minutes of the proceedings of the convention of delegates from the Abolition Societies established in the United States, assembled at Philadelphia. Philad. 1794—1817.

706. Constitution of the American Colonization Society. 1818.

" Address to the American Society for Colonizing the Free People of Colour of the United States. Washington, 1818.

706. Address of the managers of the American Colonization Society to the public. 1819.

" Annual reports of the American Society for colonizing the Free People of Colour in the United States, with an appendix, from 1819 to 1822. Washington.

706. Address of the Board of Managers of the American Colonization Society to the Auxiliary Societies and the people of the United States. Washington, 1820.

280. Essay on Slavery and the Commerce of the human species, translated from a Latin dissertation, which obtained the first prize in the University of Cambridge in the year 1785. London, 1786.

244, 698. A summary of the evidence produced before the committee of the Privy Council and before a committee of the House of Commons relating to the slave trade. London, 1792.

---

8. STATISTICS.

Connecticut. 522. Statistical account of the city of Newhaven, by T. Dwight. Newhaven, 1811.

Denmark, see *Russia*.

District of Columbia. 836. A chronographical and statistical description of the District of Columbia, by D. B. Warden. Paris, 1816.

Europe. 7. *F. Beaufort, (M.)* Le grand portefeuille politique, en 19 tableaux, contenant les constitutions, population, revenus, dépenses, &c. des divers États de l'Europe. Dédié aux hommes d'état. Paris, 1789.

France. 389. Letters concerning the present state of the French Nation, by Arthur Young. London, 1769.

405. Recherches sur la population de la France, par M. Moheau. Paris, 1778.

1027½. Notice sur l'exposition des produits de l'industrie Française. Paris, 1806.

1041. Statistique générale & particulière de la France & de ses colonies, par M. Peuchet, & autres, 7 vol. Paris, 1807.

1028. De l'industrie Française, par M. Chaptal, 2 vol. Paris, 1819.

318. Résultats d'un ouvrage intitulé "De la richesse territoriale du Royaume de France, par M. Lavoisier." Paris, 1819.

15, 1064. Exposé des moyens de mettre en valeur la Guiane, par M. Lescallier. Paris, 1798.

Great Britain. 967. Present state of England, by John Chamberlayne. London, 1707.

113. *F.* Exports and imports of England from 1698 to 1762. MS.

38. *Q.* Estimate of the comparative strength of Great Britain, by George Chalmers. London, 1782.

426. *Q.* A treatise on the wealth, power, and resources of the British Empire, by P. Colquhoun. London, 1815.

965. On the police of London, by the same. Philadelphia, 1798.

997. View of the rising resources of Bengal, by Thomas Law. London, 1792.

Ireland. 1317. Statistical Observations on the County of Kilkenny, by William Tighe, 1802.

1318. ——— ——— on the County of Armagh, by Sir Charles Coote, 1802.

1319. ——— ——— on the County of Wexford, by Robert Fraser, 1807.

1320. ——— ——— on the County of Kildare, by T. J. Rawson, 1807.

1321. Statistical Observations on the County of Cork, by Rev. H. Townsend, 1810.

Maine. 810. Statistical View of the province of Maine, by Moses Greenleaf. Boston, 1816.

Netherlands. 1051. Observations upon the United Provinces of the Netherlands, by Sir William Temple, 2 vols. London, 1705.

1080. Etat présent des Indes Hollandaises. Batavia, *(no date.)*

N. York. 739. A Brief Topographical and Statistical Manual of the State of New York. Albany, 1811.

730. A Topographical and Statistical Account of the State of New York. New York, 1822.

729. A Review of the Administration and Civil Police of the State of New York, from 1807 to 1819, by Ferris Pell. New York, 1819.

Peru. 100. Guia politica, ecclesiastica y militar do Virreynato de Peru. Lima, 1813.

Russia. 1059. Statistische Schilderung von Russland, von B. F. T. Hermann. St. Petersburg, 1790.

1082. Observations on the present state of Russia, Denmark, and Switzerland. London, 1784.

Spain. 67. *Q*. Estado de la poblacion de España, 1793.
Switzerland, see *Russia*.

United States. 632, 720. Census of the United States for 1790.
221. *F*. ——— ——— for 1800, 1810, 1820, 3 vols.
877. List of the Post Offices of the United States, 1808, 1811, 3, 7, 1319.
844½. View of the United States of America, by Tench Coxe. Philadelphia, 1794.
4. View of the United States of America, by W. H. Winterbotham, 4 vols. New York, 1796.
696. A Statistical Manual for the United States, by Samuel Blodget. Washington, 1806.
604. A Brief Review of the policy and resources of the United States, by Robert Hare. Philadelphia, 1810.
882. A Statistical view of the Commerce of the United States, by Timothy Pitkin. Hartford, (C.) 1816.
294. *Q*. Statistical Annals, containing views on the population, commerce, &c. of the United States of America, founded on Official Documents, from 1789 to 1818, by Adam Seybert. Philadelphia, 1818.
884. Resources of the United States of America, by John Bristed. New York, 1818.
43. Description Statistique, Historique & Politique des Etats Unis, par D. B. Warden, 5 vol. Paris, 1820.

Virginia. 839. Notes on the State of Virginia, by Thomas Jefferson, 1782.

XVI. LOCAL AND OCCASIONAL POLITICS;

INCLUDING TRACTS, ESSAYS, PAMPHLETS, SERMONS, &c.

(In order of dates.)

1598.

1441. Pseudo Fridericus; Comœdia Nova, quâ recensetur Historia impostoris cujusd. Fridericum II. Cæsarem se ementiti, &c. auctore Johanne Hildebrando Virtebirgio. Tubingæ, 1598.

1652.

1442½. Johannis Miltoni Defensio contrà Salmasium. London, 1652.

1711.

1409. High Church displayed, or history of the affair of Dr. Sacheverell. London, 1711.

1747.

631, 672. Plain Truth, or serious considerations on the present state of the City of Philadelphia and Province of Pennsylvania, by B. Franklin. 1747.

1748.

613. Necessary Truth, in reply to Plain Truth, or considerations for the inhabitants of Pennsylvania. Philadelphia, 1748.

1754.

672. Serious Considerations on the present state of the affairs of the Northern Colonies. New York, 1754.

630. Sermon preached before the Legislature of Massachusetts on the 29th of May, 1764, by Jonathan Mayhew. Boston, 1754.

618. A Sermon preached before the Governor and both Houses of Assembly of Maryland at Annapolis, December 13, 1754, by James Sterling. Annapolis, 1755.

1755.

670. Observations on the late and present conduct of the French, with regard to their encroachments upon the British colonies in North America. Boston, 1755.

384, 16. Q. Answer to a letter representing the impropriety of sending forces to Virginia, &c. by Lewis Evans. Philadelphia, 1756.

677. A Sermon on occasion of the present encroachments on the French, preached at Philadelphia, June 22, 1755, by the Rev. Mr. Reading. Philadelphia, 1755.

680. A Sermon preached at Philadelphia the 24th January, 1755, before the Free Masons, by William Smith. Philadelphia.

677. A Sermon preached at Carlisle, soon after General Braddock's defeat, by Thomas Barton. Philadelphia, 1755.

705. A Sermon preached at Newburyport, May 22, 1755, at the desire, and in the audience of Colonel Moses Titcomb and many others inlisted under him, and going with him in an expedition against the French, by John Lowell. Newburyport, 1806.

682. *Keewanaia che Keeteru;* a true relation of a bloody battle fought between George and Lewis in the year 1755. Printed, 1756.

674. A brief state of the province of Pennsylvania.

" A brief view of the conduct of Pennsylvania for the year 1755, being sequel to a late well-known pamphlet, intituled, A brief state of Pennsylvania. London, 1756.

1757.

384, 23. Q. The Curse of Meroz, or the danger of neutrality in the cause of God and our Country, a sermon preached at Nottingham, Pennsylvania, 1757, by Samuel Finley. Philadelphia, 1757.

677. A sermon preached in Lewis, Delaware, on July 8, 1757, being the day appointed for fasting, by Matthew Harris. Philadelphia, 1757.

" A Sermon preached in Philadelphia, April 5, 1757, to the first battalion of his Majesty's Royal American Regiment, by William Smith. Philadelphia, 1757.

1758.

56. The conduct of Major Shirley fairly stated. London, 1758.

1759.

626. An enquiry into the causes of the alienation of the Delaware and Shawanese Indians from the British interest, and into the measures taken for recovering their friendship, by Charles Thompson. London, 1759.

384, 16. Q. Inquiry concerning the trade, commerce, and policy of America. London, 1759.

1760.

617. The late regulations respecting the British colonies considered. About 1760.

1761.

982. Consideration on the present German war. London, 1761.

245. The interest of Great Britain considered with regard to her colonies, and the acquisitions of Canada and Guadaloupe. London, 1761.

1762.

384, 10. Q. Coloniæ Angl. Illustratæ, or Plantation of colonies by the British in America, with the rights of the colonies. London, 1762.

1763.

1743. Political Controversy, or Weekly Magazine of ministerial and antiministerial Essays, by J. C. Wilkes. 5 vols. London, 1762–3.

1764.

645. Remarks on a late protest against the appointment of B. Franklin an agent for this Province, by B. Franklin. Philadelphia, 1764.

" 682. An answer to B. Franklin's remarks on a late protest. Philadelphia, 1764.

682. Cool thoughts on the present situation of our public affairs, in a letter to a friend in the country. Philadelphia, 1764.

" The Plain Dealer, or remarks on Quaker politics in Pennsylvania, No. 3. Philadelphia, 1764.

624, 682. An address to the freeholders and inhabitants of the province of Pennsylvania in answer to a paper called the Plain Dealer. Philadelphia, 1764.

740. The Quaker Unmasked, or Plain Truth, humbly addressed to the consideration of all the freemen of Pennsylvania. Philadelphia, 1764.

613, 682. The Quaker Vindicated, or observations on a late pamphlet, entitled the Quaker Unmasked, or Plain Truth. 1764.

740. Looking-Glass for Presbyterians, or a brief examination of their loyalty, merit, and other qualifications for government, with some animadversions on the Quaker Unmasked. Philadelphia, 1764.

645. Dialogue containing some reflections on the late declaration and remonstrance of the back inhabitants of the province of Pennsylvania. Philadelphia, 1764.

682. A battle! a battle! a battle of squirt, where no man is killed, and no man is hurt! to the tune of three blue beans in a blue bladder; rattle bladder, rattle. *(In verse.)* 1764.

682. King Wampum, or harm watch, harm catch. Philadelphia, 1764.

681. The conduct of the Paxton men impartially represented. Philadelphia, 1764.

740. Paxtoniade, a poem, by Christopher Gymnast, with the prolegomena and exercitations of Scriblerus. Philadelphia, 1764.

1765.

682, 711. A humble attempt at scurrility, in imitation of those great masters of the art, the Rev. Dr. S—th, &c. being a full answer to the observations on Mr. H—s's advertisement, by Jack Retort. *(William T. Franklin.)* Quilsylvania, 1765.

" An address to the Rev. Mr. Allison, the Rev. Mr. Ewing, &c. being a vindication of the Quakers against certain aspersions, &c. 1765.

617. The claims of the Colonies to an exemption from internal taxes, imposed by authority of Parliament, examined. London, 1765.

20. Q. Considerations on the propriety of imposing taxes on the British Colonies, by Daniel Delany. Annapolis, 1765.

592. Same work reprinted. London, 1766.

1766.

593. A short history of the conduct of the present Ministry with regard to the American Stamp-Act. London, 1766.

670. The importance of the Colonies of North America and the interest of Great Britain with regard to them considered, together with remarks on the stamp-duty, by N. Ray. London, 1766.

682. Considerations upon the rights of the Colonists to the privileges of British subjects. New York, 1766.

644, 723. Four dissertations on the reciprocal advantages of a perpetual union between Great Britain and her American Colonies, written for Mr. Sargent's Prize Medal. Philadelphia, 1766.

592. The late occurrences in North America, and policy of G. Britain, considered. London, 1766.

592. The late regulations respecting the British Colonies on the Continent of America considered, by John Dickinson. Philadelphia, 1766.

618. Some important observations on account of the particular circumstances of the present day. Newport, (R. I.) 1766.

592. An application of some general political rules to the present state of Great Britain, Ireland, and America, in a letter to the Earl Temple. London, 1766.

597. An address to the Committee of Correspondence in Barbadoes, occasioned by a late letter from them to their agent in London. Philadelphia, 1766.

1767.

593. The conduct of the late administration examined relative to the American Stamp-Act, with an appendix, containing original and authentic documents. London, 1767.

592. Two papers on the subject of taxing the British Colonies in America. London, 1767.

1768.

596, 723, 725. Letters from a farmer in Pennsylvania to the inhabitants of the British Colonies, by John Dickinson. Philadelphia, 1768.

593. The true sentiments of America. London, 1768.

676. A letter to the Bishop of Landaff, occasioned by some passages in his sermon on the 20th of February, 1767, in which the American Colonies are loaded with great and undeserved reproach, by William Livingston. New York, 1768.

679. A vindication of the Bishop of Landaff's sermon from the gross misrepresentations, &c. contained in William Livingston's letter to him. New York, 1768.

598. The administration of the Colonies, wherein their rights and constitution are discussed and stated, by Thomas Pownall, 4th ed. London, 1768.

For the second part to this work see under the year 1774.

1769.

673. The case of Great Britain and America, addressed to the King and both houses of Parliament, by B. Franklin. London, 1769.

593. A vindication of the British Colonies, by James Otis. Boston, 1769.

592. An enquiry into the rights of the British Colonies, by Richard Bland. Williamsburg, 1769.

594. The controversy between Great Britain and her Colonies reviewed, the several pleas of the colonies stated and considered, with an appendix. London, 1769.

716. Observations on the late state of the nation. London, 1769.

681. Sermons to Asses, 3d edit. Philadelphia, 1769.

1770.

589. Collection of scarce and interesting tracts, on political and commercial subjects, from 1763 to 1770, 4 vols. London, 1788.

716. The False Alarm. London, 1770.

" Letter to Lord Mansfield to prove the rights of the people of America to petitioning to the King, by John Missing. London, 1770.

595. A short narrative of the horrid massacre in Boston, perpetrated in the evening of the 5th of March, 1770. Boston, 1770.

716. Additional observations to the above. Boston, 1770.

711. The Partnership, or the history of the rise and progress of the Pennsylvania Chronicle, by William Goddard, Nos. 1 & 2. Philadelphia, 1770.

1773.

592. Collection of tracts on the subject of taxing the British Colonies, 4 vols. London, 1773.

617, 726. A sermon preached in London before the Society for the propagation of the Gospel in foreign parts, at their anniversary meeting on the 19th of February, 1773, by Jonathan, Lord Bishop of St. Asaph. London, 1773.

1774.

616. Speech of Edmund Burke on American Taxation. London, 1774.

617, 674, 726. A true state of the Proceedings in the Parliament of Great Britain, and in the Province of Massachusetts Bay, relative to the giving and granting the money of the people of that province and of all America, in the House of Commons in which they are not represented. London, 1774.

616, 726. A Declaration of the People's natural right to a share in the Legislature, which is the fundamental principle of the British Constitution of State, by Granville Sharp. London, 1774.

726. The American Querist, or some questions proposed relative to the present disputes between Great Britain and her American colonies, by a North American. 1774.

660. Rules for reducing a great empire to a small one, by B. Franklin. London, 1793, *(Reprinted.)*

269, 596, 726. Considerations on the nature and the extent of the Legislative authority of the British Parliament. Philadelphia, 1774.

674. The true interest of Great Britain set forth, in regard to the colonies, by J. Tucker. Norfolk, 1774.

597. A Letter to Dr. Tucker on his proposal of a separation between Great Britain and her American colonies. London, 1774.

597, 726. Four Tracts on Political and Commercial subjects, by Josiah Tucker. Glocester, 1774.

" The rights of the British Legislature to tax the American colonies vindicated, and the means of asserting that right proposed. London, 1774.

598. An argument in defence of the exclusive right claimed by the colonies to tax themselves. London, 1774.

599, 711, 716, 725. A Summary View of the rights of British America, set forth in some resolutions intended for the inspection of the present Delegates of the People of Virginia now in convention. London, 1774, Williamsburg, 1774, Philadelphia, 1774.

598. The Administration of the British colonies, Part II. wherein a line of government between the Supreme Jurisdiction of Great Britain and the rights of the Colonies is drawn, and a plan of pacification suggested. With an appendix, &c. by Thomas Pownall. London, 1774.
For the first part of this work, see above, sub anno 1768.

599. Great Britain's right to tax her colonies, placed in the clearest light, by a Swiss. London, 1774.

674. America Vindicated from the high charge of ingratitude and rebellion, by a friend to both countries. Devizes, 1774.

614, 674. A Friendly Address to all reasonable Americans on the subject of our political confusions. New York, 1774.

724. Strictures on a pamphlet entitled a Friendly Address to all reasonable Americans, on the subject of our political confusions, addressed to the People of America. Philadelphia, 1774.

597. American Independence, the interest and glory of Great Britain, in a series of letters to the Legislature. London, 1774.

599. The interest of the Merchants and Manufacturers of Great Britain in the present contest with the colonies stated and considered. London, 1774.

617. Considerations, &c. on American rights. London, 1774.

595. Observations on several Acts of Parliament, (Boston Port Bill, &c.) *(No imprint.)*

727. The causes of the present distractions in America, explained in two letters to a merchant in London, by F—— B——. 1774.

726. A Letter from a Virginian to the Members of the Congress to be held at Philadelphia, on the 1st of September, 1774.

727. A full vindication of the measures of the Congress, from the calumnies of their enemies, in answer to a letter under the signature of A. W. Farmer. New York, 1774.

673. Strictures on a pamphlet entitled, an Address to all reasonable Americans on the subject of our political confusions. Philadelphia, 1774.

725. Political reflections submitted to the consideration of the British colonies by Richard Wells. Philadelphia, 1774.

716. A new essay, (by the Pennsylvania Farmer,) on the Constitutional power of Great Britain over the colonies in America. Philadelphia, 1774.

726. Americanus examined, and his principles compared with those of the approved advocates of America, by a Pennsylvanian. Philadelphia, 1774.

596. An Essay on the Constitutional power of Great Britain over the colonies in America, with the resolves of the Committee for the province of Pennsylvania, and their instructions to their representatives in Assembly, by William Smith and John Dickinson. Philadelphia, 1774.

727. An Address occasioned by the late invasion of the liberties of the American colonies by the British Parliament, delivered at Charleston, South Carolina, by William Tennant. Philadelphia, 1774.

596, 672, 726. Considerations on the measures carrying on, with respect to the British colonies in America. Philadelphia, 1774.

726. Observations on the late popular measures, offered to the serious consideration of the sober inhabitants of Pennsylvania, by John Drinker. Philadelphia, 1774.

681, 726. A Speech intended to have been spoken on the bill for altering the charter of the colony of Massachusetts Bay, by Jonathan Shipley. Lancaster, 1774.

726. An Oration delivered March 5, 1774, at the request of the inhabitants of the town of Boston, to commemorate the bloody tragedy of the 5th of March, 1770, by John Hancock. [illegible]

646. A dialogue between a southern delegate and his spouse, on his return from the grand Continental Congress, a fragment inscribed to the married ladies of America, by Mary V. V. 1774.

683. O tempora, O mores! or the best New-Year's gift for a Prime Minister, by William Scott, dedicated to Lord North. Philadelphia, 1774.

725. An address to protestant dissenters of all denominations on the approaching election of members of Parliament, with respect to the state of public liberty in general, and of American affairs in particular, by Joseph Priestley. London, 1774.

599. The justice and policy of the late act of Parliament for making more effectual provision for the government of the province of Quebec, written by Knox, under Secretary of State of G. Britain. London, 1774.

" A letter to the Earl of Chatham on the Quebec bill. London, 1774.

645. The singular and diverting behaviour of Dr. Marriot, his Majesty's Advocate-General, who was examined concerning the religion and laws of Quebec, on the 3d of June, 1774. Philadelphia, 1774.

612. Considerations on the present state of Virginia. 1774.

716. Additional preface to a pamphlet entitled, An appeal to the public, on the subject of the national debt. London, 1774.

672. A few more words on the freedom of the press, addressed by the Printer to the friends of Liberty in America. 1774.

740. A pretty story, written in the year of our lord 2774, by Peter Grievous, A. B. C. D. E. Philadelphia, 1774.

612. The poor man's advice, a ballad. New York, 1774.

614. The American Crisis, No. 1 a 11, by Thomas Paine.

" Strictures on the above. Philadelphia, 1774.

1775.

727. A plan of a proposed union between Great Britain and the American Colonies, which was produced by one of the delegates from Pennsylvania in Congress. 1775.

716. A speech intended to have been delivered in the House of Commons, in support of the petition from the General Congress at Philadelphia. London, 1775.

727. What think ye of the Congress now? or an enquiry how far the Americans are bound to abide by, and execute the decisions of the late Congress? New York, 1775.

617. The policy of Great Britain to restrain and restrict the colonial trade.

86½. Remarks on the principal acts of the 13th Parliament of Great Britain, by the author of Letters concerning the present state of Poland, *(ascribed to Gov. Pownall.)* London, 1775.

612. A candid examination of the mutual claims of Great Britain and the Colonies, with a plan of accommodation on constitutional principles, by William Rogers. New York, 1775.

617. Taxation tyranny, addressed to Samuel Johnson. London, 1775.

716. A letter to Samuel Johnson, occasioned by his late political publications, with an appendix containing some observations on a pamphlet lately published by Dr. Shebbeare. London, 1775.

661. The sentiments of a foreigner on the disputes of Great Britain with America, translated from the French. Philadelphia, 1775.

616, 646, 672. An appeal to the justice and interests of the people of Great Britain in the present disputes with America. London, 1775.

337. A second appeal on the same. London, 1775.

646, 672, 711. The address of the people of Great Britain to the inhabitants of America, by John Dalrymple. London, 1775.

727. The Patriot of North America, a (poetical) sketch with explanatory notes. New York, 1775.

724. Remarks on the Patriot, including some hints respecting the Americans, with an address to the electors of Great Britain. London, 1775.

725. The Middle Line: or an attempt to furnish some hints for ending the differences subsisting between Great Britain and the colonies. Philadelphia, 1775.

674, 727. The Political Family, or a discourse pointing out the reciprocal advantages which flow from an uninterrupted union between Great Britain and her American Colonies, by Isaac Hunt. Philadelphia, 1775.

716. Thoughts upon the present contest between administration and the British Colonies in America, addressed to the merchants of the city of London and all the sea ports and manufacturing towns in Great Britain and Ireland. London, 1775.

727. A candid examination of the mutual claims of Great Britain and the Colonies, with a plan of accommodation on constitutional principles. New York, 1775.

726. An alarm to the legislature of the province of New York, occasioned by the present political disturbances. New York, 1775.

626. Facts and observations vindicating the absolute rights of the Indian nations or tribes of America to their respective countries. London, 1775.

612. The first book of the American Chronicles of the Time, chap. II. Published about 1775.

727. An earnest address to such of the people called Quakers as are sincerely desirous of supporting and maintaining the Christian testimony of their ancestors. Philadelphia, 1775.

727. The testimony of the people called Quakers, given forth by a meeting of the representatives of said people in Pennsylvania and New Jersey, held at Philadelphia the 24th of January, 1775.

727. An epistle from the meeting for sufferings, held in Philadelphia for Pennsylvania, the 5th of January, 1775.

644. Sermon preached before the Congress of the Colony of the Massachusetts Bay, on the 31st of May, 1775, being the day of election, by Samuel Langdon. Watertown, 1775.

612, 675, 683. A sermon on the American affairs, preached at Philadelphia, June 23, 1775, by William Smith. Philadelphia, 1775.

675, 683. A sermon preached at Philadelphia, on July 20, 1775, being the day of a general fast, by Thomas Combe. Philadelphia, 1775.

689. The American Vine, a sermon preached before the Congress at Philadelphia, July 20th, 1775, by J. Duché. Philadelphia, 1775.

683. Defensive war in a just cause sinless, a sermon preached on the day of the Fast at Tredyffryn, in Chester County, by David Jones. Philadelphia, 1775.

" A sermon preached at Yorktown, on July 20, 1775, being the day for a general fast, by Daniel Batwell. Philadelphia, 1775.

" The duty of standing fast in our spiritual and temporal liberties, a sermon preached in Philadelphia, July 7, 1775, by J. Duché. Philadelphia, 1775.

339. Schreiben des Evangelisch-Lutherisch und Reformirter, Kirchen-Raths, wie auch die beamten der Deutschen Gesellschaft in der stadt Philadelphia an die Deutschen Einwohner der Provinzen von New York und Nord Carolina. Philadelphia, 1775.

1776.

614. Common Sense, addressed to the inhabitants of America, by Thomas Paine, 2d ed. Philadelphia, Bradford, 1776.

614½. Same work, English edition. London, 1791.

614, 673. Plain Truth, addressed to the inhabitants of America, containing remarks on a late pamphlet, entitled Common Sense, by Candidus. Philadelphia, 1776.

646. Remarks on a late pamphlet, entitled Plain Truth, by Rusticus. Philadelphia, 1776.

614. The true interest of America, impartially stated in certain stricture on a pamphlet entitled Common Sense. Philadelphia, 1776.

" The Deceiver Unmasked, or loyalty and interest united, in answer to a pamphlet entitled Common Sense. Philadelphia, 1776.

616, 629, 748. Observations on the nature of civil liberty, the principles of government, and the justice and policy of the war with America, by Richard Price. London, 1776.

740. Thoughts on government, applicable to the present state of the American colonies, in a letter from a gentleman to his friend. Supposed to be written by John Adams. Philadelphia, 1776.

644. The rights of Great Britain asserted against the claims of America, being an answer to the declaration of the General Congress; to which is now added, a refutation of Dr. Price's State of the National Debt. London, 1776.

711. The plea of the Colonies on the charges brought against them by Lord Mansfield and others, in a letter to his Lordship, by a native of Pennsylvania. London, printed 1776. Philadelphia, reprinted 1777.

612. Observations on the reconciliation of Great Britain and the Colonies. Philadelphia, 1776.

612. The Patriots of North America, a sketch with explanatory notes. New York, 1775.

672. The rights of Great Britain asserted against the claims of America, being an answer to the declaration of the General Congress, said to be written by Lord G. Germaine. London, 1776.

612. Address of a Carolinian to Admiral Howe and General Howe, on their proclamation. Charleston, 1776.

661. Four letters on interesting subjects on the American revolution. Philadelphia, 1776.

6. Les Droits de la G. Bretagne établis contre les prétentions des Américains, par M. Fréville. La Haye, 1776.

" Exposé des Droits des Colonies Britanniques. Amsterd. 1776.

" Justification de la résistance des colonies Américaines, &c. Leide, 1776.

683. The Church's flight into the wilderness, an address on the times, by Samuel Sherwood. New York, 1776.

675. An Oration in memory of General Montgomery, and of the officers and soldiers who fell with him, December 31, 1775, delivered the 19th February, 1776, by William Smith. Philadelphia, 1776.

1777.

269. Address of the Convention of the Representatives of the State of New York to their constituents. Philadelphia, 1777.

661. Observations upon the present government of Pennsylvania in four letters addressed to the people of Pennsylvania, by B. Rush. Philadelphia, 1777.

672. A Letter to the English nation on the present war with America, by an officer returned from that service. London, 1777.

644. Discourse addressed to his majesty's provincial troops in camp at King's-Bridge, the 28th, September, 1777, by Samuel Seabury. New York.

740. The prowess of the Whig club, and the manœuvres of Legion. Baltimore, 1777.

1778.

245. Thoughts on the present state of affairs with America, and the means of conciliation, by William Pultney. London, 1778.

681. Thoughts on the letter of E. Burke to the Sheriffs of Bristol on the affairs of America, by the Earl of Abingdon. Oxford, 1778.

245, 630. A Serious Address to such of the people called Quakers on the continent of North America, as profess scruples relative to the present government, 2d edition. Philadelphia, 1778.

328. Mystagogus Candidus. Considerations on the mode and terms of a Treaty of Peace with America. London, 1778.

6. Le vœu de toutes les nations & l'interêt de toutes les puissances dans l'abaissement de la G. Bretagne, 1778.

1779.

619, 670. Remarks on Governor Johnstone's speech in parliament, with a collection of all the letters and authentic papers relative to his proposition to engage the interest of one of the Delegates of the State of Pennsylvania, in the Congress of the United States of America, to promote the views of the British Commissioners. Philadelphia, 1779.

616. Anticipation, containing the substance of his majesty's speech to both Houses of Parliament, on the opening of the approaching session. London, 1779.

740. The Constitution and frame of Government of the free and independent State and Commonwealth of New Ireland. 1779.

612. A Discourse delivered at Easton, 17th of October, 1779, to the officers and soldiers of the Western army, by Israel Evans. Philadelphia, 1779.

6. Lettres d'un Membre du Congrès Américain à divers Membres du Parlement d'Angleterre. Philadelphie, (Paris) 1779.

669. An Essay on Free Trade and Finance, offered to the consideration of the public, by a citizen of Philadelphia. Philadelphia, 1779.

" A second Essay on Free Trade and Finance, offered to the consideration of the public, by a citizen of Philadelphia. Philadelphia, 1779.

1308. Lettres sur la validité des mariages des Protestans. Londres, 1779.

1780.

618. Extract from a Letter written to the President of Congress, by A. Lee, in answer to a libel published in the Pennsylvania Gazette of the 5th of December, 1778, by Silas Deane. Philadelphia, 1780.

660. An Appeal to the people of Massachusetts State against arbitrary power. Boston, 1780.

673. Public Good, being an examination into the claim of Virginia to the vacant Western Territory, by Thomas Paine. Philadelphia, 1780.

669. A fifth Essay on Free Trade and Finance, offered to the consideration of the public, by a citizen of Philadelphia. Philadelphia, 1780.

1515, 30. Free Address to those who have petitioned for the repeal of the act in favour of the Roman Catholics, by Joseph Priestley. London, 1780.

1781.

614. On the Revolution of America, by the Abbé Raynal, translated from the French. Philadelphia, 1781.

660, 748. Observations on the nature and use of paper credit, and the peculiar advantages to be derived from it in North America, including proposals for founding a National Bank. Philadelphia, 1781.

1782.

335, 614, 669. Letter addressed to the Abbé Raynal on the affairs of North America, in which the mistakes of the Abbé's account of the revolution of America are corrected and cleared up, by Thomas Paine. Philadelphia, 1782.

335. Consolatory thoughts on American Independence, by a merchant. Edinburgh, 1782.

724. A representation on behalf of the people called Quakers, to the President and Executive Council, and the General Assembly of Pennsylvania. London, 1782.

1783.

343. Observations on the commerce of the American States with Europe and the West Indies; also, an Essay on Canon and Feudal Law, by John Adams. Philadelphia, 1783.

629. A memorial addressed to the Sovereigns of America, by T. Pownall. London, 1783.

335. Considerations on the provisional treaty with America, and the preliminary articles of peace with France and Spain. London, 1783.

245. The case and claim of the American loyalists impartially stated and considered. London, 1783.

" Address to the independent citizens of the United States of North America, by Silas Deane. 1783.

269. Consideration on the Society or Order of Cincinnati, by Cassius, (*Ædanus Burke.*) Philadelphia, 1783.

612. An address to the freemen of the state of South Carolina on various political subjects, ascribed to Ædanus Burke, one of the Chief Justices of South Carolina. Philadelphia, 1783.

660. Remarks on a late publication, with a short address to the people of Pennsylvania, by J. Reed. Philadelphia, 1783.

613, 669. Reply to Gen. J. Reed's remarks on a late publication in the Independent Gazetteer, by John Cadwalader. Philadelphia, 1783.

267. The United States elevated to glory and honour, a sermon preached May 8, 1783, before the Governor and General Assembly of the state of Connecticut, (*Historical*) by Ezra Stiles. Newhaven, 1783.

675. The divine goodness displayed in the American revolution, a sermon preached at New York, Dec. 11, 1783, by John Rodgers. New York, 1784.

1302. Tracts published by the Society for constitutional information. London, 1783.

1784.

87. Considerations on the present situation of Great Britain and the United States of America. with a view to their future commercial connexions, by Richard Champion. London, 1784.

87½. Observations on the commerce of the United States, by Lord Sheffield. Dublin, 1784.

245, 672. A letter from an American to a member of Parliament on the subject of restraining proclamation, and containing strictures on Lord Sheffield's pamphlets on the commerce of the American States, by William Bingham. London, 1784.

645. Considerations on the present state of the intercourse between his Majesty's sugar Colonies and the dominions of the United States of America, at a meeting of the West India planters and merchants. London, 1784.

673. A letter from Phocion to the considerate citizens of New York, on the politics of the day. New York, 1784.

740, 747. Considerations upon the present Test-Law of Pennsylvania, addressed to the Legislature and freemen of the state. Philadelphia, 1784.

740. A candid examination of the address of the minority of the Council of Censors to the people of Pennsylvania, together with remarks upon the danger and inconvenience of the principal defects of the Constitution of Pennsylvania, by one of the majority. Philadelphia, 1784.

748. Proceedings of the Pennsylvania Society of the Cincinnati; to which is prefixed, the general institution of the Order, as originally framed, and afterwards altered at the general meeting in May, 1784. Philadelphia, 1785.

660. Address to every freeman, but especially to the free citizens of Pennsylvania, concerning a tyrannical embargo now laid upon the free sale of books by auction, by Bell. Philadelphia, 1784.

629. Remarks on a late pamphlet, entitled, A vindication of Governor Parr (of Nova Scotia) and his Council, &c. by a consistent loyalist. London, 1784.

748. Considerations on the Order of Cincinnatus; to which are added, several original papers relative to that institution, by the Count de Mirabeau. Translated from the French.

249. Tableau de la situation actuelle des Anglais dans les Indes Orientales, par Brissot de Warville. Londres, 1784.

1785.

669. A summary explanation of the principles of Mr. Pitt's intended bill for amending the representation of the people in Parliament, by C. Wyvill. London, 1785.

748. Observations on the importance of the American Revolution, and the means of making it a benefit to the world, by Richard Price. Philadelphia, 1785.

739. Concise View of the controversy between the proprietors of East and West Jersey. Philadelphia, 1785.

673. Remarks on a pamphlet, entitled, Considerations on the Bank of North America. Philadelphia, 1785.

270. Considerations on the Bank of North America, (ascribed to Gouverneur Morris.) Philadelphia, 1785.

270, 740. Address to the Assembly of Pennsylvania on the abolition of the Bank of North America. Philadelphia, 1785.

673. Cool thoughts on the subject of the Bank, addressed to the Legislature of Pennsylvania. 1785.

1786.

673. The Commercial conduct of the United States considered, by a citizen of New York. New York, 1786.

748. The true interest of the United States, and particularly of Pennsylvania, considered, with respect to the advantage resulting from a State paper money, with some observations on the subject of a Bank, by an American. Philadelphia, 1786.

270, 673. The true interest of the United States with respect to a State paper money, by an American. Philadelphia, 1786.

614. Dissertation on Government, the affairs of the Bank, and paper money, by Thomas Paine. Philadelphia, 1786.

660. Reasons for repealing the act of the Legislature of Pennsylvania, for supporting and incorporating the Bank of North America, by a citizen of Philadelphia. Philadelphia, 1786.

384, 2. Q. Observations on Mr. Pitt's plan for reducing the National Debt, by Charles Earl Stanhope. London, 1786.

1787.

674, 748. A View of the proposed Constitution of the United States as agreed to by the Convention held at Philadelphia, 17th of September, 1787, compared with the present Confederation, by J. Nicholson. Philadelphia, 1787.

660. Observations leading to a fair examination of the system of Government proposed by the late Convention, 1787.

" An Examination into the leading principles of the Federal Constitution proposed by the late Convention held at Philadelphia. Philadelphia, 1787.

245. An Enquiry into the principles on which a Commercial System for the United States of America should be founded, by R. Aitkin. Philadelphia, 1787.

258. A short view of the political state of Great Britain, at the year 1787. Dublin, 1787.

660. An Essay on the Domestic Debt of the United States of America, by Mathew M'Connell. Philadelphia, 1787.

1788.

715, 935. The Letters of Fabius on the Federal Constitution, written by John Dickinson, in 1788. Philadelphia, 1797.

275, 673. A View of the principles, operations, and probable effect of the Funding System of Pennsylvania. Philadelphia, 1788.

312. The Prospect before us, being a series of papers upon the great question, (the appointment of a regent,) which now agitates the public mind. London, 1788.

277. Comparative Statement of the two Bills for the better Government of the British Possessions in India, brought into Parliament by Mr. Fox and Mr. Pitt, by R. B. Sheridan. Dublin, 1788.

317. Considérations sur la guerre actuelle des Turcs, par M. de Volney. Londres, 1788.

42. Considerations on the relative situation of France and the United States of America, by Brissot de Warville. London, 1788.

1789.

660. An Essay on the seat of the Federal Government and the exclusive jurisdiction of Congress over a ten miles district. Philadelphia, 1789.

248, 721. A Discourse on the love of our country, delivered on November 4, 1789, to the Society for commemorating the Revolution in Great Britain, by Richard Price. London, 1789.

1790.

660. A Plea for the old soldiers, or an essay to demonstrate that the soldiers and other public creditors, who really and actually supported the burden of the late war, have not been paid! ought to be paid! can be paid! and must be paid! Philadelphia, 1790.

1791.

720. Observations upon the Government of the United States of America, by James Sullivan. Boston, 1791.

297. Rights of Man, by Thomas Paine, Part I. London, 1791.

614½. Same work, Parts I. & II. London, 1792.

720. Letter addressed to the yeomanry of the United States, by a Farmer. Philadelphia, 1791.

260, 711. Examination of Sheffield's Observations on the Commerce of the United States, in seven letters. Philadelphia, 1791.

1515, 42. Letters to Mr. Burke on the revolution in France, &c. by Joseph Priestley. Birmingham, 1791.

719. Letters addressed to the yeomanry of the United States on the bank and funding system, by a farmer, (G. Logan.) Philadelphia, 1791—1793.

1792.

269. Five letters addressed to the yeomanry of the United States, containing some observations on the dangerous scheme of Governor Duer and Secretary Hamilton to establish national manufactures, by a farmer. Philadelphia, 1792.

660. The politics and views of a certain party displayed. 1792.

614½. Letters to Secretary Dundas and to Lord Onslow, by Thomas Paine. London, 1792.

601. Letters on the impolicy of a standing army in time of peace. London, 1792.

1793.

320. Answer to Paine's Rights of Man, by John Adams. Dublin, 1793.

715. Letters of Pacificus, written in justification of the President's proclamation of neutrality, published originally in the year 1793, (by Alexander Hamilton.) Philadelphia, 1796.

333, 715. Letters of Helvidius in reply to Pacificus on the President's proclamation of neutrality, published originally in 1793. Philadelphia, 1794—1796.

747. A serious expostulation with the members of the House of Representatives of the United States. Philadelphia, 1793.

970. Letters on the concert of Princes, and the dismemberment of Poland and France. London, 1793.

1794.

312. A view of the relative situation of Great Britain and the United States of America. London, 1794.

702. An address to the citizens of the district of York, in Virginia, by their representative John Page of Rosewell. 1794.

269, 334. An inquiry into the principles and tendency of certain public measures. Philadelphia, 1794.

720. The Political Fugitive, being a brief disquisition into the modern system of British politics, by John Butler. New York, 1794.

319. J. P. Brissot to his constituents on the situation of the National Convention, translated from the French. London, 1794.

666. Analyse des débats entre les accusateurs & les accusés dans l'affaire de la Colonie de Saint Domingue, par le Cit. Guillois. Paris, *(no date, supposed* 1794.)

1795.

591. American Remembrancer, or an impartial collection of essays, resolves, speeches, &c. relative, or having affinity, to the treaty with Great Britain, by Mathew Carey, 3 vols. Philadelphia, 1795.

702. Features of Mr. Jay's treaty; to which is annexed, a view of the commerce of the United States as it stands at present, and as it is fixed by Mr. Jay's treaty, ascribed to A. J. Dallas. Philadelphia, 1795.

641. Defence of the treaty entered into between the United States of America and Great Britain, as it has appeared in the papers under the signature of Camillus. New York, 1795.

269. Candid examinations of the objections to the treaty between Great Britain and the United States. Charleston, 1795.

641. Speech of Mr. J. Thompson at a meeting of the citizens of Petersburg, convened August 1, 1795, to debate on the pending treaty with Britain.

641. Letters of Franklin on the conduct of the executive, and the treaty negotiated by the Chief Justice of the United States with the Court of Great Britain. Philadelphia, 1795.

299, 722. The political progress of Great Britain from the revolution in 1688, to the present time, by James Thomson Callender. Philadelphia, 1795.

659, 722. A bone to gnaw for the democrats, or observations on a pamphlet, entitled "The political progress of Great Britain, by W. Cobbett. Philadelphia, 1795.

250, 325. Extract of a letter from a gentleman in America to a friend in England on the subject of emigration. 1795.

297. A letter addressed to the people of Piedmont on the advantages of the French revolution, by Joel Barlow. London, 1795.

969. Manual of Liberty, or testimonies in behalf of the rights of mankind. London, 1795.

319. Precis du Compte rendu a la Convention Nationale, par N. X. Ricard, commandant de St. Lucie, de sa conduite publique depuis son départ de France. Philadelphie, 1795.

320. A cursory view of the assignats and remaining resources of French Finance, by F. D. Ivernois, translated from the French. Dublin, 1795.

1796.

641. Address to the House of Representatives of the United States on Lord Grenville's treaty. Philadelphia, 1796.

641. Remarks on the treaty concluded between Lord Grenville and Mr. Jay, by a citizen of the United States. Philadelphia, 1796.

" A Review of the question in whom has the Constitution vested the Treaty power, by a Senator of the United States. Philadelphia, 1796.

659. A New Year's Gift to the Democrats, or observations on a pamphlet entitled, "A Vindication of Mr. Randolph's Resignation," by P. Porcupine, (William Cobbett.) Philadelphia, 1796.

" The Political Censor, or a review of the most interesting political occurrences relative to the United States, by the same. Philadelphia, 1796.

" The Political Censor for November, 1786. Containing observations on the insolent and seditious notes communicated to the people of the United States, by the late French Minister, Adet, by William Cobbett. Philadelphia, 1796.

" The Blue Shop, or impartial and humourous observations on the life and adventures of Peter Porcupine, by James Quicksilver. Philadelphia, 1796.

" British Honour and Humanity, or the Wonders of American Patience, by a friend to regular government. Philadelphia, 1796.

628. A Letter to G. Washington, President of the United States, containing strictures on his address of the 17th of September, 1796, notifying his relinquishment of the Presidential Office, by Jasper Dwight. Philadelphia, 1796.

614, 628. Letter to G. Washington, President of the United States, on affairs public and private, by Thomas Paine. Philadelphia, 1796.

715. A Poem on the President's, (G. Washington,) Farewell

Address, with a sketch of the character of his successor. Philadelphia.

655. The pretensions of Thomas Jefferson to the Presidency examined, and the charges against John Adams refuted, by Phocion. United States, 1796.

702, 733. The Federalist, containing some strictures upon a pamphlet, entitled, "The pretensions of T. Jefferson to the Presidency examined, and the charges against J. Adams, refuted." Philadelphia, 1796.

633. The Decline and Fall of the English system of Finance, by Thomas Paine. Philadelphia, 1796.

631½. Same work. Paris, 1796.

633. Strictures on E. Burke's Letter to a noble lord, on the attacks made upon him and his pension in the House of Lords, by the Duke of Bedford and Lord Lauderdale. London, 1796.

" A Letter from an Aristocrat to William Pitt, on the anti-aristocratical tendency of E. Burke's letter to a noble lord, with hints for amending Lord Grenville's and Mr. Pitt's patriotic bills. London, 1796.

1797.

628. Remarks occasioned by the late conduct of G. Washington as President of the United States, in 1796. Philadelphia, 1797.

715, 935. The Letters of Fabius in 1788, on the Federal Constitution, and in 1797, on the situation of public affairs, by J. Dickinson. Wilmington, 1797.

632. Observations on the despatch written the 16th of January, 1797, by Mr. Pickering, Secretary of State of the United States of America, to Mr. Pinckney, Minister Plenipotentiary of the United States, near the French Republic, by C. C. Tanguy de la Boissiere, translated from the French, by Samuel Chandler. Philadelphia, 1797.

655. Observations on certain documents contained in No. V. and VI. of the history of the United States for the year 1796, in which the charge of speculation against Alexander Hamilton is fully refuted, written by himself. Philadelphia, 1797.

345, 637. Reflections on Monroe's view of the conduct of the executive as published in the Gazette of the United States, under the signature of Scipio. 1797.

637, 703. What is our Situation? and what our Prospects? a few pages for Americans, by Joseph Hopkinson. 1797.

637. The Antigallican, or the lover of his own country, by a citizen of New England. Philadelphia, 1797.

659. Political Censor for March, 1797, by William Cobbett.

333. A View of the causes and consequences of the present war with France, by Thomas Erskine. Dublin, 1797.

296. Same work. Boston, 1797.

637. Same work. Philadelphia, 1797.

340. Same work, 22d edition. London, 1797.

91. View of the causes and consequences of the American Revolution, by Jonathan Boucher. London, 1797.

333. Agrarian Justice opposed to Agrarian Law and to Agrarian Monopoly, by Thomas Paine. Philadelphia.

1798.

614. An answer to Paine's Letter to General Washington, by P. Kennedy. Philadelphia, 1798.

611. Observation on the speech of A. Gallatin in the House of Representatives of the United States, on the foreign intercourse bill, by Alexander Addison. Washington, 1798.

659. The Democratic Judge, or the equal Liberty of the Press, as exhibited in the prosecution of William Cobbett, by P. Porcupine. Philadelphia, 1798.

719. Sedgwick & Co. or a Key to the Six per cent. Cabinet. Philadelphia, 1798.

642. Truth will out! The foul charges of the Tories against the Editor of the Aurora, repelled by positive proof and plain truth, and his base calumniators put to the shame. Philadelphia, 1798.

331. Copies of Original Letters recently written by persons in Paris to Dr. Priestley in America, taken on board of a neutral vessel. London, 1798.

1799.

655. Joel Barlow to his fellow citizens. Paris, 1799.

633, 646. A View of the New England Illuminati who are indefatigably engaged in destroying the Religion and Government of the United States. Philadelphia, 1799.

601, 728. A Letter from George Nicholas of Kentucky to his friend in Virginia, justifying the conduct of the Citizens of Kentucky, as to some of the late measures of the general Government. Lexington, 1799.

728. Three Letters written and originally published under the signature of a South Carolina Planter.

The first on the case of Jonathan Robbins decided under the 26th article of the treaty with Great Britain in the District Court of the United States.

The second on the recent captures of American vessels by British cruisers, contrary to the Laws of Nations, and treaty between the two countries.

The third on the right of expatriation, by Charles Pinckney. Philadelphia, 1799.

285. Reflexiones sobre el Comercio de España con sus colonias en America en tiempo de guerra, por el Marques de Casa-Yrujo. Philadelphia, 1799.

" Same work, English translation.

313. An Impartial View of the causes leading this country to the necessity of union. Dublin, 1799.

1800.

610, 646, 728. Letter from Alexander Hamilton concerning the public conduct and character of John Adams, President of the United States. New York, 1800.

632. A Letter to General Hamilton, occasioned by his letter to President Adams, by a Federalist. 1800.

655. An impartial review of the rise and progress of the controversy between the parties known by the names of the Federalists and Republicans, by Charles Pettit. Philadelphia, 1800.

646. Address to the people of the United States, with an epitome and vindication of the public life and character of Thomas Jefferson, by John Beckley. Philadelphia, 1800.

655. Address to the Federal Republicans of the State of New Jersey, on the choice for Representatives in the Congress of the United States. Trenton, 1800.

" Connecticut Republicanism, an Oration delivered in Newhaven, 1800, by Abraham Bishop. Philadelphia, 1800.

744. Analysis of the Report of the Committee of the Virginia Assembly on the proceedings of sundry of the other states, in answer to their resolutions, by Alexander Addison. Philadelphia, 1800.

341. On the character and conduct of Louis XVI. king of France, subsequent to the revolution of 1789, by William Belsham. London, 1800.

270. Observations on the Commerce of Spain, with her Colonies, in time of war, by a Spaniard. Philadelphia, 1800.

1801.

702. An Address to the Republican Citizens of New York, on the inauguration of Thomas Jefferson, President of the United States, delivered on the 4th of March, 1801, by Tunis Wortman. New York, 1801.

699. Letter to a Member of the General Assembly of Virginia, on the late conspiracy of the slaves, with a proposal for their colonization. Baltimore, 1801.

277. H. Dundas's Letter to the Court of Directors of the East India Company on the Indian debt, 30th June, 1801. London, 1801.

1802.

609. An Address to the People of the United States on the subject of a Committee of the House of Representatives, appointed to "examine and report, whether monies drawn from the Treasury have been faithfully applied to the objects for which they were appropriated," which report was presented 29th April, 1802, by Oliver Wolcott. Boston, 1802.

655. A Series of Letters addressed to Thomas Jefferson, President of the United States, concerning his official conduct and principles, with an appendix, by Tacitus. Philadelphia, 1802.

" Letters to Alexander Hamilton, being intended as a reply to a scandalous pamphlet published under the sanction, as it is presumed, of Mr. Hamilton, and signed Julius Philænus, by Tom Callender. New York, 1802.

719. Narrative of the suppression of John Wood's history of the administration of John Adams. New York, 1802.

702. A correct statement of various sources from which the history of the administration of John Adams was compiled, and the motives for its suppression, by John Wood. New York, 1802.

628. Letters from Thomas Paine to the Citizens of America, on his arrival from France, after an absence of fifteen years in Europe. Washington, 1802.

711. Same work, reprinted. London, 1804.

261, 702. An Oration delivered at Plymouth, December 22, 1802, at the anniversary commemoration of the first landing of our ancestors at that place, by John Quincy Adams. Boston, 1802.

604. An Address to the People of the United States on the policy of maintaining a permanent navy, by Charles Fenton Mercer. Philadelphia, 1802.

1803.

728. An address to the government of the United States on the cession of Louisiana to the French, and on the late breach of treaty by the Spaniards; including the translation of a memorial on the war of St. Domingo, and cession of the Mississippi to France, drawn up by a French Counsellor of State. Philadelphia, 1803.

739. Reflexions on the late cession of Louisiana to the United States, by Allan D. Magruder. Lexington, 1803.

702. An examination of the question, who is the writer of two forged letters, addressed to the President of the United States, attributed to John Rutledge. Washington, 1803.

820. Les cinq promesses. Tableau de la conduite du Gouvernement Consulaire envers la France, l'Angleterre, l'Italie, l'Allemagne & surtout la Suisse, par F. d'Ivernois. Londres, 1803.

1804.

664. The Constitutionalist, addressed to men of all parties in the United States, by an American. Philadelphia, 1804.

647. Memorial presented by the inhabitants of Louisiana to the Congress of the United States, translated from the French. Washington, 1804.

" View of the political and civil situation of Louisiana from the 13th of November, 1803, to the 1st of October, 1804, by a native, translated from the French. Philadelphia, 1804.

" Reflections on the cause of the Louisianians, submitted by their agents. 1804.

648. An address to the government of the United States on the cession of Louisiana, &c.

647. Analysis of the third article of the treaty of the cession of Louisiana. 1804.

609. A defence of the conduct of Commodore Morris during his command in the Mediterranean, with strictures on the report of the Court of Enquiry. New York, 1804.

269. Valedictory discourse delivered before the Cincinnati of Connecticut, July 4, 1804, by David Humphreys. Boston, 1804.

719. A reply to Aristides, by James Cheetham. New York, 1804.

605. Various pamphlets, by James Cheetham, John Wood, and others, respecting the conduct of Aaron Burr, the political party then called Clintonian, &c. *(Polemic.)* Philadelphia and New York, 1802—1804.

270. Answer to Lord Sheffield's pamphlet on the navigation system, by S. Cock. London, 1804.

1805.

661. Constitution of the Democratic Society of Friends to the people, established at Philadelphia, 1805. Philadelphia.

" The circular letter of the Society of "Friends of the People," addressed to the republicans of the state of Pennsylvania generally. Philadelphia, 1805.

" An address to the people of Pennsylvania on the approaching election for governor, in favour of James Ross. 1805.

628. Thomas Paine to the citizens of Pennsylvania on the proposal for calling a convention. Philadelphia, 1805.

282. War in disguise, or the frauds of the neutral flags, by Stephens. London, 1805.

" An examination of the British doctrine which subjects to capture a neutral trade not open in time of peace, by James Madison.

632. Samson against the Philistines, or the reformation of lawsuits, 2d edit. Philadelphia, 1805.

1806.

282. An answer to War in disguise, or remarks on the new doctrine of England concerning neutral trade, *(ascribed to Gouverneur Morris.)* New York, 1806.

328. The memorial of the merchants and traders of Baltimore against the British Orders in Council, *(ascribed to W. Pinkney.)* Baltimore, 1806.

281, 329. Observations on John Randolph's speech in Congress on the non-importation of British merchandise during the present war with America, by the author of "War in disguise." London, 1806.

604, 656. An inquiry into the present state of the foreign relations of the Union affected by the late measures of administration. Philadelphia, 1806.

275, 642. Cursory reflexions on the system of taxation established in the city of Philadelphia, with a brief sketch of its unequal and unjust operation, by M. Carey. Philadelphia, 1806.

88½. Strictures of the necessity of inviolably maintaining the navigation and colonial system of Great Britain, by Lord Sheffield. London, 1806.

656, 703. Thoughts on the subject of naval power in the United States of America, and on certain means of encouraging and protecting their commerce and manufactures, by Tench Coxe. Philadelphia, 1806.

604. An inquiry into the effects of our foreign carrying trade, by Columella. New York, 1806.

1807.

281. The dangers of the Country, by the author of War in disguise. Philadelphia, 1807.

703. An examination of the conduct of Great Britain respecting neutrals. Philadelphia, 1807.

631½. Experience the test of government, in 18 essays, written during the years 1805 and 1806, by a Senator of Pennsylvania. Philadelphia, 1807.

607. Peace without dishonour, war without hope, by J. Lowell. Boston, 1807.

609. To the People of the United States on the Convention of 1803, between the United States and France relative to the claims of America on France, by William M'Clure. Philadelphia, 1807.

329. A Narrative of Facts relative to the conduct of some of the Members of the Legislature of Pennsylvania, professing to be Democrats, at the election of a Senator. Philadelphia, 1807.

320. Les quatre conicidences de dates. Bruxelles, 1819.

This pamphlet relates to the events in Portugal in 1807, *and the emigration of the Portuguese Court to Brazil.*

1808.

281. An Enquiry into the causes and consequences of the Orders in Council, and examination of the conduct of Great Britain towards the neutral Commerce of America, by Alexander Baring. New York, 1808.

312. Britain independent of Commerce, by William Spence. London, 1808.

281. Speech of Henry Brougham in the House of Commons, April 1, 1808, in support of the petitions of London, &c. against the Orders in Council. Philadelphia, 1808.

743. View of the whole ground. A brief History of the proposed impeachment of the governor of Pennsylvania, Thomas M'Kean, to which is added his Message of January 28th, 1808, comprising a dignified and satisfactory defence. Lancaster, 1808.

" Interesting Correspondence between Governor Sullivan and Colonel Pickering, in which the latter vindicates himself against the groundless charges and insinuations, made by the Governor and others. Boston, 1808.

607. Letter of Timothy Pickering to his Constituents, exhibiting a view of the imminent danger of an unnecessary and ruinous war. Boston, 1808.

" Letter to Mr. Harrison Gray Otis, on the present state of our National affairs, with remarks upon T. Pickering's letter, by John Quincy Adams. Philadelphia, 1808.

702. A Letter to John Quincy Adams, occasioned by his letter to Mr. Otis, by Alfred. 1808.

607. Letter addressed to J. Madison, Secretary of State of the United States. *Printed in America,* 1808.

641. A view of the rights and wrongs, power and policy of the United States of America, by Charles Jared Ingersoll. Philadelphia, 1808.

604. The British Treaty, addressed to those members of Congress who have the sense to perceive, and the spirit to pursue the true interests of their country, by Charles B. Brown. New York, 1808.

664. An Address to the People of New England, by Algernon Sidney, (supposed by Gideon Granger,) Dec. 15, 1808. Washington, 1808.

607. The Honest Politician, Part I. by Luther Martin. Baltimore, 1808.

283. Exposition of the practices and machinations which led to the usurpation of the crown of Spain, by Don Pedro de Cevallos. Translated from the Spanish. New York, 1808.

1809.

664. Considerations on the Executive Government of the United States of America, by Augustus Woodward. Flatbush, (N. Y.) 1809.

607. Examination of the conduct of our executive towards France and Great Britain, by Senex. Baltimore, 1809.

637. Causes and queries on neutral rights, submitted to every citizen of the United States. New York, 1809.

664. Ten hints addressed to wise men, concerning the dispute which ended November 8, 1809, in the dismission of Mr. Jackson, the British Minister to the United States, by J. Lowell. Boston.

607. Analysis of the late correspondence between our administration and Great Britain and France, by J. Lowell. 1809.

" Interesting political discussion, the diplomatic policy of Mr. Madison unveiled, by the same.

664. A cursory sketch of the motives and proceedings of the party which sways the affairs of the Union, together with some remarks on the nature of the present crisis. Philadelphia, 1809.

" A Discourse delivered before the Legislature of Massachusetts, May 31, 1809, being the day of the General Election, by David Osgood. Boston, 1809.

" Oration delivered at Washington, July 4th, 1809, at the request of the Democratic citizens of the District of Columbia, by Joel Barlow. Washington, 1809.

703, 733. A Memoir on the subject of a navigation act, including the encouragement of the manufactory of boats and sea vessels, and the protection of mariners, by T. Coxe. Philadelphia, 1809.

637. Memoir concerning the Commercial relations of the United States with England, by Talleyrand, (read at the National Institute the 15th Germinal, in the year V.) To which is added, an essay upon the advantages to be derived from new colonies in the existing circumstances, (read the 15th Messidor, in the year V.) translated from the French. Boston, 1809.

604. An Address to the Congress of the United States on the utility and justice of restrictions upon foreign commerce, by Charles B. Brown. Philadelphia, 1809.

1810.

" An Appeal to the People, being a review of the late correspondence and documents relating to the rejection of the British Minister, by ——— Coleman. New York, 1810.

637. An Exposition of the conduct of France towards America, illustrated by cases decided in the Council of Prizes at Paris, by L. Goldsmith. London, 1810.

285. The Anti-Gallican Sentinel, second part, translated from the Spanish of Don Antonio Capmany. Philadelphia, 1810.

" Carta sobre la antigua costumbre de convocar las Cortes de Castilla. Londres, 1810.

319. Letter on the genius and dispositions of the French Government, including a view of the taxation of the French empire, by Robert Walsh, jun. Baltimore, 1810.

312. The question concerning the depreciation of our currency stated and examined, by W. Huskisson. London, 1810.

1811.

743. An Enquiry into the origin, nature, and object of the British Order in Council of May 16, 1806, by E. Bronson. Philadelphia, 1811.

608. A review of Robert Smith's address to the people of the U. States. Philadelphia, 1811.

733. Oration delivered before the Pennsylvania Society of Cincinnati, on the 4th of July, 1811, by Nicholas Biddle. Philadelphia, 1811.

277. Inquiry into the effects produced on the national currency and rates of exchange by the bank restriction bill, by R. Mushet. London, 1811.

1812.

" Speech in the House of Commons, on the 16th June, 1812, upon the present state of commerce and manufactures, by H. Brougham. (Reprinted.) Philadelphia, 1812.

703. An address to the citizens of the United States, but more particularly to those of the middle and eastern states, against the war, by James Sloan. Philadelphia, 1812.

329. The conduct of Washington compared with that of the present administration. Boston, 1812.

654, 702. Touchstone to the people of the United States on the choice of a President. New York, 1812.

606. A dispassionate inquiry into the reasons alleged by Mr. Madison for declaring an offensive and ruinous war against Great Britain, by John Lowell. Boston, 1812.

606. Perpetual war the policy of Mr. Madison, by the same. Boston, 1812.

733. An oration delivered on the 4th of July, 1812, in the hall of the House of Representatives, at the Capitol, Washington, by Richard Rush.

699. Slave representation, by Boreas. Awake! O spirit of the North! 1812.

313, 659. An address to the people of England, by William Cobbett. Philadelphia, 1812.
(An invective against the United States.)

283. Resources of Russia in the event of a war with France, by Mr. Eustaphieve. Boston, 1812.

733. The Portrait, a poem, delivered before the Washington Benevolent Society of Newburyport, by John Pierpont. Boston, 1812.

1813.

711. War without disguise, or brief considerations on the political and commercial relations of Great Britain and Ireland with the United States of America, at the close of the year 1811, by Edgar Corrie. Liverpool, 1813.

654. A sketch of our political condition, addressed to the citizens of the United States, without distinction of party, by a citizen of New York. New York, 1813.

733. The new States, or a comparison of the wealth, strength, and population of the northern and southern States, by Massachusetts. Boston, 1813.

648. Observations on the conduct of our Executive towards Spain, by Verus, *(Don Luis de Onis.)*

283. Case of J. Soren, owner of the ship Enterprize, when seized at the moment of saving 300 English troops from sinking. London, 1813.

305, 1087. Correspondence respecting Russia between R. Goodloe Harper and Robert Walsh, jun. Philadelphia, 1813.

305. Reflexions on the war of 1812, by M. Tchuykevitch, translated from the Russian by M. Eustaphieve. Boston, 1813.

664. Reply to the Edinburgh Reviewers, by the author of "The resources of Russia," &c. Boston, 1813.

319. An appeal to the nations of Europe against the continental system, translated from the French of Madame de Stael Holstein. London, 1813.

369. Epitre a Mr. Aug. Guil. Schlegel, bel esprit actuellement aux gages du Prince Royal de Suède, par un Suedois. Stockholm, 1813.

1814.

36. Les Etats Unis & l'Angleterre, ou souvenirs & réflexions d'un citoyen Américain, *(William Lee.)* Bordeaux, 1814.

948. The Olive Branch, or faults on both sides, by Mathew Carey, 7th edition. Philadelphia, 1815.

648. Remarks on a dangerous mistake made as to the eastern boundary of Louisiana. Boston, 1814.

699. A calm address to the people of the eastern states, on the subject of the representation of slaves, the representation in the Senate, and the hostility to commerce ascribed to the southern states, by Mathew Carey. Philadelphia, 1814.

1815.

657. The vindication of Captain Joseph Treat against the atrocious calumny comprehended in Major General Brown's official report of the battle of Chippeway. Philadelphia, 1815.

667. Réflexions addressées aux Haytiens du parti de l'ouest & de sud, sur l'horrible assasinat du General Delvare, commis au Port-au-Prince, dans la nuit du 25 Decembre, 1815, par les ordres de Pétion, par le Baron de Vastey. Cap-Henry.

1816.

654. Documents and facts relative to the military events during the late war, by Gen. P. Boyd. Boston, 1816.

666. Réflexions sur une lettre de Mazères, ex-colon Français, addressée à J. C. L. Sismonde de Sismondi, sur les Noirs & les Blancs, la civilisation de l'Afrique, le Royaume de Hayti, &c. par le Baron de Vastey. Cap-Henry, 1816.

317. Correspondence politique & administrative, commencée en 1814, par J. Fiévée. Paris, 1816.

1817.

648. Observations on the existing differences between the government of Spain and the United States, by Verus, *(Don Luis de Onis.)* Philadelphia, 1817.

305. Sketch of the military and political power of Russia in 1817, by Sir Robert Wilson. New York, 1817.

665, 718. South America, a letter on the present state of that country to James Monroe, President of the United States, by an American. Washington, 1817.

1818.

850. Observations made on Mr. Monroe's journey in 1817. Philadelphia, 1818.

746. Considerations and documents relating to the claim of Massachusetts for expenditures during the late war. Washington, 1818.

718. Spanish America and the United States, or views of the actual commerce of the United States with the Spanish colonies, and the effects of a war with Spain on that commerce, by James Yard. Philadelphia, 1818.

294. Letter of Timothy Pickering, containing a narrative of the outrage committed on him at Wyoming. 1818.

642. A plan to lessen and equalize the burden of taxation in the

city of Philadelphia, which will produce a saving of ten thousand dollars annually, by a citizen. Philadelphia, 1818.

665. The necessity of protecting and encouraging the manufactures of the United States, in a letter to James Monroe, President of the United States, by John Melish. Philadelphia, 1818.

1819.

869. An appeal from the judgments of Great Britain, respecting the United States of America, by Robert Walsh, jun. Part I. Philadelphia, 1819.

294, 699. The Missouri question, by D. Raymond. Baltimore, 1819.

294, 699. Free remarks on the Federal Constitution, the practice of the Federal Government, and the obligations of the Union respecting the exclusion of slavery from the territories and new states, by a Philadelphian, *(Robert Walsh, jun.)* Philadelphia, 1819.

735. Essay on the necessity of improving our national forces, by William Theob. Wolfe Tone. New York, 1819.

294, 703. An appeal to the government and Congress of the United States against the depredations committed by American privateers on the commerce of nations at peace with us, by an American citizen, *(Thomas Cooper.)* New York, 1819.

665. A letter to Thomas Brand on the practicability and propriety of a resumption of specie payment, by Erick Bollman. Philadelphia, 1819.

1820.

699. Considerations on the impropriety and inexpediency of renewing the Missouri question, by a Pennsylvanian. Philadelphia, 1820.

718. Monarchal projects, or a plan to place a Bourbon king on the throne of Buenos Ayres, in opposition to British interests. London, 1820.

978. Europe after the Congress of Aix-la-Chapelle, by the Abbé de Pradt, translated from the French. Philadelphia, 1820.

730. Remarks on the present state of currency, credit, commerce, and national industry, in reply to an address of the Tammany Society of New York, by Oliver Wolcott. New York, 1820.

951. The New Olive Branch, or an attempt to establish an identity of interest between Agriculture, Manufactures, and Commerce, by Mathew Carey. Philadelphia, 1820.

1821.

1880. Europe and America in 1821, with an examination of the plan laid before the Cortes of Spain, for the recognition of the Independence of South America, translated from the French of the Abbé de Pradt, by J. D. Williams, 2 vols. London, 1822.

703. National and State rights considered, by "One of the People," in reply to "The Trio." Charleston, 1821.

702. An Address delivered at Washington on the occasion of reading the Declaration of Independence on the 4th of July, 1821, by John Quincy Adams. Washington, 1821.

" Review of the Address of John Quincy Adams, at Washington, 4th of July, 1821. Boston, 1821.

317. The cause of Greece, the cause of Europe, translated from the German. London, 1821.

707. An Examination of the new Tariff proposed by H. Baldwin, a representative in Congress, by one of the people. New York, 1821.

1822.

737. Reflections occasioned by the late disturbances in Charleston, by Achates. Charleston, 1822.

699. To the Public of Charleston on the insurrection, by William Johnson. Charleston, 1822.

737. A Refutation of the Calumnies circulated against the Southern and Western States, respecting the institution and existence of Slavery among them, by a South Carolinian. Charleston, 1822.

707, 946. An Appeal to Common Sense and Common Justice, to prove the injustice and impolicy of the present tariff, illustrated by the policy of other nations, by M. Carey. Philadelphia, 1822.

XVII. COMMERCE AND MANUFACTURES.

1. Commerce. 2. Manufactures and Useful Arts.

1. COMMERCE.

Q. *Anderson, (James)* Observations on the means of exciting a spirit of national industry, chiefly intended to promote the agriculture, commerce, manufactures, and fisheries of Scotland, by James Anderson. Edinburgh, 1777.

37. Q. *Arnould.* Atlas de la balance du Commerce.

553. Q, *Bails, (Benito da)* Arismética para Negociantes. Madrid, 1790.

1036, 3. *Baker, (John M.)* A view of the commerce of the Mediterranean. Washington, 1819.

9. Q. *Baldwin, (Samuel)* A survey of the British customs, con-

taining the rates of merchandise as established by Stat. 12. Car. II. c. 4. 11 Geo. I. c. 7, and other statutes, with tables of duties, drawbacks, &c. London, 1770.

1045. *Beaujour, (Felix)* Tableau du commerce de la Grèce, 2 vol. Paris, 1800.

1011. *Biddle, (Nicholas)* Commercial regulations of the foreign countries with which the United States have commercial intercourse, collected under the direction of the President of the United States, conformably to a resolution of the Senate, of 3d March, 1817. Washington, 1819.

103. *Brissot de Warville.* On the commerce of America with Europe. New York, 1795.

641, 674. *Coxe, (Tench)* An enquiry into the principles on which a commercial system for the United States of America should be founded. Philadelphia, 1787.

1881. *Dearborn, (Henry A. S.)* A memoir on the commerce and navigation of the Black Sea, and the trade and maritime geography of Turkey and Egypt, 2 vols. and one of charts. Boston, 1819.

1016. *Huet.* Histoire du commerce & de la navigation des anciens. Lyon, 1763.

384, 14. Q. *Jöransson.* Tabeller af Sveriges och andra Länders Mynt, Vigt och Matt. Stockholm, 1777.

1043½. *Jackson, (John)* Reflexions on the commerce of the Mediterranean. New York, 1809.

497. Q. *Krusen, (T. E.)* Contorist, 2 vols. Hamburg, 1782.

707. *Mendenhall, (A.)* Tariff, &c. payable on goods, wares and merchandises, imported into the United States. Philadelphia, 1818.

413. Q. *Milburn, (William)* Oriental commerce, 2 vols. London, 1813.

154. *Nemnich.* Waaren Lexikon, in zwölf sprachen; a dictionary of merchandise in twelve languages. Hamburg, 1797.

2. Q. *Peuchet, (J.)* Dictionnaire Universel de Géographie commerçante, 5 vol. Paris, an 7.

1019. *Rordans, (C. W.)* European commerce, a complete mercantile guide to the continent of Europe. London, 1818.

87½. *Sheffield, (John, Lord)* Observations on the commerce of the American States. Dublin, 1784.

1013. *Ustariz, (Don Geronimo)* Theory and practice of commerce, translated from the Spanish by John Kippax. Dublin, 1752.

147½. *Wagener, (J. D.)* Allgemeines Waaren-Lexikon in Spanischer, Portugiesischer, Französischer, Italiänischer, und Englischer sprache. Hamburg, 1810.

ANONYMOUS.

1014. Dictionnaire du Citoyen, ou abrégé historique, théorique & pratique du commerce. Amsterdam, 1762.

1418. Histoire du commerce & de la navigation des peuples anciens & modernes, 2 vol. Amsterdam, 1750.

1419½. Almanach des monnoies, année 1788. Paris.

731. Constitution of the East India Marine Society of Salem, with a list of their members, and a catalogue of their museum. Salem, 1821.

154. *F.* Pauta Geral para a Alfandega Grande de Lisboa. Lisboa, 1782.

---

2. MANUFACTURES AND USEFUL ARTS.

IN GENERAL.

1506. Journal des arts & manufactures, publié sous la direction de la commission exécutive d'agriculture & des arts, vol. 2. Paris, an 3.

1535. Repertory of arts and manufactures, 15 vols. London, 1794—1801.

1536. Same work, new series, vols. 3, 4, and 5. London, 1803—1804.

520. The Register of Arts, or a compendious view of some of the most useful modern discoveries and inventions, by Thomas Green Fessenden. Philadelphia, 1808.

620. The Useful Cabinet, published in monthly numbers for the New England Association of Inventors and Patrons of Useful Arts, vol. 1, for 1808. Boston.

510. The Artist's Manual, a dictionary of practical knowledge in the application of philosophy to arts and manufactures, by James Cutbush, 2 vols. Philadelphia, 1814.

263. Rules, orders, and premiums of the Bath and West of England Society for the encouragement of arts, manufactures, and commerce. Bath, 1802.

PARTICULAR ARTS.

Bleaching. 1132. Essay on the new method of bleaching by means of oxygenated muriatic acid, by Berthollet, translated from the French, by Robert Kerr. Edinburgh, 1790.

Brass Foundery. 222. *F.* L'art de convertir la cuivre rouge en laiton ou cuivre jaune, au moyen de la pierre kalaminaire, de le fondre en tables; de le battre sous le martinet, & de le tirer à la filière, par M. Gallon. Paris, 1764.

Cannon Foundry. 188. *Q.* Description de l'art de fabriquer les canons, par M. Monge. Paris, 1795.

Coining. 23. *Q.* Description de la nouvelle machine pour battre monnoye, écrite en Russe par le Comte Jean Potocki, traduite du Russe en Français, par N. O. (French and Russian.) St. Petersburg, 1811.

Distilleries. 384, 1. *Q.* Nouvelle construction d'Alambic pour la distillation des Eaux-de-vie. Paris, 1781.

Dyeing. 1167½. Practical treatise on dyeing, by Thomas Cooper. Philadelphia, 1815.

Engraving. 283. A complete course of lithography, by Senefelder. London, 1819.

384, 21. *Q.* Rapport sur la lithographie, par Engelmann. Paris, 1816.

Glass Manufacturing. 1166. Essai sur l'art de la verrerie, par Loysel. Paris, 1800.

286. Sur l'art de fabriquer du flint-glass bon pour l'optique, par d'Artigues.

Inventions. 1404. Recueil de découvertes & inventions nouvelles. Berillon, 1773.

701. Rules and regulations adopted October 22, 1807. by the New England Association of Inventors and Patrons of Useful Arts. 1807.

1029. Archives des découvertes & des inventions nouvelles, faites pendant l'année 1816. Paris, 1817.

701. Letter from the Secretary of State, transmitting a list of the names of persons to whom patents have been granted for any useful invention from the 1st of Jan. 1818, to the 1st of Jan. 1819. Washington, 1819.

Machines for Husbandry. 86. *F.* Copper plates (106) of mechanical machines, and implements of husbandry, recommended and adopted by the Society for the encouragement of arts, manufactures, and commerce, by Alexander Mabyn Bailey, 2 vols. London, 1782.

Miller. 441. Millwright and Miller's Guide, by Oliver Evans. Philadelphia, 1795.

262. New invention and improvement on saw-mills, by Moses Coates. Lancaster, 1802.

384, 5. *Q.* Exposé succinct des avantages des moulins à roues inclinées, inventés par A. G. Eckhardt.

384, 23. *Q.* Improvement in mills for the purpose of removing back water.

Paper Making. 388. *Q.* Sämmtliche Papier versuche, (specimen of paper from vegetables,) by Jac. Chr. Schæffer. Regensburg, 1772.

384, 6. *Q.* Mém. sur les papeteries, par Desmarets. Paris, 1774.

384, 9. *Q.* Specimen and observations relative to straw paper. London, 1801.

707. Certificates respecting the machine paper made at the Brandywine paper mills. 1818.

" The Memorial of the Society of Paper Makers of the States of Pennsylvania and Delaware, to the Congress of the U. States. Philadelphia, 1820.

Pot and Pearl Ashes. 325. Principles and observations applied to the manufacture and inspection of Pot and Pearl Ashes, by David Townsend. Boston, 1793.

Oil. 453. *Q.* Mem. Sobre o modo de aperfeiçoar a manuf. do azeite de oliveira em Port. Por J. A. Dalla Bella. 1784.

Saltpetre. 188½. *Q.* L'Art du Salpêtrier, par Bottée & Riffault. Paris, 1813.

Scale-beam. 384, 16. *Q.* Description of Allan Pollock's patent scale-beam. Boston.

Ship-building. 695. An Essay on the propulsion of navigable bodies, by C. A. Busby. New York, 1818.

Steel. 295. Mémoire sur la conversion des Fers de Lorraine en Acier, par Nicolas. Nancy, 1783.

Tapestry. 318. Notice sur la Manufacture Nationale des Gobelins, par C. A. Guillaumot. Paris, an 8.

Typography. 384, 6. *Q.* Nouv. Systême Typographique. Paris, 1776.

1540. Specimen of Printing Types, by Edmund Fry. London, 1788.

210. Manuel Typographique, par Fournier, le jeune, 2 vol. Paris, 1764.

848. History of Printing in America, by Isaiah Thomas, 2 vols. Worcester, 1810.

266. Specimens of Printing on paper and satin, containing the *Somnium Scipionis* in golden letters on a black ground, by J. Fry and Son. London, 1785.

Varnishing. 363. Lak, vernis en verf konst, om alle soorten van Lakken, vernisse en verwen te bereiden. Amsterdam, 1767.

Wheel Carriages. 695. Some cursory observations on the ordinary construction of wheel carriages, with an attempt to point out their defects, and to show how they may be improved, by Horatio Gates Spafford. Albany, 1815.

Windlass. 384, 5. *Q.* Exposé des avantages du Cabestan de A. G. Eckhardt. 1773.

384, 5. *Q.* Rapport sur le nouveau Cabestan de Cardinet, par Borda & La Grange. Paris, an 2.

XVIII. NAVIGATION.

577. *Anon.* The Navigator, containing directions for navigating the Monongahela, Alleghany, Ohio, and Mississippi rivers, and a description of the adjacent countries, with an appendix, containing an account of Louisiana, and of the Missouri and Columbia rivers, as discovered by Lewis and Clarke. Pittsburg, 1814.

466. *Arnold.* American Practical Lunarian and Seamen's Guide. Philadelphia, 1822.

741. *Baron, (George)* Exhibition of the genuine principles of common navigation, being the synopsis of a lecture delivered in New York on the 26th of March, 1803. New York, 1803.

117, 4. *F. Boland.* Observations on the Streights of Gibraltar, and the tides and currents. London, 1704.

465. *Bowditch, (Nathaniel)* The new American Navigator. Newburyport, (Mass.) 1807.

695. ——— ——— Directions for sailing into the harbours of Salem, Marblehead, Beverley, and Manchester. Newport, 1806.

392. *Q. Clarke.* Seamen's Desiderata. New Brunswick, 1801.

734. *Clark, (Edward)* Description of a plan for navigating the rapids in rivers. Philadelphia, 1823.

330. *Fitch, (John)* An Explanation for keeping a ship's traverse at sea, by the Columbian ready reckoner. London, 1793.

263. *Fothergill, (A.)* Essay on the preservation of shipwrecked mariners. London, 1800.

238. *Franklin, (Benjamin)* Lettre à Monsieur David Le Roy contenant differentes observations sur la marine, en mer à bord du Paquebot le London, Capt. Truxtun, au mois d'Août, 1785. Paris, 1787.

95. *Furlong, (Lawrence)* American Coast Pilot. Newburyport, 1800.

247. *Gower, (R. H.)* Description of several instruments for measuring a ship's way through the water. London, 1792.

741. *Guest, (Hensy)* Observations on sheathing vessels, seasoning timber, the proper time to fell timber, the nature and what force it is that causes the sap to rise, with a number of other valuable observations. 1805.

695. *Jones, (William)* Reflections upon the perils and difficulties of the winter navigation of the Delaware. Philadelphia, 1822.

271. *Leard, (J.)* Sailing Directions for the Island of Jamaica, and St. Domingo, and the Windward Passages. London, 1792.

292. *Leguin*. Abrégé de navigation & d'astronomie appliqué à des machines. Paris, 1811.

247. *Lelyveld, (De)* Mém. sur l'usage des Huiles & du Goudron, &c. pour diminuer les dangers sur Mer, traduit du Hollandais. Amsterdam, 1775.

95. Q. *Lescallier*. Traité pratique du gréement des Vaisseaux & autres bâtimens de mer. Paris, 1791.

97. Q. ——— Vocabulaire des termes de marine Anglais & Français, 3 vol. Paris, an 6.

438. *Liddel, (R.)* Seaman's new Vade Mecum. London, 1794.

10. F. *Martin, (Benjamin)* New principles of Geography and Navigation. London, 1758.

117, 3. F. *Monson, (William)* Naval Tracts, treating of all the actions of the English by sea, under queen Elizabeth and king James the first; the office of high admiral and his inferior officers; discoveries and enterprizes of the Spaniards and Portuguese; projects and stratagems; and on fish and fishery. London, 1704.

188. *Neuman, (Henry)* A Marine Pocket Dictionary of the Spanish, Portuguese, Italian, and German languages, with an English-French and French-English Index, 2d ed. London, 1808.

292. *Raleigh, (W.)* Two Essays relating to shipping. I. On the first invention of shipping. II. On the royal navy and sea service, published in 1650, and supplement.

1882. *Romme, (Charles)* Tableau des Vents, des marées & des courants sur toutes les mers du globe, 2 vol. avec une carte. Paris, 1806.

292. *Sayer, (Robert)* Catalogue of Pilots, Neptunes, and Charts. London, 1787.

339. *Spafarieff, (Leontey)* A new guide for the navigation of the Gulf of Finland. St. Petersburg, 1813.

247, 646. *Williams, (Jonathan)* A Memoir on the use of the thermometer in navigation. Philadelphia, 1799. See also our transactions, vol. 3. p. 82.

1478. ——— ——— Same work, translated into Spanish, by order of H. C. M. Madrid, 1794.

P. 1. *Yeates, (W.)* Chart of the Variation of the Magnetic Needle for all the Seas.

NOTE. *For other Marine Charts, see Title* GEOGRAPHY AND ETHNOGRAPHY, § MAPS AND CHARTS.

XIX. MILITARY ART.

1. Discipline and Tactics.
2. Fortifications.
3. Navy.

1. DISCIPLINE AND TACTICS.

1329. *Kosciuszko, (General)* Manœuvres for the horse-artillery, translated from the French, by J. Williams. New York, 1808.

1458. *La Fontaine, (De)* La doctrine militaire, ou le parfait général d'armée. Paris, 1671.

1654. *Lafosse.* Dictionnaire raisonné d'Hippiatrique, cavalerie, manège & maréchalerie, 2 vol. Bruxelles, 1776.

1459. *Lamont, (De)* Les Fonctions de tous les officiers de l'Infanterie. Paris, 1671.

661. *Pickering, (Timothy, jun.)* An easy plan of discipline for a militia. Salem, (Mass.) 1775.

1335. *Scheel.* A treatise on Artillery. Philadelphia, 1800.

1460. *Steuben, (the Baron de)* Regulations for the order and discipline of the troops of the United States. Philadelphia, 1800.

---

673. The manual exercise ordered by His (Britannic) Majesty, in 1764. Philadelphia, 1775.

283. Sketch of the military system of France. Baltimore, 1812.

1457. Ordenanzas de S. M. (Católica) para el regimen de sus exercitos, 4 vol. Madrid, 1768.

673. Rules and articles for the troops raised by the twelve United English Colonies. Philadelphia, 1775.

1461, 1468. Articles of war and regulations for the army of the United States, with lists of officers, &c. 1800—1808.

735. A compendious exercise for the garrison and field ordnance, as practised in the United States, (Dec. 31, 1810.) Washington, 1810.

1338. Exercise for garrison and field ordnance, with manœuvres of horse-artillery. New York, 1812.

1326. Regulations for the field exercise, manœuvres, and conduct of the Infantry of the United States, by R. Smyth. Philadelphia, 1812.

1334. Rules and articles of war, with the different acts of Congress on military affairs. Burlington, (Vt.) 1813.

1324. Regulations for the discipline of the Infantry of the United States. Philadelphia, 1813.

1462. Military laws, and rules and regulations for the army of the United States. Washington, 1813.

1464, 1469. Same work. Washington, 1814.

1463, 1469. Instructions to the deputy, district, and other sub-paymasters of the United States. Washington, 1814.

1464½. Organization of the military peace establishment of the United States, in conformity to the act of Congress of March 3, 1815. Washington, 1815.

1467. Military laws, and rules and regulations for the army of the United States. Washington, 1816.

1325. Rules and regulations for the field exercise of infantry. New York, 1815.

1327. System of Cavalry manœuvres in line. London, 1815.

---

2. FORTIFICATIONS.

113. Q. *Belidor.* La science des Ingénieurs. Paris, 1739.

134. F. *Coehorn.* Nieuwe Vestingbouw. Leeuwaarden, 1685.

1332. *Le Blond.* Elémens de fortification. Paris, 1764.

" —— Traité de l'attaque des places. Paris, 1780.

" —— Traité de la défense des places. Paris 1783.

1331. *St. Paul, (G. N.)* Traité complet de fortifications. Paris, 1764.

1465. *Vauban.* Véritable manière de bien fortifier les places. Amst. 1692.

ANONYMOUS.

29. F. Profile, elevation, views, and plans of Castle Williams in New York harbour, and of the fort at the Pea-Patch in the river Delaware.

186. Q. Essai général de fortification & d'attaque & défense des places. Berlin, 1797.

156. F. Plates to the same work. Berlin, 1797.

1336. The elements of fortification, translated from the French, by Jonathan Williams. Philadelphia, 1801.

145. F. A short treatise of fortification and geometry, MS. 2 vols. *(No date.)*

---

3. NAVY.

442. *Dupin, (Charles)* Mémoire sur la marine & les ponts & chaussées de France & d'Angleterre. Paris, 1818.

123. Q. *Juan, (George)* Examen maritime théorique & pratique ou traité de mécanique appliquée à la construction & manœuvre des Vaisseaux, traduit de l'Espagnol, par Levêque, 2 vol. Nantes, 1783.

425. *Lescallier.* Vocabulaire des termes de Marine Anglais & Français. Paris, 1800.

120. *Limpo, (M. do Espirito Santo)* Principios de tactica naval. Lisboa, 1697.

426. *Le Roy.* Les navires des anciens considérés par rapport à leurs voiles. Paris, 1783.

427. *Le Roy*. Lettre à M. Franklin sur les navires des anciens. Paris, 1787.

428. ——— Nouvelle voilure pour les Vaisseaux de toutes grandeurs. Paris, 1799.

463. *Mackay, (Andrew)* Description and use of the sliding gunter in navigation. Aberdeen, 1802.

424. *Montgéry*. Règles de pointage à bord des Vaisseaux. Paris, 1816.

296. ——— Mémoire sur les mines flottantes, & les petards flottans, ou machines infernales maritimes. Paris, 1819.

384, 22. Q. *Romieu*. Mém. sur la Marine. 1762.

---

332. Plan of the London Dock. London, 1794.

735. Marine rules and regulations of the United States. Boston, 1799.

1466. Laws of the United States in relation to the naval establishment. Washington, 1814.

735. Memoirs on the progress of military discipline, and on the means of establishing uniformity throughout the United States' army in the shortest practicable period, and the best manner.

" Register of the commission and warrant officers of the navy of the United States, including officers of the marine corps. Washington, 1818.

701. Concluding address of Mr. Fulton's lecture on the mechanism, practice, and effects of torpedoes. Delivered at Washington, Feb. 17, 1810.

1518. System of general signals for night and day. Boston, 1817.

XX. GEOGRAPHY AND ETHNOGRAPHY.

---

1. General Geography.
2. Local Geography and Ethnography.
3. Voyages and Travels.
4. Maps and Charts.

---

1. GENERAL GEOGRAPHY.

29. Q. *Anon*. La Géographie ancienne, moderne & historique, 3 vol. Paris, 1689.

1416. —— Geographical compilation for the use of schools, 2 vols. Baltimore, 1806.

18. Q. —— Mémoires & observations géographiques & critiques

sur la situation des pays Septentrionaux de l'Asie & de l'Amérique, d'après les relations les plus récentes. Lausanne, 1765.

384, 19. Q. *Bugge, (Th.)* Beschreibung der ausmessungs-methode, welche bey der Dänischen, Geog. Karten angewendet worden. Mit Kupf. Dresden, 1787.

1. Q. *Busching, (A. F.)* A new system of geography with 36 maps, translated from the German, 6 vols. London, 1762.

1061½. *Butler, (Samuel)* Geographica Classica. New York, 1821.

72. Q. *Clarke, (James Stanier)* The progress of maritime discovery from the earliest period to the close of the eighteenth century, forming an extensive system of hydrography. London, 1803.

28. Q. *Cluverus, (Philip)* Introductio in universam geographiam tam veterem quam novam: tabulis geographicis 46 ac notis ornata a J. Bunone. Jàm verò completa additamentis & annotationibus J. F. Hekelii & J. Reiskii. Londini, 1709.

1094. *Darby, (William)* Brooke's Universal Gazetteer, 3d American edition, augmented and improved, (the American articles are entirely new.) Philadelphia, 1823.

1399. *Hemso, (Graberg de)* Leçons élémentaires de Cosmographie, de Géographie & de Statistique. Gênes, 1813.

325. *J. F.* Remarks on Morse's American Universal Geography. Boston, 1793.

304. *Malte-Brun.* Discours lû dans la séance du 15 fevrier, 1823, de la Société de Géographie. Paris.

153. F. *Martinière, (Bruzen de la)* Le Grand Dictionnaire Géographique, Historique & Critique, 6 vol. Paris, 1768.

1092. *Mayo, (Robert)* Ancient and Modern Geography. Philadelphia, 1813.

131. F. *Mela, (Pomponius)* De Orbis situ, libri tres, accuratissimè emendati, unà cum Commentariis Joachimi Vadiani. Parisiis, 1540.

955. *Melish, (John)* Geographical description of the world. Philadelphia, 1818.

1031. *Mentelle.* Geographie comparée ou analyse de la Géographie Ancienne & Moderne. Paris, 1781.

554. *Morse, (Jedidiah)* Abridgment of the American Gazetteer, Boston, 1798.

1093. *Payne, (John)* Universal Geography, 4 vols. New York, 1798.

1091. *Pinkerton, (John)* Modern Geography, 2 vols. Philadelphia, 1804.

432½. Q. *Waln, (Robert, jun.)* Description of China, with remarks on the European embassies to China, 1st, 2d, and 3d parts. Philadelphia, 1823.

1095. *Worcester, (T. E.)* Universal Gazetteer, 2 vols. Andover, 1817.

2. LOCAL GEOGRAPHY AND ETHNOGRAPHY.

Africa. 1072. *Bowditch, (T. Edward)* Essay on the Geography of North Western Africa. Paris, 1821.

424. Q. ——— ——— Essay on the superstitions, customs, and arts, common to the ancient Egyptians, Abyssinians, and Ashantees. Paris, 1821.

541. Q. *Gaver, (A. D.)* Relacion general de las plazas de Oron y Mazalquivir, su importancia, &c. 2 vol. MS. *(No date.)*

1391. *Jackson, (James Grey)* Account of the empire of Morocco. Philadelphia, 1810.

706. *La Servière.* Notice Historique sur la Colonie de Sierra Leone. Paris, 1816.

19. Q. *Leo, (John,* commonly called *Leo Africanus,)* Description of Africa, first written in Arabic, afterwards translated into Italian and French, translated into English, by John Pory. London, 1600.

Alabama. 746. *Cummins, (Ebenezer)* A Summary Geography of Alabama. Philadelphia, 1819.

America. 35. *Anon.* Lettere Americane, 3 vol. Cremona, 1782.

84. —— Account of the European settlements in America, 2d edition improved, 2 vols. London, 1758.

61. F. *Bertius, (Petrus)* Description d'Amérique, qui est le nouveau monde. Amst. 1622.

" F. *Cevallos, (Pedro Ordonnez de)* Particulière Description de l'Inde Occidentale. Amst. 1622. *Published with the French translation of Herrera's West Indies.* See *Herrera.*

Ebeling, see above, p. 116.

61. F. *Herrera, (Ant. de.)* Description des Indes Occidentales, traduit de l'Espagnol, avec le voyage de Jacques le Maire. Amsterdam, 1622.

69. F. *Laet, (Joannes de)* Novus Orbis, seu descriptiones Indiæ Occidentalis. Lugd. Bat. 1633.

1039. *Pauw, (De)* Recherches philosophiques sur les Américains, 7 vol. Paris, 1795.

American Indians. 89. Q. *Adair, (James)* The History of the American Indians, particularly those nations adjoining to the Mississippi, East and West Florida, Georgia, South and North Carolina, and Virginia. London, 1775.

224. *Barton, (Benjamin S.)* Remarks on the Speech attributed by Mr. Jefferson to the Indian Chief Logan. Philadelphia, 1798.

645, 681. *Benezet, (Anthony)* Some remarks on the situation, disposition and character of the Indian natives of the continent. Philadelphia, 1784—1786.

558. *Colden, (Cadwallader)* History of the Five Nations of Indians. London, 1755.

879. *Heckewelder, (John)* An account of the history,

manners and customs of the Indian nations who once inhabited Pennsylvania and the neighbouring states. Philadelphia, 1819.

879½. ——— ——— Histoire, mœurs & coutumes des Nations Indiennes qui habitaient autrefois la Pennsylvanie & les États voisins, par le Rev. Jean Heckewelder, Missionnaire Morave, traduit de l'Anglois, par le Chevalier du Ponceau, *(being a translation of the above work.)* Paris, 1822.

524. *Q.* ——— ——— Communications made to the historical and literary committee and to members of the American Philosophical Society, on the subject of the history, manners and languages of the American Indians, MS. 1821.

626. *Hopkins.* Abridgment of Hopkins' Historical Memoirs relating to the Housatunnak, or Stockbridge Indians. Philadelphia, 1757.

853. *Hunter, (John D.)* Account of the manners and customs of the several Indian tribes west of the Mississippi. Philadelphia, 1823.

341, 611. *Jefferson, (Thomas)* An Appendix to the Notes on Virginia, relative to the murder of Logan's family. Philadelphia, 1800.

British American Colonies. 53. *Anon.* Present state of Nova Scotia, with an account of Canada and the British Islands on the coast of North America. Edinburgh, 1787.

862. *Coxe, (Daniel)* Description of the English province of Carolana, by the Spaniards called Florida. London, 1741.

384, 10. *Q.* 384, 16. *Q. Evans, (Lewis)* Two essays relative to a General Map of the middle British Colonies in America. Philadelphia, 1755–6.

California. 31. *Venegas, (Miguel)* Noticia de la California y de su conquista, 3 vol. Madrid, 1757.

Canada. 80. *Bouchette, (Joseph)* Topographical Description of Lower Canada. London, 1815.

848. *Smith, (M.)* Geographical view of Upper Canada. Trenton, 1813.

Chili. 27. *Molina, (Juan Ignacio)* Compendio de la historia geographica, natural y civil del Regno de Chile, 2 vol. Madrid, 1788.

28. ——— ——— The geographical, natural, and civil history of Chili, translated from the Italian, by an American Gentleman, 2 vols. Middletown, (Con.) 1808.

China. 398. *Q. Missionaries of Pekin.* Mémoires concernant l'histoire, les sciences, les arts, les mœurs, les usages, &c. des Chinois, par les Missionaires de Pekin, 11 vol. Paris, 1776—1786.

England. 74. *Q. Anon.* Modern London, being the history of the present state of the British metropolis. London, 1805.

77. Q. *Malcolm, (James Seller)* Anecdotes of the manners and customs of London during the 18th century. London, 1808.

391. *Pilkington, (James)* A view of the present state of Derbyshire, with an account of its most remarkable antiquities. Illustrated by an accurate map and plates, 2 vols. Derby, 1789.

1281. *Tunnicliff, (William)* Survey of the Counties of Harts, Wilts, Dorset, Devon, &c. Salisbury, 1791.

Europe. 1054. *Stuart, (Gilbert)* View of society and manners in Europe. Dublin, 1778.

Florida. 717. *Anon.* An original memoir on the Floridas, with a general description from the best authorities, by a Gentleman of the South. Baltimore, 1821.

" —— Notices of East Florida, with an account of the Seminole nation of Indians, by a recent traveller in the province. Charleston, 1822.

" *Chazotte, (Peter Stephen)* Facts and observations on the culture of vines, olives, capers, almonds, &c. in the southern states, and of coffee, cocoa, and cochineal in East Florida. Philada. 1821.

" *Darby, (William)* Memoir on the geography and natural and civil history of Florida, attended by a map of that country. Philadelphia, 1821.

" *Forbes, (James Grant)* Sketches, historical and topographical of the Floridas, more particularly of East Florida. New York, 1821.

France. 47. Q. *Cassini de Thury.* Description géométrique de la France. Paris, 1783.

Georgia. 250. *Sibbald, (George)* Notes and observations on the pine lands of Georgia. Augusta, 1801.

Greenland. 1047. *Crantz, (David)* History of Greenland, 2 vols. translated from the German. London, 1769.

1083. *Egede, (Hans)* A Description of Greenland, translated from the Danish. London, 1745.

1084. *O'Reilley, (Bernard)* Greenland, the adjacent seas, and the north west passage to the Pacific Ocean. New York, 1818.

Guiana. 13. *Anon.* Essai historique sur la colonie de Surinam. Paramarib. 1788.

14. —— Essay on the Natural History of Guiana. London, 1769.

Lescallier, see above, p. 155.

Hudson's Bay. 281. Q. *Dobbs, (Arthur)* An account of the countries adjoining the Hudson's Bay in the north-west part of America. London, 1744.

50. *Umfreville, (Edward)* Present state of Hudson's Bay. London, 1790.

Japan. 117, 1. F. Curious remarks on the Empire of Japan, translated from the High Dutch. London, 1704.

Java. 1001. *Anon.* Sketches, civil and military, of the island of Java. London, 1812.

Iceland. 1056. *Von Troil, (Uno)* Letters on Iceland. London, 1783.

Illinois. 849. *Birkbeck, (Morris)* Letters from the Illinois. Philadelphia, 1818.

India. 304. *Morenas, (J.)* Des castes de l'Inde, ou lettres sur les Hindous à l'occasion de la tragédie du Paria de Casimir Delavigne. Paris, 1822.

Ireland. 3. Q. *Seward, (William Wenman)* Topographia Hiberniæ, or the Topography of Ireland, ancient and modern. Dublin, 1795.

Louisiana. 72. *Anon.* Relations de la Louisiane & du Fleuve Mississippi. Amsterdam, 1720.

75. —— Vue de la Colonie Espagnole du Mississippi ou des provinces de Louisiane & Floride occidentale, en 1802. Paris, 1803.

647. —— An Account of Louisiana, being an abstract of documents in the offices of the Departments of State, and of the Treasury, with an appendix.

871. *Brackenridge, (H. M.)* Views of Louisiana. Pittsburg, 1814.

168. F. *Dannemours, (le Chevalier)* Mémoire sur le district de Ouachita, dans la Louisiane, MS.

872. *Darby, (William)* Geographical Description of Louisiana. Philadelphia, 1816.

717. *Garret, (Elliot Pendegrast)* A Physical and Topographical Sketch of the Mississippi Territory, Lower Louisiana, and a part of West Florida. Philadelphia, 1808.

250. *Hutchins, (Thomas)* Historical Narrative and Topographical Description of Louisiana and West Florida. Philadelphia, 1784.

874. *Stoddard, (Amos)* Sketches of Louisiana. Philadelphia, 1812.

Vergennes, (le Comte de) see above, p. 113.

Maine. 251. *Bingham, (William)* Description of the situation, climate, &c. of certain tracts of land in the District of Maine. 1793.

Whipple, see above, p. 110.

Massachusetts. 623. *Dickinson, (Rod.)* A Geographical and Statistical View of Massachusetts proper. Greenfield, 1813.

Mexico. 285, 718. *Arispe, (Miguel Ramos de)* Memorial on the natural, political, and civil state of the Province of Cohauila in the kingdom of Mexico, presented by him to the august congress, translated from the Spanish. Philadelphia, 1814.

Clavigero, see above, p. 113.

Humboldt, see further, *Voyages and Travels.*

Netherlands. 324. *Bouge, (J. B. de)* Description du cours de l'Escaut occidental, avec une carte. 1806.

111. *F. Guicciardini.* Descrizione di tutti i Paesi Bassi. Anvers, 1567.

N. York. 250. *Anon.* Description of the settlement of the Genessee country in the State of New York. New York, 1799.

686. *Eaton, (Amos)* Geological and Agricultural survey of Rensselaer County in the State of New York. Albany, 1822.

826. *Spafford, (Horatio Gates)* New York Gazetteer, and Statistical account of the State of N. York. Albany, 1813.

Ohio. 576. *Drake, (Daniel)* Natural and Statistical View, or picture of Cincinnati and the Miami country, illustrated by Maps. Cincinnati, 1815.

623. ——— ——— Notices concerning Cincinnati. Cincinnati, 1810.

746. *Kilbourn, (John)* The Ohio Gazetteer, or topographical dictionary of the State of Ohio. Columbus, 1819.

Paraguay. 23. *Muratori.* Relation of the Missions of Paraguay, translated from the Italian. London, 1759.

Pennsylvania. 582. *Johnson, (C. B.)* Letters from the British settlement in Pennsylvania. Philadelphia, 1819.

570. *Mease, (James)* Picture of Philadelphia. Philadelphia, 1811.

Russia. 1061. *Pleschéef, (Sergey)* Survey of the Russian empire. London, 1792.

Scotland. 973. *Anon.* Scotland Delineated, or a geographical description of every shire in Scotland, including the Isles. Edinburgh, 1791.

South Carolina. 863. *Drayton, (John)* View of South Carolina as it respects its moral and civil concerns. Charleston, 1802.

Spanish America. 9. *Bonnycastle, (R. H.)* Spanish America, or an account of the Spanish dominions in the Western Hemisphere. Philadelphia, 1819.

Tartary. 425. *Q. Bacon.* Quelques observations sur les parties Septentrionales du monde, principalement sur les Tartares, tirées de l'Histoire de R. Wendover & M. Paris. Leide, 1729.

" *Q. Bergeron, (Pierre)* Traité sur les Tartares. Leide, 1729.

" *Q. Salcon.* Histoire Orientale, ou des Tartares, de Haiton, Parent du Roi d'Arménie, contenant l'Etat de plusieurs Roiaumes Orientaux en 1300, & une relation de choses remarquables, arrivées aux peuples de ces Pais, traduit du Latin sur l'édition de A. M. Müller Greiffenhag. Leide, 1729.

Sweden. 1057. *Catteau.* General View of Sweden. London, 1790.

Switzerland. 993. *Anon.* Dictionnaire Géographique, historique, & politique de la Suisse. Geneva, 1776.

Tennessee. 623. *Anon.* Short description of the Tennessee government, or the territory of the United States south of the river Ohio, to accompany and explain a map of that country. Philadelphia, 1793.

361. —— A short description of the state of Tennessee. Philadelphia, 1796.

Turkey. 1008. *Hammer, (Joseph von)* Constantinopolis und der Bosporos, 2 vol. Pesth, 1822.

United States. 671. *Anon.* A topographical description of Virginia, Pennsylvania, Maryland, and North Carolina, the climate, soil, and produce, &c. with an appendix containing Mr. Patrick Kennedy's journal up the Illinois river, and a correct list of the different nations and tribes of nations, &c. London, 1778.

38. *Beaujour, (Felix de)* Aperçu des Etats Unis au commencement du XIXe siècle. Paris, 1814.

48. *Crevecœur, (St. John de)* Lettres d'un cultivateur Américain, 3 vol. Paris, 1787.

794. *Darby, (William)* The Emigrants Guide to the western and southwestern states and territories, comprising a geographical and statistical description of the same. New York, 1818.

867. *Hutchins, (Thomas)* Topographical description of Virginia, Pennsylvania, Maryland, and North Carolina. London, 1778.

647. *Jefferson, (Thomas)* Message of the President of the United States, communicating discoveries made in exploring the Missouri, Red River, and Washita, by Lewis, Clarke, &c. with a statistical account of the countries adjacent, February 19, 1806. Washington, 1806.

881½. *Imlay, (George)* Topographical description of the Western Territory of N. America. Lond. 1793.

33. *Mandrillon, (J.)* Le Spectateur Américain, ou remarques générales sur l'Amérique Septentrionale. Amsterdam, 1784.

39. *Mazzei, (Philip)* Recherches historiques & politiques sur les Etats Unis de l'Amérique Septentrionale, 4 vol. Colle, 1788.

898. *Melish, (John)* A geographical description of the United States. Philadelphia, 1816.

795. —— —— Same work. Philadelphia, 1818.

746. —— —— A description of the roads in the United States. Philadelphia, 1814.

Vermont. 623. *Dean, (John)* An alphabetical Atlas, or Gazetteer of Vermont. Montpellier, (Vermont) 1808.

W. Indies. 384, 4. *Q. Arthaud, (M.)* Recherches sur la constitution des naturels de l'Isle de St. Domingue, sur leurs arts, leur industrie, & leurs moyens de subsistance. Cap François, 1786.

57. F. *Davies, (John)* The history of the Caribbee Islands, with a Caribbean vocabulary. London, 1666.

70. Q. *Moreau de St. Méry, (L. E.)* Description topographique, physique, civile, politique, & historique de la partie Française de l'Isle de St. Domingue, 2 vol. Philadelphie, 1797.

986. ——— ——— Description de la partie Espagnole de l'Isle de St. Domingue, 2 vol. Philad. 1796.

985. Same work in English, translated by W. Cobbett. Philadelphia, 1796.

See under the following head, Acosta, Pleschéef, Humboldt, &c.

---

3. VOYAGES AND TRAVELS.

432. Q. *Abel, (Clarke)* Narrative of a Journey in the interior of China, and a voyage to and from that country in 1816 and 1817. London, 1818.

Acarete, see *Acugna.*

30. *Acosta, (Joseph)* Naturall and moral historie of the East and West Indies, translated from the Spanish by E. G. London, 1600.

8½. *Acugna, (Christopher d')* Voyage up the river of Amazons to Quito in Peru, and back again to Brazil, performed at the command of the King of Spain, with M. Acarete's voyage up the river of La Plata, and thence by land to the mines of Potosi, and Grillet and Béchamel's from Cayenne into Guayana, in search of the Lake of Porima. London, 1698.

1074. *Adams, (Robert)* Narrative of his shipwreck on the western coast of Africa, and residence for several months in Tombuctoo. Bulor, 1817.

1069. *Adamson, (M.)* Voyage to Senegal, the Isle of Goree and the river Gambia. London, 1759.

77. *Anbury, (Thomas)* Voyages dans les parties intérieures de l'Amérique Septéntrionale pendant la dernière Guerre, 2 vol. Paris, 1780.

117, 1. F. *Angelo, (M.)* and *Denis Carli.* Account of a voyage to Congo, in the years 1666 and 1667, translated from the Italian. London, 1704.

20. *Azara, (Don Felix de)* Voyages dans l'Amérique Meridionale, 4 vol. avec Atlas. Paris, 1809.

706. *Bacon, (E.)* Abstract of a Journal of E. Bacon, Assistant Agent to the United States to Africa, with an Appendix containing extracts from Proceedings of the Church Missionary Society in England, from the years 1819-20, to which is prefixed, an abstract of the Journal of J. B. Cates, one of the missionaries from Sierra Leone to Grand Bassa. Philadelphia, 1821.

117, 2. F. *Backoff, (Feodor Iskonitz)* Voyage into China, translated from the High Dutch. London, 1704.

117, 3. F. *Baldæus, (Philip)* A description of the East India Coast of Malabar and Coromandel, and of the Island of Ceylon, with all the adjacent Countries, translated from the High Dutch. London, 1704.

1421. *Barrington, (George)* Voyage to New South Wales. Philadelphia, 1796.

332. ——— ——— Sequel to the same. London, 1800.

1883. *Barrow, (John)* An account of Travels into the interior of Southern Africa, in 1797 and 1798, with a map. New York, *(Reprinted)* 1802.

332. *Bartram, (John)* Observations on the Inhabitants, Climate, Soil, &c. in his travels from Pennsylvania to Onondago, Oswego and the Lake Ontario, to which is annexed an account of the Cataracts at Niagara, by Peter Kalm. London, 1751.

866. *Bartram, (William)* Travels in North and South Carolina and Georgia. Philadelphia, 1791.

117, 1. F. *Baumgarten, (M.)* Travels through Egypt, Arabia, Palestine and Syria, with the Author's Life, translated from the Latin. London, 1704.

117, 1. F. *Beauplan, (Sieur de)* A description of Ukraine, translated from the French. London, 1704.

425. Q. *Benjamin.* Voiage autour du Monde, commencé en 1173, écrit originairement en Hébreu, traduit en Latin par B. A. Montan, & traduit du Latin en Français. Leide, 1729.

1030. *Berchtold.* Essai pour diriger & étendre les recherches des Voyageurs, qui se proposent l'utilité de leur patrie, 2 vol. Paris, 1797.

1066. *Betagh, (William)* Voyage round the World in 1719. London, 1728.

106. *Birkbeck, (Morris)* Notes of a journey in America. Philadelphia, 1817.

117, 2. F. *Borri, (Christ.)* An Account of Cochinchina. London, 1704.

59. *Bossu.* Voyage through Louisiana, 2 vols. London, 1771.

49. Q. *Bougainville, (De)* Voyage autour du Monde de 1766 à 1769. Paris, 1771.

1073. *Bowdich, (T. Edwards)* British and French expedition to Teembo in Africa. Paris, 1821.

423. Q. *Bowdich, (Edward)* Mission from Cape Coast castle to Ashantee, with a statistical account of that kingdom, and geographical notices of other parts of the interior of Africa. London, 1819.

8. *Brackenridge, (H. M.)* Voyage to South America, 2 vols. Baltimore, 1819.

117, 1. F. *Brawern, (H.)* A Voyage to the kingdom of Chili, translated from the High Dutch. London, 1704.

41. *Brissot de Warville, (J. P.)* Nouveau Voyage dans les Etats Unis de l'Amérique Septentrionale, en 1788, 3 vol. Paris, 1791.

623. ——— ——— A Critical Examination of the Marquis de Chastellux's travels in North America, translated from the French, *see next page.* Philadelphia, 1798.

564. Q. *Bruce, (James)* Travels to discover the source of the Nile, from the year 1768 to 1773, 5 vols. Edinburgh, 1790.

36. Q. *Bruyn, (Corneille le)* Voyage au Levant, en Asie Mineure & dans les Isles de Chio, Rhodes, Chypre, &c. 5 vol. La Haye, 1732.

414. Q. *Buchanan, (Francis)* Journey from Madras through the countries of Mysore, Canara, and Malabar, 3 vols. London, 1807.

1086. *Burney, (James)* Chronological History of the north-eastern discovery and the early navigations of the Russians. London, 1819.

356. Q. *Camus, (A. G.)* Mémoires sur la collection des grands & petits voyages, & sur la collection des voyages de M. Thevenot. Paris, 1802.

117, 1. F. *Candidius, (G.)* An Account of the Island of Formosa, translated from the High Dutch. London, 1704.

Candiss, see *Magellan*.

Carvajal, see *Magellan*.

60. *Carver, (Jonathan)* Travels through the interior of North America. Philadelphia, 1796.

64. *Castiglioni, (il Conte di)* Viaggio negli Stati Uniti dell' America Settentrionale, fatto negli anni 1785 à 1787, 2 vol. Milano, 1790.

1081. *Catteau, (Jean Pierre)* Tableau des Etats Danois, 3 vol. avec une carte. Paris, 1802.

61. F. *Cevallos, (Pedro Ordonnez de)* Description particulière de l'Inde Occidentale, traduite de l'Espagnol en Français. Amsterdam, 1622.

48. Q. *Chabert, (De)* Voyage fait en 1750 & 1751, dans l'Amérique Septentrionale, pour rectifier les cartes des Côtes de l'Acadie, de l'Isle Royale & de l'Isle de Terre Neuve, & pour en fixer les principaux points par des observations Astronomiques. Paris, 1753.

63. Q. *Champlain.* Voyages de la nouvelle France occidentale, dicte Canada, *(with MSS. notes by Albert Gallatin.)* Paris, 1632.

144. Q. *Chappe d'Auteroche.* Voyage en Sibérie, fait en 1761, 3 vol. & un volume atlas & planches. Paris, 1768.

46. Q. ——— ——— Voyage à la Californie. Paris, 1772.

69. *Charlevoix.* Voyage to Canada, and travels through that country and Louisiana. London, 1763.

47. *Chastellux, (Marquis de)* Travels in North America, 1780, 1, and 2, translated from the French London, 1787.

60. Q. *Clarke, (Edward)* Letters concerning the Spanish Nation, written at Madrid during the years 1760 and 1761. London, 1763.

1029½, 1048. *Clarke, (Edward Daniel)* Travels in various countries of Europe, Asia, and Africa. Philadelphia, 1811.

706. *Coker, (Daniel)* A descendant of Africa, journal from the time of leaving New York, in a voyage for Sherbro in Africa, in company with three agents and about ninety persons of colour. Baltimore, 1820.

Columbus, (Christopher) see Title BIOGRAPHY.

430. *Q.* *Collins, (David)* An Account of the English colony in New South Wales, from its first settlement in January, 1788, to August, 1801. London, 1801.

40. *Q.* *Condamine, (de la)* Journal du Voyage fait par ordre du Roi, à l'équateur, servant d'introduction historique à la mesure des trois premiers degrés du Meridien. Paris, 1751.

29. ——— ——— Relation abrégée d'un voyage fait dans l'interieur de l'Amérique Meridionale. Maestricht, 1778.

425. *Q.* *Contarini. (Ambroise)* Voiage de Perse comme Ambassadeur de la Republique de Venise, fait en 1473. Leide, 1729.

Cordes, (Simon de) See *Magellan.*

578. *Cumming, (F.)* Tour in the Western Country. Pittsburg, 1810.

421. *Q.* *Dalrymple, (Alexander)* Historical collection of the several Voyages and Discoveries, in the Pacific Ocean. London, 1770.

977. *Dampier, (William)* Voyage round the World, 3 vols. London, 1699.

823. *Darby, (William)* Tour from New York to Detroit. New York, 1819.

1077. *Delano, (Amasa)* Voyages and Travels round the World. Boston, 1817.

34. *F.* *Denon, (Vivant)* Voyage dans la Basse & la Haute Egypte, pendant les Campagnes du Général Bonaparte, 2 vol. dont un de cartes, planches, &c. Paris, 1802.

289. *Q.* Le même, 2 vol. Londres, 1802.

23. *F.* Planches pour le même. Londres.

Drake, (Francis) See *Magellan.*

36. *F.* *Du Halde.* A description of the Empire of China and Chinese Tartary, together with the kingdoms of Korea and Tibet, translated from the French. London, 1738.

518. *Q.* *Dunbar, (William) and George Hunter,* Journal of a voyage to the Red, and Washita rivers, and Hot Springs in 1804, MSS.

35. *Q.* *Ellicott, (Andrew)* Journal containing occasional remarks on the Situation, Soil, Rivers, Natural productions and Diseases on the Ohio, Mississippi and Gulf of Mexico. Philadelphia, 1803.

83. *Q.* *Forster, (John Reinold)* Observations made during a voyage round the World, on Physical Geography, Natural History and Ethic Philosophy. London, 1778.

1049. ——— ——— History of the Voyages and Discoveries made in the North. Dublin, 1786.

101. *Gage, (Thomas)* Survey of the West Indies, with a journal of 3300 miles within the main land of America. London, 1699.

560. *Gass, (Patrick)* Journal of the Voyages and Travels of a Corps of discovery, under the command of captains Lewis and Clarke. Pittsburg, 1807.

117, 4. *F.* *Gemelli Carreri, (John Fr.)* A voyage round the World, translated from the Italian. London, 1704.

1542. *Graberg, (Giacomo)* Annali di Geografia e di Statistica, 2 vol. Genova, 1802.

5. *Q.* *Grant, (James)* Narrative of a Voyage of Discovery to New South Wales, 1800, 1, 2. London; 1803.

117, 2. *F.* *Greaves, (John)* A description of the Pyramids in Egypt. London, 1704.

Grillet & Béchamel, see *Acugna.*

1043. *Guys.* Voyage littéraire de la Grèce, ou lettres sur les Grecs anciens & modernes, 4 vol. Paris, 1783.

7. *Q.* *Hanway, (Jonas)* Journal of eight days journey from Portsmouth to Kingston, to which is added an essay on Tea. London, 1756.

870. *Harris, (Thaddeus Mason)* Tour North-west of the Alleghany Mountains. Boston, 1805.

54. *Hearne, (Samuel)* Journey from Hudson's Bay to the Northern Ocean. Dublin, 1796.

62. *Henry, (Alexander)* Travels in Canada, and the Indian Territories, 1760–1776. New York, 1809.

61. *F.* *Herrera, (Ant. de)* Description des Indes occidentales, traduite de l'Espagnol en Français. Amsterdam, 1622.

68, 739. *Herriot, (George)* Travels through the Canadas, containing a description of the picturesque scenery on some of the rivers and lakes, with an account of the productions, commerce and inhabitants of those Provinces. Philadelphia, 1813.

1046. *Hinlock, (Francis)* Letters from Geneva and France, by a Virginian, 2 vols. Boston, 1819.

1080. *Hop, (Henri)* Nouvelle description du Cap de Bonne Espérance, avec un Journal d'un Voyage fait dans l'intérieur de l'Afrique. Amsterd. 1778.

347. *Q.* *Humboldt, (Alex. de)* & *Bonpland.* Voyage de, 3e partie, Essai politique sur le Royaume de la nouvelle Espagne, 2 vol. Paris, 1811.

16. ——— ——— Voyage aux régions équinoxiales du nouveau continent, fait en 1799—1804, 4 vol. Paris, 1816.

17. ——— ——— Vues des Cordillères & monumens des peuples indigènes de l'Amérique, 2 vol. Paris, 1816.

70, 71. *Hennepin, (L.)* Discovery of a vast country in America, between New France and New Mexico. London, 1698.

428. *Q.* *Hunter, (John)* An historical journal of the transactions at Port Jackson and Norfolk Island, with the discoveries that have been made in New South Wales and in the Northern Ocean, since the publication of Philips's voyage. London, 1793.

117, 2. *F.* *James, (Thomas)* A voyage intended to discover a North West Passage into the South Sea, in the years 1631 and 1632. London, 1704.

402. *Kalm, (Peter)* Travels in North America, 3 vols. Warrington, 1770.

94. *Kendall, (Edward A.)* Travels through the northern parts of the United States, 3 vols. New York, 1809.

1884. *Klaproth, (Jules)* Voyage au mont Caucase & en Géorgie, avec une carte de la Géorgie, 2 vol. Paris, 1823.

72½. Q. *Krusenstern, (A. J. von)* Reise um die Welt, in den Jahren 1803—1806, auf Befehl S. K. M. Alexander I. auf den Schiffen Nadeshda und Newa, 3 vol. and one folio vol. of maps and plates. St. Petersburgh, 1810—1812.

57. *Lambert, (John)* Travels through Canada and the United States, 2 vols. London, 1816.

66. *La Hontan, (the Baron)* Voyages to North America, translated from the French, 2 vols. London, 1703.

88. Q. *Laval, (R. P.)* Voyage de la Louisiane fait en 1720, dans lequel sont traitées diverses matières de physique, astronomie, géographie, & marine. Paris, 1728.

12. *Lavaysse, (J. J.)* Voyage aux iles de Trinidad, Tabago, &c. 2 vol. Paris, 1813.

61. F. *Lemaire, (Jacques)* Journal & mémoire de la navigation Australe de. Amsterdam, 1722.

87. Q. Le même, 1615. *Sans lieu d'impression.*

235½. *Lewis & Clarke.* Original journals, notes and memoranda, taken by them and their fellow-travellers, 18 vols. MSS.

881. ——— ——— History of the expedition under their command to the sources of the Missouri, thence across the Rocky Mountains, and down the river Columbia to the Pacific Ocean, performed during the years 1804, 5, 6, by order of the government of the United States, 2 vols. Philadelphia, 1814.

Loaysa, see *Magellan.*

880. *Long, (Major Stephen)* Expedition from Pittsburg to the Rocky Mountains, 2 vols. and Atlas. Philadelphia, 1823.

1389. *Luillier.* Nouveau voyage aux grandes Indes. Amsterdam, 1726.

882. Q. *Mackenzie, (George Stuart)* Travels in the island of Iceland during the summer of the year 1790. Edinburgh, 1811.

61½. F. *Magellan, (F. de)* Recueil & abrégé de tous les voyages qui ont été faits devers le Détroit de Magellan, par F. de Magellan, en 1519—1520. Don Gutieres Carvajal, Don Frere Garcia de Loaysa en 1525. François Drake, en 1577—1580. Pedro Sarmiento, en 1579—1581. Candiss en 1586—1595. Jacques Mahu & Simon de Cordes en 1598—1599. Olivier du Nort, en 1598—1601. Amsterdam, 1622.

Mahu, (Jacques) see *Magellan.*

55. *Mackenzie, (Alexander)* Voyages from Montreal to the Frozen and Pacific Ocean, 2 vols. in one. Philadelphia, 1802.

991. *Macneven, (William James)* Rambles through Switzerland, in 1802. Dublin, 1803.

55. F. *Maldonado, (Lor. Ferrer)* Viaggio dal mare Atlantico al Pacifico, per la via del nord-ouest, Tradotto da un Manoscritto Spagnuolo inedito, da Carlo Amoretti. Milano, 1811.

34. *Mandrillon, (Jr.)* Le Voyageur Américain. Amsterdam, 1782.

425. Q. *Mandeville, (J. de)* Recueil ou Abrégé des voyages de J. de Mandeville, en Asie & Afrique en 1332, par M. Bale. Leide, 1729.

425. Q. *Marc Paul.* Voyages faits en Asie, Tartarie, Mangi, Japon, Indes Orientales, Isles adjacentes & l'Afrique, commencé en 1252: le tout divisé en III Livres, conféré avec un manuscrit de la Bibliothèque de S. A. E. de Brandebourg, & enrichi de plusieurs Notes & additions tirées du dit manuscrit, de l'Edition de Ramuzio, de celle de Purchas, & de celle de Vitriare. Leide, 1729.

117, 4. F. *Merin.* A journey to the Mines in Hungary, with an account of his observations in relation to them, and subterraneous passages in general, translated from the Latin. London, 1704.

868. *Melish (John)* Travels in the United States of America, 2 vols. Philadelphia, 1812.

117, 1. F. *Monck, (J.)* A voyage to Hudson Straits, in order to discover a passage that way to the West Indies, with a description of Old and New Greenland, translated from the High Dutch. London, 1704.

61. F. *More, (Jean de)* Relation de deux caravelles envoyées par le Roi d'Espagne en 1618, sous la conduite du capitaine Don Jean de More pour découvrir le passage de Le Maire, traduit de l'Espagnol en Français. Amsterdam, 1622.

417. Q. *Morier, (James)* Journey through Persia, Armenia, and Asia Minor to Constantinople. London, 1812.

117, 1. F. *Navarette, (D. F.)* An account of the Empire of China, historical, political, moral and religious, translated from the Spanish. London, 1704.

117, 2. F. *Nieuhoff, (John)* Voyages and travels into Brazil, and the best parts of the East Indies, translated from the Low Dutch. London, 1704.

51. F. *Norden, (Fred. Lew.)* Travels in Egypt and Nubia, translated from the Danish, by T. Templeman. London, 1757.

Nort, (Olivier du) see *Magellan.*

564. *Ogden, (John C.)* A Tour through Upper and Lower Canada, containing a view of the present state of religion, learning, commerce, agriculture, colonization, customs and manners, among the English, French and Indian settlements. Litchfield, 1799.

739. Same work. Wilmington, 1800.

21. Q. *Olafsen, (B. L.)* and *B. Povelsens.* Reise durch Island veranstaltet von der koeniglichen Societät der Wissenschaften in Kopenhagen, 2 vol. Copenhagen & Leipzig, 1775.

43. Q. *Outhier*. Journal d'un Voyage au Nord, en 1736 & 1737. Paris, 1756.

117, 3. F. *Ovalle, (Alonso de)* An Historical relation of the kingdom of Chili, translated from the Spanish. London, 1704.

408. Q. *Pallas, (P. S.)* Voyages en differentes Provinces de l'empire de Russie & dans l'Asie Septentrionale, 5 vol. Paris, 1788.

409. Q. Cartes & gravures pour les voyages de Pallas. Paris, 1793.

1075. *Park, (Mungo)* Travels in the interior districts of Africa, in 1795, 1796, and 1797. Philadelphia, 1800.

1076. ——— ——— Journal of a mission to the interior of Africa in 1805. Philadelphia, 1815.

540. Q. *Parras, (P. S.)* Viage desde Aragon à Yndias, en 1748—1759, MS.

1085. *Parry, (William Edward)* Voyage for the discovery of a north-west passage to the Pacific. Philadelphia, 1821.

117, 4. F. *Pelham*. Preservation of eight men in Greenland, nine months and twelve days. London, 1704.

1038. *Pérouse, (La)* A Voyage round the World, performed in 1785 to 1788, translated from the French, 3 vols. London, 1799.

20. F. Charts and Plates for the Voyages of La Pérouse. London, 1798.

117, 2. F. *Peyrère, (La)* An account of Iceland, translated from the French. London, 1704.

117, 2. F. ——— ——— An account of Greenland, translated from the French. London, 1704.

1003. *Phillips, (Governor)* Voyage to Botany Bay. Dublin, 1790.

98. Q. *Phipps, (Constantine John)* A Voyage towards the North Pole in 1773. London, 1774.

56. F. *Pigafetta, (Antonio)* Primo Viaggio intorno al globo Terracqueo, ossia Ragguaglio della Navigazione alle Indie Orientali per la via d'occidente, sulla squadra del capit. Magaglianes negli anni 1519—1522, publicato da Carlo Amoretti. Milano, 1800.

425. Q. *Plan Carpin, (Jean de)* & *N. Ascelin*. Voiages faits en Tartarie & autres peuples orientaux comme Légats Apostoliques & Ambassadeurs du Pape Innocent IV. en 1246. Leide, 1729.

623. *Pike, (Zebulon M.)* An account of a Voyage up the Mississippi River from St. Louis to its source, made under the orders of the War Department in the years 1805 and 1806, compiled from Mr. Pike's journal. *(No imprint.)*

519. Q. ——— ——— Journal of the above voyage, MS.

876. ——— ——— An account of Expeditions to the Sources of the Mississippi, and through the western parts of Louisiana to the sources of Arkansaw, Kans, La Platte, and Pierre Jaune Rivers, performed by order of the Government of the United States, during the years 1805,

1806, and 1807, and a tour through the interior parts of New Spain in the year 1807. Philadelphia, 1810.

53. Q. *Pingré.* Journal du voyage de M. le Marquis de Courtanvaux, sur la frégate l'Aurore, pour essayer par ordre de l'Académie plusieurs instrumens relatifs à la longitude. Paris, 1768.

10. Q. *Pinkerton, (John)* A collection of the best and most interesting voyages in all the parts of the world, 6 vols. Philadelphia, 1810.

10. *Pons, (F. A. de)* Voyage to the eastern part of Terra Firma on the Spanish Main, in 1801—4, 3 vols. translated from the French. New York, 1806.

22. Q. *Potocki, (J. Comte)* Voyage en Russie en 1797, MSS.

116. F. *Purchas, (Samuel)* Pilgrimage or relation of the world, and the religions observed in all ages and places, discovered, from the creation unto this presents. London, 1614.

1071. *Riley, (James)* Authentic Narrative of the loss of the American brig Commerce. Hartford, 1817.

79. *Robin, (C. C.)* Voyage dans l'interieur de la Louisiane, de la Floride & dans les Isles de la Martinique & de St. Domingue, 1802—1806, 3 vol. Paris, 1807.

285. *Robinson, (William D.)* A cursory view of Spanish America. Georgetown, (D. C.) 1813.

67. *Robson, (Joseph)* Account of six years' residence in Hudson's Bay, 1733—1736 and 1744 to 1747. London, 1752.

76. Q. *Rochefoucault Liancourt, (le Duc de la)* Travels through the United States of North America, the country of the Iroquois, and Upper Canada, in the year 1795 to 1797, with an account of Lower Canada, translated from the French. London, 1799.

1004. *Rochon, (Alexis)* Voyage aux Indes orientales & en Afrique. Paris, 1807.

117, 1. F. *Roe, (Thomas)* Journal of his voyage to the East Indies, and observations there during his residence at the Mogul's Court, as Embassador from King James the First of England, taken from his own MSS. London, 1704.

425. Q. *Rubruquis, (Guillaume)* Voiage en Tartarie, à la Chine & autres parties de l'orient, comme Ambassadeur de Louis IX. Roi de France, en 1253, traduit de l'Anglais, par de Bergeron. Leide, 1729.

Sarmiento, see *Magellan.*

1078. *Salt, (Henry)* Voyage to Abyssinia, with a map. Philadelphia, 1817.

990. *Sansom, (Joseph)* Letters during a tour through Switzerland and Italy, 2 vols. Philadelphia, 1805.

562. ——— ——— Sketches of Lower Canada. New York, 1817.

493. Q. *Saussure, (de)* Voyage dans les Alpes, précédé d'un essai sur l'histoire naturelle des environs de Genève, 2 vol. Neuchatel, 1779.

294. *Schelechof, (Grigori)* Erste and Zweyte reise von Ochotsk

in Sibirien durch den Ostlichen Ocean nach den kusten von Amerika in den Jahren 1783 bis 1789, aus den Russischen übersezt von J. Z. Logan. St. Petersburgh, 1793.

847. *Schoolcraft, (Henry R.)* Journal of travels from Detroit to the sources of the Mississippi. Albany, 1821.

904. *Schœpf, (Johan David)* Reise durch einige Nord Amerikanischen Staaten. Erlangen, 1788.

1008½. *Scoresby, jun. (William)* Journal of a voyage to the Northern Whale Fishery, including researches and discoveries on the eastern coast of Greenland, made in 1822. Edinburgh, 1823.

875. *Shultz, (Christian)* Travels in New York, Pennsylvania, Virginia, Ohio, Kentucky, and Tennessee, 2 vols. New York, 1810.

1042. *Serres, (Marçel de)* Voyage en Autriche ou essai statistique & géographique sur cet empire, 4 vol. Paris, 1814.

117, 4. F. *Sepp, (Anthony)* and *Anthony Behme.* An account of a voyage from Spain to Paraquaria, translated from the High Dutch. London, 1704.

122. F. *Shaw, (Thomas)* Travels, or observations relating to several parts of Barbary and the Levant. Oxford, 1738.

974. *Silliman, (Benjamin)* Travels in England, Holland, and Scotland, in 1805 and 1806. New York, 1810.

399. Q. *Sonnerat.* Voyage aux Indes orientales & à la Chine, depuis 1774 a 1781, 2 vol. Paris, 1782.

80. Q. *Sonnini, (C. S.)* Travels in Upper and Lower Egypt, translated from the French. London, 1800.

117, 2. F. *Smith, (John)* His travels and adventures in Europe, Asia, Africa, and America, from the year 1592 to 1629. London, 1704.

838. Same work, 2 vols. Richmond, 1819.

117, 1. F. *Sorrento, (T. M. de)* A voyage to Congo and several other countries in the southern Africk, in the year 1682. London, 1704.

1070. *Sparrman, (Andrew)* Voyage to the Cape of Good Hope, towards the antarctic polar circle, and round the world, 2 vols. London, 1785.

1088. *Stœhlin, (J. Von)* Account of the new northern Archipelago lately discovered by the Russians. London, 1774.

1000. *Staunton, (George)* Account of the embassy from the king of Great Britain to China. Philadelphia, 1799.

901. *Sutcliff, (Robert)* Travels in some parts of North America. Philadelphia, 1812.

117, 4. F. *Ten Rhyne.* Account of the Cape of Good Hope, and the Hottentots. London, 1704.

1393. *Tollot.* Nouveau voyage fait au Levant en 1731–2. Paris, 1742.

1067. *Tournefort.* Voyage into the Levant, containing the ancient and modern state of the islands of the Archipelago, 3 vols. London, 1741.

983. *Townson, (Robert)* Voyage en Hongrie, traduit de l'Anglais, par Cantwell, 3 vol. Pasis, 1799.

422. Q. *Tuckey, (J. K.)* Expedition to explore the river Zaire, usually called the Congo, in South Africa. London, 1818.

1079. Same work. New York, 1818.

420. Q. *Turner, (Samuel)* Embassy to the Court of the Teshoo Lama in Thibet. London, 1800.

93. Q. *Vaillant, (F. le)* Premier voyage dans l'intérieur de l'Afrique par le Cap de Bonne Esperance. Paris, *(sans date.)*

94. Q. ——— ——— Second voyage fait en 1783 à 1785. Paris, an 4.

56. Q. *Ulloa, (Antoine de & George Juan)* Voyage historique de l'Amérique Méridionale, avec des observations astronomiques & physiques, 2 vol. *(1st wanting.)* Amsterdam, 1752.

57. Q. ——— ——— Relacion historica del Viage a la America Meridional para medir algunos grados del meridiano Terrestre, 4 vol. *(2d wanting.)* Madrid, 1748.

117, 2. F. *Wagener, (Z.)* A voyage through a great part of the world into China, translated from the High Dutch. London, 1704.

429. Q. *White, (John)* Journal of a voyage to New South Wales. London, 1790.

1005. *Wittmair, (William)* Travels in Turkey, Asia Minor, Syria and across the desert to Egypt. Philadelphia, 1804.

983½. *Woodward, (Captain)* Narrative of his shipwreck on the coast of the island of Celebes, with an account of that island. London, 1804.

1044. *Zalony, (Marcaky)* Voyage a Tine, l'une des isles de l'Archipel de la Grèce. Paris, 1809.

ANONYMOUS AND MISCELLANEOUS.

117. F. A collection of voyages and travels, some now first printed from original manuscripts, other translated out of foreign languages, and now first published in English, 4 vols. London, 1704.

425. Q. Recueil de divers voyages faits en Tartarie, Perse & ailleurs. Leide, 1729.

The different voyages contained in the above volumes are also separately inserted in this Catalogue, under the names of their respective authors.

117, 2. F. Two journals: the first kept by seven Sailors, in the isle of St. Maurice in Greenland, in the year 1633 and 1634, who passed the winter, and all died in the said island. The second kept by seven other Sailors, who in the years 1633 and 1634, wintered at Spitzbergen, translated from the Low Dutch. London, 1704.

117, 2. F. An account of 42 persons, who perished by shipwreck near Spitzbergen, in the year 1646, translated from the Low Dutch. London, 1704.

54. *Q.* Voyage en Siam des Pères Jesuites envoyés par le Roy aux Indes & à la Chine; avec leurs observations astronomiques & leurs remarques de Phisique, de Geographie d'Hydrographie & d'Histoire. Paris, 1686

117, 4. *F.* An account of the shipwreck of a Dutch vessel, on the coast of the isle of Quelpaert, together with the description of the kingdom of Corea, translated from the French. London, 1704.

117, 4. *F.* A fragment concerning the discovery of the islands of Salomon, translated from the Spanish. London, 1704.

425. *Q.* Traité de la navigation & des voiages de découverte & conquête Modernes & principalement des Français. Leyde, 1729.

704. Amerikanisches magasin, oder authentische Beytträge zur Erdbeschreiburg, staatskunde, und geschichte von Amerika herausgegeben von Hegewisch in Kiel, und Professor Ebeling in Hamburg, Erster Band. Hamburg, 1797.

1006. Voyage dans l'Inde, en Perse, &c. traduit de l'Anglais. Paris, 1801.

49. Voyage dans la Haute Pennsylvanie & dans l'état de New York, traduit par St. John de Crevecœur, 3 vol. Paris, 1801.

32. Relacion del viage hecho por las Goletas Sutil y Mexicana, en el año de 1792, para reconocer el Estrecho de Fuca. Madrid, 1802.

285. Notes Statistiques, Physiques & Politiques, Sur l'Amérique Espagnole, extraites des ouvrages de Humboldt, & autres voyageurs, traduites de l'Espagnol. Philadelphie, 1812.

144. *F.* Journal of a voyage to Russia, and a journey from Petersburgh by Moscow, Pultowa, Kiow, and through a part of Poland, MSS.

---

4. MAPS AND CHARTS.

ATLASSES AND BOUND COLLECTIONS OF MAPS AND CHARTS.

4½. *F.* *Alagna, (T. Giacomo)* Charts of the coast of Portugal and Mediterranean Sea. London, 1764.

145. *Q.* *Anon.* Atlas Maritime; recueil de cartes & plans des quatre parties du monde, en cinq volumes. Paris, 1764.

4. *Q.* *Arrowsmith* and *Lewis.* A new Atlas, comprising all the new discoveries to the present time. Philadelphia, 1804.

287. *Q.* *Bonne* & *Desmarets.* Atlas Encyclopédique, contenant la Geographie ancienne & quelques Cartes Sur la Geographie du moyen âge, la Géographie moderne & les cartes relatives a la Géographie Phisique, 2 vol. Paris, 1787.

31. *F.* *Brué, (H.)* Atlas Universel. Paris, 1814–1816.

45. *F.* *Carey, (H. C.)* and *I. Lea.* A complete Historical, Chro-

nological and Geographical Atlas of America, on the plan of Le Sage. Philadelphia, 1822.

159. Q. *Churchman, (John)* Magnetic Atlas, or Variation Charts of the whole terraqueous Globe. London, 1794.

6. F. *Danville.* Atlas Antiquus. Norimbergæ, 1784.

3. F. *Des Barres, (J. F. W.)* Charts of the sea coast and harbours of Nova Scotia and New England. Surveyed by order of the Lords of the Admiralty, 2 vols.

2. F. *Dewitt.* Atlas, containing Europe, Asia, Africa and America. Amsterdam.

9. F. *Dunn, (S.)* A new Atlas of the Mundane system of Geography and Cosmography. London, 1776.

4. F. *Homan.* Atlas Germaniæ Specialis. Norimbergæ, 1753.

33½. F. *Humboldt, (Alexander)* Atlas de la Nouvelle Espagne, see No. 347, quarto, above p. 207.

8. F. *Jeffery, (J.)* Neptune Occidental, a complete pilot for the West Indies. London, 1782.

44. F. *Lavoisne.* A complete genealogical, historical, and geographical atlas, edited by M. Carey. Philadelphia, 1820.

5. F. *Mackenzie, (M.)* Maritime survey of Ireland and the west coast of England, 2 vols. London, 1775.

48. *Mayo, (Robert)* An Atlas of Ancient Geography, with a chronological chart of Universal History, being intended as an accompaniment of his ancient geography and history. Philadelphia, 1814.

21. F. *Melish, (J.)* Juvenile Atlas. Philadelphia, 1814.

12. F. ——.—— Military Atlas. Philadelphia, 1814.

32. F. *Pinkerton, (T.)* Modern Atlas. Philadelphia, 1818.

5½. F. *Rennell, (James)* The Bengal Atlas, containing maps of the theatre of war and commerce on that side of Hindoostan. 1780.

3½. F. *Tanner, (H. S.)* New American Atlas, 5 Nos. Philadelphia, 1818—22.

2½. F. Collection de cartes de l'Allemagne, des Pays Bas & de l'Italie Septentrionale. Par Homan, Mayer, Sanson, Inselen, le P. Placide & autres, 2 vol.

SEPARATE MAPS, CHARTS, PLANS, &C.

America. C. 1. Carte Encyclopédique de l'Amérique Méridionale, par H. Brue. Paris, 1815.

P. 2. Nuevo Mapa Geographico de la America Septentrional perteneciente al Virreynato de Mexico. Por Don J. A. de Alzate y Ramirez. 1768.

Canada. P. 1. Map of Lower Canada, by A. Say.

R. 3. A Map of Upper Canada, describing all the new settlements, townships, &c. with the countries adjacent, from Quebec to Lake Huron, by David William Smyth. New York, 1813.

Denmark. P. 2. Collection of Maps of the Danish European Dominions, containing the islands and ports of Jutland and of the Dutchy of Schleswig, made under the direction of the Royal Society of Sciences, and executed by Wessel, Shanke, Harbol, and others, 17 sheets. 1768—1805.

P. 2. Grund Tegning af den Kongelige Residenz Stad Kiöbenhavn.

Europe. R. 4. A Geographical Chart of Europe, by J. Jameson.

P. 2. Nouvelle Carte de l'Europe après le traité de Vienne & la réunion de la Hollande à l'Empire Français, divisé en 130 Départements, comprenant en outre une partie de l'Asie, le golfe Persique, le bassin de la Méditerranée & toute la Côte d'Afrique, en 4 feuilles, par Hérisson. Paris.

Florida. P. 1. Map of Florida.

P. 1. Chart of the Coast of Florida, Cuba, &c. by J. J. de Ferrer.

P. 1. Plan of lands in East Florida, purchased by Mess. Forbes from the Indians.

P. 1. Plan of the town of Colinton in East Florida.

France. C. 2. Carte de France.

17. *F.* Plan de Paris, commencé en 1734, & acheve en 1739, par L. Bretz, 20 sheets, bound.

C. 3. Plan de Paris, 1800.

Germany. R. 5. Karte von Deutschland nach des Hrn. O. C. Busching Erdbeschreibung, und der besten Hülfsmitteln entworffen, von D. F. Soltzman. Berlin, 1789.

P. 2. Basis Novæ Chartæ Palatinæ. 1773.

G. Britain. R. 6. Plan of the proposed London Docks.

Italy. P. 2. Italia; cioè tutte le grandi e picciole Sovranità e Repubbliche d' Italia, da Ignazio Heyman. Trieste.

P. 2. Carte de l'Isle d'Elbe, par Picquet. Paris, 1814.

P. 2. Isola dell'Elba.

Kentucky. R. 7. A Map of the State of Kentucky, also part of Indianna and Illinois, by Luke Mansel. Frankfort, 1816.

Louisiana. R. 8. A Map of the State of Louisiana, with part of the Mississippi Territory, by William Darby.

R. 9. Carte générale du territoire d'Orléans, comprenant aussi la Floride occidentale & une portion du Territoire du Mississippi, dressée par B. Lafon.

P. 1. Plan of New Orleans, as it was at the time of the cession.

R. 10. Plan of the city and environs of New Orleans, by B. Lafon. 1816.

Madeira. P. 2. Geo-Hydrographic Survey of the Isle of Madeira, with the Dezertas and Porto Santo Island, geometrically taken in 1788, by William Johnston. Published London, 1791.

Maine. P. 1. A Map of the District of Maine, by Moses Greenleaf. 1815.

Maryland. R. 11. A Map of the State of Maryland, principal waters, public roads, and division of counties therein; and of the Federal Territory, as also a sketch of the State of Delaware, by Dennish Griffith. 1794.

P. 1. A Plan of Charles Town from a survey of Edward Crisp in 1704.

Massachusetts. P. 1. Chart of the harbours of Salem, Marblehead, Beverly and Manchester, in 1804–6, by Bowditch.

P. 1. A map of Boston and its vicinity, by John G. Hales.

C. 4. The same.

Netherlands. P. 2. A new map of the Netherlands or Low Countries, with some part of the Provinces of Holland, Utrecht and Gelders, and the whole of Zeeland, by Laurie & Whittle. London.

New York. R. 12. A map of the state of New York, including the turnpike roads now granted, as also the principal common roads connected therewith, by William M'Alpin. Oxford, 1808.

P. 1. Map of the northern part of the state of New York, by Lay.

P. 1. Part of Onondago Lake, in the state of New York.

P. 1. Map of the Waldo Patent.

P. 1. Map of Morris's purchase of West Genessee in the state of New York, exhibiting the boundaries of the lands purchased by the Holland Land Company, by Joseph & B. Ellicott, 1800.

R. 27. Map of the Hudson between Sandy Hook and Sandy Hill, with the post road between New York and Albany.

North Carolina. R. 13. A map of the state of North Carolina, by John Price and John Strother. 1808.

Ohio. R. 14. A map of the state of Ohio, by B. Hough and A. Bourne. 1815.

Pennsylvania. C. 5. Map of Pennsylvania, by N. Scull. Philadelphia, 1759.

P. 1. Map of Pennsylvania as it was in 1791, by Reading Howell.

R. 15. A map of the state of Pennsylvania, by Reading Howell, 1792.

R. 16. A map of the state of Pennsylvania, by Reading Howell, revised 1811.

C. 6. The map of Wayne and Pike Counties, with an Index, by Jason Torrey. Philadelphia, 1814.

R. 1. A map exhibiting a general view of the roads and inland navigation of Pennsylvania, and part of the adjacent States, by John Adlum and John Wallis.

P. 1. Plan of the City of Philadelphia and its environs, by J. Hills. Philadelphia, 1801-7.
P. 1. Plan of the City of Philadelphia and its environs.
P. 1. Map of Philadelphia.
P. 1. Map of Philadelphia for the use of firemen.
P. 1. An east prospect of the City of Philadelphia, by G. Heap.
R. 17. An east prospect of the City of Philadelphia, taken by George Heap from the Jersey shore, under the direction of Nicholas Scull.
R. 18. Plan of Pittsburg and the adjacent country, surveyed by William Darby, 1817.
P. 1. Draft of the city of Germany, founded on the 25th of Sept. 1810, by Samuel F. Conover, situated in the county of Somerset, state of Pennsylvania.

Poland. P. 2. Map of Poland, by Komarzewsky. Paris, 1809.

Polynesia. P. 2. Karta over Polynesien eller Femte Delen af Jordklotet, af Djurberg. Stockholm, 1780.

South Carolina. P. 1. Map of South Carolina, by John Wilson, (made and published under the authority of the state.) 1822.
P. 1. Sketch of the Santee Canal.

Switzerland. C. 7. Rhœtia fœderata delineata, Wallesia Canton.
C. 8. Rhœtia fœderata, Wallesia.
Canton Underwalden.
——— Schweitz.
——— Solothurn.
——— Freiburg.
——— Glarus.
——— Lucern.
——— St. Gallen, Toggenburg, Appenzl, Thurgau und Reinthal.
The above nine maps by Gabriel Walser.
Mappa Geographica Bernensis.
Pagus Uriensis.
Canton Schaffhausen.
The above three maps by Matth. Scutter.
Graffschafft Toggenburg, von J. Jac. Büler.
Turgoviæ Chorographica Tabula, à J. A. Rizzi Zannoni.
Carte en perspective des Montagnes de la Suisse, d'après le plan du Gen. Pfyffer, gravé par Clausner.
Carte en perspective du Nord au Midi, ou Suisse, par Pfyffer.
Die Eisgebürge der Schweizerlandes, von J. S. Grüner.

Tennessee. P. 1. Map of Tennessee.
P. 1. A sketch of the Muscle Shoals of the Tennessee River, by General Wilkinson.

United States. P. 1. Map of the United States of America, with the British and Spanish Possessions, according to the Peace of Versailles, 20th January 1783. London, 1783.

R. 19. A Map of the United States, with the contiguous British and Spanish possessions by John Melish. Philadelphia.

R. 20. A new and correct map of the United States, exhibiting the Counties, Towns, Roads, &c. by Samuel Lewis. Philadelphia, 1815.

R. 2. A Map of the United States, exhibiting the Post Roads, the situations, connexions, and distances of the Post Offices, Stage Roads, Counties and principal Rivers, by Abraham Bradley, junr.

Washington. R. 22. Plan of the City of Washington.

Vermont. R. 1. A map of the State of Vermont, exhibiting the County and Town Lines, Rivers, Lakes, Ponds, Mountains, Meeting Houses, Mills, Public Roads, &c. by James Whitelan, 1796.

Virginia. P. 1. Frederick, Berkeley, and Jefferson Counties, in the State of Virginia.

West Indies. P. 2. Charta öfver Canalerna och utloppen δarna frän St. Barthelemy, till Dog och Prickle Pear, af Samuel Fahlberg, 1792.

R. 23. A Map of the French part of St. Domingo, by Bellin, and augmented by C. P. Varle.

P. 2. Special map representing Man of War Shoal, its distance from the Island of St. Martin's, conformably to the discovery of Captain Fowke, commanding the British frigate Proselyte in the month of May, 1801. By Samuel Falbergs, chief Engineer to the Government. *MS. Drawing.*

World. P. 2. Carte des parties principales du globe terrestre, pour Servir à l'Histoire des deux premiers Siècles depuis la création du monde, par Luneau de Boisjermain. Paris, 1765.

R. 24. Map of the World, on a globular projection, by Arrowsmith, engraved by Samuel Lewis. Philadelphia, 1809.

P. 2. The World horizontally divided, in two sheets. *(German Map.)*

P. 2. Carte Magnétique des deux Hémisphères.

MISCELLANEOUS.

P. 1. Navigation Chart from America to the British Channel, by T. Garnett. 1816.

P. 1. Two Maps of the boundary line between the United States and Upper Canada.

P. 1. Chart containing the Coast of California, New Albion, and Russian discoveries to the North; with the peninsula of

Kamtschatka in Asia, opposite thereto, and islands dispersed over the Pacific Ocean to the North of the Line.

R. 25. A Map of Mexico, Louisiana, and the Missouri Territory, including also the State of Mississippi, Alabama Territory, East and West Florida, Georgia, South Carolina, and part of the Island of Cuba, by John H. Robinson.

R. 26. A Map of the most inhabited part of Virginia, containing the whole province of Maryland and part of Pennsylvania, New Jersey, and North Carolina, drawn by John Fry and Peter Jefferson in 1775. Published in London, 1794.

P. 1. Lewis Evans's Map of Pennsylvania, New Jersey, New York, and Delaware, 1749.

P. 1. The Seat of the War of the Revolution in the Southern States.

P. 1. Map of the Mississippi River, by King.

P. 1. Geographical, Historical, and Biographical Chart of the United States.

In the marginal indications for Maps, Charts, &c. throughout this Catalogue, C. *stands for* Case, P. *for* Portfolio, *and* R. *for* Roll, *with the appropriate numbers.*

XXI. PHILOLOGY.

1. Languages in General. 2. Particular Languages.

1. LANGUAGES IN GENERAL.

Adelung, (J. C.) see *Vater.*

276. Q. *Adelung, (Fred.)* Catherinens der Grossen Verdienste um die vergleichende Sprachenkunde. St. Petersburgh, 1815.

182. ——— ——— Uebersicht aller Sprachen und ihrer Dialekte. St. Petersburgh, 1820.

Beattie, (James) The theory of language, in two parts: 1. Of the origin and general nature of speech; 2. Of universal grammar, new edition, enlarged and corrected. London, 1788.

336. *Blacklock.* An essay on universal etymology, or the analysis of a sentence. Edinburgh, 1756.

161. *Brerewood, (Edward)* Enquiry touching the diversity of languages and religions throughout the chief parts of the world. London, 1614.

167. Same work, to which is subjoined, an account of the languages of the people of Europe, collected out of J. Scaliger. London, 1674.

1490. *Cascales.* Cartas Philologicas. Madrid, 1779.

410. Q. *Catharine, (the Great)* Linguarum totius orbis vocabularia comparativa, augustissimæ curâ collecta, 2 vol. Petrop. 1786—1787.

411. Q. The same work, alphabetically arranged, with the addition of African and American words, by Theodore Jankewitsch, 4 vols. St. Petersburgh, 1790—1791.

174. *Chazotte, (Peter S.)* Essay on the best method of teaching foreign languages. Philadelphia, 1817.

685. ——— ——— An introductory lecture on the metaphysics and philosophy of languages. Philadelphia, 1819.

1539. *Fry, (Edm.)* Pantographia, containing accurate copies of all the known alphabets in the world. London, 1799.

337. Q. *Gébelin, (Court de)* Le monde Primitif, analysé & comparé avec le monde moderne, 9 vol. Paris, 1773—1778.

386. ——— ——— Histoire naturelle de la Parole, ou Grammaire Universelle, avec des notes, par M. Lanjuinais. Paris, 1816.

318. *Goulianoff.* Discours sur l'etude fondamentales des Langues écrit et traduit par lui du Russe. Paris, 1822.

Q. *Jacobson, (Johan Carl Godfried)* Technologisches Wörter-Buch, mit Rosenthals fortsetzung, 8 vol. Berlin und Stettin, 1781—1795.

685. *Jahn.* Dissertations on the importance and best method of studying the original languages of the Bible, by Jahn and others, translated from the originals, and accompanied with notes, by M. Stuart. Andover, 1821.

" *Lanjuinais, (J. D.)* Notice du Livre intitulé Origine des langages, par Zalkind Hourwitz, par J. D. Lanjuinais, (extrait du Moniteur, No 201, 1808.)

——— ——— see *Gebelin.*

211. Q. *Le Brigant.* Observations fondamentales sur les langues anciennes & modernes, ou prospectus de l'ouvrage intitulé "La langue primitive conservée." Paris, 1787.

1550, 2. *Maupertuis.* Réflexions philosophiques sur l'origine des langues, avec les remarques critiques de M. Turgot.

165. *Rüdiger, (J. C. C.)* Grundriss einer Geschichte der menschlichen sprache, nach allen bisher bekannten Mund- und-Schriftarten, mit proben und Bücherkenntniss; Erster Theil, von der sprache. Leipzig, 1782.

385. *Sicard.* Journal d'instruction d'un sourd muet de naissance. Paris, 1803.

185. *Tooke, (John Horne)* 'Επεα πτερόεντα, or the diversions of parley, by John Horne Tooke, 2 vols. Philadelphia, 1806.

1550, 2. *Turgot.* Remarques critiques sur les réflexions philosophiques de M. Turgot, sur l'origine des langues.

109. *Vater, (J. S.)* Untersuchungen über Amerikas Bevölkerung aus dem alten Kontinente. Leipzig, 1810.

153. —— Mithridates, oder Allgemeine Sprachenkunde, von J. C. Adelung, und J. S. Vater, vol. 3, part 2, and vol. 4. (The remainder is wanting.) Berlin, 1817.

179. ——— Analekten der sprachenkunde. Leipzig, 1821.

384, 13. *Q. Volney*. Rapport fait à l'Académie Celtique, Sur l'Ouvrage Russe de M. le Professeur Pallas, intitulé "Vocabulaires comparés des langues de toute la terre." Paris.

187. *Wilson, (James P.)* An essay on Grammar, the principles of which are exemplified and appended in an English Grammar. Philadelphia, 1817.

---

2. PARTICULAR LANGUAGES.

For Bibles and other religious works in various languages, see Title RELIGION, *above, p.* 71.

African Languages. 423. *Q.* Numerals in 31 African languages, Appendix No. VI. at the end of Bowditch's Mission to Ashantee, p. 503.

For particular languages of this part of the world, see under their respective names.

Algonkin. 66. 2. *Q.* Short Dictionary of the most universal language of the Savages—At the end of the 2d vol. of La Hontan's Travels. London, 1703.

63. *Q.* L'oraison Dominicale (& autres prières) traduites en langage des Montagnards du Canada, Par le R. P. Massé—At the end of Champlain's Voyages de la nouvelle France. Paris, 1732.

Mr. Gallatin in a MS. note in the said Book calls these Montagnards *Algonquins inférieurs*, and so by their Dialect they appear to be. He has subjoined a MS. vocabulary of this language from the Relation of Father Lejeune, a work now very rare.

55. Examples of the Knisteneaux and Algonkin Tongues—In M'Kenzies voyages to Montreal, &c. p. cii.

60. A short vocabulary of the Chippeway language—In Carver's Travels, C. 17 p. 278.

American Languages. 374, 63. *Q.* Extracts of some letters from Sir William Johnson, to Arthur Lee, on the customs, manners, and languages of the Northern Indians of North America. (In the Philosophical Transactions.) London, 1773.

224. New views of the origin of the tribes and nations of America. By Benjamin S. Barton. 2d edit. Philadelphia, 1798.

This work principally consists of comparative vocabularies of the languages of the American Indians.

879. Report of Peter S. du Ponceau, Corresponding Secretary of the Historical and Literary Committee of the American Philosophical Society, on the general characters and forms of the language of the American Indians. Philadelphia, 1819.

879. A Correspondence between the Rev. John Heckewelder and Peter S. du Ponceau, respecting the languages of the American Indians. Philadelphia, 1819.

153. Mithridates oder allgemeine sprachen kunde, von J. S. Vater, vol. 3, part 2. Berlin, 1817.

This volume treats exclusively of the languages of South America, and there is a dissertation prefixed to it, on the American languages in general. See also on this subject, Vater's *Untersuchungen über Amerikas Bevölkerung*, above, page 221.

685. A Discourse on the religion of the Indian tribes of North America, by Samuel F. Jarvis. New York, 1820.

This work contains much information on the Indian languages, particularly the Delaware and the Iroquois.

See further under the head of each particular language, and see also Asiatic languages.

Amharic. 73. *F.* Grammatica Liguæ Amharicæ, quæ vernacula est Habessinorum, autore Jobo Ludolfo. Franc. ad Mœn. 1698.

Anglo-Saxon. 177. Angelsaksisk Sproglare, tilligemed en kort Læsebog, ved R. K. Rask. Stockh. 1817.

Arabic. 163. Elementa linguæ Arabicæ, ex Erpenii Rudimentis ut plurimum desumpta, cujus Praxi Grammaticæ novam legendi praxin addidit Leonardus Chappelow. London, 1730.

49. *F.* Diccionario Español-Latino-Arabigo, por D. Francisco Canes, Tomo I. Madrid, 1787.

449. *Q.* Vestigios da lingoa Arabica em Portugal, por J. de Sousa. 1789.

1071. A Vocabulary of the Arabic language, as spoken by the Moors at Morocco, by William Wiltshire, at the end of Riley's Narrative of the loss of the American Brig Commerce, &c. appendix, p. xxiv.

Aramaic. Languages. 1885. Caroli Schaafs opus Aramæum, complectens Grammaticam Chaldaico-Syriacam, Saluta Targumin, cum versione latinâ & annotationibus; Lexicon Chaldaicum, Libris V. T. Chaldæis, item Salutis Targumicis accommodatum. Lugd. Bat. 1686.

322. Chrestomathia Chaldaica, Edidit J. J. Marcel. Lutet. 1803.

307. *Q. Hottingeri.* Grammatica quatuor linguarum, Hebraicæ, Chaldaicæ, Syriacæ, et Arabicæ. Heidelberg, 1659.

Armenian. 371. Lettre au sujet de la nouvelle Grammaire Arménienne, publiée par M. Cirbied, par M. J. Zorab, Docteur Arménien. Paris, 1823.

Aruwak. 1578. Grammatische Sätze von der Aruwakkischen Sprache, von Theodor Schulz, MS.

521. *Q.* Aruwakkisch-Deutsches Wörter-Buch, vermehrt von Theodor Schulz, 1803, MS.

Ashantee. 423. *Q.* A Vocabulary of the Ashantee language, appendix, No VI. at the end of Bowditch's mission to Ashantee, p. 506.

Asiatic Languages. 56. *Q.* Asia Polyglotta, von Julius Klaproth, mit einem Sprach-Atlas, in folio. Paris, 1823.

404. *Q.* Wörter. Sammlungen aus den Sprachen einiger Völker des Oestlichen Asiens und der Nordwest Küste von Amerika, von A. J. von Krusenstern. St. Petersburgh, 1813.

371. Première & seconde lettre à la Société Asiatique, par Louis de l'Or. Paris, 1823.

See further under the head of each particular language.

Atacapas. 179. Vocabulaire de la langue des Atakapas, par Martin Duralde, dans les *Analekten der sprachen kunde* du Prof. Vater. Leipz. 1821, p. 63.

Atnah. 55. Words of the language of the Atnah or Chin Indians, in M'Kenzie's voyages, C. 3, p. 246.

Basque. 153. Berichtigungen und Zusätze zum ersten Abschnitte des zweyten Band des Mithridates, über die Cantabrische oder Baskische sprache, von Wilhelm von Humboldt, (Im Mithridat. vol. 4.) Berlin, 1817.

Bengalee. *Q.* A grammar of the Bengalee language, by Nathaniel Brassey Halhed Hoogly, in Bengal, 1778.

157. An extensive vocabulary Bengalese and English. Calcutta, 1793.

Berber. 122. *F.* A vocabulary of the Showiah dialect of the language of the Berbers of Africa, by Thomas Shaw. Oxford, 1738.

In his travels to some parts of Africa.

Booroom. 423. *Q.* A vocabulary of the Booroom language, Appendix No. VI. at the end of Bowditch's Mission to Ashantee, p. 506.

Caribbee. 57. *F.* A vocabulary of the language of the Caribbee Indians, by John Davies. London, 1666.

In his history of the Caribbee Islands.

Caucasian Languages. Vocabulaires des diverses langues Caucasiennes comparées entre elles & avec d'autres langues, par Jules Klaproth. Paris, 1823.

In the second volume of his voyage to Mont Caucase, page 289 to the end.

Remarques grammaticales sur la langue Tcherkesse, par le même. Ibid, p. 383.

Grammaire de la langue des Ossètes, par le même. Ibid, p. 437.

Celtic. 200. Grammaire Celto-Bretonne, par M. Le Gonidec. Paris, 1807.

201. Dictionnaire Celto-Breton, ou Breton-Français, par le même. Paris, 1821.

200½. Eléments succincts de la langue des Celtes-Gomérites ou Bretons, par Le Brigant, 2d edit. Brest, an. 7.

See *Irish*, *Welsh*.

Chaldaic, see *Aramaic languages*.

Chetimachas. 179. Vocabulaire de la langue des Chetimachas, par Martin Duralde.

Dans les *Analekten der sprachenkunde* du Prof. Vater, p. 73. Leipzig, 1821.

Cherokee, see *Oto*.

Chepewyan. 55. Examples of the Chepewyan Tongue. In M'Kenzie's voyages to Montreal, &c. p. cxxiii.

Chippeway, see *Algonkin*.

Chilese. 28. An essay on the Chilian language, in the 2d vol. of Molina's history of Chili, p. 285. (Eng. trans.) Middletown, (Con.) 1808.

Chinese. 433. *Q.* A grammar of the Chinese language, by the Rev. Robert Morrison. Serampore, 1815.

434. *Q.* A dictionary of the Chinese language, by the same, 3 vols. (third part of vol. 1 wanting.) Macao, 1815—1822.

50. *F.* Dictionnaire Chinois-François, Latin, par M. de Guignes. Paris, 1813.

64. *F.* Dictionarium linguæ Sinensis, MS. Macao, 1810.

227. *F.* An explanation of the elementary characters of the Chinese, with an analysis of their ancient symbols and hieroglyphics, by Joseph Hager. London, 1801.

401. Q. Dissertation on the characters and sounds of the Chinese language, including tables of the elementary characters, and of the Chinese monosyllables. Serampore, 1809.

431. *Q.* View of China for Philological purposes, by the Rev. Robert Morrison. Macao, 1817.

1886. Dialogues and detached sentences in the Chinese language, with a free and verbal translation in English. Digested as an initiating work for the use of students of Chinese, by the same. Macao, 1816.

322. Essai sur la langue, & la littérature Chinoise, par Abel Remusat. Paris, 1811.

685. Revue de l'ouvrage ci dessus, par M. Lanjuinais. (Extrait du Moniteur.) Paris, 1811.

435. *Q.* Chinese almanacs for 1805, 1810, 1820.

" The speech of the Emperor Kien-Long on the first chapter of the Ta-Hio, or Great Science. Printed in Chinese, at St. Petersburgh, 1819.

" A Chinese essay on Vaccination.

31

435. A map of the Chinese Empire, (in Chinese.)
" A number of a Chinese magazine, printed at Macao.
" A Chinese primer.
The above are introduced here as helps for the student.

Congo. 117, 1. *F.* A short vocabulary of the language of Congo, in Merolla's voyage to that country, in an anonymous collection of voyages and travels, vol. 1. p. 755.

Danish. 407. *Q.* En Dansk og Engelsk Ord-Bog: af Ernst Wolff. London, 1779.

Delaware. 512. *Q.* A Grammar of the language of the Lenni-Lenape or Delaware Indians; translated from the German MS. of the Rev. David Zeisberger, and presented to the American Philosophical Society by Peter S. Duponceau, MS.

1584. A Delaware and English Spelling Book, by the Rev. David Zeisberger, 1st edit. Philadelphia, 1776.

1584½. Same work, 2d. edit. Philadelphia, 1806.
There are material differences in these two editions; the first contains the Lord's prayer, commandments and belief in Delaware and English.

879. Words, phrases and short dialogues in the languages of the Leni-Lenape or Delaware Indians, by the Rev. John Heckewelder. (In the first vol. Histor. Transact. p. 453.) Philadelphia, 1819.
See also as to this language Mr. Heckewelder's correspondence with Mr. Duponceau, in this volume.

108. Lutheri Catechismus, Oefwersatt på American-Virginiske Språket. Stockh. 1696.
This language is that which was spoken by the Delaware Indians of New Sweden; the Catechism is in Indian and Swedish, with a vocabulary and phrases at the end.

179. Verbal-Biegungen der *Chippewayer*, von David Zeisberger. In Vater's *Analekten der Sprachen kunde.* Leipz. 1821.
These are *Delaware* conjugations, by mistake here called *Chippeway.*

Dutch. 312. *Q.* English and Dutch, and Dutch and English Dictionary, by William Sewel. Amsterd. 1802.

148. Neues Holländisches-Deutsches und Deutsch-Holländisches Wörter buch, von Matthias Kramer. Leipz. 1759.

148. Het nieuwe Neder-Hoog-Duitsch en Hoog-Neder-Duitsch Worden-Boek, door Matthias Kramer. Leipz. 1759.

157. Hollandsch-Hoog Duitsch en Hoog Duitsch-Hollandsch Woorden-Boek, Door O. R. F. Winkelmann. Amsterdam, 1796.

Embomma. 1079. A Vocabulary of the Embomma language. In the Appendix to Tuckey's expedition to the river Zaire, p. 395.

English. 159. English Grammar, by Lindley Murray. Hallowell, (Maine) 1823.

540. A Dictionary of the English language, by Samuel Johnson, to which are added, Walker's Principles of English Pronunciation, 4 vols. Philadelphia, 1818.

277. *Q.* A Critical Pronouncing Dictionary and expositor of the English language, by John Walker. London, 1797.

194. Volkome Engelsche Spraak-konst, door George Smith. Rotterdam, 1758.

173. Traité complet de la prononciation Angloise, par Charles Carré. Philadelphia, 1818.

685. A vocabulary or collection of words and phrases, which have been supposed to be peculiar to the United States of America, by John Pickering. Boston, 1816.

365. *Q.* English Phonology, or an essay towards an analysis and description of the component sounds of the English language, by Peter S. Duponceau. (In the 1st vol. Am. Philos. Trans. N. S.) Philadelphia, 1818.

399. Cadmus, or a treatise on the elements of written language, by William Thornton. Philadelphia, 1793.

1581. Orthography corrected, or a plan proposed for improving the English language, by uniting orthography with pronunciation, by Thomas Embree. Philadelphia, 1813.

260, 1581. The Columbian Alphabet, being an attempt, to new model the English alphabet, so as to work every simple sound by an appropriate character, by James Ewing. Trenton, 1798.

205. A System of Notation, representing the sounds of alphabetical characters, by a new application of the accentual marks in present use, with such additions as were necessary to supply deficiencies, by William Pelham. Boston, 1808.

685. Elements on Orthography, or an attempt to form a complete system of letters. Philadelphia, 1817.

Etchemins. 69. *F.* Aliquid de eorum linguâ. In De Laet's Novus Orbis, p. 54. Lugd. Bat. 1633.

Ethiopic or Gheez. 73. Jobi Ludolfi Grammatica Æthiopica; Editio Secunda, ab Autore solicitè revisa, correcta & aucta, cum Appendicibus, &c. Francof. ad Mœn. 1702.

European Languages. 207. A collection of phrases and vocabulary in the Latin, French, Flemish, German, Spanish, Italian,

English and Portuguese languages. Printed in 1585. *(Title page wanting.)*

Fantee. 423. *Q.* A Vocabulary of the Fantee language. Appendix No. VI. at the end of Bowditch's mission to Ashantee, p. 506.

Finnish. 180. Finnische Sprachlehre, von Z. Strahlmann. St. Petersb. 1816.

178. Finska Språkets Grammatik; af Jac. Juden. Wiborg, 1818.

302. *Q.* Fennici Lexici tentamen; Finsk-Orda-Boks Försök, Sammansökt af D. J. (Daniel Juslenius.) Stockh. 1745.

Flemish. 177. *Q.* Le Grand Dictionnaire Français-Flamand, par François Halma. La Haye & Leyde, 1781.

178. *Q.* —— —— Flamand & Français, par le même. La Haye & Leyde, 1781.

French. 197. Principes généraux & particuliers de la langue Française, par M. de Wailly. Huitième Edit. Paris, 1777.

139. Nature displayed in her mode of teaching language to man. Adapted to the French, by N. G. Dufief, 2 vols. Philadelphia, 1804.

176. Abridgment of a French and English Grammar, by M. A. Texier de la Pommeraye. Philadelphia, 1822.

175. Mestre Francez, ou Novo Methodo para aprender a lingoa Franceza por meio da Portugueza; por F. B. D. L. Lisboa.

192. Novo Mestre Francez, ou Nova Grammatica da lingoa Franceza. Lisboa, 1797.

169½. *Γραμματικὴ της Γάλλικης διάλεκτȣ; Συντεθεῖσα μὲν παρὰ Γεοργιȣ Βεντοτη, αφιερωθεισα δε τοῖς Εὐγενεστάτοις Κυρίοις Αὐταδέλφοις Ζωσιμα, παρὰ Σπυρίδωνος Βλαντη. Ενετιησιν,* 1810.

108. *F.* Dictionnaire de l'Académie Française, 3 vol. Paris, 1694.

180. *Q.* Le même, cinquième edition. Paris, 1800.

107. *F.* Dictionnaire universel, contenant tous les mots Français anciens & modernes, & les termes de Sciences & Arts. Par Furetière. Rotterd. 1690.

145. A new and universal pronouncing Dictionary of the French and English languages, by N. G. Dufief, 3 vols. Philadelphia, 1810.

1887. Dictionnaire universel des Synonimes de la langue Française publiés par Girard, Beauzée, Roubaud & autres, 3 vol. Paris, 1802.

Georgian. 141. *Kratkaia Grusinskaia Grammatika;* A Grammar of the Grusinian language, in Russian. St. Petersb. 1802.

See also Klaproth's *Voyage au Mont Caucase,* and his Asia Polyglotta, above, p. 208.

German. 278. *Q.* Dictionnaire Royal Français & Allemand, pour l'une & l'autre nation, par Matthias Kramer, 5 vol. Nuremberg, 1715.

150. Phraseologia Anglo-Germanica, or a collection of more than 50,000 phrases, collected from the best English classics and translated into German, with a vocabulary of words not comprehended in the said Phraseology, by F. W. Haussner. Strasburg, 1798.

See *Dutch.*

Gheez, see *Ethiopic.*

Greek 137. Primitives of the Greek tongue, by M M. de Port-royal. London, 1748.

1888. Græcæ Grammaticæ Compendium, (The Westminster Greek Grammar.) London, 1785.

168½. D. Jacobi Welleri Grammatica Græca nova, antè à B. Abrahamo Tellero quoad Dialectos completa. Lipsiæ, 1708.

176. *Q.* Hederici Lexicon Manuale Græcum, Recensitum & plurimùm auctum à Sam. Patrick. Tertia Editio, auctior & emendatior, curâ Gulielmi Young. London, 1755.

102. *F.* Glossarium ad Scriptores mediæ & infimæ Græcitatis. Auctore Carolo Dufresne Du Cange. Lutetiæ Parisiorum, 1688.

384, 17. *Q.* An essay on the pronunciation of the Greek language, as published in the Memoirs of the American Academy of Arts and Sciences, by John Pickering. Cambridge, (Mass.) 1818.

For *Modern Greek*, see *Romaic.*

Greenland. See the 17th chapter of Egede's Description of Greenland, above, p. 199, and the 6th chapter of the 3d book of Crantz's History of Greenland, vol. 1, p. 217, above, p. 199.

Gros Ventres, see *Oto.*

Guiana, (Indians of.) 69. *F.* De barbarorum horum, (scil. Yaiorum, Arwacorum, & Shebayorum) idiomate. In De Laet's Novus Orbis, p. 642. Lugd. Bat. 1633.

Hebrew. 1889. An easy introduction to the knowledge of the Hebrew language, without the points, by James P. Wilson. Philadelphia, 1812.

1890. A Hebrew grammar, with a praxis or select portions of Genesis and the Psalms, by Moses Stuart, 2d edit. revised and enlarged. Andover, (Mass.) 1823.

322. Chrestomathia Hebraica, varios textus exhibens, quas additâ eorum Lectione, subjuncto que Glossario edidit J. J. Marcel. Lut. Par. 1802.

168. L'Hebreu simplifié, par la méthode alphabétique de C. F. Volney. Paris, 1820.

Hindostanee. 155. A compendious grammar of the current corrupt dialect of the Jargon of Hindostan, commonly called Moors, with a vocabulary English and Moors, Moors and English, by John Hadley. London, 1796.

415. *Q.* The Oriental Linguist; an introduction to the popular language of Hindostan, vulgarly but improperly called the Moors, with an extensive vocabulary, English and Hindostanee, and Hindostanee and English, by John Gilchrist. Calcutta, 1798.

Hochelaga. 69. *F.* Barbarorum qui has partes (Hochelagam) incolunt idioma, in De Laet's Novus Orbis, p. 46. Lugd. Bat. 1633.

Huastecan. 536. *Q.* Noticia de la lengua Huasteca, con Catechismo y Doctrina Christiana, por D. Carlos de Tapia Zenteno. Mexico, 1767.

Hudson's Bay Indians. 281. *Q.* Vocabularies of the languages of the Eskima, *(Eskimaux)* Indians, and of the Indians inhabiting the north-west part of Hudson's Bay. In Dobbs' account of Hudson's Bay, p. 203.

50. A specimen of the languages of sundry Indian nations, inhabiting the inland parts of Hudson's Bay, between that Coast and the Coast of California, viz. the Nehethawa, or Kalisteno, *(Knistenaux,)* the Assinepoetuc, *(Assinipoils,)* or Stone Indians, the Fall Indians, Black Foot, Snake and Sussee Indians. In Umfreville's present state of Hudson's Bay, p. 203.

Huron. 1574. Dictionnaire de la langue Huronne, par Gabriel Sagard. Extrait de son grand voyage au pays des Hurons, imprimé à Paris en 1732, MS.

63. *Q.* Doctrine Chrestienne, traduicte en langage Canadois autre que celui des Montagnars, par le R. P. Brebeuf. At the end of Champlain's Voyages de la nouvelle France. Paris, 1632.

See *Wyandot.*

Icelandic. 181. Undersögelse om det gamle Nordiske, eller Islandske Sprogs Oprindelse, af R. K. Rask. Kiöbenh. 1818.

Italian. 195. Nouvelle méthode de Messieurs de Port Royal, pour apprendre la langue Italienne, 4e edit. Amsterd, 1736.

198½. Le maitre Italien, ou la Grammaire Française & Italienne de Veneroni. Lyon, 1787.

196. Die Volkommene Italiänische Grammatica, von Matthias Kramer. Nürnberg, 1722.

106. *F.* Vocabulario degli accademici della Crusca. Venezia, 1686.

181. *Q.* Nouveau Dictionnaire Français Italien & Italiano-Francese, par l'Abbé François d'Alberti de Villeneuve, 2 vol. Marseille, 1796.

Irish. 170. A grammar of the Iberno-Celtic or Irish language,

2d edit. with additions. To which is prefixed, An essay on the Celtic language, by Charles Vallancey. Dublin, 1781.

175. *Q.* The English-Irish Dictionary, by MacCuirtin. Paris, 1732.

Iroquois. 532. *Q.* Essay towards an Onondago grammar, or a short introduction to learn the Onondago or Macqua tongue, by David Zeisberger, MS.

527. *Q.* Onondagoische Grammatica, von David Zeisberger, with an English translation, by Peter S. Duponceau, MS.

528. *Q.* Same work, in an incomplete form, appearing to be the author's first attempt, MS.

531. *Q.* Onondago words and phrases explained into German, by Chr. Pyrlæus, MS.

523. *Q.* Deutsch und Onondagoisches Wörter-Buch, von David Zeisberger, 7 Bänd. MS.

530. *Q.* Onondago and German Vocabulary, by David Zeisberger, MS.

529. *Q.* Adjectiva, Nomina & Pronomina Linguæ Macquaicæ, auctore Christoph. Pyrlæo, MS.

526. *Q.* Affixa, nominum & verborum linguæ Macquaicæ, auctore Christoph. Pyrlæo, MS.

525. *Q.* Lexicon der Macquaischen sprachen, von Chr. Pyrlæus, MS.

685. *Gaiatonsera Jonteweienstakwa Ongweonwe Gawennontakon;* a spelling book in the language of the seven Iroquois nations, by Eleazer Williams. Plattsburgh, 1813.

Konza, see *Oto.*

Knisteneaux, see *Algonkin.*

Laponic. 314½. *Q.* Lexicon Lapponicum, cum interpretatione, Sueco-Latinâ & Indice Suecano-Lapponico, illustratum præfatione Latino-Suecana Johannis Ihre; nec non auctum Grammaticâ Lapponicâ à Dom. Erico Lindahl et Johanne Oehrling. Holmiæ, 1780.

Latin. 138. New Method of learning the Latin Tongue, by Messrs. de Portroyal, 2 vols. London, 1758.

166. Grammatica Latina, för begynnare, och them som mognare i thet Latinska Språket, af Johann Streling. Wexiö, 1773.

112. *F.* Ambrosii Calepini Dictionarium. 1570.

518. An Abridgment of Ainsworth's Dictionary, English and Latin, for the use of schools, by Thomas Morell. Philadelphia, 1812.

101. *F.* Glossarium ad Scriptores mediæ & infimæ Latinitatis. Auctore Carolo Dufresne Du Cange, 3 vol. Lutetiæ Parisiorum, 1678.

149. Kirschii Cornucopiæ Linguæ Latinæ et Germanicæ. Lipsiæ, 1778.

Mahratta. 156. A Grammar of the Mahratta language, to which are added, dialogues on familiar subjects, by W. Carey, 2d ed. Serampore, 1808.

Malabar. 117, 3. *F.* A short orthography of the Malabar language London, 1704.

Malay. 172. Maleische spraakunst, door G. H. Worndly. Amsterd. 1736.

416. *Q.* A dictionary of the Malay tongue, in two parts, English and Malay and Malay and English, to which is prefixed a grammar of that language, by James Howison. London, 1801.

Malemba. 1079. A vocabulary of the Malemba language, appended to Tuckey's Expedition to the river Zaire, p. 395.

Mandingo. 1075, 1. A vocabulary of the Mandingo language. At the end of the first vol. of Mungo Park's Travels into Africa.

Mantchou. 685. Notice de l'ouvrage intitulé Alphabet Mantchou, rédigé, par L. Langlès, par J. D. Lanjuinais. Paris, 1808.

Massachusetts. 537. *Q.* The Indian Grammar begun, or an essay to bring the Indian language into rules, by John Eliot. Cambridge, 1666.

685. Same work, a new edition, with notes and observations, by P. S. Duponceau, and an introduction and supplementary observations, by J. Pickering. Boston, 1822.

Mexican. 69. *F.* Mexicanorum idioma. In De Laet's Novus Orbis, p. 240. Lugd. Bat. 1633.

1570. Arte Mexicana, compuesta por el P. Antonio del Rincon, de la Comp. de Jesus. Mexico, 1595.

535. *Q.* Arte Novissima de lengua Mexicana, por D. Carlos de Tapia Zenteno. Mexico, 1753.

1568. Compendio del arte de la lengua Mexicana, del P. Horacio Carocchi de la Comp. de Jesus. Mexico, 1759.

59. *F.* Vocabulario en lengua Castellana y Mexicana, compuesto por el muy R. P. Fray Alonso de Molina, de la Comp. de Jesús. Mexico, 1571.

Under this title this book contains a very ample Spanish-Mexican and Mexican-Spanish Dictionary.

Mohawk, see *Iroquois.*

Minetaree, see *Oto.*

Mohegan. 685. Observations on the language of the Muhhekaneew Indians, by Jonathan Edwards. New Haven, 1788.

731. Same work, new edition, with notes, by J. Pickering. Boston, 1823.

1579. Miscellanea linguæ nationis Indicæ, Mahikan dicta, auctore Johan Jacob Schmick, 2 vol. MS.

Nagailer. 55. A specimen of the language of the Nagailer or Carrier Indians. In Mackenzie's Travels, p. 246.

Naudowessie. 60. A short vocabulary of the Naudowessie (or *Sioux*) language. In Carver's Travels, c. 17, p. 288.

New Zealand. 179. Grammatik der Neu-Seeländischen Sprache. In Vater's Analekten der sprachenkunde, s. 1. Leipzig, 1821.

Nootka. 32. Vocabulario de los habitantes de Nutka. (*At the end of the Spanish relation of the voyage made in 1792, by the schooners Sutil and Mexicana.*)

Omawha, see *Oto*.

Onondago, see *Iroquois*.

Oriental Languages. 685. Dissertations on the importance and best method of studying the oriental languages of the Bible, by Jahn and others, translated from the originals, with notes, by M. Stuart. Andover, (Mass.) 1821.

315½. *Q.* Etymologicum Orientale sive Lexicon Harmonicum ἑπτάγλωττον, quo non tantum Hebraicæ linguæ, sed et Chaldaicæ, Syriacæ, Arabicæ, Samaritanæ, Ethiopicæ, et Talmudico-Rabbinicæ Dialectorum voces exhibentur. A Joh. Henr. Hottingero. Francof. 1661.

156½. Primitiæ Orientales, vol. II. containing the Theses in the oriental languages, (Persian, Arabic, Hindostanee, and Bengalee,) pronounced at the public disputation, 29th March, 1803, by the students of the College of Fort William, in Bengal, with translations. Calcutta, 1803.

Osage. 179. Wörter der Osage-sprache, aufgenommen von Dr. Murray. In Vater's Analekten der sprachen kunde, s. 53. Leipzig, 1821.

Othomi. 1571. Reglas de orthographia, y diccionario y arte del idioma Othomi, por D. Luis Neve y Molina. Mexico, 1767.

Oto. 731. Vocabularies of the languages of the Oto, Konza, Omawha, Yankton-Sioux, Minnetarees or Gros Ventres, Pawnee and Cherokee Indians; by Thomas Say. Extracted from the account of Major Long's Expedition. See *Ultra-Mississippian Indians.* Philadelphia, 1822.

Pamticough. 13. *Q.* A vocabulary of the language of the Pamticough Indians. In Lawson's History of Carolina, p. 225.

Pawnee, see *Oto*.

Persian. 419. *Q.* Grammar of the Persian language, by William Jones, 2d edit. London, 1775.

184. Tooti Nameh, or Tales of a Parrot in the Persian language, with an English Translation. *Help for the student.* London, 1801.

405. *Q.* Persian Poem in honour of Catharine II. by the Persian Ambassador Mohamed son of Mahomed Mochsin, surnamed Askrefi, with a Russian translation in verse, 1793. *Help for the student.*

Peruvian. 69. *F.* De Peruvianorum Idiomate atque Poesi. In De Laet's Novus Orbis, p. 477. Lugd. Bat. 1633.

1571½. Arte y vocabulario de la lengua Quichua, general de los Indios del Peru, qui compusò el Padre Diego de Torres Rubio, de la Comp. de Jesus, y añadiò el P. Juan de Figueredo, de la misma Compañia. Reimpreso en Lima, 1754.

Poconchi. 101. Rules for the better learning of the Indian tongue called Poconchi or Pocoman, commonly used about Guatemala and some other parts of Honduras. By Thomas Gage. London, 1699.

In Gage's new survey of the West Indies.

Portuguese. 199. A new Portuguese Grammar, by Anthony Vieyra Transtagano. London, 1801.

193. Maitre Portugais, ou nouvelle Grammaire Portugaise, composée d'après Vieyra & autres Grammairiens. Lisbonne, 1799.

462. *Q.* Dictionary of the Portuguese and English languages, in two parts, Portuguese and English and English and Portuguese, by Anthony Vieyra. London, 1794.

147. Dictionnaire Français & Portugais. Barcelona, 1772.

159. *F.* Diccionario da Lingoa Portugueza publicado pela Academia das Sciencias de Lisboa, tomo I. Lisboa, 1793.

437. *Q.* Catal. dos livros, que se haõ de ler, para a Continuaçaõ do Diccion. da Ling. Port. 1799.

Romaic Greek. 102. *F.* Simonis Portii Romani grammatica linguæ Græcæ vulgaris. At the beginning of the first volume of Ducange's *Glossarium ad Scriptores mediæ & infimæ Græcitatis.* Lugd. 1688.

564. *Q.* Θεσαυρος τῆς ἐγκυκλοπαιδικῆς βάσεως τετράγλωσσος. A Dictionary of the Modern Greek, Latin, French, and Italian languages, beginning with the Modern Greek, by Gerasimus Vlachus of Crete. Venice, 1784.

276. *Q.* Ἑλληνικος Τηλεγραφος, περιοδικὴ ἐφημερὶς πολιτική, φιλολογική τε καὶ ἐμπορική. Εν Βιέννη, Φεβρ. 1812. Νοεμβρ. 1815.

Help for the student, (see *Turkish,* and see above p. 73 and p. 88.)

Russian. 142. Elémens de la langue Russe, *(no author's name.)* Petersbourg, 1805.

143. Elémens raisonnés de la langue Russe, par J. B. Maudru, 2 vol. Paris, 1802.

427. *Q. Novy i Rossiisko-Franzousko-Nemetzkii Slovar.* Nouveau Dictionnaire Russe, François & Allemand, par Jean Heyon. Moscow, 1799.

144. *Polnoi Frantzousskoi i Rossiiskoi Lexikon.* Dictionnaire complet, François & Russe, par J. Tatischeff, 2 vol. St. Petersburgh, 1798.

Sankikani. 69. *F.* De Sankikaniorum lingua. In De Laet's Novus Orbis, p. 75. Lugd. Bat. 1633.

Sanscrit. 436. *Q.* A Grammar of the Sungskrit language, by W. Carey. Serampore, 1806.

158. The Sungskrit Grammar, called Moogdhu boodha, by Vopa Deva.

276. *Q.* Rapports entre la langue Sanscrit & la langue Russe. Présentés à l'Académie Impériale Russe. (Par Fréderic Adelung.) St. Petersb. 1811.

Serbian. 202. Wolf Stephansohns Serbisch-Deutsch und Latinisches Wörter Buch. Lupi Stephani Filii Lexicon Serbico-Germanico-Latinum. Vindob. 1818.

Slavonic. 311. *Q.* Dictionarium trilingue, hoc est, Dictionum slavonicarum, Græcarum & Latinarum thesaurus. *(No imprint or date.)*

South Sea Islands. 61. *F.* Dictionnaire du langage des Isles de Salomon, Isle de Cocos, Nouvelle Guinée & Isle de Moyse, par Jacques Lemaire. Amsterd. 1622.

In the Journal of his Austral navigation.

Souriquois. 69. *F.* Souriquosiorum idioma. In De Laet's Novus Orbis, p. 52. Lugd. Bat. 1633.

Spanish. 190. Gramática de la lengua Castellana, compuesta por la Real Academia Española. Quarta Edic. Madrid, 1796.

191. Gramática de la lengua Castellana, por D. Benito Martinez Gomez Gayoso. Madrid, 1769.

140. Dufief's Nature Displayed in her mode of teaching language to man; adapted to the Spanish by Don Manuel de Torres and L. Hargous, 2 vols. Philadelphia, 1811.

104. *F.* Diccionario de la lengua Castellana, compuesto par la real academia Española. Madrid, 1780.

179. *Q.* Nouveau Dictionnaire Espagnol, François & Latin, par Séjournant, 2 vol. Paris, 1775.

146. Dictionnaire portatif & de prononciation, Espagnol-François & François-Espagnol, par J. L. B. Cormon, 2 vol. Lyon, 1800.

Swedish. 183½. A short introduction to the Swedish Grammar, adapted to the use of Englishmen; by Gustavus Brunnmark. London, 1805.

174. *Q.* Dictionnarium Anglo-Suethico-Latinum, à Jacobo Serenio. Hamburg, 1734.

This work is in two parts, one beginning with the English, the other with the Swedish.

173. *Q.* An English and Swedish Dictionary, by Jacob Serenius, 2d edit. enlarged. Nykoping, 1757.

189. English and Swedish pocket Dictionary, by P. A. Granberg. Stockh. 1807.

Syriac, see *Aramaic languages.*

Tagala. 534. *Q.* Compendio de la Arte de la lengua Tagala, por el P. Fr. Gaspar de San Augustin. Manila, 1703.

Tamul. 164. Grammatica Latino Tamulica, ad usum Missionarium Soc. Jesu, by C. J. Beschius. Trangambariæ, 1737.

162. Rituale Trangambaricum, (Linguâ Tamulicâ.) *Help for the student.* Trangambariæ.

Tartar. 402. Q. *Grammatika Tartarskago Yazwika*, a grammar of the Tartar language, by Joseph Higanoff. St. Petersburgh, 1801.

406. Q. *Slovar Rossiisco-Tartarskii*, a Russian and Tartar dictionary, by Joseph Higanoff. St. Petersburgh, 1804.

371. Sur les Boukhares, par M. Klaproth. Paris, 1823.

Tarascan. 1469. Arte de la lengua Tarasca, por el R. P. Diego Basalenque, Sacalo à luz, el R. P. Nicolas de Quixas. Mexico, 1714.

Tcheremiss. 403½. Q. *Sotchinenia prinadlezhaschtschiya v' grammatikè Tcheremiscago Yazwika*—A grammatical treatise on the Tcheremiss language. St. Petersburgh, 1775.

Turkish. 563. Q. Elémenta de la langue Turque, ou tables analytiques de la langue Turque usuelle, avec leur développement, par M. Viguier, Préfet Apostolique des Missions du Levant, sous les auspices de M. Le Comte de Choiseul-Gouffier, Ambassadeur de S. M. T. C. près la Porte Ottomane. Constantinople, Imprimerie du Palais de France, 1790.

198. Grammatica, Dizionarj e Colloquj per imparare le lingue Italiana, Greca-volgare e Turca, da Bernardino Pianzola. Venezia, 1701.

Tuscarora. 13. Q. A vocabulary of the Tuskeruro (Tuscarora) language. In Lawson's History of Carolina, p. 225.

Uigur. 228. F. Abhandlung über die sprache und Schrift der Uiguren, nebst einem Wörterverzeichnisse und anderen Uigurischen sprachproben, aus dem Kaiserl. Uebersetzungshoff, zu Peking. Herausgegeben von Julius Klaproth. Paris, 1820.

Ultra-Mississippian Indians. 880. Vocabularies of the languages of the Wahtoktata, or Otoes, Konzas, Omawhas, Yancton-Sioux, Minnetarees, or Gros Ventres, Pawnees, Shoshonees, and Upsarokas, or Crow Indians, and also of the Cherokees. (At the end of the 2d vol. of Major Long's Expedition to the Rocky Mountains.) Philadelphia, 1823.

Welsh. 306. A brief introduction to the Welsh or ancient British language, by Thomas Richards. Bristol, 1753.

171. A new English-Welsh Dictionary, by William Evans. Carmarthen, 1771.

Woccon. 13. Q. A vocabulary of the language of the Woccon Indians. In Lawson's History of Carolina, p. 225, above, p.

Wyandot, see *Huron*.

Yankton, see *Oto*.

XXII. ARCHÆOLOGY & BIBLIOGRAPHY.

1. Archæology. 2. Bibliography.

1. ARCHÆOLOGY.

American Antiquarian Society, see above, page 8, under *Worcester*.

Antiquarian Society of London, see above, page 4, under *London*.

Asiatic Society of Bengal, see above, p. 2, under *Calcutta*.

1068. *Ancora, (Gaetano d')* Guida ragionata per le antichità e par le curiosità naturali di Pozzuoli, e de' luoghi circonvicini. Napoli, 1792.

111. *Anon.* La science des Médailles, antiques & modernes, 2 vol. Paris, 1715.

1305. —— Réflexions philosophique sur l'origine de la civilisation. Amsterdam, 1781.

1032. —— La Scava, or some account of an excavation of a Roman town on the hill of Châtelet in Champagne, discovered in the year 1772; to which is added, a journey to the Simplon, by Lausanne, and to Mont Blanc, through Geneva. London, 1818.

85. Q. *Arbuthnot, (John)* Tables of ancient coins, weights and measures, explained and exemplified in several dissertations, by John Arbuthnot, with an appendix, containing observations, by Benjamin Langwith. London, 1754.

224. *Barton, (Benjamin S.)* Observations on some parts of natural history; to which is prefixed, an account of several ancient vestiges discovered in North America, Part I. (containing the account of the vestiges.) London, *(no date.)*

The remainder was not published.

341. *Belknap, (Jeremy)* A discourse on the discovery of America by Columbus, with four dissertations. 1. On the circumnavigation of Africa by the ancients. 2. On the pretensions of Martin Boehm to the discovery of America. 3. On the question whether the honey-bee is a native of America. 4. On the colour of the native Americans, and the recent population of this Continent. Boston, 1792.

318. *Boulard, (A. M. H.)* Dissertation sur les découvertes des anciens en Asie, traduit de l'Anglais. Paris, 1820.

161. *Brerewood. (Edward)* De ponderibus & pretiis veterum nummorum, Liber unus. London, 1614.

See above, p. 220, *Brerewood*.

1451. *Cellarii, (Christophori)* Antiquitates Romanæ. Londini, 1711.

1385. *Chiniac.* Histoire des Celtes & particulièrement des Gaulois & des Germains, 8 vol. Paris, 1770.

384. 6. Q. *Chaulnes, (de)* Mém. sur un monument Egyptien. Paris, 1777.

96. Q. *Clarke, (E. D.)* The Tomb of Alexander, a dissertation on the Sarcophagus brought from Alexandria and now in the British Museum. Cambridge, 1805.

38. F. *D'Herbelot.* Bibliothèque orientale. Maestricht, 1776.

1397. *Dubos, (l'Abbé)* Histoire des quatre Gordiens prouvée & illustrée par les Médailles. Paris, 1695.

101. F. *Ducange, (Car. Dufresne)* De Imperatorum Constantinopolitanorum, seu de inferioris ævi, vel imperii, uti vocant, numismatibus, Dissertatio. *(At the end of the 3d volume of his* "Glossarium ad Scriptores mediæ & infimæ Latinitatis.) Lutet. Paris, 1678.

242. *Fabbroni.* Dissertazione del Bombice e del Bisso degli Antichi. Perugia, 1782.

1456. *Fabricii, (Georgii)* Romanorum antiquitatum libri duo. Basiliæ, 1560.

371. *Ferlus, (L. D.)* Explication du Zodiaque de Denderah. Observations curieuses sur ce monument & sur sa haute antiquité, 2e edit. Augmentée de l'explication de la précession des Equinoxes, & des différences qui existent entre les Zodiaques Grecs & le Zodiaque de Denderah. See *Saulnier, fils.* Paris, 1822.

412. Q. *Franklin, (William)* Inquiry in the site of ancient Palibothra, conjectured to lie within the limits of the modern district of Bhangulpoor, according to researches made on the spot in 1811 and 1812. London, 1815.

291. *Gama, (Antonio de Leon y)* Descripcion historica y chronologica de las Piedras que con occasion del nuevo empedrado que se esta formando en la plaza principal de Mexico se hallaron en ella el año de 1790. Mexico, 1792.

337. Q. *Gébelin, (Court de)* Monde Primitif, analysé & comparé avec le monde moderne, 9 vol. Paris, 1779.

138. F. *Goltz, (Hubert)* Thesaurus rei antiquariæ uberrimus. Antverpiæ, 1618.

117, 2. F. *Greaves, (John)* A discourse of the Roman Foot and Denarius, from whence as from two principles the Measures and weights used by the Ancients may be deduced. London, 1704.

299. Q. *Gusseme, (Thomas Andres de)* Diccionario Numismatico general, para la inteligencia de las medallas antiquas. Madrid, 1773.

85. F. *Hammer, (Joseph de)* and others; Les Mines d'Orient 6 vols, 4, 5, and 6, *(1st. 2d. and 3d. wanting.)* Vienne, 1814.

229, F. R. 28. ——— ——— Copie figurée d'un rouleau de papyrus trouvé en Egypte, publié par M. Fontana, & expliquée par M. de Hammer. Vienne, 1822.

998. *Jones, (W.) Chambers, (Wm.) &c.* Dissertations and Mis-

cellaneous pieces relating to the history, antiquities, &c. of Asia, 2 vols. London, 1792.

1891. *Kennett, (Basil)* Romæ Antiquæ Notitia; or the antiquities of Rome, to which are prefixed two essays concerning Roman learning and Roman education, first Amer. edit. Philadelphia, 1822.

322. *Klaproth, (Julius)* Sur l'origine du Papier-Monnaie, (lu à la Soc. Asiatique.) Paris, 1822.

" ——— ——— Mémoire dans lequel ou prouve l'identité des Ossètes, peuplade du Caucase, avec les Alains du moyen Age, (lu à la Soc. Asiat.) Paris, 1822.

371. ——— ——— Examen des Extraits d'une Histoire des Khans Mongols, insérés par M. J. J. Schmidt dans le 6e vol. des Mines de l'orient. Paris, 1823.

" ——— ——— Sur quelques antiquités de la Sibérie, Mémoire lu à la Société Asiatique, le 2 Dec. 1822. Paris, 1823.

425. *Le Roy.* Les navires des anciens considérés par rapport à leurs voiles. Paris, 1783.

427 ——— Lettre à M. Franklin sur les navires des anciens. Paris, 1787.

125. *F. Loon, (Gerard van)* Histoire métallique des Pays-Bas, 5 vol. La Haye, 1732.

228. *F. Middleton, (J. J.)* Grecian Remains in Italy; a description of Cyclopian Walls and Roman Antiquities, with Topographical and Picturesque views of ancient Latium. London, 1812.

1050. *Mallet.* Northern Antiquities: or description of the Manners, Customs, Religion and Laws of the Ancient Danes and other Northern Nations, translated from the French, 2 vols. London, 1770.

336. *Q. Muratori.* Dissertazioni sopra le antichità Italiane, 3 vol. *(2d vol. wanting.)* Milan, 1751.

414½. *Q. Ousely, (William)* Oriental Collections for January, February and March, 1797. London, 1797.

963. *Parker, (Richard)* History and Antiquities of the University of Cambridge. London.

1039. *Pauw, (de)* Recherches Philosophiques sur les Egyptiens, les Chinois, les Grecs, & les Américains, 7 vol. Paris, an 3.

1. *F. Pitiscus, (Samuel)* Lexicon antiquitatum Romanorum, 2 vol. Lewardiæ, 1713.

23. *Q. Potocki, (le Comte Jean)* Chronologie des deux prémiers livres de Manéthon. St. Petersb. 1805.

" ——— ——— Examen critique du fragment Egyptien connu sous le nom d'ancienne Chronique, tiré à cent Exemplaires. St. Petersb. 1808.

287. *Quatremere de Quincy.* Sur les vases Céramographiques appellés jusqu' à présent vases Etrusques. Paris, 1807.

444. *Q. Ribeiro, (João Pedro)* Observações historicas e criticas para servir de Memorias ao Systema da Diplomatica Portugueza. Lisboa, 1798.

384, 5. Q. *Sargent, (Winthrop)* and *Barton, (B. S.)* Papers relative to certain American antiquities. Philadelphia, 1796.
Barton, (B. S.) see *Sargent.*

371. *Saulnier (fils)* Notice sur le voyage de M. le Lorrain en Egypte & Observations sur le Zodiaque circulaire de Denderah avec un Dessin de ce Zodiaque. Paris, 1822.

643. *Schröder, (Joh. Henry)* Om Skandinavernes Fordna Upptäckts-resol till Nord-Amerika. Upsala, 1818.

371. *Spassky, (Georg.)* De Antiquis sculpturis & inscriptionibus in Sibiriâ repertis. Petrop. 1822.

568. *Stiles, (Rev. Ezra)* Anniversary election sermon.
(Takes a view of the origin of the North American Indians, and Asiatic Tartar Tribes.)
Worcester, (Mass.) 1785.

99. Q. *Tassie, (James)* Descriptive Catalogue of ancient and modern engraved gems, cameos, and intaglios, French and English, 2 vols. London, 1791.

109. *Vater, (Johann Severin)* Untersuchungen über Amerikas Bevölkerung aus dem alten Kontinente. Leipzig, 1810.

64. Q. *Velasquez, (J. J.)* Ensayo sobre los alphabetos de las lettras Desconocidas en los antiguas medallas y monumentos de España, 1752.

1035. *Wilcocks, (Joseph)* Roman Conversations, or a short description of the antiquities of Rome; interspersed with characters of eminent Romans, and reflections, religious and moral on Roman History, 2 vols. London, 1797.

326. *Williams, (John)* An Enquiry into the truth of the tradition concerning the discovery of America, by Prince Madog ab Owen Gwynedd, about the year 1170.
London, 1791.

326. ——— ——— Further observations on the discovery of America. London, 1792.

2. BIBLIOGRAPHY.

14. Q. Bibliothecæ Americanæ primordia. An attempt towards laying the foundation of an American Library.
London, 1713.

285. Q. Bibliotheca Americana. London, 1789.

1809. Catalogue of the books, maps, and charts, belonging to the Library established at the capitol in Washington.
Washington, 1812.

1810. Catalogue of the Library of the United States.
Washington, 1815.

1803. Catalogue of books belonging to the Library of Friends of Philadelphia. Philadelphia, 1813.

" Catalogue of Books in Friends' Library.

696. Catalogue of the Library of the Athenæum of Philadelphia, (with its Charter and By-laws.) Philadelphia, 1820.

1808. Catalogue of the Medical Library belonging to the Pennsylvania Hospital. Philadelphia, 1806.

1800. Catalogue of the books, pamphlets, &c. in the Library of the Massachusetts Historical Society. Boston, 1811.

1801. Catalogus Bibliothecæ Harvardianæ Cantabrigiæ Nov-Anglorum. Bostoniæ, 1790.

1802. Catalogue of the books, tracts, &c. in the Library of the New York Historical Society. New York, 1813.

1803. Catalogue of books in the Library of the American Academy of Arts and Sciences. Boston, 1802.

1811. Catalogue of books, belonging to the Charleston Library Society. Charleston, 1811.

1796. Catalogue of the Library of the Royal Institution of Great Britain. London, 1809.

1797. Catalogue of books contained in the Library of the Medical Society of London. London, 1803.

1798. Catalogue of books belonging to the Edinburgh Library. Edinburgh, 1808.

1799. Catalogue of books belonging to the Dublin Society. Dublin, 1807.

210. Q. Catalogue of the Library of the writers to his majesty's signet. Edinburgh, 1805.

1515, 43. Catalogue of books written by J. Priestley.

1805. The Charter, Laws, and Catalogue of books of the Library Company of Philadelphia. Philadelphia, 1770.

1806. Catalogue of the books belonging to the Library Company of Philadelphia, with four Supplements. Philadelphia, 1807—1820.

1807. Catalogue of the books belonging to the Loganian Library. Philadelphia, 1795.

618. The Charter, Laws, Catalogue of books, list of Philosophical instruments, &c. of the Juliana (Penn.) Library Company in Lancaster. Philadelphia, 1766.

1803. Laws and Regulations of the Trenton Library Company. Trenton, 1819.

203. Memoria ed Orazione del P. Paolo Ma. Paciaudi, intorno la Biblioteca Parmense. Parma, Bodoni, 1815.

143. F. Epitome de Bibliotheca Oriental y Occidental, Nautica y Geografica, de Don Antonio de Leon Pinelo, en que se contienen los Escritores de las Indias Orientales y Occidentales, y Reinos convecinos, China, Tartaria, Japon, Persia, Armenia, Etiopia y otras partes, por el Marques de Torre Nueva, 3 vol. Madrid, 1737.

1794. Handbuch fur Bücherfreunde und Bibliothekare, 9 vol. Halle, 1788—1792.

220. Manuel du Libraire & de l'amateur de livres, par Brunet, 4 vol. Paris, 1814.

221. Nouveau Dictionnaire portatif de Bibliographie, par F. J. Fournier. Paris, 1809.

1812. Versuch einer medicinischen handbibliothek von J. J. Palm. Erlangen.

XXIII. LITERATURE AND FINE ARTS.

1. Poetical and Prose Writings. 2. Literary Journals.
3. Fine Arts.

1. POETICAL AND PROSE WRITINGS.

535. *Adams, (John Quincy)* Lectures on Rhetoric and Oratory, 2 vols. Cambridge, 1810.

615. ——— ——— An Inaugural Oration delivered at the author's installation as Boylston professor of Rhetoric and and Oratory at Harvard University, in Cambridge, Massachusetts, June 12, 1806. Boston, 1806.

1055. *Ælian.* Αιλιανȣ (Κλ.) Ποίκιλη Ἱςορία; Æliani variæ Historiæ; cum versione Justi Vutteri & perpetuo Commentario Jacobi Perizonii, 2 vol. Lugd. Bat. 1701.

1443. *Alciati, (Andreæ)* Omnia emblemata cum commentariis. Paris, 1618.

160. *Ali Ben Abi Taleb.* Carmina Arabicè & Latinè; Edidit & notis illustravit Gerardus Kuypers. Lugd. Bat. 1745.

1492. *Andres, (D. Juan)* Cartas familiares à sũ hermano dandole noticia del viage que hizo à varias Ciudades de Italia en 1785, 5 vol. Madrid, 1791.

1495. ——— ——— Cartas à su hermano, dandole noticia de la litteratura de Viena. Madrid, 1794.

89. F. *Anon. Panteon Rossiiskich Awtorow.* The Pantheon of Russian authors—containing the portraits of Boian, Nestor, Nicon, Matweeff, and several others with short notices, (in Russian.) Moscow, 1801.

1603. *Apuleius.* Apuleii Madaurensis Platonici Opera omnia quæ exstant. Francof. 1621.

1162. *Aratus.* Αρατȣ Διοσημεῖα. Notis & collatione Scriptorum illustravit Thomas Forster. London, 1815.

292. Q. *Barlow, (Joel)* The Columbiad, a poem. Philadelphia, 1807.

643. ——— ——— Revüe du Poëme de la Colombiade. (Extrait du Magasin Encyclopédique.) 1809.

" ——— ——— Observations critiques sur le poëme de la Columbiade, par Grégoire. Paris, 1809.

" ——— ——— Letter to Henry Gregoire, in reply to his letter on the Columbiad, by J. Barlow. Washington, 1809.

622. *Biddle, (Nicholas)* Oration delivered before the Pennsylvania State Society of Cincinnati, on the 4th of July, 1811. Philadelphia, 1811.

213. *Botta, (Carlo)* Camillo, o Veia conquistata. Parigi, 1815.

206. *Browne, (Thomas)* Viridarium Poeticum, seu Delectus Epithetorum in Latinis Scriptoribus sparsorum, in Scholarum usum. Londini, 1799.

1591. *Buchleri, (Joannis)* Phrasium Poeticarum Thesaurus, edit. 13a. London, 1642.

972. *Busby, (Thomas)* Arguments to prove that De Lolme was the author of Junius's Letters. London, 1816.

114. *Caminha, (Pedro de Andrade)* Poezias de —— 1791.

1476. *Capmany, (Antonio de)* Filosofia de la Eloquencia, Madrid, 1777.

1487. *Cascales, (Francisco)* Tablas poeticas; añadese Epistola Q. Horatii Flacci de Arte Poeticâ, in methodum redacta, cum novis in Grammaticam observationibus. Madrid, 1779.

287. *Catullus.* Les nôces de Thétis & de Pélée, de Catulle; traduites en vers Français avec le Latin en regard. Paris, 1809.

1426. *Cervantes, (Miguel)* El ingenioso Hidalgo Don Quixote de la Mancha, nueva edicion, corregida por la Real Academica Española, 4 vol. Madrid, 1782.

1427. La misma obra, corregida de nuevo, con nuevas notas de Pellicer, 8 vol. Madrid, 1798.

1020. *Chapman, (Nathaniel)* Select speeches, forensic and parliamentary, 5 vols. Philadelphia, 1808.

287. *Chézy, (A. L.)* Yadjnadatta-Budha ou la mort d'Yadjnadatta; Episode extrait & traduit du Ramayana, Poëme épique Sanskrit. Paris, 1814.

1547. *Dante Alighieri.* La divina Commedia, 3 vol. col comento di G. Biagioli. Parigi, 1818.

213½. *Delille, (Jacques)* Les trois Règnes de la Nature, avec des notes par Cuvier. La Haye, 1809.

310½. *Erasmus.* The Complaint of peace, translated into English. London, 1802.

460. Q. *Euripides.* Εὐριπίδου Ἱππόλυτος Στεφανοφόρος. Hippolito de Euripides, vertido do Griego em Portugues. Lisboa, 1803.

1486. *Florez, (Don C.)* La Poetica de Aristoteles dada a nuestra Lengua Castellana. Madrid, 1778.

906. *Franklin, (Benjamin)* His works, 6 vols. Philadelphia, 1818.

—— —— Political, miscellaneous, and philosophical pieces, with plates. London, 1779.

459. Q. *Gomez, (Francisco Dias)* Obras Poeticas de —— 1739.

1552. *Gregoire.* De la littérature des Nègres. Paris, 1808.

451. *Gudin, (P. Ph.)* L'Astronomie, Poëme. Paris, 1810.

418. Q. *Hafiz.* Persian Lyrics, or scattered poems from the Diwan of Hafiz. London, 1800.

1921. *Hammer, (Joseph von)* Memnons Dreyklang, nachgeklungen in Dewajani, einem indischen Schäferspiele; Anahid, einem persischen Singspiele und Sophie, einem Türkishen Lustspiele. Wien, 1823.

——, see *Spenser.*

129. F. *Hawkesworth.* The adventurer, *(editio princeps.)* London, 1752—1754.

940. *Hopkinson, (Francis)* Miscellaneous works, 3 vols. Philadelphia, 1792.

214. *Horace.* Horatii Flacci Opera, in usum Delphini, cum notis Ludovici Desprez. Philadelphia, 1804.

845. *Humphreys, (David)* Miscellaneous Works. New York, 1804.

321. *Hupfeld, (Herm.)* Animadversiones philologicæ in Sophoclem. Marburgi, 1817.

995. *Jones, (G.)* Poeseos Asiaticæ commentariorum libri VI. Londini, 1774.

1589. *Junii, (Melchioris)* Scholæ Rhetoricæ de contexendarum epistolarum ratione. Argerlinæ, 1592.

384, S. Q. *Kirkpatrick, (W.)* Introduction to the history of the Persian Poets.

244. *Kirkland, (John Thornton)* Oration delivered at the request of the Soc. of Φ. B. K. in the chapel of Harvard College on the day of their anniversary, July 19, 1798. Boston, 1798.

159½. *Lescallier.* Bakhtiar Nameh, ou la Favorite de la Fortune; Conte traduit du Persan. Paris, 1805.

152. *Lempriere.* Classical Dictionary. Philadelphia, 1822.

747. *M'Henry, (James,)* Waltham, an American Revolutionary Tale, in three cantos. New York, 1823.

984. *Mandrillon, (J.)* Fragmens de politique & de litterature. Paris, 1788.

285. *Martinez de la Rosa, (Francisco)* Zaragoza, Poema. Londres, 1811.

1541. *Muret*, see *Neufchâteau*, above, p. 89.

391. Q. *Oppian.* Oppiani Poeti Halieuticon, sive de Piscibus. Argentorati, 1534.

1253. ——— The same work, in English. Oxford, 1722.

212. *Petrarca.* Le opere di—con le osservazioni di Messer Francesco Alunno. Venetia, 1539.

129. *Pope, (Alexander)* Essay on Man, in five languages—English, Latin, Italian, French and German. *(All in verse.)* Strasburg, 1772.

1424. *Ramsay, (Allan)* Poems, with the life of the author, and his collection of Scots proverbs, 2 vols. Philadelphia, 1813.

1548. *Raynouard.* Choix des Poësies originales des Troubadours, 3 vol. Paris, 1816.

622. *Rush, (Richard)* An oration delivered on the 4th of July, 1812, in the Hall of the House of Representatives, at the Capitol, Washington.

349. *Sacombe.* La Luciniade, ou l'art des accouchemens; Poëme didactique. Paris, an 1.

1485. *Salas, (Gonzales de)* Nueva idea de la Tragedia antigua ò ilustracion de las Poetica de Aristoteles. Madrid, 1778.

1489. *Sanchez, (D. T. A.)* Colleccion de Poesias Castellanas Anteriores al Siglo XV. 4 vol. Madrid, 1770.

1690. *Sarbievius, (Matthias Casimir.)* Lyricorum Libri IV. Epodon, Liber Unus, alterq. Epigrammatum. Antwerp, 1634.

1498. *Sedano, (Juan Joseph Lopez de)* Jahel, tragedia. Madrid, 1763.

213. Q. *Sheridan.* Lectures on Elocution. London, 1762.

313. Q. *Spenser.* His sonnets, with a translation into German verse, by Joseph de Hammer. Vienna, 1814.

128. F. *Steele, (Richard)* The Tattler, or the Lucubrations of Isaac Bickerstaff, from April 12, 1709, to January 2, 1710-11, *(editio princeps.)* London, 1709.

126. *Stockler, (F. de Borja Garção)* Obras de, Tomo 1. Lisboa, 1805.

396. ——— ——— Poesias Lyricas. Londres, 1821.

1546. *Tacitus, (Cornelius)* De moribus Germanorum et vitâ Agricolæ, (Italian translation.) Genova, 1814.

1425. *Thomas.* Œuvres de, 2 vol. Paris, 1773.

1430. ——— Essai sur les Eloges, 2 vol. Paris, 1812.

290. ——— Elogium on Marcus Aurelius, translated from the French. New York, 1808.

1543. *Thomson, (James)* The Seasons, a Poem, with a French translation. Paris, 1802.

346. Q. *Tiraboschi, (G.)* Storia della Letteratura Italiana, 9 vol. Modena, 1787—1794.

1604. *Valerii Maximi.* Factorum dictorumque memorabilium exempla. Francofurti, typis Brubacchii.

308. Q. *Van Merken, (Lucretia Wilhelmina)* Germanicus, in zestien gezangen. Amsterdam, 1787.

1516. ——— The same work, translated into French. Amsterdam, 1787.

88. F. *Various Authors.* Pacis Annis 1814 and 1815, Foederatis Armis restitutæ Monumentum, Orbis Terrarum de Fortuna reduce Gaudia Linguis interpretans Principibus Piis Felicibus Augustis Populisque Victoribus Libertatis Dicatum, *(being poetical and prose pieces in a great variety of languages and in appropriate characters, elegantly engraved.)* Wratislav. *(No date.)*

127. F. ——— ——— The World, from January the 4th, 1753, to December, 1756, by Adam Fitz-Adam, 2 vols. *(Editio princeps.)* London 1753—1756.

1479. *Velasques, (D. J.)* Origenes de la Poesia Castellana. Malaga, 1797.

1597. *Villette.* Oeuvres du Marquis de. Londres, 1786.

90. F. *Virgil.* Georgicorum Publii Virgilii Maronis libri IV. Æneidos libri I. a IV.—Græco Carmine heroico expressi. Studio, &c. E. de Bulgaris. Petrop. 1786.

87. F. *Woodward, (A. E. B.)* A system of Universal Science. Philadelphia, 1816.

1431. *Young.* Noites Selectas de Young. Lisboa, 1783.

ANONYMOUS.

1519. Exhortations à M. de Voltaire, avec le Parallèle entre lui & Rousseau. Londres, 1770.

725. A Poem on the rising glory of America, being an exercise

delivered at the public commencement at Nassau Hall, September, 25, 1771. Philadelphia, 1772.

326. A Norfolk Tale, or a Journal from London to Norwich, with a prologue and an epilogue. London, 1792.

460. *Q.* Osmia, Tragedia de asumpto Portuguez, em cinco actos. Coroada pela acad. Real de Sciencias. Lisboa, 1795.

339. Fanny, (a Poem.) New York, 1819.

1429. Choix d'Eloges Français, 5 vol. Paris, 1812.

---

2. LITERARY JOURNALS.

556. *Q.* Allgemeine Literatur Zeitung, 1815-1818, 6 vol. Halle and Leipzig, 1815, 1818.

730. The American Magazine, a monthly miscellany, conducted by H. Gates Spafford, vol. 1, No. 4, September, 1815. New York.

1874. The American Monthly Magazine and Critical Review, from May 1817, to March 1819, 4 vols. New York, 1817-1819.

1737. Annals of Oriental Literature, Parts I. and II. London, 1820.

1523. Annual Review and History of Literature; Arthur Aikin, Editor, 6 vols. (1802—1807.) London, 1803—1808.

1588. Bibliothèque Française, Ouvrage périodique, rédigé par Ch. Pougens, 9 vol. *(vol. 1 et 3 manquent.)* Paris, 1801—1802.

585. Columbian Magazine, 4 vols. Philadelphia, 1787—1790.

1554. Edinburgh Review, 37 vols. 1802—1823.

1563. Journal général de la littérature de France, 24 vol. *(les 4 premiers volumes manquent.)* Paris, 1803—1821.

1875. The Literary and Scientific Repository and Critical Review, No. 1 to No. 6, 3 vols. New York, 1821.

1524. Monthly Magazine, 40 vols. 1809—1823. *(vols. 1 and 2 wanting.)* London.

439. *Q.* Memorias de Litteratura Portugueza, 1792—1806, 7 vol.

552. North American Review, 8 vols. Boston, 1815, 1823.

586. Pennsylvania Magazine, 2 vols. Philadelphia, 1775-6.

1537. The Portfolio, (a Literary Journal,) by Oliver Oldschool, from 1816 to 1823, 16 vols.

1876. The Portico, a repository of science and literature, from January, 1816, to March, 1818, 5 vols. Baltimore.

1555. Quarterly Review, 27 vols. 1809—1823. London, 1813—1823.

1565. Revue encyclopédique, ou analyse raisonnée des productions les plus remarquables dans la littérature, &c. 16 vol. Paris, 1819—1822.

562. *Q.* The Literary Gazette, or Journal of Criticism, Science, and the Arts, being a third series of the Analectic Magazine, from January 6, 1821, to Dec. 29, 1821.

3. FINE ARTS.

11. *F.* *Anon.* Omaggio delle Provincie Venete alla Maestà di Carolina Augusta, Imperatrice d'Austria, *(being elegant engravings of ancient monuments.)* Venezia, 1818.

452. —— Essai sur le perfectionnement des beaux arts, 2 vol. Paris, 1803.

499. —— Essay on town and country architecture, in Russian. St. Petersburgh, 1802.

223. *F.* *Bemetzrieder.* New lessons for the Harpsichord. London, 1783.

238. ——— Précis d'une nouvelle Méthode de Musique. Londres, 1783.

240. ——— On the principles of Music. London, 1783.

1500. *Boettiger, (C. A.)* Amalthea, oder Museum der Kunst-mythologie und bildlichen Alterthumskunde. Leipzig, 1820.

1403. *Brissot de Warville.* Tableau des sciences & des arts en Angleterre. London, 1784.

1033. *Lafolie, (J.)* Mémoires historiques relatifs à la statue équestre de Henry IV. Paris, 1819

1553½. *Liron, (Chev. D.)* Explication du systême de l'harmonie, pour abréger l'Étude de la composition. Londres, (Paris,) 1785.

204. *Moreau de St. Mery.* Discours sur l'utilité du Musée établi a Paris. Parma, 1805.

146. *F.* *Palladio, (Andrea)* Four books of architecture, translated by Isaac Ware. London.

147. *F.* *Pozzo, (Andrea)* Prospettiva de' pittori e architetti. Roma, 1764.

148. *F.* Same work, with an English translation, by J. Sturt. London, 1693.

273. *Tatham, (W.)* Circular architecture, being a new mode of building. London, 1803.

398. *Vinci, (Leonardo da)* Traité élémentaire de la Peinture. Paris, 1803.

132. *F.* *Vitruvii* Architectura. Venise, 1497.

ANONYMOUS.

640, 741. Report of the committee appointed to examine into the rise, progress, and present state of the Society of Artists of the United States, read April 15, 1812. Philadelphia, 1812.

620. The constitution of the Society of Artists of the United States, established at Philadelphia, 1810. Philadelphia, 1810.

640. Annual exhibitions of the Society of Artists of the United States, 1811—1819. Philadelphia.

" . Exhibition at the Pennsylvania Academy of the Fine Arts of Mr. Allstone's picture of the Dead Man restored to Life, by touching the bones of the Prophet Elisha, May 1816. Philadelphia, 1816.

244. Constitution of the Columbianum, or American Academy of the Fine Arts. Philadelphia, 1795.

" Exhibition of the Columbianum, or American Academy of the Fine Arts. Philadelphia, 1795.

640. Catalogue of statues, busts, &c. in the collection of the Pennsylvania Society of the Fine Arts. Philadelphia, 1807.

640. Guide to the Philadelphia Museum.

" Description of the picture of Christ healing the sick in the temple, painted by B. West. Philadelphia, 1817.

620. Articles for the establishment of a Society for the printing and publishing of the works of Grecian, Roman, Hebrew, and other Oriental Literature, to be denominated the "American Classic Association." Philadelphia, 1808.

384, 16. Q. Catalogue of the exhibition of the American Academy of Arts, 1816. New York.

" Catalogue of paintings, statues, busts, &c. exhibited by the American Academy of the Fine Arts, Sept. 1, 1817. New York.

640. The charter and by-laws of the American Academy of the Fine Arts, instituted Feb. 12, 1802, under the title of American Academy of the Arts; with an account of the statues, busts, &c. belonging to the Academy. New York, 1817.

XXIV. MISCELLANEA.

1. Miscellaneous Dictionaries and Collections.
2. Miscellaneous Writings.
3. Almanacs, &c.

1. MISCELLANEOUS DICTIONARIES AND COLLECTIONS.

350. Q. Encyclopédie Méthodique ou par ordre de Matières, Par une Société de Gens de Lettres, de Sçavans & d'Artistes. Paris, 237 vol. divisés en:

Art Aratoire, 1 vol.
Antiquités, 10 vol.
Agriculture, 7 vol. A-EYM.
Arts & Métiers, 16 vol.
Amusemens des Sciences, 1 vol.
Assemblée Nationale, 1 vol.
Système Anatomique des Animaux, 2d. vol. *(le 1 vol. manque.)*
Architecture, 3 vol. A-ESC.
Beaux-Arts, 4 vol.
Botanique, 8 vol. A-PAN.
Chasse, 1 vol.

Chimie, 3 vol. A-CHI.
Chirurgie, 4 vol.
Commerce, 5 vol.
Economie Politique & Diplomatique, 8 vol.
Equitation, Escrime, Danse & l'art de nager, 1 vol.
Encyclopediana, 1 vol.
Finances, 4 vol.
Forêts & Bois 1re partie, 1 vol.
Géographie, 6 vol. avec un Atlas en 2 vol. par Bonne & Desmarets, *(Voyés p. 214.)*
——— Ancienne, 6 vol.
——— Physique, 2 vol. A-LAV.
Grammaire & Littérature, 6 vol.
Histoire, 10 vol.
Histoire Naturelle.
——— Quadrupèdes, 1 vol.
——— Vers, 2 vol. A-CON.
——— Oiseaux, 3 vol.
——— Poissons, 1 vol.
——— Insectes, 7 vol. A-MAN.
Jurisprudence, 18 vol. *(la 2e partie du 8e manque.)*
Logique, 8 vol.
Mathématiques, 5 vol.
Jeux Mathématiques & Familiers, 1 vol.
Manufactures & Arts, 5 vol.
Marine, 6 vol.
Médecine, 14 vol. A-JUS.
Art Militaire, 6 vol. & supplément, 2 vol.
Philosophie Ancienne & Moderne, 6 vol. & supplément. A-PAS.
Musique, 1re partie, 1 vol. A-CYN.
Phisique, 1 vol. A-BUF.
Pêches, 1 vol.
Théologie, 6 vol.

PLANCHES.

Art Aratoire, 1 vol.
Histoire Naturelle, 22 vol.
Chirurgie, 1 vol.
Planches générales, 8 vol. *(le 7e manque.)*
In all 204 vols. of text, 31 vols. of plates, and 2 vols. of maps.

506. The British Encyclopedia, or Dictionary of Arts and Sciences. By William Nicholson, (American edition,) 12 vols. Philadelphia, 1819.

267. Q. Encyclopedia, or a Dictionary of Arts, Sciences and Miscellaneous Literature. First American edition, 18 vols. Philadelphia, Dobson, 1798.

268. Q. Supplement to the above, 3 vols. Philada. Dobson, 1803.

269. Q. The Cyclopædia, or Universal Dictionary of Arts, Sciences and Literature, by Abraham Rees, 41 vols. Philadelphia, Bradford.

270. Q. Plates belonging to the above, 6 vols. Philada. Bradford.

34

100. *F.* Lexicon Technicum, or an Universal English Dictionary of Arts and Sciences. By John Harris, 2 vols. London, 1704.

103. *F.* Johannis Henrici Alstedii Encyclopædia, 2 vol. Herborn, Nassov, 1630.

150. *F.* Chambers' Dictionary of Arts and Sciences, 3 vols. *(imperfect.)* London, 1753.

126. *F.* Athenian Gazette, or casuistical mercury, 2 vols. London, 1691.

1921. Archives of Useful Knowledge, a work devoted to Commerce, Manufactures, Rural and Domestic Œconomy, Agriculture, and the useful Arts, by James Mease, M. D. 2 vols. Philadelphia, 1811.

893. The American Register, or a summary review of history, politics and literature, by Robert Walsh, junr. 2 vols. Philadelphia, 1817.

587. The American Museum, or Repository of ancient and modern fugitive pieces, prose and poetical. Edited by Mathew Carey, 12 vols. Philadelphia, 1787—1792.

These volumes, besides the literary collections, contain a great number of political pieces and documents illustrating the history of the times.

1557. Emporium of Arts and Sciences, 5 vols. the two first by J. R. Coxe, the others by T. Cooper. Philadelphia.

1171. Edinburgh Essays and Observations, Physical and Literary, 3 vols. Edinburgh, 1754.

25. Mercurio Peruano, 2 vols. Lima, 1791.

---

2. MISCELLANEOUS WRITINGS.

944. *Abercrombie, (Rev. James)* Academical discourses, and miscellaneous publications. Philadelphia, 1809, 1810.

580. *Alden, (Timothy)* Collection of American Epitaphs, 5 vols. New York, 1814.

1437¼. *Ali-Gier-Ber.* La Certitude des preuves du Mahométisme. Londres, 1780.

384, 16. *Q. Allen, (Andrew)* Claim and Answer with the subsequent proceedings in the case of A. Allen against the United States. Philadelphia, 1799.

696. *Beck, (Paul)* A Proposal for altering the eastern front of the City of Philadelphia. Philadelphia, 1820.

723. *Beveridge, (John)* Epistolæ familiares et alia quædam Miscellanea. Familiar epistles and other miscellaneous pieces, wrote originally in Latin verse by John Beveridge, to which are added several translations into English verse by different hands. Philadelphia, 1765.

638. *Birkbeck, (Morris)* Extracts from a supplementary letter from the Illinois dated January 31st, 1819, addressed to British emigrants arriving in the Eastern ports, July 19th, 1819, reply to William Cobbett, July 31st, 1819. New York, 1819.

1422. *Brown, (William Lawrence)* Prize essay on the natural equality of man. Philadelphia, 1793.

250. *Cooper, (Thomas)* Some information respecting America. London, 1795.

712. *Courtauld, (George)* Address to those who may be disposed to remove to the United States of America, including remarks on Mr. Birkbeck's opinions upon this subject. Sudbury, 1820.

741. *Davis, (John)* The Philadelphia Pursuits of Literature, a satirical poem, by Juvenal Junius. To which is added, a candid and dispassionate dissertation on the merits of the writers in the Portfolio, &c. Philadelphia, 1805.

496. Q. *Delesclache.* L'art de discourir des passions, des biens, & de la charité. Paris, 1660.

58. *Du Calvet, (Pierre,* of Montreal,) Narrative of his case and persecutions, French and English. London, 1774.
This shows the state of the British colony of Canada, immediately after the conquest.

1534. *Du Pont de Nemours.* Irénée Bonfils sur la religion de ses pères & de nos pères. Paris, 1808.

153½. F. *Eisenberg, (Le Baron de)* Description du manège moderne dans sa perfection, par le Baron d'Eisenberg, avec gravures par B. Picart. La Haye, 1733.

1501. *Fernagus de Gelone.* Relation de la déportation & de l'exil à Cayenne d'ùn jeune Français. Paris, 1816.

1477. *Foronda, (Valentin de)* Miscellanea, ò colleccion de varios discursos, segunda edic. Madrid, 1793.

63. *Grece, (Charles F.)* Facts in respect to emigration to Canada and the United States. London, 1819.

306. *Hoyle.* An Essay towards making the game of chess easily learned. London, 1761.

641. *Ingersoll, (C. J.)* Inchiquin, the Jesuit's Letters during a late residence in the United States of America, being a fragment of a private correspondence, accidentally discovered in Europe, by some unknown foreigner. New York, 1810.

582. *Johnson, (C. B.)* Letters from the British settlement in Pennsylvania. Philadelphia, 1819.

102. *Mandrillon.* Mémoire addressé à l'Académie de Lyon sur la question si la découverte de l'Amérique a été utile ou nuisible au genre humain, MS.

577½. *Melish, (John)* Information and advice to emigrants to the United States. Philadelphia, 1819.

1405. *Moreau de St. Méry.* Abrégé des Sciences & des arts, à l'usage de la jeunesse. Philadelphia, 1796.

1406. Same work in English. Philadelphia, 1797.

1342. *Neild, (James)* Account of the society for the discharge of persons imprisoned for small debts. London, 1808.

632. *Paine, (Thomas)* The Age of Reason, being an investigation of true and of fabulous theology. Paris, an 2.

224. Q. *Palissy, (Bernard)* Œuvres de, avec des notes par Faujas de St. Fond & Gobet. Paris, 1777.

968. *Porney, (M. A.)* Elements of Heraldry. London, 1795.

318. *Robinson, (W. D.)* Memoir addressed to persons of the Jewish religion in Europe, on the subject of emigration to, and settlement in, one of the parts of the United States of North America. London, 1819.

390. Q. *Rollenhagius, (Gabriel)* Nucleus emblematum selectissimorum, *(being an engraved selection of devices and mottos.)*

663. *Sampson, (William)* Trial of Captain H. Whitby for the murder of J. Pierce, with his dying declaration, also the trial of Captain G. Crimp, for piracy and man stealing. New York, 1812.

" ——— ——— Is a Whale a Fish? An accurate report of the case of J. Maurice against S. Judd, tried in the Mayor's Court of New York on the 30th and 31st of December, 1818. Wherein the above problem is discussed, theologically, scholastically, and historically. New York, 1819.

1436. *Sharp, (Granville)* His Works, 5 vols. London, 1774—1777.

463. Q. *Trithemius.* Steganographia, hoc est, ars per occultam scripturam animi sui voluntatem absentibus aperiendi certa. Darmstadii, 1621.

ANONYMOUS.

American Army. 1468. Registers of the army of the United States, from 1813 to 1817.

1333. Registers of the officers and agents, civil, military, and naval, in the service of the United States. Washington, 1818.

Blacks. 364. Narrative of the proceedings of the black people during the late awful calamity in Philadelphia, in 1793. Philadelphia, 1794.

Boston Athenæum. 620. Memoir of the Boston Athenæum, with the act of incorporation. Boston, 1807.

British Museum. 234. Synopsis of the contents of the British Museum, 2 parts. London, 1810—1821.

Commissioners on the British Treaty. 619. Sundry resolutions and proceedings in cases before the board of commissioners for carrying into effect the sixth article of the treaty between his Britannic Majesty and the United States of America. Philadelphia, 1799.

Connecticut Claims in Pennsylvania. 642. A brief statement of the origin and progress of the Connecticut intrusion in the State of Pennsylvania. 1803.

627, 240. An examination on the Connecticut claim to lands in Pennsylvania. Philadelphia, 1774.

627. A brief exhibition of the rights of jurisdiction and soil of the State of Pennsylvania. 1782.

" Connecticut claims examined on its ground, their private title, their Indian deed of 1754, &c. 1795.

627. Petitions to Congress of inhabitants of Pennsylvania, settled on lands under Connecticut claims, previous to 1795.

273. Important statement of facts relative to the Connecticut claimants of Pennsylvania lands, by T. Coxe. Lancaster, 1801.

627. An important statement of facts relative to the invalidity of the pretensions formerly made upon the Pennsylvania lands by the unincorporated companies of Connecticut claimants, by Tench Coxe. Lancaster, 1801.

Free-Masonry. 347. A few notices of the history of Free-Masonry in several parts of Europe, Asia, and Africa. Boston, 1798.

336. A master key to Free-Masonry, by which all the secrets of the society are laid open. London, 1760.

Gold-Mine. 384, 16. Q. Account of the North Carolina Gold-Mine Company.

Greenwich Hospital. 182. Q. Historical account of the Royal Hospital at Greenwich. London, 1789.

Illinois and Ouabache Companies. 273. Account of the proceedings of the Illinois and Ouabache Land Companies, in pursuance of their purchase made of the Independent Natives, 1773 & 1775. Philadelphia, 1803.

Indians. 339. A new society for the benefit of Indians, organised at the City of Washington, 1822.

Lord Selkirk. 668. Statements respecting the Earl of Selkirk's settlement of Kildonan upon the Red River in North America; its destruction in the years 1815 and 1816; and the massacre of governor Temple and his party, with a map. London, 1817.

668. A narrative of the occurrences in the Indian countries of North America, since the connexion of the Earl of Selkirk with the Hudson's Bay Company. London, 1817.

627. Memorial of the Illinois and Ouabache Land Companies to the Congress of the United States, and their prayer for redress, presented 1802.

" An account of the proceedings of the Illinois and Ouabache Land Companies in pursuance of their purchases made of the independent natives, July 5th, 1773, and 18th October, 1775. Philadelphia, 1796.

Migration to America. 638. Hints to emigrants on the choice of lands, particularly addressed to the farmers in the north-eastern states, by Agricola. Albany, 1817.

638. Thoughts on emigration, in a letter from a gentleman in Philadelphia to his friend in England. London, 1794.

250. Extract of a letter from a gentleman in America

to a friend in England on the subject of emigration.

Monkish Orders. 248. Specimen of the natural history of the various Orders of Monks, after the manner of Linnæan system, by Physiophilus, translated from the Latin, by Born. London, 1783.

Philadelphia City. 384, 16. *Q.* Reports of the city councils of the title to the state house yard of Philadelphia. 1813.

Richmond Theatre. 746. A narrative of the conflagration of the Theatre in the city of Richmond, on the 26th of December, 1811. Philadelphia, 1812.

Sandwich Islands. 738. Narrative of five youths from the Sandwich Islands now receiving an education in this country. New York, 1816.

Swiss Colony in Brazil. 718. Providencias para a jornada da Colonia Suissa desde o Porto do Rio de Janeiro até á Nova Friburgo. Disposition concernant le voyage de la colonie Suisse dès le port de Rio Janeiro jusqu' à la nouvelle Fribourg, in Portuguese and French. Rio de Janeiro, 1819.

Washington, (General.) 741. An eulogium on General Washington being appointed commander in chief of the Federal army in America, (in verse.) Philadelphia, 1781.

Widow's Scheme. 214. *F.* Calculations with the principles and data on which they are instituted, relative to the Widow's Scheme. Edinburgh, 1748.

Yazoo Claims. 627. Sundry papers in relation to the claims commonly called the Yazoo Claims, Dec. 18, 1809. Washington, 1809.

S. ALMANACS, &c.

FOREIGN.

1861. A collection of London Almanacs, for the years 1663, 1672, 1677, 1679, 1682, 1694, 1697, 1705, 1706, and 1708 a 1752 inclusive. The years 1726, 1727 and 1737, are wanting.

These almanacs were collected by the late Dr. Benjamin Franklin, and are bound together in volumes, each volume containing several almanacs all for the same year. Each of the years 1706 and 1708 has three volumes, the years 1709, 1710, 1711, 1718, 1734, and 1735, have each two, chiefly duplicates.

London Court and City Registers, or Court Kalendars, under different names for the years 1746, 1758, 1760, 1763, 1765, 1766, 1767, 1775, 1776, 1777, 1778, (duplicates) 1779, 1783, 1800—List of the British Parliament for 1806.

1862. Edinburgh Town and Country Almanacs, for the years 1783, 1784.

1863. The Glasgow Almanac for 1779, 1804.
1863½. The Oxford Almanac (Christian and Jewish) for 1692.
967½. A new Pocket Companion for Oxford, or Guide through the University, containing an accurate description of public edifices, buildings, &c. Oxford, 1814.
393. Almanach Impérial pour 1812 and 1813. Paris.
394, 1869. Almanach Royal pour 1814, 1815, and 1816, par Testu. Paris.
1868. Almanach du Commerce de Paris, pour 1809, 1811, 1812, 1813, and 1815, par de la Tynna. Paris.
1867. Almanak Mercantil, o Guia de Commerciantes, para los años 1802, 1803, and 1808. Madrid.
398½. Q. Kongelig Dansk Hof og Stats Calender for 1813. Kiöbenhavn.
107. Guia de Forasteros de la isla de Cuba. Habana, 1820.
666. Almanach Royal d'Hayti pour les années 1814, 1815, 1816, par P. Roux au Cap-Henry.

AMERICAN.

113. Philadelphia almanacs from 1719 to 1744 inclusive, collected by Dr. B. Franklin, and bound together in one volume. Among these are several printed by himself under the name of Richard Saunders or Poor Richard. The year 1720 is wanting.
" Poor Richard's (Franklin's) Almanac for 1758, in which the Doctor's celebrated moral piece "*The way to Wealth*," is published for the first time.
" The same for 1764.
" Philadelphia Almanac for 1765.
1865. United States Register for 1794, 1795. Philadelphia.
1864. Philadelphia Almanacs for 1812, 13, 14.
1864½. American Almanacs in the German language for the years 1817, 1818, 1820, 1823. Printed at Philadelphia and Reading in Pennsylvania, and Baltimore and Hagerstown in Maryland.
1872. Philadelphia Directory, 1794—1798, 1785—1797, 1800—1811, 1813, 1816, 1820, 27 vols. Philadelphia.
1873. The Massachusett's Register, 1802, 1811, 2 vols. Boston.
1873½. Baltimore Directory, 1819.
581. Alden's New Jersey Register. Newark, 1811.

XXV. SUPPLEMENT,

Containing the books that have been added to the Library while this Catalogue was in the press, and those that have been accidentally omitted, misplaced, or inaccurately described in this catalogue.

1. MEMOIRS AND TRANSACTIONS, &c.

1522. Mémoires de l'Académie de Dijon, de 1746 à 1773, 2 vols. Dijon, 1769—1774.

1672. Transactions of the College of Physicians of Philadelphia, vol. 1. part 1. Philadelphia, 1793.

1165. Discours prononcé à l'ouverture de la première séance publique du cercle des Philadelphes tenue au Cap-Français le 11 Mai, 1785, avec une description de la ville du Cap, par Arthaud. Paris, 1785.

749. A discourse concerning the influence of America on the mind, being the annual oration delivered before the American Philosophical Society on the 18th Oct. 1823, by C. J. Ingersoll. Philadelphia, 1823.

749. A discourse delivered before the New York Alpha of the Phi Beta Kappa, by De Witt Clinton. Albany, 1823.

2. ASTRONOMY.

204½. *Q.* Le Mastigophore, ou Précurseur du Zodiaque, en trois parties contenant la connoissance des temps, les tables de déclinaison, ascension, &c. par le Sr. Laisné. Brest, 1700.

1892. Voyage to California to observe the transit of Venus, with an historical description of the author's route through Mexico, by M. Chappe d'Auteroche. Also a voyage to Newfoundland and Sallee to make experiments on Le Roy's time keepers, by M. de Cassini. London, 1778.

1893. An account of the astronomical discoveries of Kepler, including an historical view of the systems which had successively prevailed before his time, by Robert Small. London, 1804.

3. MATHEMATICS.

1894. Mémoire sur quelques changemens faits à la Boussole & au Rapporteur, suivi de la description d'un nouvel instrument nommé Grammomètre, par M. Maissiat. Paris, 1818.

142½. *Q.* Trigonométrie rectiligne & sphérique, par Antoine Cagnoli, traduit de l'Italien, par N. M. Champré. Paris, 1808.

4. NATURAL PHILOSOPHY.

574. *Q.* Renati Descartes principia Philosophiæ; accedunt specimina Philosophiæ and Tractatus de Passionibus animæ. Amstelod. (Elzevir) 1664.

140. *F.* Micrographia, or some physiological description of minute bodies made by magnifying glasses, with observations and inquiries thereupon, by R. Hooke. London, 1667.

580. *Q.* The works of Robert Boyle, to which is prefixed the life of the author, 6 vols. London, 1772.

See above, p. 28, No. 320. Q.

1599. Traité du Mouvement des Eaux & des autres corps fluides, par Mariotte. Paris, 1700.

5. CHEMISTRY.

1201½. Chimie appliquée à l'Agriculture, par M. le Comte Chaptal, 2 vol. Paris, 1823.

575. *Q.* Elementa Chemiæ, quæ anniversario labore docuit in publicis privatisque Scholis Hermannus Boerhaave. Duo Tomi in uno. Lugd. Bat. 1732.

For Translation, see above, p. 29, No. 209.

1209½. Chemical Essays principally relating to the arts and manufactures of the British dominions, 2d edit. by Samuel Parkes, 2 vols. London, 1823.

6. NATURAL HISTORY.

565. *Q.* Emanuelis Kœnig, dicti Avicenna, Regnum Minerale. Basil. Raurac, 1686.

566. *Q.* A Natural History of Fossils, by Emanuel Mendez da Costa, vol. 1. part 1. London, 1757.

567. *Q.* Mémoires pour servir à l'histoire & à l'anatomie des Mollusques, par le Chevalier Cuvier. Paris, 1817.

375. Première Décade Ichthyologique, ou description complete de dix espèces de poisons nouvelles ou imparfaitement connues, habitant la mer qui baigne les côtes de l'Isle de Cuba. Paris, 1823.

35. *F.* Beata ruris otia fungis Danicis impensa, à Theod. Holmskjold. Havniæ, *(no date.)*

234. *F.* Icones plantarum Japonicarum, auctore Car. Petr. Thunberg. *(Inserted by mistake in this catalogue under the name of Smyth, above p. 45.)*

235½. American Entomology, or description of the Insects of North America, with coloured plates, by Thomas Say. Philadelphia, 1817.

263½. *Q.* History and description of the Royal Museum of Natural History, published by order of the administration of that establishment, translated from the French of M. Deleuze, with three plans and fourteen views of the galleries, gardens and menagerie, 2 vol. Paris, 1823.

316. *Q.* Elementos de Orictognosia ó del conocimiento de los Fósiles,

dispuestos segun los principios de A. G. Werner, por D. A. M. Del Rio. Mexico, 1795.

41. *F.* Museum Carlsonianum in quo novas et selectas Aves coloribus ad vivum brevique descriptione illustratas, exhibet Andreas Sparrman, 2 vol. Holmiæ, 1788.

2. *Q.* Histoire des conferves d'eau douce, contenant leur différente méthode de reproduction, & la description de leurs principales espèces, par Jean Pierre Vaucher. Genève, 1803.

167. *Q.* Icones Pictæ rariorum Fungorum; Figures coloriées de Champignons rares. Paris, 1803.

169. *F.* Mineralogical Journal in Europe, descriptive of the minerals, which Thomas P. Smith left to the American Philosophical Society, MS.

451. *Q.* Breves Instrucções aos correspondentes da Academia das Sciencias de Lisboa sobre as remessas dos productos e noticias pertencentes à Historia da Natureza, para formar hum Museo Nacional. Lisboa, 1781.

1918. A history of the earth and animated nature, by Oliver Goldsmith, 5 vols. Philadelphia, 1823–4.

1919. A supplement to the History of animated nature, by Oliver Goldsmith, selected principally from the animals peculiar to North America, by John D. Goodman, 2 vols. Philadelphia, 1824.

7. RURAL AND DOMESTIC ECONOMY.

291. *Q.* Letters from George Washington to John Sinclair on agricultural and other interesting topics, all in a fac simile of his handwriting. London, 1800.

321. *Q.* A new digester or engine for softening bones, by Denys Papin. London, 1681.

8. MEDICINE AND SURGERY.

1895. D. Jo. Frid. Blumenbachii Institutiones Physiologicæ. Gottingæ, 1787.

110. *F.* The works of Ambrose Paré, Surgeon, translated out of the Latin and compared with the French, by A. Sprigelius. London, 1618.

1898. The Institutes and Practice of Surgery, being outlines of a course of lectures, by Wm. Gibson, M. D. Philadelphia, 1824.

465. *Q.* Mémoires sur les Hôpitaux de Paris, par M. Tenon. Paris, 1788.

296. *Q.* An account of the principal Lazarettos in Europe, with various papers relating to the plague, by John Howard. London, 1791.

384, 14. *Q.* Commentatio Anatomico-Physiologica, sistens disquisitionem an verum organorum digestioni inservientium discrimen inter animalia herbivora, carnivora & omnivora reperiatur, auctore J. W. Neergaard. Göttingæ, 1804.

576. Q. Observations on the structure of hospitals for the treatment of lunatics, and on the general principles on which the cure of insanity may be most successfully conducted by Andrew Duncan, jun. Edinburgh, 1809.

1698. Collection of Inaugural Dissertations on Medical subjects. New York, 1797—1813.

1917. Ueber Psychische Heil-mittel und Magnetismus, von J. D. Brandis. Kopenh. 1818.

192. Q. London Medical Dictionary, by B. Parr, 2 vols. Philadelphia, 1819.

295. Q. System of Surgical Anatomy, by William Anderson. New York, 1822.

1896. Essays on various subjects connected with Midwifery, by William P. Dewees. Philadelphia, 1823.

1897. A Treatise on the Diseases of the Chest, by R. T. H. Laennec. Philadelphia, 1823.

1666. Tracts on Suspended Animation, by W. Hawes & A. Fothergill. London, 1783.

1924. A Treatise on the Diseases of the Eye, by George Frick. Baltimore, 1823.

---

9. RELIGION.

231. F. Biblia Sacra Vulgatæ Editionis, Sixti V. Pont. Max, jussu recognita atque edita cum expositionibus priscorum Patrum litteralibus et mysticis ipsorum verbis fideliter prolatis. Antverpiæ, 1630.

568. Q. Biblia Pentapla, das ist, die Bücher des heiligen schrift des alten und neuen Testaments, nach fünf-facher Deutscher Verdollmetschung, 3 vol. Hamburg, 1710–12.

569. Q. Francisci Mayronis Doctoris illuminati Sermones. Venet. 1491.

1600. Miscellanea, in quibus continetur Responsio ad nuperas D. Simoni in libro super fide græcorum de dogmate Transubstantionis cavillationes. Londini, 1690.

1899. An Apology for the true Christian Divinity, being an explanation and vindication of the principles and doctrines of the people called Quakers, written in Latin and English, by Robert Barclay. Philadelphia, 1805.

1900. Apologie de la vraie Théologie Chrétienne, contenant l'explication & la défense des principes & de la doctrine de de la Société dite des Quakers, par Robert Barclay. Traduit en Français, par E. P. Bridel. Londres, 1797.

1901. A Treatise on Church Government, by Robert Barclay. Philadelphia, 1822.

1902. A Journal or Historical Account of the life, travels, sufferings, Christian experiences, and labours of love, in the work of the ministry, of that ancient, eminent, and faithful servant of Jesus Christ, George Fox, 2 vols. Philadelphia, 1808.

190 . No Cross, No Crown, by William Penn. Philadelphia, 1807.

1904. Point de Croix, Point de Couronne, par Guillaume Penn. Traduit de l'original, par Claude Gay. Bristol, (Eng.) 1746.

1905. The Journal of Thomas Chalkley, to which is annexed a collection of his works. New York, 1808.

1906. The Works of John Woolman, 5th edit. Philadelphia, 1818.

1907. The Christian experiences, gospel labours, and writings, of that ancient servant of Christ, Stephen Crisp. Philadelphia, 1822.

1908. The original and present state of man briefly considered, by Joseph Phipps. Philadelphia, 1818.

954. Acts and Proceedings of the Presbyterian and Associate Reformed churches in America, from 1785 to 1814. Wilmington, Philadelphia, &c. 1785—1815.

10. MORAL SCIENCES.

214. *Q.* Dalla perfettione della vita politica, di M. Paolo Parutti, Nobile Venetiano. Venetia, 1599.

1909. Elements of the Philosophy of the human mind, by Dugald Stuart, 2 vols. in one. Albany, 1822.

1341. Observations on the old and new views and their effects on the conduct of individuals, as manifested in the proceedings of the Edinburgh Christian Instructor, and M'Owen, by Abraham Combe. Edinburgh, 1824.

384, 14. *Q.* Analysis and Analogy recommended as the means of rendering experience and observation useful in education, by H. G. M'Nab. Paris, 1818.

11. JURISPRUDENCE.

71. *Q.* Lois & Constitutions des Colonies Françaises de l'Amérique sous le vent de 1550 a 1785 par Moreau de St. Mery. 6 vol. Paris, *(no date.)*

141. *F.* Ordenanzas de la Ilustre universidad y casa de contratacion de la muy Noble y muy leal villa de Bilbao. Madrid, 1796.

25. *Q.* Mémoire & consultation pour la Dame Marquise d'Anglure, contre le Sieur P. Petit; Question d'Etat. Paris, 1783.

1910. The Laws of the Commonwealth of Massachusetts from 1780 to 1816, published by order of the General Court, 4 vols. Boston, 1807—1816.

1911. A Digest of the Laws of Maryland, by Thomas Herty. Baltimore, 1799.

1786. Ordinances of the corporation of the city of Philadelphia from 1701 to 1812, collected by John C. Lowber. Philadelphia, 1812.

" A digest of the ordinances of the corporation of the city of

Philadelphia and of the Acts of Assembly relating thereto, by John C. Lowber and C. S. Miller. Philadelphia, 1822.

749. Two addresses to "The associated Members of the Bar of Philadelphia," pronounced by William Rawle, Chancellor of the Institution. Philadelphia, 1824.

---

12. BIOGRAPHY.

749. A discourse on the death of Col. James Morrison, delivered at Lexington, Kentucky, by Horace Holly. Lexington, 1823.

120. *Q.* An account of the life, writings, and inventions of John Napier of Merchiston, by David Stewart, Earl of Buchan, and Walter Minto. Perth, 1787.

---

13. HISTORY AND CHRONOLOGY.

384, 10. *Q.* Coloniæ Anglicanæ illustratæ: or the acquest of dominion, and the plantation of colonies made by the English in America, with the rights of the colonists examined, stated and illustrated. London, 1762.
This work contains, among other things, the Bull of Pope Nicholas I. of the 8th of January, 1454, conferring the empire of Guinea, on Alphonso, King of Portugal.

30. *Q.* Von dem Regiment des Lobl. Eydgenootschaft, von Josias Simlar. Zurich, 1722.

163. *F.* Memoria historica, politica, y economica, de esta provincia de Misiones de Indios Guaranis, por Gonzalo de Doblas, MS.

137. *F.* An impartial account of what passed most remarkable in the parliament relating to the case of Dr. Henry Sacheverell. London, 1710.

61. *Q.* Joannis Genesii Sepulvedæ Opera cum edita, tum inedita, accurante Rigiâ Historiæ Academiâ, 4 vol. Madrid, 1780.

1915. Justini Historiæ Philippicæ, cum Versione Anglicâ Johannis Clarke. London, 1780.

570. *Q.* The History of the United Provinces of the Netherlands from the death of Philip II. King of Spain to the truce made with Albert and Isabella, by William Lothian. London, 1780.

230. *F.* A chronological history of the European States, with their discoveries and settlements from the treaty of Nimeguen in 1678, to the close of the year 1794, by Charles Mayo. Bath, 1795.

1913. Mémoires de Sully, principal ministre de Henri le Grand, 6 vol. Paris, 1814.

1914. Histoire du Brésil, depuis sa découverte en 1500 jusqu'en 1810, por Alphonse de Beauchamp, 3 vol. Paris, 1815.

1912. An epitome of ancient and modern history, for the use of schools, by Benjamin Tucker. Philadelphia, 1822.

14. HISTORICAL DOCUMENTS.

1916. A collection of the parliamentary debates in England, from the year 1668 to 1740, 18 vols. London, 1739—1741.

16. Q. A journal of the proceedings in the detection of the conspiracy, formed by some white people, in conjunction with negro and other slaves, for burning the city of New York in America, and murdering the inhabitants, by the Recorder of the city of N. York. N. York, 1744.

24. Q. Procès-verbal de ce qui s'est passé au Lit de Justice tenu par le Roi à Paris, le 12 Novembre, 1774. Paris, 1774.

51. An account of the proceedings of the British and other Protestant inhabitants of the province of Quebec in North America, in order to obtain a house of assembly in that province. London, 1775.

674. The constitution proposed for the government of the United States, by the federal convention held at Philadelphia, with the ratification thereof by the delegates of Pennsylvania, in the state convention. Philadelphia, 1787.

571. Q. A selection from the Harleian Miscellany of Tracts which principally regard English history, of which many are referred to by Hume. London, 1793.

297. Speech by Mr. Fox in the House of Commons, January 4th, 1793, on the alien bill. London, 1793.

899. Debates in the House of Representatives of the United States, during the first session of the fourth congress upon the constitutional powers of the house with respect to Treatises. Philadelphia, 1796.

1756. Journal of the Senate of the United States of America, being the first session of the tenth congress, begun at Washington, October 26, 1807. Washington, 1807.

" Journal of the House of Representatives of the same date. Washington, 1807.

114. F. Minutes of evidence taken before the House of Commons of Great Britain, on the petitions against the orders in Council. London, 1812.

890. The Naval Monument, containing official and other accounts of all the battles fought between the navies of the United States and Great Britain during the late war. Boston, 1816.

372. Mr. Alexander Baring's speech in the House of Commons 15 May, 1823, on Mr. Buxton's motion for a resolution declaring slavery to be contrary to the English Constitution and to Christianity. London, 1823.

" Mr. Canning's speech on the same motion, May 16, 1823. London, 1823.

372. The speech of G. Canning in the House of Commons on the motion of T. Fowel Buxton, for a resolution declaratory of slavery in the British Colonies, being contrary to the English Constitution and to Christianity, May 1823. London, 1823.

1765. Message of the President of the United States to Congress at the opening of the session of 1823–4, with the documents thereto annexed. Washington.

” Report of the Secretary of the Treasury on the state of the finances, January 2, 1824. Washington, 1824.

749. Mr. Webster's Speech, (in Congress,) on the Greek Revolution. Washington, 1824.

165. *F.* Collections of Treatises between the government of Pennsylvania and the Indian Nations, MS.

---

15. POLITICAL ECONOMY AND STATISTICS.

81. *Q.* European commerce, showing new and secure channels of trade with the continent of Europe: detailing the produce, manufactures and commerce of Russia, Prussia, Sweden, Denmark and Germany, by J. Jepson Oddys. London, 1805.

185. *Q.* The Political Economy of inland navigation, irrigation and drainage, with thoughts on the multiplication of commercial resources, by N. Tatham. London, 1799.

286. *Q.* An inquiry into the principles of Political Economy, by James Stewart, 2 vols. London, 1767.

226. *Q.* L'Ordre naturel & essentiel des sociétés politiques. Londres, 1767.

227. *Q.* Recherches sur la population des généralités d'Auvergne, de Lyon, de Rouen &c. par Messance. Paris, 1766.

122. *Q.* The principles of the doctrine of life-annuities, by Francis Maseres. London, 1783.

750. The Potomac Canal. Papers relating to the practicability, expediency and cost of the Potomac Canal; also the act of the Legislature of Virginia incorporating the Potomac Canal Company. Washington, 1823.

” Report of the President and Managers of the Union Canal Company of Pennsylvania to the Stockholders, Nov. 18, 1823. Philadelphia.

” Great national object; proposed connection of the Eastern and Western Waters by communication through the Potomac country. Washington, 1823.

” Letter to the Governor and Council of Maryland, transmitting a report of the commissioners appointed to survey the River Potomac, Jan. 27, 1823. Printed by order of the Senate. Washington, 1823.

” Speech of Mr. C. F. Mercer on the subject of the Chesapeake and Ohio Canal, delivered in the convention of Delegates held at Washington, Nov. 7, 1823. Washington, 1823.

” The sixth annual report of the American Society for Colonizing the free people of colour of the United States, with an appendix. Washington, 1823.

” Catalogue of the Lycæum at Gardiner in the State of Maine. Hallowell, (Maine,) 1823.

750. Catalogue of the officers and students of Bowdoin College. Brunswick, (Maine,) 1823.

" Catalogue Collegii Dartmuthensis. Portsmouth, (N. H.) 1823.

372. Note sur la population des Isles Britanniques, & quelques considérations sur celle de France. Par Coquebert-Montbret. Paris, 1823.

1786½. Collection of reports of committees of the Select and Common Councils of the city of Philadelphia, concerning their finances, water-works, &c. Philadelphia, *(various dates.)*

1341. Statements showing the power that Ireland possesses to create wealth. By Robert Owen. London, 1823.

16. LOCAL AND OCCASIONAL POLITICS.

676. A Sermon preached before the society for the propagation of the gospel, &c. Feb. 20, 1767, by the Bishop of Llandaff. London, 1767.

(Omitted in its place, and inserted by mistake, under the head RELIGION, *above, p.* 80.*)*

589. A collection of scarce and interesting tracts written by persons of eminence, upon the most important political and commercial subjects, from 1763 to 1770, 4 vols. London, 1778.

152. *F.* The true interest of Great Britain, Ireland, and our plantations, by Alexander Murray. London, 1790.

902. Gazette Publications, by H. H. Brackenridge. Carlisle, 1806.

79. *Q.* The West India Common Place-Book, compiled from official documents, showing the interest of Great Britain in the sugar colonies, by Sir William Young. London, 1807.

372. Prospérité des Finances de l'Empire Français en 1811, par Francis d'Ivernois. Londres, 1811.

699. A calm address to the people of the eastern states, on the subject of the representation of slaves; the representation in the Senate: and the hostility to commerce, ascribed to the southern states, by M. Carey. Philadelphia, 1814.

17. COMMERCE AND MANUFACTURES.

1691. A century of the names and scantlings of such inventions as I have tried down to the year 1655. By the Marquis of Worcester. Glasgow, 1794.

" Dud Dudley's Malleum Martis, or an account of the difficulties he encountered in erecting forges for making of iron, smelting it with pit-coal, sea-coal, &c. in preference to charcoal in 1654. Glasgow, 1794.

1922. De Koophandel van Amsterdam en andere Nederlandsche steden naar alle gewesten der wereld, door de l'Esping en le Long, 4 deelen. Amsterdam, 1801.

554. *Q.* O Guarda-Livros Moderno ou curso completo de instrucções elementares sobre as operações do commercio, por M. T. Cabral de Mendonça, 2 vol. Lisboa, 1815.

18. NAVIGATION.

136. *F.* Remarks, instructions, and examples, relating to the longitude and latitude, also the variation of the compass, by Thomas Truxtun. Philadelphia, 1794.

19. MILITARY ART.

325. *Q.* Real Ordenanza Naval para el servicio de los Baxeles de S. M. Madrid, 1802.

20. GEOGRAPHY AND ETHNOGRAPHY.

232. *F.* Cosmographey oder beschreibung aller länder, herrschafften-fürnemsten stetten, geschichten, gebreüchen, hantierungen, &c. von Sebastian Munster. *Mit holzgeschnitten Karten.* Basel, 1564.

51. *Q.* Dimensio Graduum Meridiani Viennensis et Hungarici. A Josepho Liesgang. Vindobonæ, 1770.

37. *F.* Maps and Plates belonging to Du Halde's description of China.

54. *F.* Ceremonies and religious customs of the various nations of the world, translated from the French, with engravings by Bernard Picart, 6 vols. London, 1733.

171. *F.* Journal of the voyage of George Hunter up the Red and Washita Rivers, with William Dunbar, 1804, by order of the United States: and up to Hot Spring, MS.
For the original, see p. 238.

1046. Letters from Geneva and France, addressed to a Lady, by Francis Kinloch, 2 vols. Boston, 1819.
Misprinted under the name of HINLOCK, *above, p. 207.*

1923. Narrative of a journey to the shores of the Polar Sea, in the years 1819—1822, by John Franklin. Philadelphia, 1824.

21. PHILOLOGY.

539. *Q.* Oratio Dominica πολυγλωττος, πολυμορφος, nimirùm plus C. linguis, versionibus aut characteribus reddita & expressa. London, 1713.
This work was first published at Berlin in 1680, by Andreas Muller, under the assumed name of Thomas Ludeken. It

was reprinted on the continent of Europe about 1690 without designation of year or place. In 1700, one B. Mottus, a printer in London, probably to display the beauty of his types, republished it, but did not preserve the geographical arrangement of the languages, which are thrown confusedly together. His edition, however, was reprinted at Augsburg about 1710, and in 1713 the present one was published at London, which is an exact copy of that printed by Mottus. All these editions are now very scarce. Adelung, who takes notice of this in the Mithridates, vol. 1, p. 663, never had seen a copy of it, and speaks of it only from the information contained in other Philological works, particularly *Fry's Pantographia.*

1920. Versuch eines practischen Unterrichts in den Anfangsgründen der Deutschen Sprache, von J. W. Berger. Cleve, 1810.

572. *Q.* La Langue Hébraique restituée & le véritable sens des mots Hébreux rétabli & prouvé par leur analyse radicale, par Fabre d'Olivet. Paris, 1815.

577 *Q.* Dictionnaire Italien, Latin, & François, par Antonini, vol. 1. commençant par l'Italien A.—Z. Paris, 1743.

344½. *Q.* A Dictionary Spanish and English and English and Spanish, by Joseph Baretti. London, 1800.

60. *F.* Vocabulario de la Lengua Tagala, por Hermano Fray Domingo. Sampaloo, 1794.

22. ARCHÆOLOGY AND BIBLIOGRAPHY.

53. *F.* Le Pitture Antiche d'Ercolano e' contorni incise con qualche spiegazione, (with a catalogue,) 7 vol. Napoli, 1757.

300. *Q.* Promptuaire des Médailles des plus renommées personnes qui ont été depuis le commencement du monde, avec brieve description de leurs vies & faits, recueillie des bons auteurs. Lyon, 1553.

309. *Q.* Laurentii Pignorii Patavini Mensa Isiaca, quâ sacrorum apud Ægyptios ratio & simulacra subjectis tabulis æneis simul exhibentur & explicantur. Amstel. 1669.

58. *F.* Origen de los Indios de el Nuevo Mundo e Indias Occidentales, por Fr. Gregorio Garcia. Madrid, 1729.

170. *F.* Historical and chronological description of two stones found under ground in the great square of the city of Mexico, in the year 1790, translated from the Spanish by Wm. E. Hulings, MS.

For the original, see page 238.

1385. *Q.* Histoire des Celtes & particulièrement des Gaulois & des Germains, depuis les tems fabuleux, jusqu' à la prise de Rome par les Gaulois, par Simon Pelloutier, 8 vol. Paris, 1770.

Inserted by mistake above, p. 238. *under the name of* Chiniac, *the Editor.*

573. *Q.* Essais sur les Isles Fortunées & l'antique Atlantide, par J. B. G. M. Bory de St. Vincent. Paris, 1804.
237. *Q.* Mémoire sur les Navires & la Marine des Anciens. 1770.
272. Index librorum ad celebranda sacra sæcularia reformationis ecclesiasticæ tertia annis 1817 & 1819, cùm in Germaniâ tum extrà Germaniam vulgatorum, quos Bibliotheca Regia Berolensis ad hunc usque diem comparavit. Berolini, 1821.

23. LITERATURE.

233. *F.* Polyanthea nova, hoc est opus suavissimis floribus celebriorum Sententiarum tam Græcarum quam latinarum refertum, Quod ex innumeris ferè cum sacris tum profanis autoribus olim collegere eruditissimi viri Dominicus Nanus Mirabellus, Bartholomæus Amantius, & Franciscus Tortius, nunc auctum, locupletatum & exornatum studio & operâ Josephi Langii Cæsaremontani. Francof. 1607.

ADDITIONAL OMISSIONS.

248. Eulogium on Benjamin Franklin, delivered in the German Lutheran Church of the city of Philadelphia, March 1, 1791, by the Rev. William Smith, D. D. Philadelphia, 1792.
538. Manuel pratique & élémentaire des poids & mesures & du calcul décimal, avec la nouvelle nomenclature, par M. Tarbé. Paris, an 10.

The following books have been received from Europe and added to the Library, while this sheet was in the press.

371. *Q.* Transactions of the Royal Society of London, 1822, Part 2, 1823, Parts 1 and 2.
363. *Q.* Transactions of the Linnæan Society of London, 8th to 13th vol. inclusive. London, 1818—1822.
169. *Q.* Transactions of the Horticultural Society of London, vol. 5, Part 3d, 1823.

LIST

OF THE NAMES OF

AUTHORS, TRANSLATORS, AND EDITORS,

MENTIONED IN THIS CATALOGUE,

With references to the pages where their works are to be found.

A

N.

ERRATA.

Page xiv. *United States*, for 117 read 115.
1. *Belfast*, for *fascicula* read *fasciculi.*
3. 438. *Q. Lisbon*, for *adiantomento* read *adiantamento.*
" 374. *Q. London*, in the last line of this article, for 1799 read 1789.
5. *Recueil, &c.* for No. 350. *Q.* read 350½. *Q.*
10. *Smith*, for No. 384–5 read 384–3. *Q.*
12. 473. For *Gummerie* read *Gummere.*
" *Le Gendre*, for No. 125 read 125. *Q.*
" Same work, &c. for No. 439 read 489.
" 136. *Q. Pingré*, add *Paris*, 1783–4.
13. *Dollond*, for No. 384. *Q.* read 384, 2. *Q.*
" No. 237, for *Ludlow* read *Ludlam.*
14. *Magellan*, for No. 235 read 238, and for *(L. F.)* read *(J. H.)*
18. 348, 19. *Q.* for *L'Hopital* read *L'Hospital.*
19. *La Place*, for No. 593½ read 493½.
21. *Prony*, for No. 396 read 397.
" *Beccaria Elettricismo, &c.* for No. 384, 8. *Q.* read 234.
22. 1127. *Cavallo*, for *Siberdas* read *Tiberius.*
" *Ingen-Housz*, for No. 384. *Q.* read 384, 1. *Q.*
23. No. 231. *Q.* for *De la Luc* read *De Luc.*
24. *Smith, (Robert)* prefix 219. *Q.* and add, 2 vols.
" 384, 2. *Q.* for *Dolland* read *Dollond.*
25. 111. *Q. De Prony* dele *De.*
27. 143. *Q.* for *Borguis* read *Borgnis.*
28. 491. *Q. Rozier*, add *Delamétherie and Blainville.*
29. 1562. *Tilloch*, for 17 vol. read 61 vol. and for 1803 read 1823.
30. 1208. *Henry*, add 2 vol.
" No. 1176, for *Parker* read *Parkes.*
" 1206. *Thénard*, add, 4 vol. and for 1811 read 1813.
32. No. 1194, for *Huggins* read *Higgins.*
33. *Ure*, for *with notes by B. F. Bache*, read *revised, with notes by Dr. Hare, assisted by Dr. Bache.*
34. 1213. *Buffon*, after 127 vol. add, including the continuation by Daudin, Denys, Montfort, Latreille & Brisseau-Mirbel, and by Sonnini, the editor.
36. 1274. *Smith, (John Coakley)* read *Smith, (James Edward.)*
" 1099. For *Systime* read *Système.*
37. 385. *Q. Blumenbach*, for *illustrata* read *illustratæ.*
" 686. for *Dandridge Peck, (William)* read *Peck, (William Dandridge)*
40. After No. 384, 12. *Q. Barton, (Wm. P. C.)* insert No. 265½. *Q. Barton, (Wm. P. C.)* Flora of North America, No. 1—30. Philadelphia, 1823.

Page 41. 226. *Bigelow*. American Medical Botany, for 6 vol. read 3 vol.

43. 225½. *Michaux*. North American Sylva, for 7 vol. read 3 vol.

" 16. *F.* and 251. *Q.* under *Michaux, (F. André)* for *F. André* read *André*, these two works being by the elder Michaux, and the others by his son.

" 1270. for *Petersoon* read *Persoon*.

44. No. 384, 22. *Q.* for *Schrœder* read *Schrader*.

" 1228. for *Smith, (Ever. Jac.)* read *(Jacob Edvar.)*

45. 224. *F.* under *Smyth*. Icones, &c. for *Smyth* read *Thunberg*, and see the supplement under the head of NATURAL HISTORY.

" 1248. *Thunberg*, for *Carpensis* read *Capensis*.

46. 104. *Q. Bournon*, dele 4 vol. Paris, 1818.

48. 384, 9. *Q.* for *Hatschett* read *Hatchett*.

49. 229. *Q. Schultter* read *Schlutter*.

52. 384, 4. add *Q.*

" 374, 12. *Q.* for *Hogermuller* read *Hogelmuller*.

58. 384, 20. *Q.* for *Fomento* read *Formento*.

61. 216. for *Hilary, (Wm.)* read *Hillary, (Wm.)*

64. Last article, Observations by J. R. Coxe, prefix No. 1719.

65. *Vaccine. Rapport de*, for No. 274 read 1720.

70. *Shoepf*, for 259 read 256.

" *Tavares*, for No. 357. *Q.* read 457. *Q.*

72. 42. *F.* La Sainte Bible, add 2 vol.

" ——— ——— for No. 1354. *Q.* read 1354.

" For No. 1346, the same in the Welsh, &c. read No. 1346½.

" Mamusse, after No. 538 add *Q.*

" *Daniel*, for No. 190. *F.* read 190. *Q.*

76. 118. *F. Bedæ, (Venerabilis)* Historia, &c. add *Anglo-Saxon and Latin.*

79. 274. *sub anno*, 1820, for *Grandverfassung* read *Grundverfassung*.

80. 676. *Llandaff, (Bishop of)* A Sermon, &c. transfer this to LOCAL AND OCCASIONAL POLITICS, page 160, *sub anno*, 1767.

88. 1251. *Delamétherie*, for *perfectabilité* read *perfectibilité*.

91. *Dumoulin, (J. T.)* read *(J. F.)*

95. 370. Constitution, &c. for *Cadix* read *Cadiz*.

97. *John Horne*, for No. 221. *F.* read 221½. *F.*

98. First article, for *alluvious* read *alluvions*.

102. *Beza*, for No. 481. *Q.* read 489. *Q.*

108. 496. *Euler*, for *vorgelisen* read *vorgelesen*.

104. 282. *Q. Green, (Nathan)* read *Greene, (Nathaniel)*

105. 294. *Napoleon*, for *prononcé* read *prononcée*.

109. Last line, for *Tirenze* read *Firenze*.

113. *Bedæ*, for No. 118, 1592. *F.* read 118. *F.* 1592.

115. *Sweden*. 1402. *Blix, (Magnus)* for 7921 read 1791.

123. 384, 17. *Q. sub anno*, 1478. Lettre inédite, &c. in the last line of this article, for 1478 read *(No imprint, no date.)*

Page 139. 1502. *Jakob, (L. H. von)* for *Erster Band* read *two vols. in one.*
140. 942. *Webster, (Petatiah)* read *Pelatiah.*
141. 266, 700. *Eddy, (George)* read *(Thomas)*
149. 631. Candid remarks, &c, prefix also No. 675.
156. View, &c. for No. 844½. read 895.
159. 682, 711. Sub anno 1765, for *(William T. Franklin,)* read *(William Franklin.)*
185. 718. sub anno 1820. *Monarchal*, &c. read *Monarchical.*
186. *Anderson, (James)* prefix No. 578. *Q.*
188. 222. *F. Brass-foundry*, for *la cuivre* read *le cuivre.*
189. 283. *Engraving*, read 283. *Q.*
207. 1046. *Hinloch* read *Kinloch.*
" 347. *Q. Humboldt*, after 2 vol. add, *(with a folio volume of plates.)*
208. *Mackenzie*, for No. 882. *Q.* read 82. *Q.*
213. No. 1005. for *Wiltmair* read *Wittman.*
" 117. *F.* A collection, &c. after "*published in English,*" add *by A. & J. Churchill.*
214. 32. *Relacion, &c.* add *con un Atlas.*
215. *Humboldt*, for No. 33½. *F.* read 33. *F.*
" 2½. *F. Collection, &c.* add 1700—1713.
" *P.* 1. *Canada*, for *A. Say* read *A. Lay.*
216. 17. *F. Plan de Paris, &c.* add *giving a bird's eye view of the City of Paris and all its buildings.*
220. *Beattie, (James)* prefix No. 186.
221. *Q. Jacobson*, prefix 579.
" 185. *Tooke, (John Horne)* for *Parley* read *Purley.*
" 1550, 2. line 2, for *Turgot* read *Maupertuis.*
222. 423. *Q.* For *Bowditch* read *Bowdich.*
224. *Q. A Grammar*, prefix, No. 415½.
226. *A Grammar*, for No. 512. *Q.* read 522. *Q.*
234. 564. *Q. Romaic Greek*. For Θισαυρος read Θισορος.
" 427. *Q.* line 3, for *Heyon* read *Heym.*
236. *Sotchinenia*, for No. 403½ *Q.* read 403. *Q.*
" 563. *Q.* Elements de la langue Turque, &c. *dele the whole article, the work being no longer in the library.*
238. 299. *Q. Gusseme*, add 6 *vol.*
" 1385. For *Chiniac* read *Pelloutier.*
255. *Kongelig*, for No. 398½. *Q.* read 298½. *Q.*
258. 1919, line 3, for *Goodman* read *Godman.*
261. 61. *Q.* line 2, for *Rigiâ* read *Regiâ.*
269. For *Amantus* read *Amantius*, and for 260 read 267.
271. *Bollman* 138 add 185.
" *Bory de St. Vincent*, for 266 read 267.
273. *Delambre*, for 12 read 11.

xiv. Internal improvements, for 141 read 142.
" Domestic manufactures, for 142 read 146.
" NAVIGATION, add 191.

CPSIA information can be obtained at www.ICGtesting.com
Printed in the USA
LVOW112232030512
280252LV00004B/40/P